BELARUSIAN NATION-BUILDING
in Times of War and Revolution

BELARUSIAN
NATION-BUILDING
in Times of War and Revolution

Lizaveta Kasmach

Central European University Press
Budapest–Vienna–New York

Published in 2023 by

Central European University Press

Nádor utca 11, H-1051 Budapest, Hungary
Tel: +36-1-327-3138 or 327-3000
E-mail: ceupress@press.ceu.edu
Website: www.ceupress.com

ISBN 978-963-386-633-7 (hardback)
ISBN 978-963-386-634-4 (ebook)

Library of Congress Cataloging-in-Publication Data

Names: Kasmach, Lizaveta, author.
Title: Belarusian nation-building in times of war and revolution
/ Lizaveta Kasmach.
Description: Budapest ; New York : Central European University Press, 2023.
| Includes bibliographical references.
Identifiers: LCCN 2023031353 (print) | LCCN 2023031354 (ebook) |
ISBN 9789633866337 (hardback) | ISBN 9789633866344 (adobe pdf)
Subjects: LCSH: Belarus—History—1917-1991. | Belarus—Politics and
government—1917-1945 | Nationalism—Belarus. | BISAC: HISTORY / Europe
/ Eastern | HISTORY / Wars & Conflicts / World War I
Classification: LCC DK507.73 .K375 2023 (print) | LCC DK507.73 (ebook) |
DDC 320.5409478--dc23/eng/20230808
LC record available at https://lccn.loc.gov/2023031353
LC ebook record available at https://lccn.loc.gov/2023031354

Contents

Acknowledgments

This book is based on my academic journey across different countries and continents. It would not have been possible without the help and support of my academic advisors, colleagues, friends, and most importantly, my family, whose history inspired me and guided me on my way.

I am grateful to the University of Alberta in Canada and everyone at the Department of History and Classics who provided a stimulating environment for my professional and intellectual growth. David Marples encouraged me to develop my research interests, offered his expertise and insights, and provided extensive feedback on my work. John-Paul Himka helped me to become more outspoken and confident in discussions, giving me faith in my abilities and the path I chose as a historian. I am also grateful to Heather Coleman for her invaluable advice and comments and for inviting me to the Eastern Europeanists' Circle, where I could present some of my work. I also appreciated the opportunity to discuss my research with the late Mark von Hagen, who urged me to develop my ideas and publish this book.

My research benefited from a number of awards and scholarships, among them the University of Alberta Doctoral Recruitment Scholarship, the Frank W. Peers Graduate Research Scholarship, and the Mary Louise Imrie Graduate Student Award. They facilitated my work in archives and gave me valuable time and space for writing. I am grateful to everyone at the CEU Press who welcomed me as an author and helped me in the final stages of shaping this project into a book.

I was lucky to have people in my life, who stood by my side as I worked on this project, especially my friends and colleagues from the University of Alberta and the wider Ukrainian community of Edmonton. I am also grateful to my family as I would not have been able to complete this project without their unconditional love and support. I dedicate this book to the memory of my grandmothers, Halina Kalačyk and Maryja Kasmač, who always encouraged my curiosity and intellectual pursuits.

Notes on transliteration, translation, and calendars

This book follows the UN guidelines for the transliteration of Belarusian names and geographical locations which is a simplified version of the historical Belarusian Latin script (known as Lacinka), used in the nineteenth and early twentieth centuries. In the past, Lacinka developed as a Belarusian identity-building element opposing imperial practices and competing nationalisms, as shown in this book. In present times, Belarusian media often use the historical Latin script for the transliteration of Belarusian names in recognition of its potential. It also appears logical to move beyond the artificially constructed transliteration systems which often ignore the phonetic peculiarities of Belarusian. Last but not least, the choice of Belarusian Latin script serves to emphasize the anti-colonial aspect of Belarusian nation-building, the main subject of this book.

The Library of Congress (LoC) system is used for the transliteration of other Cyrillic-based languages.

TRANSLITERATION TABLE		
Belarusian Cyrillic alphabet	**Simplified Belarusian Latin script**	**Library of Congress transliteration**
A a	A a	A a
Б б	B b	B b
В в	V v	V v
Г г	H h	H h
Д д	D d	D d
Е е	Je je (*), ie (**)	E e
Ё ё	Jo jo (*), io (**)	Io io
Ж ж	Ž ž	Zh zh

Belarusian Cyrillic alphabet	Simplified Belarusian Latin script	Library of Congress transliteration
З з	Z z	Z z
I i	I i	I i
Й й	J j	I i
К к	K k	K k
Л л	L l	L k
М м	M m	M m
Н н	N n	N n
О о	O o	O o
П п	P p	P p
Р р	R r	R r
С с	S s	S s
Т т	T t	T t
У у	U u	U u
Ў ў	Ŭ ŭ	Ŭ ŭ
Ф ф	F f	F f
Х х	Ch ch	Kh kh
Ц ц	C c	Ts ts
Ч ч	Č č	Ch ch
Ш ш	Š š	Sh sh
Ы ы	Y y	Y y
Ь	' (soft sign)	' (soft sign)
Э э	E e	E e
Ю ю	Ju ju (*), iu (**)	Iu iu
Я я	Ja ja (*), ia (**)	Ia ia

* Initially, and after vowels, apostrophe, soft sign, and ŭ

** After consonants

Some texts cited in this book were originally written in Belarusian Latin script where the spelling may differ slightly from the above table. In this case, the original spelling has been maintained. The case of Vil'nia/Wilno/Vilnius is a complicated one. Without questioning its current status as a Lithuanian city, it is transliterated from Belarusian here due to the historical context with a primary focus on Belarusian life in the city and its importance as one of the chief centers of the Belarusian national movement in the early twentieth century.[1] All modern references to the city use its current name of Vilnius. All other Polish and Lithuanian geographical locations are rendered in their modern form unless there is a more common English form. For instance, Warsaw is used instead of Warszawa; the same applies to Moscow and St. Petersburg.

Archival signatures throughout the text are used in the original language; hence, for Belarusian archives the following abbreviations are used: f. (fond), vop. (vopis), spr. (sprava), ark. (arkuš); for Lithuanian archives: f. (fondas), ap. (aprašas), b. (byla), l. (lapas).

The difference between the old-style (Julian) and new-style (Gregorian) calendars in Soviet Russia was eliminated on February 14, 1918. The switch to the Gregorian calendar resulted in missing the first thirteen days of the month of February 1918. Those chapters dealing with the eastern Belarusian territories administered by the Russian Empire and later under Bolshevik control will use the Julian calendar (old-style, O.S.) for dates up until the calendar change in 1918. Gregorian calendar (new-style, N.S.) dates will be indicated in parentheses in cases where it is appropriate, especially, at the turn of 1918. After February 14, 1918, the Gregorian calendar style will be used. The chapters dealing with the German occupation of the Belarusian territories will use the new-style dates of the Gregorian calendar, since the German authorities had already introduced it for the occupied territories in Eastern Europe on May 25, 1915.

There are different ways to translate into English the name of the first Belarusian state—Bielaruskaja Narodnaja Respublika. In the research literature, it is most often referred to as the Belarusian People's Republic, the Belarusian National Republic, or the Belarusian Democratic Republic. The last option is used in this book as the most precise and free of negative connotations. Correspondingly, the abbreviation of the BDR and not the BNR is used. All abbreviations, along with full forms and English translations, are listed separately below.

---

[1]   This remains an under-researched topic, while studies about Vilnius and its declining fortunes as a multicultural city throughout the twentieth century fail to address the role of Belarusians in shaping its diversity. See Theodore R. Weeks, *Vilnius between Nations, 1795–2000* (DeKalb, IL: NIU Press, 2015).

List of abbreviations

Bielnackam	Bielaruski Nacyjanaľny Kamisaryjat (Belarusian National Commissariat)
BNK	Bielaruski Nacyjanaľny Kamitet (Belarusian National Committee)
BNPS	Bielaruskaja Narodnaja Partyja Sacyjalistaŭ (Belarusian People's Party of Socialists)
BDR	Bielaruskaja Narodnaja Respublika (Belarusian Democratic Republic)
BOK	Bělorusskii Oblastnoi Komitet (Belarusian Oblasť Committee)
BPSF	Bielaruskaja Partyja Sacyjalistaŭ-Federalistaŭ (Belarusian Party of the Socialists-Federalists)
BPSR	Bielaruskaja Partyja Sacyjalistaŭ-Revalucyjaneraŭ (Belarusian Party of the Socialist-Revolutionaries)
BRH	Bielaruskaja Revaliucyjnaja Hramada (Belarusian Revolutionary Hramada)
BRP	Bielaruskaja Revaliucyjnaja Partyja (Belarusian Revolutionary Party)
BSDP	Bielaruskaja Sacyjal-Demakratyčnaja Partyja (Belarusian Social Democratic Party)
BSDRP	Bielaruskaja Sacyjal Demakratyčnaja Rabočaja Partyja (Belarusian Social Democratic Workers' Party)
BSH	Bielaruskaja Sacyjalistyčnaja Hramada (Belarusian Socialist Hramada)
BSSR	Bielaruskaja Saveckaja Sacyjalistyčnaja Respublika (Belarusian Soviet Socialist Republic)
CBVR	Centraľnaja Bielaruskaja Vajskovaja Rada (Central Belarusian Military Rada)
GDL	Grand Duchy of Lithuania
Narkomnats	Narodnyi Komissariat po Delam Natsionaľnostei (People's Commissariat for Nationality Affairs)
Ober Ost	Oberbefehlshaber Ost (German Supreme Command in the East)
Obliskomzap	Oblastnoi Ispolniteľnyi Komitet Sovetov Rabochikh, Soldatskikh i Krest'ianskikh Deputatov Zapadnoj Oblasti i Fronta (Oblasť Executive Committee of the Soviets of Workers', Soldiers', and Peasants' Deputies of the Western Oblasť and Front)

Oblastiskomzap   Oblastnoi Ispolniteľnyi Komitet Zapadnoi oblasti (Oblast' Execu-
                  tive Committee of the Western oblast')
P.O.W.   Polska Organizacja Wojskowa (Polish Military Organization)
PPS   Polska Partia Socjalistyczna (Polish Socialist Party)
RKP(b)   Rossiiskaia Kommunisticheskaia Partiia (bolshevikov) (Russian
                  Communist Party [Bolsheviks])
RSDRP   Rossiiskaya Sotsial Demokraticheskaia Rabochaia Partiia (Rus-
                  sian Social Democratic Labor Party)
RSFSR   Rossiiskaya Sovetskaia Federativnaia Sotsialisticheskaia Respub-
                  lika (Russian Soviet Federative Socialist Republic)
SDKPiL   Socjaldemokracja Królestwa Polskiego i Litwy (Social Democracy
                  of the Kingdom of Poland and Lithuania)
SSRB   Sacyjalistyčnaja Savieckaja Respublika Bielarus' (Socialist Soviet
                  Republic of Belarus)
Sovnarkom   Sovet Narodnykh Komissarov (Council of the People's Commissars)
SVU   Soiuz Vyzvolennia Ukraïny (Union for the Liberation of Ukraine)
TsB KP(b)B   Tsentraľnoe Biuro Kommunisticheskoi Partii Belorussii (Central
                  Bureau of the Communist Party of Belarus)
TsK RKP(b)   Tsentralnyi Komitet Rossiiskoi Kommunisticheskoi Partii
                  (bolshevikov) (Central Committee of the Russian Communist
                  Party [Bolsheviks])
VBR   Vialikaja Bielaruskaja Rada (Great Belarusian Rada)

ARCHIVES

BArch   Bundesarchiv Freiburg
BDAMLIM   Bielaruski Dziaržaŭny Archiŭ-Muzej Litaratury i Mastactva
                  (Belarusian State Archive-Museum of Literature and Art)
LCVA   Lietuvos Centrinis Valstybės Archyvas (Lithuanian Central
                  State Archive)
LVIA   Lietuvos Valstybės Istorijos Archyvas (Lithuanian State Historical
                  Archive)
NARB   Nacyjanaľny Archiŭ Respubliki Bielarus' (National Archive of
                  the Republic of Belarus)
NHAB   Nacyjanaľny Histaryčny Archiŭ Bielarusi (National Historical
                  Archive of Belarus)
RGALI   Rossiiskii Gosudarstvennyi Arkhiv Literatury i Iskusstva (Russian
                  State Archive of Literature and Arts)

Introduction

"Narod tol'ki tady isnue, kali mae svaih herojaŭ."

Barys Kit[1]

Over the course of the twentieth century, Belarus transformed from several provinces of the Russian Empire into a sovereign state. Belarusians profited from imperial decline and the rise of the nation-state concept in the early twentieth century, when the First World War, revolutions, and subsequent violence disrupted traditional societies throughout Eastern Europe, opening up new opportunities for the national self-determination of so-called "small" nations.[2] Subsequently, more than seven decades of communist rule coincided with an active process of nation-building, which in the Belarusian case was directed from above. The post-Soviet period was marked by a transition to an authoritarian regime, and at the time of writing, the future poses the questions of imperial ambitions versus national affirmation once again. The peaceful protests against the rigged 2020 presidential election brought Belarusians together as a nation. Protesters quickly rallied around national symbols, prohibited and despised by the ruling regime. This demonstrated that the ideals of those who imagined Belarus over a hundred years ago still have the power to attract people and provide them with the symbolic continuity of historic tradition.[3]

---

[1] "The nation exists only when it has its own heroes." Barys Kit, *Ciarnovy šliach: Uspaminy* (Frankfurt am Main, n. p., 2001), 56.

[2] This definition of the "small" nation rests on the assumption of its subordination to a ruling nation which is reflected in the social structure of the small nation, causing its incomplete character or atypical composition. While certain social groups dominate, national elites usually remain outnumbered by the elites of the ruling nation. See Miroslav Hroch, *Social Preconditions of National Revival in Europe: A Comparative Analysis of the Social Composition of Patriotic Groups among the Smaller European Nations* (Cambridge: Cambridge University Press, 1985), 4–5, 9; Andreas Kappeler, *Der schwierige Weg zur Nation: Beiträge zur neueren Geschichte der Ukraine* (Vienna: Böhlau, 2003), 25.

[3] See, for instance, Tatsiana Kulakevich, "National Awakening in Belarus: Elite Ideology to 'Nation' Practice," *SAIS Review of International Affairs* 40, no. 2 (2020): 97–110. On the reappropriation of national symbols, see the discussion in Aliaksej Kazharski, "Belarus' New Political Nation? 2020 Anti-Authoritarian Protests as Identity Building," *New Perspectives* 29, no. 1 (2021): 69–79. https://doi.org/10.1177/2336825X20984340 (Accessed September 15, 2022).

This book is a case study of Belarusian nation- and state-building in its early stages, dating back to the Fist World War and subsequent revolution. It focuses on the path towards the creation of the first modern Belarusian state and explores in detail the roots of its duality. The proclamation of Belarusian independence on March 25, 1918, and the rival establishment of the Soviet Belarusian state on January 1, 1919, resulted in two distinct and mutually exclusive national myths, which continue to define contemporary Belarusian society. Both projects, national and Soviet, transformed into two separate concepts of alternative and official Belarusianness, respectively, which developed parallel to each other during the twentieth century.[4] By looking at their formative period, this book contributes to an analysis of the origins of modern Belarusian statehood and the problematic character of national identity. On a different level, it also addresses the impact of the First World War on Belarusian nation-building efforts, the reasons for the uneven development of Belarusian national mobilization in the early twentieth century, and their consequences for the future state-building process—consequences which are still felt in contemporary Belarusian society.

The story of the challenges and struggles of the modern Belarusian national project helps reveal the internal mechanisms of national mobilization and understand the nature of nationalism as an inherently modern phenomenon.[5] The concept of a nation is treated here in the broad sense following Ernest Renan's definition of "a large-scale solidarity," held together by two basic principles: that of the common legacy of historical memories and the present desire to live together, being in essence a "daily plebiscite."[6] Methodologically, this study is based on the modernist approach to the study of nationalism, assuming the artificial nature of every national project and treating it as a product of certain conditions, which have enabled nationalism to emerge in the capacity of a political principle, advocating the congruence of political and national boundaries.[7] Ernest Gellner, who formulated this definition of nationalism, maintained that its analysis necessitated a departure from the assumption of the "awakening" of an ancient nation, towards understanding it as a modern phenomenon.[8]

---

[4] Nelly Bekus, *Struggle over Identity: The Official and the Alternative "Belarusianness"* (Budapest–New York: CEU Press, 2010), 163–64.
[5] Ernest Gellner, *Nations and Nationalism* (Ithaca, NY: Cornell University Press, 1983), 43; Timothy Snyder, *The Reconstruction of Nations: Poland, Ukraine, Lithuania, Belarus, 1569–1999* (New Haven, CT: Yale University Press, 2003), 41.
[6] Ernest Renan, "What Is a Nation?," in *Becoming National: A Reader*, ed. Geoff Eley and Ronald Grigor Suny (New York: Oxford University Press, 1996), 52–53.
[7] Gellner, *Nations and Nationalism*, 1.
[8] Gellner, *Nations and Nationalism*, 48.

Modernization alone does not explain the emergence of nation-states in the imperial context, as the imperial power's military and economic stability in peacetime disadvantages national movements. They have a viable chance only when power shifts occur, caused by wars or military conflicts. This scenario allows national movements to accumulate strength for challenging the empire and mobilizing their followers.[9] Noting that major theories of nationalism fail to account for wars as factors in the successes of national movements, Eric Lohr suggested the concept of "sudden nationalism" or "war nationalism," departing from the view of nationalism as a linear progression and a long-term development.[10] In a similar vein, Aviel Roshwald acknowledged the significance of the First World War which launched "the idea of national self-determination toward sudden realization across a wide range of societies."[11]

This study also draws on concepts which emerged from the growing interest of historians in the complexities and peculiarities of the Great War in Eastern Europe as a whole, rather than as a catalyst of imperial decline. Klaus Richter stressed that the First World War caused the structural reformatting and fragmentation of the entire region of East-Central Europe, opening up spaces for state-building activities and national empowerment and determining the trajectory of the region's history for the twentieth century.[12] The "entangled history" approach can also open up new perspectives on nation and empire, by integrating transnational and regional history.[13] Even though it is more common for an analysis of peacetime, Mark von Hagen suggested that this approach might widen our understanding of the First World War in Eastern Europe, pointing to the inter-imperial entanglements as well as the connections of empires with ethnic and religious minorities in other empires.[14]

---

[9]   Andreas Wimmer, *Waves of War: Nationalism, State Formation and Ethnic Exclusion in the Modern World* (New York: Cambridge University Press, 2013), 22.

[10] Eric Lohr, "War Nationalism," in *The Empire and Nationalism at War*, ed. Eric Lohr, Vera Tolz, Alexander Semyonov, and Mark von Hagen (Bloomington, IN: Slavica Publishers, 2014), 93.

[11] Aviel Roshwald, *Ethnic Nationalism and the Fall of Empires: Central Europe, Russia and the Middle East, 1914–1923* (London: Routledge, 2000), 3.

[12] Klaus Richter, *Fragmentation in East Central Europe: Poland and the Baltics 1915–1929* (Oxford: Oxford University Press, 2020), 3–4.

[13] For examples of these approaches in the analysis of Belarusian history, see Thomas M. Bohn, Victor Shadurski, and Albert Weber, eds., *Ein weißer Fleck in Europa: Die Imagination der Belarus als einer Kontaktzone zwischen Ost und West* (Bielefeld: Transcript, 2011).

[14] Mark von Hagen, "The Entangled Eastern Front in the First World War," in Lohr et al., *The Empire and Nationalism at War*, 9–11. During the war, this trend was particularly evident from the forced entanglement of civilian and military spheres, illustrated by Ludendorff's aspirations towards a military utopian state in Ober Ost on the one hand, and the arbitrary military rule of Russian generals in the western borderlands under martial law on the other. Ibid., 23, 26.

Joshua Sanborn interpreted the First World War in Eastern Europe as a war of European decolonization, a complex "multiactor and multistage process," not limited to the war's outcome at Versailles.[15] In this manner, he challenged the "rise of nationalism" paradigm, noting that it placed the wrong emphasis on the struggle between nation and empire, where the opposing sides supposedly aimed for liberation and control, respectively.[16] Sanborn suggested that the road of national movements towards independence started with the failure of the imperial state, which, in the case of the Russian Empire, was marked by the introduction of martial law in the western borderlands in July 1914 and the retreat of the Russian armies, culminating in the February Revolution in 1917. The final stage in this decolonization scheme is linked to the state-building process, which can be defined as a continuous work in progress.[17]

Structure and Organization

This book covers the period between 1914 and 1918, tracing the Belarusian national movement in various settings: throughout the years of population displacement, in the German-occupied parts of western Belarus and Lithuania, as well as in the eastern Belarusian territories that remained under Russian rule in 1915. It looks at the achievements and failures of the Belarusian national elites as the chief agents of modernization, and their attempts to overcome the class divide and interact with the masses which preferred to cling to their pre-modern identities. The nation-building efforts of the Belarusian national activists are analyzed against the background of the changing dynamics of competition with the Polish and Lithuanian national movements on the one hand, and the lasting influences of the Russification policies on the other. Within this context, this book follows the evolution of Belarusian political thought from different federalist-based concepts towards thinking in terms of an independent state.

Notably, the First World War did not end on November 11, 1918, for Eastern Europe, as a series of local conflicts stretching over the following years overshadowed the defeat of the German Empire.[18] However, this study covers only the pe-

---

[15] Joshua Sanborn, "War of Decolonization," in Lohr et al., *The Empire and Nationalism at War*, 52.

[16] Sanborn, "War of Decolonization," 54.

[17] Sanborn, "War of Decolonization," 59, 62; Joshua Sanborn, *Imperial Apocalypse: The Great War and the Destruction of the Russian Empire* (Oxford: Oxford University Press, 2014), 5–7.

[18] In the Belarusian case, the Polish-Soviet war replaced the First World War until the signing of the Treaty of Riga on March 18, 1921. By its terms, Poland and Soviet Russia divided the Belarusian territories for the interwar period. On the need to incorporate the revolution and the subsequent

riod up to 1918, since this year marks the emergence of Belarusian statehood: in March 1918, the national activists in Minsk proclaimed the BDR (Bielaruskaja Narodnaja Respublika, Belarusian Democratic Republic), while almost at the same time the Soviet state developed its own version with the Belarusian Soviet Republic. Prominent Belarusian politician Anton Luckievič described this in essence as the victory of "the idea of a Belarusian republic."[19] Even though he made this enthusiastic entry in his diary in January 1919, when the days of the first SSRB (*Savieckaja Sacyjalistyčnaja Respublika Bielarus'*, Socialist Soviet Republic of Belarus) were already numbered, he was correct in noting that the idea of Belarusian statehood had taken root, even if it was to be implemented under Soviet control in the future. In this form, it survived throughout the twentieth century and eventually served as the basis of an independent Belarus after the dissolution of the Soviet Union.

This book starts with the political, social, and demographic effects of the First World War in the western borderlands of the Russian Empire, analyzing the implications of the war for the situation of the ethnically Belarusian population and the nation-building process. The military conflict between Germany and the Russian Empire resulted in new territorial divisions, drawing new borders across the Belarusian territories. After 1915, the western Belarusian lands were incorporated into Ober Ost under German administration, while the eastern areas remained within the Russian Empire. Both of these new regions experienced different policies, which in turn led to diverse conditions for the national activists and their work. While the Russian Empire mobilized all resources for the war and uprooted the population in the territories adjacent to the front line, the areas under German military rule, although also tormented by wartime issues, experienced slightly more liberal approaches in the sphere of culture and education.

The following chapters deal with the positions and evolution of the Belarusian national movement in Ober Ost under the German occupation. Chapter two examines the early phase of the occupation between 1915 and 1917, when the German military administration promised equal treatment of all local nationalities in Ober Ost. Despite the lack of resources, both human and financial, Belarusian national activists managed to achieve relative progress within the parameters

---

civil war experiences into the larger framework of the total war, see Peter Holquist, *Making War, Forging Revolution: Russia's Continuum of Crisis, 1914–1921* (Cambridge, MA.: Harvard University Press, 2002), 2–6; on violence extending to the years after 1918, see Robert Gerwarth, *Vanquished: Why the First World War Failed to End (1917–1923)* (London: Allen Lane, 2016).

[19] Lietuvos Mokslų Akademijos Vrublevskių Biblioteka, Rankraščų Skyrius (hereafter LMAVB, RS), f. 21, b. 319, l. 38 r.

defined by the Germans, advancing their cause of nation-building, especially in contrast to eastern Belarus during the same period. Vil'nia was a focal point of Belarusian national activism at this time, where the first schools with Belarusian as the principal language of instruction appeared as early as 1915. However, by early 1917, German *Ostpolitik* had already assumed a more pronounced anti-Polish and Lithuanian-oriented character, placing the Belarusian national movement on the margins. Outside of Vil'nia, the Belarusian movement was instrumentalized by the occupation authorities as a tool to undermine Polish national politics.

Chapter three addresses the evolution of Belarusian political thinking in the context of the modified German national politics in East-Central Europe between 1916 and 1918. By looking at the interplay of regional and national interests in the Belarusian-Lithuanian-Polish borderlands, it explores why federalism, rather than a nation-state concept, enjoyed popularity among the Belarusian activists, both in western and eastern Belarus, while the Lithuanian and Polish national movements reoriented towards the nation-state concept. It concludes with an account of the Brest-Litovsk peace negotiations between Soviet Russia and the Central Powers, with particular attention devoted to the question of how the concept of national self-determination was misused by the great powers to ensure dominance in East-Central Europe.

Moving to the revolutionary period, Chapter four examines the re-organization of the Belarusian national milieu in the Russian-controlled territories of eastern Belarus between the two revolutions in 1917, when liberalization and democratization enabled the national elites across the former Russian Empire to consolidate and strengthen their national movements. Similar to other nationalities, the chief demands of Belarusians throughout 1917 remained limited to different forms of autonomy within a hypothetical future Russian federative democratic state. Reflecting on the political organization of the Belarusian movement after the February Revolution, this chapter analyzes its internal dynamics and provides an insight into the intense political competition in Minsk during 1917, while paying attention to the changing fortunes of the Belarusian national parties.

Chapter five deals with the preparations for and convocation of the First All-Belarusian Congress in December 1917 in Minsk. Often described as the Belarusian version of a constituent assembly,[20] the Congress was the major event

---

[20]   Ja. Varonko, *Bielaruski ruch ad 1917 da 1920 hodu: Karotki ahliad* (Kaunas: n. p., 1920), 7; A. Cvikievič [Tsvikevich], *Kratkii ocherk vozniknoveniia Belarusskoi narodnoi respubliki* (Kyiv: n. p., 1918), 8.

of Belarusian national life in 1917 and, on a larger scale, one of the key events in the modern history of Belarus. The Congress marked an important transition in the thinking of Belarusian national activists. In the wake of its violent dissolution by the Minsk Bolshevik authorities, national elites started to re-evaluate their political views, abandoning their aspirations for autonomy within a federative Russian republic, which had remained the prevalent attitude throughout 1917.

Chapter six provides a comparative perspective of the early state- and nation-building efforts of the Belarusian national activists from the national and Bolshevik-friendly camps during the crucial period in the history of Belarusian statehood in 1918. It addresses the conditions under which the idea of a separate Belarusian nation-state emerged, examining its meaning for the Belarusian national movement. Dating back to resolutions of the First All-Belarusian Congress in late December 1917 and the aftermath of its dissolution, its implementation was prompted by the unfavorable international situation and, in particular, the Brest-Litovsk peace treaty signed by Soviet Russia and the Central Powers. The departure from Russia-oriented state-building concepts was evident with the proclamation of the Belarusian Democratic Republic (BDR) on March 9, 1918, which was followed by the declaration of its independence on March 25. Immediately thereafter, the Bolsheviks hurried to appropriate the Belarusian national idea and make use of it to secure the borders of the Soviet state.

This book is based on an analysis of primary sources and archival holdings from Belarusian and Lithuanian archives, complemented by collections of published archival materials in Belarusian, Russian, and German languages as well as official and personal documentation and correspondence, protocols of meetings, and analytical reports. It also refers to the writings and memoirs of prominent Belarusian national activists, including Anton Luckievič, Ivan Luckievič, Vaclaŭ Lastoŭski, Jazep Varonka, Adam Stankievič, Aliaksandr Cvikevič, and others.[21] Another type of source is the periodical press, its correspondence with officials, journalists, and ordinary readers, as well as censored materials which did not appear in print.

Unfortunately, documentation pertaining to Belarusian national activism during the First World War is not preserved in full, leaving voids which cannot

---

[21] For instance, see Anton Luckievič, *Da historyi bielaruskaha ruchu*; Anatoľ Sidarevič, ed., *Pra Ivana Luckieviča: Uspaminy, sviedčanni* (Minsk: Knihazbor, 2007); Julijana Vitan-Dubiejkaŭskaja, *Maje ŭspaminy* (Vilnius: Niezaležnaje vydaviectva Technalohija, 1994); Cvikievič, *Kratkii ocherk*; F. Turuk, *Belorusskoe dvizhenie: Ocherk istorii natsionalnogo i revoliutsionnogo dvizheniia belorussov* (Moscow: Gosudarstvennoe izdatelstvo, 1921); Adam Stankievič, *Z Boham da Bielarusi: Zbor tvoraŭ* (Vilnius: Instytut bielarusistyki, 2008); Varonko, *Bielaruski ruch*.

be filled in. For instance, BDR-related source materials suffered a difficult fate throughout the twentieth century. The location of some key documents is unknown and they are inaccessible for researchers. These include, but are not limited to, documentation concerning the All-Belarusian Congress in 1917, the protocols of its Executive Committee, which continued operating after the dissolution of the Congress, and documents reflecting the early activities of the BDR government. From late 1918, the archives of the BDR were in the custody of different people and some materials were either lost or destroyed after the BDR institutions were forced to leave Minsk in December 1918. Currently, the majority of the surviving documentation is scattered between the National Archive of the Republic of Belarus (NARB) and the Lithuanian Central State Archive (LCVA). The latter's BDR files were published in a two-volume document collection in 1998.[22] Recently, it has been expanded with another important collection of BDR documents from the State Archive of the Russian Federation.[23]

Historical Background of the Belarusian National Movement

After the final partition of the Polish-Lithuanian Commonwealth in 1795, the Russian Empire incorporated most of the ethnically Belarusian territories. It was still cautious with the newly acquired lands in the first half of the nineteenth century, aiming to coopt the local elites into the administrative structure and prioritizing the integrity of the empire.[24] However, the Russian authorities started giving up on this approach after the November Uprising of 1830–31, while the January Uprising of 1863 marked a definitive turn in the imperial nationalities policies. Their primary aim shifted towards depriving the Poles of their influence in the western borderlands which became the site of assimilatory nationalities policies.[25]

---

[22]   For a more detailed summary regarding the fate of the BDR archives, see Hanna Surmač, "Bielaruski zahraničny archiŭ," *Bielaruskaja Miniuŭščyna*, no. 1 (1993): 18–23; Siarhiej Šupa, "Bielaruskaja Narodnaja Respublika i jaje archivy," in *Archivy Bielaruskaj Narodnaj Respubliki*, ed. Siarhiej Šupa (Vilnius: Bielaruski instytut navuki i mastactva, 1998), v–xviii; Janka Zaprudnik, "Da zahadki dziaržaŭnaha archivu BNR u Mikoly Abramčyka," *Zapisy*, no. 32 (2009): 450–76.

[23]   Aliaksandr Horny and Andrej Buča, eds., *Archivy Bielaruskaj Narodnaj Respubliki*, vol. 2, bk. 1 (Minsk: Knihazbor, 2021).

[24]   On the integration and Russian administration of the former territories of the Grand Duchy of Lithuania in the first half of the nineteenth century, see Jörg Ganzenmüller, *Russische Staatsgewalt und Polnischer Adel: Elitenintegration und Staatsausbau im Westen des Zarenreiches (1772–1850)* (Cologne: Böhlau Verlag, 2013).

[25]   Alexei Miller refers to these territories as a "laboratory of nationalisms" in the nineteenth and twentieth centuries. See Alexei Miller, "The Role of the First World War in the Competition between

More confrontational and uncompromising than elite cooptation, these policies affected various national groups in different ways. For instance, there was a consensus that Poles could not be assimilated, while Belarusians, on the other hand, became the primary target of Russification policies. In the case of Lithuanians, there was a less clearly expressed intention toward full assimilation, which allowed for more leeway in the activities of the national movement, as compared to the Belarusian case.[26]

The Polish-Lithuanian-Belarusian region became the arena of struggle between the Russian Empire and the Polish national movement. While the latter aimed to advance a modern national project with vertical ties uniting the elites and the masses, the Russian imperial government focused on the idea of Slavic unity, in particular the notion of the tri-partite Russian nation, where the Great Russian, Little Russian, and White Russian nationalities were conceived as branches of the same tree. Therefore, de-Polonization was treated as an essential tool for depriving the Polish nobility of their influence in the region, and asserting Russian dominance over the Eastern Slavs. The turn towards assimilation manifested itself, among other things, in the Russian approach to religion. The Uniate Church was liquidated by 1839 and former Uniates were forced to convert to Orthodoxy.[27]

Imperial authorities started to interpret the Belarusian past in terms of Russian dominance in opposition to the Poles.[28] The turn towards full assimilation appeared to be an impediment to the Belarusian nation-building process. It prevented the emergence of sufficient numbers of dedicated activists supporting and promoting the national project, defined exclusively in Belarusian terms. Combined with the predominantly peasant character of society and the linguistic closeness of Slavic languages, these factors collectively accounted for the belated Belarusian nation-building. At the same time, comparisons with the Ukrainian

---

Ukrainian and All-Russian Nationalism," in Lohr et al., *The Empire and Nationalism at War*, 73. On Russification, see also Serhii Plokhy, *Lost Kingdom: The Quest for Empire and the Making of the Russian Nation from 1470 to the Present* (New York: Basic Books, 2017), 85–104; Darius Staliūnas, *Making Russians: Meaning and Practice of Russification in Lithuania and Belarus after 1863* (Amsterdam: Rodopi, 2007), 297; Andrew Savchenko, *Belarus: A Perpetual Borderland* (Leiden: Brill, 2009), 53.

[26] Staliūnas, *Making Russians*, 302–5.

[27] For a detailed analysis of Russian imperial confessional policies, see Theodore Weeks, "Religion and Russification: Russian Language in the Catholic Churches of the 'Northwest Provinces' after 1863," *Kritika: Explorations in Russian and Eurasian History* 2, no. 1 (2001): 87–110; M. D. Dolbilov, *Russkii krai, chuzhaia vera: Etnokonfessional'naia politika imperii v Litve i Belorussii pri Aleksandre II* (Moscow: Novoe literaturnoe obozrenie, 2010).

[28] Rainer Lindner, *Historiker und Herrschaft: Nationsbildung und Geschichtspolitik in Weissrussland im 19. und 20. Jahrhundert* (Munich: R. Oldenbourg, 1999), 71.

situation reveal that despite similar social structures, Ukraine had more favorable conditions due to the presence of universities in its cultural life and its different history of partitions.[29] Since all ethnically Belarusian territories were administered by the Russian Empire, the chance that a significant emigre community would emerge to initiate and uphold alternate projects was rather limited,[30] unlike in the Ukrainian and Lithuanian cases.

In the second half of the nineteenth century, the imperial authorities tried to prove the close connections and common historical roots of all East Slavic peoples in the newly constructed imperial region. This approach eventually led to the emergence of West-Russism ideology.[31] Belarusian identification within this framework was subordinated to the larger All-Russian project and had to remain within its regional boundaries.[32] However, from another angle, the Russian imperial nationalities policies also had an important side-effect in the unintended recognition of local Belarusian, Ukrainian, and Lithuanian[33] nationalisms, contributing to a process of cultural accumulation[34] and the subsequent strengthening of corresponding national movements. More importantly, from a long-term perspective, even the controlled interim construction of new regions and identities from above within a colonial context created a space and premise for an "imaginable" project of modern Belarus,[35] facilitating the task of the emerging national elites.

Modern Belarusian national discourse developed parallel to the imperially promoted West-Russism, demonstrating the inherent duality of the modern Belarusian project already in its early formative period. Rainer Lindner terms these two competing positions as integrative and national conceptions, noting that both had a political dimension.[36] The latter gradually gained strength in the second half of the nineteenth century, separating the history of the Belarusians from their neighbors and creating myths of a "golden age," as for instance Adam Kirkor did by idealizing the Grand Duchy of Lithuania.[37]

---

[29]   Lindner, *Historiker und Herrschaft*, 57, 69.

[30]   Lindner, *Historiker und Herrschaft*, 57.

[31]   Valer Bulgakov, *Istoriiia belorusskogo natsionalizma* (Vilnius: Institut belorusistiki, 2006), 151.

[32]   Dolbilov, *Russkii krai, chuzhaia vera*, 195.

[33]   Alexei Miller, "The Romanov Empire and the Russian Nation," in *Nationalizing Empires*, ed. Alexei I. Miller and Stefan Berger (Budapest–New York: CEU Press, 2015), 330–31.

[34]   Ales' Smaliančuk, "Licvinstva, zachodnierusizm i bielaruskaja ideja XIX–pačatak XX st," in *Białoruś w XX stuleciu: W kręgu kultury i polityki*, ed. Dorota Michaluk (Toruń: Wydawnictwo Naukowe Uniwersytetu Mikołaja Kopernika, 2007), 60.

[35]   P. V. Tereshkovich, *Etnicheskaia istoriia Belarusi XIX–nachala XX v. v kontekste Tsentralno-Vostochnoi Evropy* (Minsk: BGU, 2004), 187.

[36]   Lindner, *Historiker und Herrschaft*, 72.

[37]   Lindner, *Historiker und Herrschaft*, 76–77.

During the 1863 Uprising, the insurgents started to use the Belarusian language as a means of political struggle in an attempt to mobilize the support of the peasantry. Kanstancin (Kastus') Kalinoŭski, who commanded the uprising in Belarus and Lithuania, tried to reach out to the broad masses with the irregular newspaper *Myžyckaja Praŭda* (Peasant Truth). Shortly after the defeat of the uprising, his *Listy z-pad šybenicy* (Letters from beneath the Gallows) addressed the issue of the Belarusian language and its suppression by the educational system.[38] Kalinoŭski would become an important symbolic figure within the Belarusian national discourse in the future. Most likely, the uprising caused the evolution of his views from support for the regional patriotic allegiance to the former Grand Duchy of Lithuania towards the national concept.[39]

The last decades of the nineteenth century represented the key turning point for modern Belarusian nationalism. Between 1880 and 1900, the anticolonial counter-narrative espoused by the lawyer and poet Francišak Bahuševič marked this transition.[40] Bahuševič framed the Belarusian national idea in the introduction to his poetry volume *Dudka Białaruskaja*.[41] Mediating between the past and the present, he established the tradition of the Belarusian Revival/Renaissance, based on the interpretation of Belarus as the core of the former Grand Duchy of Lithuania, glorifying its history and emphasizing the value of the Belarusian language.[42] These steps were instrumental in creating a common legacy of memories for Belarusians. The French theorist of nationalism, Ernest Renan, considered such images of heroic history, great men, and past glory to be at the core of a national idea.[43]

In an attempt to convey the national message to the broad masses, Bahuševič constructed the ideal type of its recipient, a Belarusian peasant with a distinctly differing identification from Russians and Poles.[44] However, the major drawback of this narrative, adopted later by the emergent Belarusian national elites, was the focus on peasant culture. In fact, it was unattractive not only for the nobles, who were unlikely to identify with peasant culture, but for the broad masses as well,

[38] Kastus' Kalinoŭski and Henadz' Kisialoŭ, *Za našuju vol'nasc': tvory, dakumenty* (Minsk: Bielaruski knihazbor, 1999), 40–46.

[39] Aleksandr Kravtsevich, Aleksandr Smolenchuk, and Sergei Tokt', *Belorusy: natsiia Pogranich'ia* (Vilnius: EGU, 2011), 123–24.

[40] Bulgakov, *Istoriia*, 233.

[41] Maciej Buraczok, *Dudka Białaruskaja* (Kraków: Wł. L. Anczyc i Ska, 1891). The book was published in Belarusian using the Latin script.

[42] Bulgakov, *Istoriia*, 226–27, 229.

[43] Renan, "What Is a Nation?," 52.

[44] Bulgakov, *Istoriia*, 267; Tereshkovich, *Etnicheskaia istoriia*, 133.

since the latter were more inclined to strive for inclusion into the cultural world of nobles and intellectuals (Polish or Russian) in hopes of future social mobility.[45] The lack of social groups dedicated primarily to the modern Belarusian project, especially in a situation where religion was a divisive factor rather than a unifying one, slowed down the process of nation-building. The ban on the Uniate Church back in 1839 deprived the future Belarusian movement of its potentially active social base,[46] especially as, in the subsequent decades, religious identifications tended to be equated with national ones, where being Roman Catholic or Orthodox often meant being identified as Polish or Russian, respectively.

The final project of the modern Belarusian nation was also heavily influenced by the colonial discourses of West-Russism and modern Polish nationalism,[47] which presented Belarus as a marginalized region with a predominantly peasant culture. The political context of the second half of the nineteenth century, along with the assimilatory pressures on Belarusians and Ukrainians, slowed down the development and evolution of their respective national movements.[48] National movements of largely peasant nations were highly dependent on the coincidence of confessional, social, and political antagonisms,[49] most of which were not pronounced in the Belarusian case, as demonstrated by the religious divide between the masses and the national activists, who belonged to different confessions and social strata.

Similarly to the Ukrainians, the Belarusians were more receptive to socialist rather than nationalist slogans, due to their peasant-dominated society. In this respect, the convergence of social and national demands could be used as an effective means of mobilizing the masses, which explains the popularity of the socialist parties within the Belarusian national milieu.[50] On the other hand, the socialist character of the leading Belarusian political parties and their emphasis on social liberation rather than national self-determination precluded the inclusion of all social strata in the process of modern nation construction. Socialists focused on

---

[45]   Ryšard Radzik, *Vytoki sučasnaj bielaruskasci: Bielarusy na fone nacyiatvorčych pracesaŭ u Centralna-Uschodniaj Eŭropie 19 st.* (Minsk: Medysont, 2012), 319.

[46]   Radzik, *Vytoki sučasnaj bielaruskasci*, 312–13. For instance, the Lithuanian national movement capitalized on the religious element; on the role of the Roman Catholic clergy, see Tomas Balkelis, *The Making of Modern Lithuania* (New York: Routledge, 2009), 87–88.

[47]   Bulgakov, *Istoriiia*, 115–28.

[48]   Kappeler, *Der schwierige Weg*, 34.

[49]   Kappeler, *Der schwierige Weg*, 96–97.

[50]   Per Anders Rudling, *The Rise and Fall of Belarusian Nationalism, 1906–1931* (Pittsburgh, PA: University of Pittsburgh Press, 2014), 22; Kappeler, *Der schwierige Weg*, 31.

their own narrow vision of a nation, rooted in the perceptions of Belarusians as predominantly peasant masses, Orthodox by religion, and populating the countryside. Within this socialist framework, the nation was interpreted in exclusivist terms, leaving no place for the nobles or even, often, the Roman Catholics.[51]

By contrast, the long-lasting identification of the elites with the pre-modern Grand Duchy of Lithuania and their orientation towards regional patriotism resulted in a reluctance to embrace the new nationalist thinking, which was especially characteristic for Belarusians, or Polonized Belarusians to be exact. In contrast to the Lithuanians, whose elites had strong connections to the peasantry,[52] Belarusian activists had different backgrounds: most of them belonged to the smallholding gentry with strong ties to Polish culture, magnified through a common religion and language affinity. Thus, the broad masses of the ethnically Belarusian peasant population, Orthodox or converted to Orthodoxy, had little in common with its largely Roman Catholic elites with noble backgrounds. Moreover, the linguistic closeness of Slavic languages did not bring out the need for the exclusive use of Belarusian for communication with the peasant masses, who could understand other languages too. With the increased emphasis that national movements placed on language and religious distinctions in the late nineteenth century, this was a certain drawback.[53]

The Revolution of 1905 marked a turn towards a more flexible nationalities policy in the western borderlands and changed the Russian imperial hierarchy of internal threats, where the revolutionary peasantry replaced the Poles as the primary danger. At the same time, the revolution contributed to the revival of national activities and their inclusion into the political realm. Duma election campaigns led to the nationalization of the peasantry, causing a growing interest in politics.[54] However, in the case of Belarusian nation-building, the period of liberalization proved to be ambiguous and challenging. Despite the concessions to nationalities in the sphere of education, schools with Belarusian as the principal language

[51] Dorota Michaluk, *Białoruska Republika Ludowa, 1918–1920: u podstaw białoruskiej państwowości* (Toruń: Wydawnictwo Naukowe Uniwersytetu Mikołaja Kopernika, 2010), 320; Nelly Bekus, "Nationalism and Socialism: 'Phase D' in the Belarusian Nation-Building," *Nationalities Papers* 38, no. 6 (2010): 834.

[52] Wiktor Sukiennicki and Maciej Siekierski, *East Central Europe during World War I: From Foreign Domination to National Independence*, vol. 1 (New York: Columbia University Press, 1984), 53–54.

[53] Snyder, *Reconstruction of Nations*, 40, 45–47.

[54] M. D. Dolbilov and A. I. Miller, *Zapadnye okrainy Rossiiskoi imperii* (Moscow: Novoe literaturnoe obozrenie, 2006), 343–53.

of instruction were not tolerated, unlike the Polish or Lithuanian schools.[55] The demands for education in the mother tongue for Belarusians remained one of the chief aims of the short-lived Belarusian Teachers' Union, established in 1907 in Vil'nia.[56]

Nevertheless, following the Revolution of 1905, the role of the urban-based intellectuals in articulating national interests became more pronounced. In the Belarusian case, this meant growing influence and increased nation-building activities within the intellectual circles in Vil'nia. One of the positive outcomes was the growth of their publishing activities in the subsequent decade.[57] In 1906, the first legal Belarusian newspaper, conceptualized by Ivan Luckievič, appeared in print.[58] The first issue of *Naša Dolia* was published on September 14, 1906, with a run of 10,000 copies. Five other issues followed, yet the newspaper soon closed down after confiscations by the tsarist authorities and the political persecution of its authors.

Its successor, *Naša Niva*, turned out to be a more stable long-term project. Its first issue dates back to November 10, 1906. Its circulation of 3,000 copies was notably lower due to the reactionary tsarist policies, yet the newspaper existed until August 7, 1915, and acted as "the main forge of the Belarusian revival ideology,"[59] giving a name to a whole period in the early history of modern Belarusian

[55] On the effects of the Revolution of 1905 on Polish culture in the Belarusian territories, see Andrzej Romanowski, "The Year 1905 and the Revival of Polish Culture between the Neman and the Dnepr," *Canadian Slavonic Papers/Revue Canadienne Des Slavistes* 41, no. 1 (1999): 45–67.

[56] Sviatlana Snapkoŭskaja, *Adukacyjnaja palityka i škola na Bielarusi ŭ kancy XIX–pačatku XX stst.* (Minsk: Ministerstva Adukacyi Respubliki Bielarus', Nacyjanal'ny Instytut Adukacyi, 1998), 70.

[57] Lindner, *Historiker und Herrschaft*, 56–57. A similar situation was also characteristic for the Lithuanian national movement, which expanded its cultural activities after 1905 in an attempt to forge links between the national elites and the population. See Balkelis, *The Making of Modern Lithuania*, 102.

[58] Ivan Luckievič (1881–1919) and his brother Anton (1884–1942) were born in Kaunas province to the family of a railway official. In 1895, the family moved to Minsk, where Ivan could pursue his interests in history, antiquity, and archeology. In 1902, Ivan Luckievič was admitted to St. Petersburg University to study law, while simultaneously enrolling at the Institute for Archeology. Ivan Luckievič's collections became the basis of the Belarusian Museum in Vil'nia, which officially opened in 1921 and was named after him. It became one of the major Belarusian educational and cultural centers, with a rich library and archival holdings. Ivan and his brother Anton kept close contacts with all future major Belarusian national activists, including Alaiza Paškievič (literary pseudonym—Ciotka), Ales' Burbis, Aliaksandr Ulasaŭ, Branislaŭ Epimach-Šypila, and Vaclaŭ Lastoŭski. See Sidarevič, *Pra Ivana Luckieviča*, 13–15.

[59] Anton Luckievič, *Da historyi bielaruskaha ruchu: vybranyja tvory*, ed. Anatol' Sidarevič (Minsk: Bielaruski knihazbor, 2003), 134.

nationalism. Brothers Ivan and Anton Luckievič along with the editor Aliaksandr Ulasaŭ formed the core of the *Naša Niva* milieu, grouping together the Belarusian poets Maksim Bahdanovič, Jakub Kolas, Janka Kupala, Ales' Harun, the writers Zmitrok Biadulia, Ciška Hartny, Maksim Harecki, Jadzvihin Š., Siarhiej Palujan, and others.[60] While *Naša Dolia* focused on the social liberation of the poor Belarusian peasantry, *Naša Niva* assumed a more moderate tone and essentially served as a tool of ethnic nationalism. Belarusian activists also used regional patriotism as a means of promoting the national idea to broader audiences. The so-called "clerical-patriotic" version of the Belarusian national project emphasized the national unity of Orthodox and Roman Catholic Belarusians. It gave rise to the Belarusian Christian Democrats, who were represented by the activists around the newspaper *Biełarus*, which started to appear in 1913 and was edited by Baliaslaŭ Pačobka.[61]

In 1910, Vaclaŭ Lastoŭski[62] published his *Short History of Belarus*[63] pioneering the construction of the Belarusian historical narrative in exclusively national terms. In the vein of Bahuševič's nation-foundation mythology, he provided the modern Belarusian narrative with historical continuity. Remarkably, it was defined by its defensive character, emphasizing victimization and suffering rather than progress and development. Moreover, this aspect was magnified by statements that Russia and Poland had detrimentally influenced Belarusian cultural, linguistic, and social development.[64] Remarkably, these tropes proved to be rather persistent almost one hundred years later, when Belarus gained independence after the dissolution of the Soviet Union.

The inception of an organized Belarusian political movement dates back to the establishment of the first illegal Belarusian party, the BRP (Belarusian Revolutionary Party), which originated in the Belarusian student circles organized around Vaclaŭ Ivanoŭski in St. Petersburg in 1902. Ivanoŭski soon switched his interests to the cultural and educational sphere, popularizing Belarusian publishing, while the brothers Ivan and Anton Luckievič assumed the leading roles in the political establishment of the Belarusian national movement in the

---

60 Luckievič, *Da historyi bielaruskaha ruchu*, 135–36.

61 Smialančuk, "Licvinstva, zachodnierusizm i bielaruskaja ideja XIX–pačatak XX st," 62–66.

62 Vaclaŭ Lastoŭski was a writer, politician, and historian, and is sometimes referred to as a "herald of the Belarusian national reawakening." See Victor Sienkevich, "Lastoŭski the Historian and His Historical Views," *Journal of Belarusian Studies* 5, nos. 3–4 (1984): 4.

63 Vaclaŭ Lastoŭski, *Karotkaja historyja Biełarusi z 40 rysunkami* (Vilnius: Drukarnia Marcina Kuchty, 1910).

64 Lindner, *Historiker und Herrschaft*, 115–17.

early twentieth century.[65] They initialized the transformation of the BRP into the Belarusian Revolutionary Hramada (BRH) in 1904.[66] In late 1905, the BRH held a congress in Minsk where it decided on a socialist direction and was renamed the Belarusian Socialist Hramada (BSH), with branches in Minsk, Vil'nia, and St. Petersburg.[67] The BSH did not operate during the reactionary period following the failed 1905 revolution and resurfaced in the political arena only after the February Revolution of 1917, when it immediately claimed the leadership of the Belarusian national movement.[68]

[65]   Jury Turonak, *Madernaja historyja Bielarusi* (Vilnius: Instytut bielarusistyki, 2008), 166–67.

[66]   Turonak, *Madernaja historyja Bielarusi*, 174.

[67]   Luckievič, *Da historyi bielaruskaha ruchu*, 152–53.

[68]   Z. Žylunovič, "Liuty—Kastryčnik u bielaruskim nacyjanalnym ruchu," in *Bielarus': Narysy historyi, ekanomiki, kul'turnaha i revoliucyjnaha ruchu*, ed. A. Stašeŭski, Z. Žylunovič, and U. Ihnatoŭski (Minsk: Vydannie Centralnaha Komitetu Bielaruskae Savieckae Socyjalistyčnae Respubliki, 1924), 184–85.

Chapter 1

The First World War on Belarusian Territories

Until recently, the First World War in Eastern Europe remained in the shadows of the battles and trench warfare of the Western Front and the revolutionary period of 1917 in Russia. For a long time, Norman Stone's account of the military operations on the Eastern Front, dating back to the 1970s, was one of the few studies which addressed this aspect of the Great War.[1] Yet, with the advent of the war's centennial, the historiography of the First World War in Eastern Europe experienced rapid growth. Along with the traditional topics of military,[2] diplomatic,[3] economic, and social history,[4] recent historiography has also addressed the cultural aspects of the Great War and the experiences of the civilian populations and soldiers on the Eastern Front.[5] Finally, new methodological approaches of transnational and entangled histories have concentrated on the implications of the First World War for the process of imperial collapse, decolonization, and the radicalization

1   Norman Stone, *The Eastern Front, 1914–1917* (New York: Scribner, 1975).
2   David R. Stone, *The Russian Army in the Great War: The Eastern Front, 1914–1917* (Lawrence, KS: University Press of Kansas, 2015); Gerhard P. Groß, ed., *Die Zeitalter der Weltkriege: Die vergessene Front—der Osten 1914/15: Ereignis, Wirkung, Nachwirkung* (Paderborn: Schöningh, 2006).
3   Dominic Lieven, *The End of Tsarist Russia: The March to World War I and Revolution* (New York: Viking, 2015); Borislav Černev, *Twilight of Empire: The Brest-Litovsk Conference and the Remaking of East-Central Europe, 1917–1918* (Toronto: University of Toronto Press, 2019).
4   See Peter Gatrell, *Russia's First World War: A Social and Economic History* (Harlow: Pearson/ Longman, 2005); Jennifer Siegel, *For Peace and Money: French and British Money in the Service of Tsars and Commissars* (New York: Oxford University Press, 2014).
5   See, for instance, Murray Frame, Boris Kolonitskii, Steven G. Marks, and Melissa K. Stockdale, eds., *Russian Culture in War and Revolution, 1914–22* (Bloomington, IN.: Slavica Publishers, 2014); Alfred Eisfeld, Guido Hausmann, and Dietmar Neutatz, eds., *Besetzt, interniert, deportiert: Der Erste Weltkrieg und die deutsche, jüdische, polnische und ukrainische Zivilbevölkerung im östlichen Europa* (Essen: Klartext, 2013); Bernhard Bachinger and Wolfram Dornik, eds., *Jenseits des Schützengrabes: Der Erste Weltkrieg im Osten: Erfahrung—Wahrnehmung—Kontext* (Innsbruck, Vienna, Bolzano: Studien Verlag 2013); Oksana S. Nagornaia, *Drugoi voennyi opyt: rossiiskie voennoplennye Pervoi mirovoi voiny v Germanii (1914–1922)* (Moscow: Novyi Khronograf, 2010).

of violence in the region.[6] In this regard, a focus on the Belarusian dimension within these larger narratives allows one to contextualize the impact of this major military conflict on the conditions for nation-building.

In 1915, the central sector of the Eastern Front of the First World War had stabilized and would remain so for almost the next three years, dividing contemporary Belarusian territories into two parts: the German-occupied Ober Ost and the areas controlled by the Russian Empire. Belarusians who found themselves under German administration had to deal with a foreign occupation regime. To some extent, they could use German educational and cultural concessions to the local nationalities in order to advance their nation-building efforts. Yet, national politics suffered from the limitations imposed by the German military administration.[7] On the other side of the front, martial law in the western borderlands of the Russian Empire, a ban on political activities, forced migration, mass displacement of the civilian population, and evacuations of educational and cultural institutions negatively affected the nation-building efforts of Belarusian national activists up until 1917, when the February Revolution liberalized political life for all nationalities of the former Russian Empire. The aim of this chapter is to outline the major implications of the First World War on Belarusians and their national movement in the Russian Empire in the period between the start of the war and the February Revolution in 1917.

Russian Military Administration in the Western Borderlands

After the declaration of general mobilization in Russia on July 30, 1914 (N.S.), about 3.4 million reservists were called to service. Russian imperial authorities hurried with mobilization and had already started military operations against Germany in East Prussia by mid-August 1914, as they were obliged to keep their treaty promises to France.[8] Imperial Russia received the news of the war with patriotic-inspired enthusiasm, mobilizing all available resources for the war effort.[9]

---

[6] See, for instance, Sanborn, *Imperial Apocalypse*; Lohr et al, *The Empire and Nationalism at War.*

[7] See Chapters 2 and 3 for a detailed discussion of the German occupation in Ober Ost.

[8] Bruce W. Menning, "War Planning and Initial Operations in the Russian Context," in *War Planning 1914*, ed. Richard F. Hamilton and Holger H. Herwig (Cambridge: Cambridge University Press, 2010), 126, 128.

[9] On the popular moods in 1914, see the eyewitness account of Mikhail Lemke, who served in the Russian Stavka, M. K. Lemke, *250 dnei v tsarskoi stavke 1914–1915* (Minsk: Kharvest, 2003), 14–25.

On July 16, 1914, Tsar Nicholas II signed the "Regulations on the Field Administration of the Troops in Wartime," which structured the army command and introduced martial law in the Russian borderlands west of the Dnepr River. Over time, this area gradually expanded eastward, exceeding in size the combined territories of Germany and Austria-Hungary.[10]

New regulations prioritized the needs of the Russian army and allowed the military to take extraordinary measures to ensure successful military operations, fight espionage, and guarantee state security.[11] Martial law introduced the supremacy of the military over civilian authorities, fundamentally transforming governance in the western provinces. It resulted in a hybrid dual power system, where the military regime in the borderlands existed almost independently of the central civilian powers in Petrograd.[12] For instance, the entire hierarchy of the Russian army command in 1914 became independent of the Ministry of War and the civilian government. Daniel Graf has argued that in the long run, this circumstance combined with the lack of coordinated actions endangered the Russian war effort, contributing to the demise of tsarism.[13]

According to the "Regulations," Tsar Nicholas II personally picked the commanders of the armies, who were subordinate only to the Commander-in-Chief, Grand Duke Nicholas. The imperial bureaucracy and civil institutions had no authority to supervise or request any reports from the military. Along with their war-related missions, army commanders received powers to interfere in civilian matters. They could limit freedom of movement by ordering the compulsory removal of individuals deemed undesirable from the army operation areas. On the other hand, they could also prohibit certain categories of professionals from leaving, if their jobs were important for the war effort at the front. Further, army commanders had the upper hand in the management of resources and provisions, and were responsible for carrying out requisitions. They assumed responsibility for civil order and state security, controlling transportation, communications, trade, and industries, along with censoring the press.[14] The introduction of martial

---

[10] Daniel Graf, "Military Rule behind the Russian Front, 1914–1917: The Political Ramifications," *Jahrbücher für Geschichte Osteuropas* 22, no. 3 (1974): 390–92.

[11] Joshua Sanborn, "War of Decolonization," in Lohr et al., *The Empire and Nationalism at War*, 63–64.

[12] Jochen Böhler, "Generals and Warlords, Revolutionaries and Nation State Builders," in *Legacies of Violence: Eastern Europe's First World War*, ed. Jochen Böhler, Włodzimierz Borodziej, and Joachim von Puttkamer (Munich: Oldenbourg Verlag, 2014), 55–56.

[13] Graf, "Military Rule," 390.

[14] Lemke, *250 dnei*, 61–63.

law allowed Russian generals to place whole regions under their direct command, expanding zones of violence and catalyzing the overall radicalization of society.[15]

On August 16, 1914, the Russian Headquarters of the Supreme Commander, known as Stavka, started operating in the town of Baranavičy, located south-west of Minsk. Threatened by the German advance in the summer of 1915, Stavka moved further east to Mahilioŭ in August 1915.[16] Concerned with strengthening the rear of the army in 1915, Stavka conducted its own policies, severely interfering with the authority of the central government. On June 16, 1915, the Russian Chief of Staff, General Yanushkevich, sent a secret telegram from Stavka to General Danilov at the North-Western Front, ordering him to evacuate all means of transportation, cattle, and provisions, to destroy the crops, and to blow up bridges and dams.[17] Following the removal of strategically important industries, the military started to evacuate administrative and cultural institutions, banks, businesses, and even church bells. Schools, public libraries, museums, and archives from the western borderlands were thus scattered across the Russian Empire. Some of the schools were permanently dismantled and closed down. Only the larger ones managed to continue working during the evacuation. Among the latter were the Minsk Pedagogical Institute in Yaroslavl and the Maladzečna Pedagogical Seminary in Smolensk.[18]

The process of evacuations was accompanied by the forced uprooting and resettlement of reservists, soon extending to entire populations behind the front, conducted both by military and civilian authorities. The army commanders did not differentiate between which categories of the population could be useful for the enemy, and which could stay.[19] Relying on the Russian experiences during the war of 1812, when civilians fled from the Grande Armée, destroying provisions and complicating the procurement of resources for the French, the Russian Commander-in-Chief, Grand Duke Nicholas, hoped that depopulated areas would slow down the German armies in the same manner. Yet, while this tactic made sense in 1812, when the French armies moved east through a narrow corridor, it was obsolete in 1915, as the German armies quickly advanced in a broad continuous

---

[15]   Eric Lohr argues that the system of military rule and increased role of the army marked the era of so-called war nationalism, which defined the transformation of nationalism during the First World War. See Lohr, "War Nationalism," 95–97.

[16]   Irina Dubeiko, *Zabytaia voina* (Minsk: Medisont, 2014), 9.

[17]   M. M. Smol'ianinov, *Belarus' v pervoi mirovoi voine 1914–1918* (Minsk: Bielaruskaja navuka, 2014), 95–96.

[18]   "Rasciarušanaje bahacce," *Bielaruski Šliach*, no. 68, June 16, 1918, 1.

[19]   Smol'ianinov, *Belarus' v pervoi mirovoi voine*, 95–96.

front, using all available roads and railways.[20] Failure to account for modernization turned the "scorched earth" tactic into another factor that discredited the Russian military in the eyes of the local populations, who suffered to a greater degree than the enemy armies. The unpredictable behavior of the Russian generals, whose actions were often not coordinated with the central government, contributed to further chaos and disorganization during the retreat.[21]

Fearing the negative reactions of the local population, Commander-in-Chief Grand Duke Nicholas tried to prevent the escalation of violent expropriations and to involve civilian authorities in securing order and providing for the army's needs. However, his intervention was not successful. The front commanders and the lower rank army officers together with the subordinate local authorities often interpreted Stavka's orders in a broader sense, accompanying them with threats and terrorizing the civilian population. In this manner, the military authorities sidelined the civilian government and expanded their own sphere of power.[22] Generals Danilov and Zabelin, acting as supreme chiefs of supplies on the Northwestern and Southwestern Fronts, respectively, were in charge of the front rear areas. In addition to the expanded authorities of the civilian governors-general, these virtual military dictators also received the power to control almost every aspect of life in the western borderlands, including the bureaucracy, censorship, requisitions, and prices.[23] In certain ways, the Russian military regime resembled Ludendorff's methods of military administration in the neighboring occupied Ober Ost lands at around the same time.[24]

Military operations in Eastern Prussia, Galicia, and Poland during the first year of the war uncovered a number of problems within the Russian imperial army. Ineffective command, a lack of munitions, unreliable intelligence, and insufficient communication between different army headquarters had already resulted in a retreat and significant human losses by the fall of 1914.[25] The Russian military soon

[20]   E. A. Nikol'skii, *Zapiski o proshlom* (Moscow: Russkii put', 2007), 212–13.
[21]   Peter Gatrell, *A Whole Empire Walking: Refugees in Russia During World War I* (Bloomington, IN: Indiana University Press, 1999), 16, 33.
[22]   Smol'ianinov, *Belarus' v pervoi mirovoi voine*, 98–99.
[23]   Graf, "Military Rule," 392–93. On the organization of requisitions and the mobilization of industries for the needs of the Russian army in 1914–1915, see Valerii N. Cherepitsa, *Gorod-krepost' Grodno v gody Pervoj mirovoj vojny: Meropriiatiia grazhdanskikh i voennykh vlastei po obespecheniiu oboronosposobnosti i zhiznedeiatel'nosti* (Minsk: Bielaruskaja Encyklapedyja imia Pietrusia Broŭki, 2009), 261–77.
[24]   See the detailed discussion of Ober Ost in Chapter 2.
[25]   Menning, "War Planning," 131–32; Smol'ianinov, *Belarus' v pervoi mirovoi voine*, 69.

discovered that prewar investment in the construction of fortresses was useless, as it only translated into wasted resources and increased numbers of POWs. Moreover, soldiers were not sufficiently prepared for trench warfare and were forced to learn new field fortification technologies by trial and error.[26] The fighting spirit of the Russian army deteriorated, as soldiers and officers lost faith in the successful outcome of the war. These moods created a fertile ground for Bolshevik anti-war agitation. The number of deserters and instances of mass surrender grew, with the first case of fraternization between Russian and German soldiers documented during Easter of 1915.[27]

The Great Retreat of the Russian army in the summer of 1915 brought military action to the western provinces of the Russian Empire. After conquering the Polish provinces, the German armies celebrated a successful offensive with the Sventsiany Breakthrough on August 27, 1915, destroying the lines of the Russian Northern and Western Fronts. Large territories of present-day Lithuania, Latvia, and Belarus came under German power, yet the strategic gains were not comparable to the scope of territorial conquest, as the Russian armies were able to fortify defenses and stabilize the front along the Riga-BaranaviČy-Pinsk-Dubno line. Mobile warfare, characteristic of the Eastern Front in the initial phase of the war, turned into positional warfare on the Belarusian territories for the next almost three years, up until 1918.[28]

Eastern Front trenches stretched over the vast territories from Riga at the Baltic Sea in the north to the Romanian border in the south. The military conflict between Germany and the Russian Empire thus led to the first major redrawing of borders in Eastern Europe since the partitions of the Polish-Lithuanian Commonwealth in the late eighteenth century. The German offensive on the Eastern front in the fall of 1915 cut through the Belarusian territories. The eastern non-occupied areas (parts of Minsk, Viciebsk [Vitebsk], Mahilioŭ [Mogilev] provinces) remained within the Russian Empire, while the areas in the west around the major cities of Vil'nia (Vilnius), Hrodna (Grodno), and Białystok were incorporated into the German zone of occupation, known as Ober Ost. The rest of the territories in the

---

[26] Lemke, *250 dnei*, 120.

[27] V. M. Chadanionak, *Sacyjalna-ekanamičnae stanovišča nasiel'nictva neakupiravanaj terytoryi Bielarusi ŭ hady Pieršaj susvietnaj vajny (kastryčnik 1915–kastryčnik 1917 hh.)* (Viciebsk: UA VDTU, 2015), 35–36.

[28] Boris Khavkin, "Russland gegen Deutschland: Die Ostfront des Ersten Weltkrieges in den Jahren 1914 bis 1915," in *Die vergessene Front—der Osten 1914/15: Ereignis, Wirkung, Nachwirkung,* ed. Gerhard Paul Gross (Paderborn: Schöningh, 2006), 82; Sanborn, *Imperial Apocalypse,* 106–7.

vicinity of the front line turned into a depopulated wasteland and massive battle-fields. For instance, the town of Smarhon', located about 120 km to the west of Minsk, was completely destroyed during the 810-day-long siege by the German armies.[29]

Demographic Crisis of 1915

In the first year of the war, the Russian military authorities decided to secure the western borderlands by deporting so-called "enemy subjects," including ethnic Germans and Austrians, who were deemed unreliable.[30] In early 1915, the policy of forced deportations was expanded towards the Jewish population.[31] These practices, along with the resettlement of reservists, foreshadowed the large-scale displacement of civilians later on in 1915, which complemented the "scorched earth" tactics. The Russian military regime soon became infamous for its arbitrary actions towards the civilian population in the rear of the front, contributing to the overall chaos and disorganization in the western provinces. Enforced migration from the areas where military actions were expected to take place resulted in a massive and unprecedented uprooting of the local population. Violence and threats, along with overzealous interpretations of the orders, were common occurrences. For instance, Cossack units were notorious in their ruthlessness, and they often forced people to move east with minimal or no possessions and provisions.[32]

Surveys conducted by the Union of Zemstvos among the refugees in 1915 confirm the forced nature of resettlement, noting that "despite the outwardly voluntary character of evacuations, available data indicate the significant role of threats and pressures exercised by the local administrations."[33] The eyewitness account of Siamion Aniščuk from the village of Husaki (Białystok province) is more explicit, describing how Cossacks rode through the village, chased people away from their homes, and set all the buildings on fire. Prior to that, Orthodox priests intimidated the villagers, demonizing the Germans as barbarians, who were allegedly

---

[29]   Vladimir Liguta, *U Smorgoni, pod znakom Sviatogo Georgiia* (Minsk: Izdatel'stvo Viktora Khursika, 2010), 102.

[30]   Eric Lohr, *Nationalizing the Russian Empire: The Campaign against Enemy Aliens during World War I* (Cambridge, MA: Harvard University Press, 2003), 122–23.

[31]   Lohr, *Nationalizing the Russian Empire*, 137–40.

[32]   A. Iu. Bakhturina, *Okrainy Rossijskoj imperii: gosudarstvennoe upravlenie i natsionalnaia politika v gody pervoi mirovoi voiny (1914–1917 gg.)* (Moscow: Rosspen, 2004), 339–40; Nikol'skii, *Zapiski o proshlom*, 212.

[33]   Nacyjanal'ny Historyčny Archiŭ Bielarusi (hereafter NHAB), f. 700, vop. 4, spr. 9, ark. 29.

blinding people and mutilating women.[34] In some cases, people resisted the orders to evacuate in 1915, refusing to leave their homes and properties. Officials of the Union of Zemstvos recorded the statements of refugees, which indicated their negative opinions of the evacuation.[35] Others remained, as the Russian army was too busy retreating and ran out of time to deal with civilians due to the quickly approaching front.[36]

Conducted in an ad hoc manner, the evacuations of the civilian population destroyed traditional peasant societies and produced millions of refugees. British historian Peter Gatrell estimated the overall number of refugees in the Russian Empire to have been around 7 million people by 1917. The exact percentage of Belarusian refugees is unknown, since they, together with Ukrainians, were represented in the official statistics under the category of "Great Russians," which comprised 67.2% of the overall number of refugees.[37] According to the statistics collected by the Union of Zemstvos, out of all registered refugees in the Russian Empire in 1916, 30.6% were from the Hrodna province, 4.82% from the Minsk province, 4.12% from the Vil'nia province, and 1.47% from the Viciebsk province.[38] Overall, as the western borderlands of the Russian Empire were the ones primarily affected by military actions, researchers concur that the total number of people evacuated from the Vil'nia, Hrodna, Minsk, Viciebsk, and Mahilioŭ provinces, where the majority of the ethnically Belarusian population resided, lies at around 1.4 million.[39] The Hrodna province was among the most severely affected: according to the official data gathered by the Tatiana Committee, the number of refugees from the Hrodna province alone exceeded 700,000 people.[40]

The distribution of refugees within the Russian Empire did not have clear patterns. Some ended up in the Far East and Turkestan, while others were scattered

[34]   Vital' Luba, ed., *Bieżanstva 1915 hoda* (Białystok: Prahramnaja rada tydniovika Niva, 2000), 24.
[35]   "We will not move anywhere, unless we are chased away and forced to leave. Where should the women go? It is cold and the children have no clothes. We will not go anywhere, unless there is shooting." See NHAB, f. 700, vop. 4, spr. 9, ark. 2.
[36]   Gatrell, *A Whole Empire Walking*, 20.
[37]   Gatrell, *A Whole Empire Walking*, 213–14.
[38]   S. F. Lapanovič, *Dzejnasc' dziaržaŭnych i hramadskich arhanizacyj pa akazanni dapamohi bežancam u Bielarusi ŭ hady Pieršaj susvietnaj vajny (1914–kastryčnik 1917 h.)* (Minsk: Akademija MUS, 2010), 23–24.
[39]   Eugeniusz Mironowicz, Siarhiej Tokć, and Ryszard Radzik, *Zmiana struktury narodowościowej na pograniczu polsko-białoruskim w XX wieku* (Białystok: Wydawnictwo Uniwersytetu w Białymstoku, 2005), 26; Michaluk, *Białoruska Republika Ludowa*, 132.
[40]   Nacyjanal'ny Archiŭ Respubliki Bielarus' (hereafter NARB), f. 325, vop. 1, spr. 21, ark. 4.

all over the inner Russian provinces.[41] Some refugees often deliberately chose to stay closer to home, in the non-occupied Belarusian provinces, especially when it became clear that the front had stabilized. In early 1917, their overall number in the unoccupied parts of the Minsk, Vil'nia, Viciebsk, and Mahilioŭ provinces comprised some 285,442 persons. The majority stayed in the Minsk and Mahilioŭ provinces: 126,496 and 91,639 persons, respectively. How many Belarusians were among them remains unknown, as the Russian imperial statistics did not differentiate the Orthodox Belarusians from Russians and the Catholic Belarusians from Poles.[42]

The first category was most likely to be evacuated, as generally the Orthodox Church actively supported resettlement along with the official war propaganda and fearmongering. Entire Orthodox parishes often evacuated east.[43] Known cases from the Białystok region testify to the eagerness of the Orthodox clergy to lead the process. Often, these priests even left their congregations behind, as later, during the occupation, the German administration documented high numbers of Orthodox Belarusians in the region, noting problems in the organization of church services for them. As of spring 1916, there were no Orthodox priests available to serve in the Białystok region.[44] According to correspondence received by the Belarusian newspaper *Homan*, the remaining Orthodox population of Białystok had to ask a German Lutheran priest for assistance. Pastor Zirknitz created an officially recognized organization for the Belarusian Orthodox population of the city and was even known to baptize children according to the Orthodox rite. Throughout 1916, the local Lutheran parish also helped provide about 50,000 free meals and financial assistance to the Orthodox population.[45]

By contrast, almost all of the Roman Catholic priests remained with their parishes.[46] Orthodox believers who chose to stay often found themselves under pressure

---

[41]   Gatrell, *A Whole Empire Walking*, 54–55.

[42]   Lapanovič, *Dzejnasc' dziaržaŭnych i hramadskich arhanizacyj*, 98–99.

[43]   "Relihijnye sprawy," *Homan*, no. 5, February 29, 1916, 3. See also Gatrell, *A Whole Empire Walking*, 212–14; Mironowicz, Tokć, and Radzik, *Zmiana struktury narodowościowej*, 24–26; Valentina Utgof, "In Search of National Support: Belarusian Refugees in World War One and the People's Republic of Belarus," in *Homelands: War, Population and Statehood in Eastern Europe and Russia, 1918–1924*, ed. Nick Baron and Peter Gatrell (London: Anthem Press, 2004), 53.

[44]   LMAVB, RS, f. 23, b. 11a, l. 25.

[45]   "Z usiaho kraju," *Homan*, no. 73, September 11, 1917, 2. Orthodox Church services in the Białystok area resumed only in April 1918, when three priests started to travel through the Białystok, Hrodna, and Svislač districts. See LMAVB, RS, f. 23, b. 15, l. 34.

[46]   *Homan*, no. 74, September 14, 1917, 1.

to convert to Catholicism, as was the case in the town of Rudomina (Vil'nia district). A letter, addressed to the German Military Administration of Lithuania, pointed out that the town had lost a significant part of its Orthodox population due to the 1915 evacuations. Using the departure of the Orthodox clergy as a pretext, local Catholics undertook steps to appropriate the abandoned church and turn it into a Catholic one.[47] In this manner, through the church, Polish nationalism often successfully claimed Catholic Belarusians, as during the war the numbers of Belarusian national activists in the countryside were low and they did not have stable support within any church structures.

With millions of civilians from the western provinces and the Kingdom of Poland blocking the roads of the army rear in the summer of 1915, Russian imperial authorities faced another unexpected problem. As the scope of the humanitarian crisis became alarming, General Danilov criticized Minsk zemstvo authorities for their lack of attention to the refugees, requesting that actions be taken immediately along the major roads leading to Minsk, Ihumen, Bierazino, and Mahilioŭ. Danilov also offered financial assistance in this matter,[48] as the military finally realized that the depopulation tactic had backfired and that thousands of refugees had become a major inconvenience for Russian military operations.

The main evacuation routes led east from the Hrodna, Vil'nia, and Minsk provinces. Those people who could afford to travel on the railways, packed passenger and cargo trains,[49] while refugee traffic on eastward roads peaked in the late summer of 1915. Peasants traveled with everything that they could take, bringing along horses, cattle, and all their possessions.[50] According to the report of the Minsk governor Aleksei Girs, addressed to the Special Commission dealing with the regulation of refugee movement in Minsk, by September 1915, the refugee crisis had heavily affected the city and its surroundings. Tens of thousands of displaced people came to Minsk with the hope of getting on trains and evacuating to safer provinces. Many were forced to sell their horses due to a lack of food for the animals. Deprived of their own means of transportation, the refugees received free tickets to move further east by railway. However, the number of available trains did not suffice, forcing about 6,000 people to camp around the railway station. Trying to make their way out, refugees besieged every train that they could see,

---

[47] Lietuvos Centrinis Valstybės Archyvas (hereafter LCVA), f. 361, ap. 5, b. 14, l. 54, 55.
[48] NHAB, f. 700, vop. 1, spr. 29, ark. 80.
[49] See the memoirs of Zos'ka Vieras, who evacuated from the Hrodna province to Minsk: Zos'ka Vieras, *Ja pomniu ŭsio: Uspaminy, listy* (Hrodna–Wrocław: Haradzienskaja biblijateka, 2013), 29–32.
[50] NHAB, f. 511, vop. 1, spr. 7, ark. 209 adv.

disrupting the operation of the railway station. Refugees still in possession of horses and carts crowded the streets of Minsk, creating serious obstacles for traffic and the transportation of soldiers and military cargo. The governor's report ended on a desperate note, complaining that the police forces could not handle the large number of displaced people and requesting reinforcement from the army to guard the railway station and major streets in the city.[51]

Thousands of people in need of accommodation stayed under the open sky in Minsk, camping in the city suburbs and antagonizing the local population by damaging property and the harvest. Some "entrepreneurs" in the city even made money by turning telephone booths into temporary accommodations and renting them to desperate people in need.[52] Refugees who stayed near the front often found themselves in limbo, not eager to look for stable jobs out of fear of being parted from their families, who could be moved further east.[53] Those who were stuck on the roads were often forced to move at a slow pace, suffering from German bombardments, as happened with refugees in the marshes of Palesse region, in the vicinity of Pinsk.[54] Unsanitary conditions, exhaustion, malnutrition, and a lack of clean drinking water led to the spread of cholera, dysentery, and typhus among the refugees, further endangering this new vulnerable social group.[55]

Many people had left in a panic at the last moment before the invasion of the enemy, or fled their homes within sight of military action. According to surveys conducted by the Union of Zemstvos in November 1915 assessing the mood of refugees in Valožyn (Vil'nia province) in November 1915, the majority came to the city from the neighboring localities of Kreva, Višnieva, and Bakšty, which had been directly affected by movement at the front. Disoriented and traumatized by the war, large families had to share accommodations, often with three or four families living in one tiny house. Deprived of their properties, cattle, and regular income, refugees survived on the bread they received from charitable canteens. The lack of food, clothes, and necessities was exacerbated by the unavailability of information about resettlement. Moreover, a majority of the refugees were not interested in moving away, as all of them hoped to return to their homes as soon

---

51 NHAB, f. 511, vop. 1, spr. 7, ark. 258, 259.
52 NHAB, f. 511, vop. 1, spr. 7, ark, 259. See also Aliaksandr Mikalaevič, "Biežancy Pieršaj susvietnaj vajny," *Spadčyna*, no. 3 (1994): 20.
53 NHAB, f. 700, vop. 4, spr. 9, ark. 40.
54 Gatrell, *A Whole Empire Walking*, 51.
55 *Kratkii otchet o deiiatel'nosti Minskago Gubernskago Komiteta V. Z. S. za 1916 god* (Minsk: Tipografiia B. L. Kaplana, 1917), 2–5.

as possible.[56] Sometimes the authorities forced the refugees to move further east, as occurred in the Rečyca district, where refugee groups tried to avoid using emergency canteens, as the local authorities would detain them there and then drive them out of the Minsk province, regardless of whether these people were from the Minsk province or from other provinces.[57]

Overall, the evacuations, both voluntary and forced, along with the army mobilization at the onset of the First World War fundamentally changed the demographic situation in the Belarusian provinces. Moreover, they severely impacted the potential of the Belarusian national movement, since people who would have been able to respond positively to nationalist slogans were physically absent for several years. As correctly noted by Eugeniusz Mironowicz, this fact is often overlooked in discussions about the weaknesses of Belarusian nationalism.[58] Anton Luckievič, who remained in the German-occupied territories, observed how "the Russian government drove out masses of people from the Hrodna and Vil'nia provinces, including nearly all Belarusian intelligentsia."[59] The First World War thus created more obstacles for the national activists, since they, too, were all suddenly scattered across Russia, Ukraine, and the unoccupied Belarusian provinces of Minsk, Viciebsk, and Mahilioŭ, where national politics was severely restricted.

Belarusian Charities within the System of Organized Refugee Relief

Refugee relief in the Russian Empire was administered by both government-sponsored and public organizations. One of the first official charitable institutions was the Tatiana Committee. Named after the tsar's second daughter, it was established on September 14, 1914, to supervise the provision of assistance to wounded soldiers, yet it soon expanded its activities to provide support to displaced civilians.[60] Committee chair, member of the State Council Aleksei Neidgardt, visited Minsk on October 5, 1914, in order to clarify the situation with the war victims

56   NHAB, f. 700, vop. 4, spr. 9, ark. 27–29.
57   NHAB, f. 700, vop. 1, spr. 29, ark. 84.
58   Mironowicz, Tokć, and Radzik, *Zmiana struktury narodowościowej*, 27.
59   NARB, f. 325, vop. 1, spr. 21, ark. 131.
60   Anastasia S. Tumanova, "The Public and the Organization of Aid to Refugees during World War I," *Russian Studies in History* 51, no. 3 (Winter 2012): 85.

in the province. After his meeting with the local authorities and representatives of the local civil society, the Minsk section of the Tatiana Committee was founded on October 29, 1914, and was chaired by the Minsk governor Aleksei Girs.[61] In the first year of the war, the Tatiana Committee acted as the central refugee relief institution, administering resettlement, running shelters, distributing food and medicine, and paying allowances. By 1915, its Minsk section managed twenty free shelters in the city, providing accommodation for over 1,000 people. Anticipating even greater numbers of displaced people in the summer of 1915, it initiated the construction of special barracks.[62]

As the refugee crisis deepened, the Russian Ministry of the Interior drafted a law "On Meeting the Needs of Refugees" on August 30, 1915. It determined the legal refugee status for all individuals who were resettled or displaced due to the wartime conditions.[63] Along with the Tatiana Committee, the local governors' offices and the network of *Severopomoshch*, administered by the Chief Plenipotentiary for Refugee Matters on the North-Western Front S. I. Zubchaninov, shared the responsibility for refugee relief in the affected areas in the western borderlands and in the vicinity of the front. Their efforts to regulate the streams of refugees and coordinate assistance were complemented by the public organizations of zemstvos and municipalities, represented by the All-Russian Union of Towns and the All-Russian Union of Zemstvos, which also contributed to the solution of the refugee problem. Yet, the activities of the government and public refugee relief organizations were often uncoordinated, while the arbitrary behavior of the army command further complicated the conditions of their work.[64]

Last but not least, national charitable organizations grew along with the mass exodus of refugees from the western borderlands of the Russian Empire in the summer of 1915. Polish, Lithuanian, Latvian, Jewish, Ukrainian, and Belarusian charities were the only kind of associations permitted for nationalities in the Russian Empire prior to the February Revolution. In most cases, these organizations not only took care of people's welfare, but they also expanded their work into other spheres, providing a range of cultural and educational activities. Along with their humanitarian mission, these charities thus served as the main centers for bringing national activists together and legalizing their activities during the war. Belarusian refugee relief organizations were not an exception, despite being

---

61   NHAB, f. 511, vop. 1, spr. 8, ark. 60, 60 adv., 65.
62   NHAB, f. 511, vop. 1, spr. 7, ark. 213 adv., 215.
63   Lapanovič, *Dzejnasc' dziaržaŭnych i hramadskich arhanizacyj*, 70.
64   NHAB, f. 700, vop. 1, spr. 29, ark. 88; Gatrell, *A Whole Empire Walking*, 34–40.

underfunded and understaffed.[65] Subjected to suspicious attitudes from both the Russian imperial authorities and public organizations, they nevertheless attempted to provide necessary assistance to the uprooted Belarusian peasants, while at the same time making their first attempts to advance the cause of national solidarity in the wartime period.

The Belarusian Committee for the Aid of War Victims (henceforth the Belarusian Committee) was established in April 1915 in Vil'nia by a group consisting of Vaclaŭ Ivanoŭski, Paviel Radkievič, Paviel Aliaksiuk, Ihnat Bindziuk, Mikalaj Mochaŭ, and Vaclaŭ Lastoŭski. The goal was to provide assistance to all inhabitants of the Vil'nia, Hrodna, Minsk, Viciebsk, and Mahilioŭ provinces who suffered from the war.[66] In the first three months before the arrival of the Germans, the Vil'nia section of the Committee helped Belarusian refugees to settle in safer eastern Belarusian provinces and established its own small regional network with three sections in the Vil'nia province, two sections in the Hrodna province, as well as branches in Minsk and Polack.[67] The arrival of the Germans in Vil'nia in September 1915 cut off all contacts with the eastern Belarusian areas, thus severing communication between the Vil'nia and Minsk sections of the Committee, which continued to operate as two separate centers of charitable activities.

It appears that the Belarusian Committee was smaller than the Jewish, Polish, and Lithuanian organizations. For instance, by 1915, the Lithuanian Committee for the Aid of War Victims supervised about ninety-eight local branches in the western provinces, which was considerably more than the Belarusian Committee.[68] By the mid-summer of 1915, Belarusian activists in Vil'nia had already complained that the Russian authorities, which supported the national charitable organizations financially, "declared a full boycott" of the Belarusian Committee, whereas private donations and membership fees did not suffice and assistance from the Union of Towns was irregular or marginal at best. The Belarusian Committee struggled to find stable funding schemes.[69]

---

[65]   Gatrell, *A Whole Empire Walking*, 156, 165.

[66]   LCVA, f. 361, ap. 5, b. 4, l. 2, l. 8.

[67]   *Homan*, no. 74, September 14, 1917, 2. See also Lapanovič, *Dzejnasc' dziaržaŭnych i hramadskich arhanizacyj*, 105.

[68]   By February 1915, 32 branches of the Lithuanian Society for the Aid of War Victims were operating in the Suwałki province, 37 in the Kaunas province, 26 in the Vil'nia province, and 3 in the Hrodna province. See *Otchet o deiatelnosti Litovskogo Obshchestva po okazaniiu pomoshchi postradavshim ot voiny za vremia s 22 noiabria 1914 po 1 iiulia 1915 g.* (Petrograd: Nauchnoe delo, 1916), 16.

[69]   Lapanovič, *Dzejnasc' dziaržaŭnych i hramadskich arhanizacyj*, 105.

By the time the Russians retreated, the Belarusian Committee was left without any substantial funds, and was unable to maintain contact with its sections
in the provinces.[70] It is likely that the Russian authorities perceived a danger of
separatism and nationalism in the Belarusian charity and tried to appropriate its
target populations. For instance, the All-Russian Society for the Aid of Refugees,
established in September 1915 and designed to assist the Russian population,
declared that the Orthodox Belarusians and Ukrainians were also in the sphere of
its responsibility. This society actively supported its local branches and enjoyed
privileges from the local Russian civilian authorities. It had a strong inclination
towards promoting the Orthodox faith and stressed its own uniqueness as opposed
to other national organizations.[71]

The Minsk section of the Belarusian Committee started operating in the
summer of 1915, in the midst of the refugee crisis. Headed by the Minsk lawyer
Viktar Čavusaŭ, it attracted about fifty members, including Zos'ka Vieras (Ludvika Sivickaja), Uladzislaŭ Halubok, Usievalad Falski, Anton Liavicki, Aliksandr
Astramovič, Albert Paŭlovič, Fabian Šantyr, as well as Belarusian poet Maksim
Bahdanovič. In the fall of 1915, the Belarusian Committee opened six free
shelters and three canteens in Minsk.[72] However, by 1916, due to its sporadic
and insufficient funding, it was forced to limit its activities to the operation of
a single dining hall.[73]

Instead of paying allowances to the refugees, the Belarusian Committee
reoriented towards the more practical tasks of finding work for them. In January
1916, it organized the distribution of flax for weaving, initially employing about
150 women for this job. Another 700 women did sewing jobs for the army. In the
spring and summer of 1916, the Belarusian Committee organized six-week long
agricultural courses for the refugees, with instruction in the Belarusian language.[74]
Yet, the majority of the refugees in the non-occupied Belarusian provinces continued to receive assistance through the Tatiana Committee, as well as through
the Union of Zemstvos and *Severopomoshch*, which boasted a better developed
institutional network, stable funding, and governmental support.[75]

---

[70]   *Homan*, no. 74, September 14, 1917, 2.
[71]   Lapanovič, *Dzejnasc' dziaržaŭnych i hramadskich arhanizacyj*, 101.
[72]   Maksim Bahdanovič, *Vybranyja tvory* (Minsk: Bielaruski knihazbor, 1996), 381.
[73]   Lapanovič, *Dzejnasc' dziaržaŭnych i hramadskich arhanizacyj*, 105.
[74]   Bahdanovič, *Vybranyja tvory*, 382.
[75]   *Kratkii otchet o deiiatel'nosti*, 1.

Displaced Belarusians in Russia and Ukraine: 1915–1917

Over 100,000 Belarusian refugees stayed in Petrograd,[76] where a section of the Belarusian Committee for the Aid of War Victims was founded on December 22, 1915, when Branislaŭ Epimach-Šypila, Časlaŭ Rodzevič, Aliaksandr Jaremič, and Uladzimir Mitkievič signed its statute. The official founding conference followed on January 31, 1916, gathering seventy-one active members, including a number of known supporters of the Belarusian national cause, among them Branislaŭ Taraškievič, Edvard Budz'ka, and Zmicier Žylunovič.[77] Chaired by Leanid Siaŭruk, the Belarusian Committee in Petrograd was the only national charitable organization of Belarusian refugees in Russia, until the creation of the Belarusian National Commissariat in 1918, which concentrated on the refugee issue as one of the major areas of its work.[78]

In order to reach out to Belarusians beyond the capital, the Petrograd section of the Belarusian Committee published two newspapers addressing the needs of the Belarusian refugees. With the reluctant approval of the Ministry of the Interior, starting in November 1916, *Dziannica* and *Svietač* appeared in Petrograd. The editors, Zmicier Žylunovič and Edvard Budz'ka, used their own funds and connections to publish these periodicals. Heavily censored, the newspapers nevertheless found their readership among the Belarusians in Russia and in the unoccupied Belarusian provinces, as confirmed by pre-orders and excited messages to the editors. However, on December 31, 1916, *Dziannica* was discontinued due to the strict censorship which prohibited all materials with a trace of links to the Belarusian national movement. The even more moderate *Svietač* shared this fate, as only five issues were ever allowed to be published.[79]

Petrograd Belarusians continued keeping track of the refugees, assisting them in everyday matters, supporting Belarusian students, overseeing medical services, and organizing social gatherings. The bulk of financial support to the Petrograd section was provided by the Tatiana Committee, although membership fees, donations, and proceeds from cultural events and concerts also contributed to its funding. However, similarly to the Minsk section of the Belarusian Committee,

---

[76] NARB, f. 325, vop. 1, spr. 211, ark. 157.
[77] NHAB, f. 511, vop. 1, spr. 8, ark. 1–2.
[78] On the Belarusian National Commissariat in 1918, see Chapter 6.
[79] Nikolai Shchavlinskii, "Deiiatel'nost' Belorusskogo obshchestva v Petrograde po okazaniiu pomoshchi poterpevshim ot voiny v 1916–1918 godakh," *Bielaruskaja Dumka*, no. 6 (2013): 63–65; Utgof, "In Search of National Support," 58.

this funding did not suffice either, as the Russian government often deliberately denied financial assistance to the Belarusian relief organizations. The latter were perceived as competitors of the already established separate departments designed to help the "refugees of Russian nationality." This broad categorization included Belarusians and Ukrainians.[80]

Thus, the Belarusian Committee in Petrograd was often not able to secure the needs of all Belarusian refugees, especially those who were resettled to the remote Russian provinces.[81] According to the eyewitness account of refugee V. Hrynievič, despite the significant number of Belarusian refugees in Kazan province, they did not have their own national charity, in contrast to the Polish, Lithuanian, and Latvian refugee committees. People applied for assistance either to the Russian or Polish committees, where along with bread, they also received a dose of corresponding "patriotism." Russian committees were in particular singled out as the most successful in their Russification attempts, as they had the advantage of operating in their own country.[82]

Refugees found themselves adjusting to new life circumstances, uprooted and displaced, away from their homes. Although their perceptions of national belonging were starting to change, it appeared to be a slow and inconsistent process, often accompanied by the pressures of assimilation to the local cultures of their new surroundings.[83] Due to the lack of strong Belarusian charitable organizations outside of Petrograd, refugees in Russia were left without a stable connection to their homeland and often found themselves in an information vacuum. Hence, they became susceptible to assimilation by the dominant Russian culture. A representative of the Belarusian National Commissariat reported that even in 1918, Belarusian refugees in the Saratov province were completely apolitical and did not have any information on the political developments in Belarus.[84] They generally viewed Belarusian national activists with suspicion, seeing in them either "Polish servants" or "intriguers."[85]

---

[80] Mikalaevič, "Biežancy Pieršaj susvietnaj vajny," 21.

[81] N. E. Kalesnik, *Belorusskoe obshchestvo v Petrograde po okazaniiu pomoshchi postradavshim ot voiny, 1916–1918: mezharkhivnyi spravochnik* (Minsk: NARB, 2008), 6.

[82] V. Hrynievič, "Na rekach Vavilonu," *Spadčyna*, no. 4 (1997): 167–68.

[83] Uladzimir Liachoŭski, *Ad homanaŭcaŭ da hajsakoŭ: čynnasc' bielaruskich maladzevych arhanizacyj u 2-oj palovie 19 st.–1-aj palovie 20 st. (da 1939)* (Vilnius: Instytut bielarusistyki, 2012), 101–2.

[84] NARB, f. 4, vop. 1, spr. 67, ark. 4.

[85] *Vol'naja Bielarus'*, no. 27, October 30, 1917, 3.

Some of the population of the Belarusian provinces was also resettled in Ukraine, where Belarusian committees existed in Kyiv, Kharkiv, Kherson, and Yekaterinoslav (currently—Dnipro). The highest number of Belarusian refugees was recorded in Odesa. According to a detailed report by Anton Balicki, who was an authorized representative of Belarusians in the Odesa district in 1918, the number of Belarusians in Odesa alone was around 20,000 in the city and about 100,000 in the whole district.[86] Their mood was described as patriotic: after having lived in a different country, they realized that they were a separate people, with their own language and customs. The refugees tended to settle in the vicinity of each other, forming their own communities, with clear ideas that they differed from the local population. They did not lose their connection to their homeland and showed interest in all news from Belarus.[87] Despite good living conditions and the availability of jobs, a lot of refugees dreamed about returning home.[88]

Odesa Belarusians established a range of cultural initiatives, including an artistic circle, a Belarusian orchestra, theatre groups, and a cultural-educational organization called "Bielaruski Haj" (Belarusian Grove).[89] By 1917, these organizations started transforming, receiving a political dimension: in particular, "Bielaruski Haj" became a base for the Belarusian Committee for the Aid of War Victims in Odesa. The Statute of the Committee pointed out that its main goals were to provide financial assistance and moral support to all Belarusians evacuated during the war, to collect information on the locations of their families, and to inform people about current events in Belarus. The Committee also emphasized the task of strengthening national consciousness among the Belarusian refugees.[90]

Despite the financial difficulties, it managed to attract people to its side by offering them effective assistance in repatriation. It also disseminated Belarusian newspapers and literature, which were popular among the refugees. Remarkably, the Odesa section of the Belarusian Committee for the Aid of War Victims clashed with the local Russian Refugee Committee. The latter claimed that there was no need to single out Belarusians, since it saw no difference between them and Russians.[91]

Refugees in Russia generally perceived the modern Belarusian national movement through the "Russian lens" of Polish intrigues. The experiences of Belarusian

---

[86] NARB, f. 325, vop. 1, spr. 21, ark. 139.
[87] NARB, f. 325, vop. 1, spr. 21, ark. 139.
[88] NARB, f. 325, vop. 1, spr. 21, ark. 139 adv.
[89] NARB, f. 325, vop. 1, spr. 21, ark. 140 adv.
[90] LCVA, f. 361, ap. 5, b. 21, l. 1.
[91] *Niezaležnaja Bielarus'*, no. 7, October 24, 1919, 4.

refugees in Ukraine represent a contrasting example to the assimilation trends among the refugees in Russia. The Odesa section of the Belarusian Committee for the Aid of War Victims successfully engaged in nation-building efforts among the displaced people, promoting a distinct Belarusian identity along with their effective refugee relief. However, as the efforts to create a national army out of the Belarusian soldiers on the Romanian front failed,[92] the Odesa Belarusians did not manage to influence the outcome of the power struggle over Belarus in 1917–1918.

Belarusian Dilemmas in Minsk

In contrast to the Belarusian areas under German occupation which had been abandoned by the refugees, the eastern Belarusian provinces were overpopulated.[93] The influx of soldiers, refugees, workers, and administrative personnel to the cities disrupted the ethnic composition of the population, creating more challenges for the Belarusian nation-building processes. The armies of the Russian Western front, which had its headquarters in Minsk, numbered over 1,500,000 soldiers and officers of non-Belarusian origin. At the same time, about 636,000 Belarusian peasants from the Minsk, Viciebsk, and Mahilioŭ provinces were mobilized into the Russian army and sent away from their homes to distant fronts. The First World War thus resulted in serious demographic changes in the Belarusian areas, where refugees and military mobilization set in motion processes of mass migration. Similarly to Ober Ost, economic life in the Russian-held provinces prioritized military needs: this was especially evident in the creation of new enterprises for the army and the employment of workers mobilized from the interior of Russia.[94]

In the early twentieth century, Minsk did not offer a lot of space for Belarusian national politics. According to the 1897 Russian Imperial Census data, the total population of Minsk was 90,912 people, of which 9% were Belarusian, 25.5% were Russian, 11.4% were Polish, and 51.2% were Jewish.[95] On the eve of the First

92   See Chapter 6.
93   Helena Głogowska, *Białoruś 1914–1929: kultura pod presją polityki* (Białystok: Białoruskie Towarzystwo Historyczne, 1996), 24.
94   Aleh Latyšonak, *Žaŭnery BNR* (Białystok: Bielaruskae Histaryčnaje Tavarystva, 2009), 33; Stanislaŭ Rudovič, "Bielarus' u čas Pieršaj susvietnaj vajny. Aspiekty etnapalityčnaj historyi," in *Białoruś w XX stuleciu: w kręgu kultury i polityki*, ed. Dorota Michaluk (Toruń: Wydawnictwo Naukowe Uniwersytetu Mikołaja Kopernika, 2007), 100–101.
95   Steven L. Guthier, *The Belorussians: National Identification and Assimilation, 1897–1970* (Ann Arbor, MI: Center for Russian and East European Studies, University of Michigan, 1977), 45.

World War, this provincial capital was dominated by Russian cultural influence. While there was some connection to local traditions and culture, as the growing interest in Belarusianness after the Revolution of 1905 indicated, overall Minsk was the result of Russification policies, which influenced even its Jewish population.[96] The ideology of West-Russism, which only allowed for regional forms of identification for Belarusians within a larger All-Russian framework, took firm roots in the city. According to the correspondence of the teacher Selenskii from Haradzišča (Minsk province) with the liberal *Vecherniia gazeta* in 1913, "Russian nationalists from Minsk" were very vocal in protesting against the hypothetical opening of a university in Vil'nia, claiming that it would "destroy their century-long work to strengthen and restore the Russian origins in the North-Western region."[97]

While many cities of the western borderlands were depopulated due to the forced uprooting of the population and military actions, Minsk was full of newcomers: mostly soldiers and refugees. Many locals became refugees and moved east, or were mobilized to serve in the army on distant fronts. By 1918, Minsk was colorfully described as the "Harbin of the rear, where all the natives have disappeared."[98] The already strong positions of Polish culture became even more prominent after 1915, when significant numbers of Polish refugees settled in the eastern Belarusian provinces. Actively participating in public life, Poles had already started publishing their own newspaper in Minsk, *Nowy Kurier Litewski*, by August 1915. It was succeeded by *Dziennik Miński* in 1917, established by the Executive Committee of the Polish Council of the Minsk Province (*Rada Polska Ziemi Mińskiej*). The Polish press in Minsk prioritized national consolidation among the refugees and the local Poles, without clearly siding with any of the Polish political parties.[99]

The Belarusian national milieu in Minsk during the First World War survived mainly through the efforts of the Belarusian Committee for the Aid of War Victims. Its Minsk section oversaw a number of Belarusian-themed cultural events in the city, thus spearheading socializing among the intelligentsia and popularizing the Belarusian language. Members of the Committee organized Christmas performances for

---

[96] Zachar Šybeka, *Minsk sto hadoŭ tamu* (Minsk: Bielarus', 2007), 293.
[97] LCVA, f. 368, ap. 1, b. 10, l. 110.
[98] *Bielaruski Šliach*, no. 12, April 6, 1918, 1.
[99] Dariusz Tarasiuk, *Między nadzieją a niepokojem: Działalność społeczno-kulturalna i polityczna Polaków na wschodniej Białorusi w latach 1905–1918* (Lublin: Wyd. Uniwersytetu Marii Curie-Skłodowskiej, 2007), 56–58. In 1915, the number of Polish refugees in Minsk province alone was estimated at more than 90,000. See Tadeusz Zienkiewicz, *Polskie życie literackie w Mińsku: w XIX i na początku XX wieku, do roku 1921* (Olsztyn: Wyższa Szkoła Pedagogiczna, 1997), 111.

children and successfully revived the traditions of *batlejka*, the ancient Belarusian puppet theatre. Usievalad Falski directed a choir, soon followed by weekly dance parties and performances of Flaryjan Ždanovič's theatre company.[100] Yet, Belarusian public space in the city remained limited, especially in contrast to Vil'nia, where the Germans allowed the publication of a Belarusian newspaper and conducted rather liberal policies in the cultural sphere for all non-Russian nationalities. At the same time, the Russian press, banned from German-occupied Vil'nia, moved to Minsk, where it prospered, in contrast to the marginalized Belarusian press, which appeared in the city only in 1917.[101]

Conclusion

With the start of the First World War, the western borderlands of the Russian Empire experienced destruction through military actions, an unprecedented demographic crisis, and a major redrawing of borders. In 1915, German military successes in Eastern Europe forced imperial Russia to relinquish to the enemy the territories of present-day Poland, Lithuania, Latvia, and parts of Belarus. The war also resulted in the elimination of the boundaries between civil and military authorities, with the establishment of military rule. This trend was characteristic for both the German-occupied Ober Ost and the Russian-controlled Belarusian provinces in the front rear under martial law, where the military assumed the upper hand in governance.

The Great War represented an unforeseen disruptive external factor for Belarusian nation-building, as its violence interfered in the process of the gradual evolution of the Belarusian national movement. Forced evacuations affected all social groups, resulting in displacement of the national intelligentsia, along with the masses of ethnic Belarusians from the western provinces. Moreover, the effects of the wartime restrictions, combined with the strong position of Russian culture in Minsk and the eastern Belarusian provinces, negatively impacted the potential of the young Belarusian national movement, weakening it structurally. By 1917, it barely survived under the guise of national charities, which had been established to solve the humanitarian catastrophe of the refugees.

Until the February Revolution in 1917, Belarusian national activists were deprived of their own distinct center, as the German authorities prohibited political

---

[100] Vieras, *Ja pomniu ŭsio*, 36–38; Bahdanovič, *Vybranyja tvory*, 383.
[101] Šybeka, *Minsk sto hadoŭ tamu*, 152–54.

activities in Vil'nia, while Minsk did not have enough potential to establish itself in this role. The introduction of martial law in the Russian-administered provinces, along with the massive population displacement and arrival of Polish refugees, further restricted opportunities for the development of the Belarusian national milieu in Minsk. Yet, on the other hand, the war resulted in the failure of the imperial state, which eventually paved the way for revolution and enabled national movements to challenge central authority.

Chapter 2

Belarusians, Lithuanians, and Poles in the Lands of Ober Ost (1915–1917)

Following the three partitions of the Polish-Lithuanian Commonwealth in the late eighteenth century, all modern Belarusian territories were incorporated into the Russian Empire.[1] This situation remained unchanged until the First World War, when Vil'nia and Hrodna provinces, and the western parts of Minsk province were occupied by the German Empire and became a part of Ober Ost,[2] while Viciebsk and Mahiliou provinces, and the eastern parts of Minsk province remained under tsarist rule. By looking at the redrawing of borders in the western parts of the Russian Empire during the First World War, this chapter focuses on Belarusian nation-building in the western Belarusian provinces under the German regime. Chronologically, it covers the period between 1915 and 1917, which represents the early phase of the occupation, when German policies proclaimed the principle of equal treatment for all Ober Ost nationalities, in contrast to a clearly Lithuanian-oriented policy that was in effect by early 1917.

The chief aim here is to determine to what degree Belarusian national politics benefited from the new political circumstances in the region. Another goal is to illustrate the influence of German policies in Ober Ost on the intensification of competition between the Belarusian, Lithuanian, and Polish national movements. Jews stood aside from this national struggle, yet some aspects relating to the Jewish population in Ober Ost will be briefly discussed in regard to their relations with the German authorities. The Latvian and German populations of Ober Ost are beyond the scope of this chapter.

---

[1] Parts of this chapter were previously published by *Canadian Slavonic Papers/Revue Canadienne des Slavistes*, see Lizaveta Kasmach, "Forgotten Occupation: Germans and Belarusians in the Lands of Ober Ost (1915–1917)," *Canadian Slavonic Papers* 58, no. 4 (2016): 321–40. DOI:10 .1080/00085006.2016.1238613.

[2] Das Land des Oberbefehlshabers Ost—German-administered occupation zone in East-Central Europe during the First World War. It included the territories of contemporary Lithuania, along with parts of Belarus, Latvia, and Poland.

This chapter follows the establishment of the occupation regime in Ober Ost and the interaction between German authorities and local nationalities, with particular attention to plans of annexation and economic exploitation, the situation of nationalities, and the evolution of German attitudes towards Belarusians as a separate ethnicity in Ober Ost. Turning from the German perspectives to those of the Belarusian national activists, it will concentrate on national activism within the Belarusian milieu in Vil'nia and beyond, discussing challenges encountered both in dealing with the occupation powers and in promoting the Belarusian national cause. In this context, the following aspects are important: the dynamics of interaction between the German authorities and Belarusian national elites in Ober Ost and the presence of stronger and more developed Polish and, to a lesser degree, Lithuanian national movements.[3]

Despite concessions to the nationalities of Ober Ost, German military interests always remained a priority in the region, while the concerns and needs of the local population, including national development, were considered to be of secondary importance. Nevertheless, Belarusian national activists were able to act within the parameters defined by the Germans, achieving more in the sphere of nation-building in comparison to the eastern Belarusian provinces which remained under Russian rule. The key question here is whether they were able to advocate for their national needs as successfully as were neighboring nationalities.

---

[3]   With regard to the second aspect, the relations of the German occupation regime with the Lithuanians and Poles in Ober Ost have been sufficiently explored in the historical research. See Eberhard Demm, *Ostpolitik und Propaganda im Ersten Weltkrieg* (Frankfurt am Main: P. Lang, 2002); Vejas G. Liulevicius, *War Land on the Eastern Front: Culture, National Identity and German Occupation in World War I* (Cambridge: Cambridge University Press, 2000); A. Strazhas, *Deutsche Ostpolitik im Ersten Weltkrieg: Der Fall Ober Ost 1915–1917* (Wiesbaden: Harrassowitz, 1993); Christopher Barthel, "Contesting the Russian Borderlands: The German Military Administration of Occupied Lithuania, 1915–1918," PhD Dissertation, Brown University, 2011. As the Belarusian national movement at that time was only starting to enter international politics, it remained in the background and its historiography is represented only by a handful of studies. See Uladzimir Liachoŭski, *Škol'naja adukacyja ŭ Bielarusi padčas niameckaj akupacyi (1915–1918 h.)* (Vilnius: Instytut bielarusistyki, 2010); Jerzy Turonek, *Białoruś pod okupacją niemiecką* (Warsaw: Książka i Wiedza, 1993); Volha Volkava "Ziemie białoruskie pod niemiecką okupacją w okresie I wojny światowej," in *Pierwsza Niemiecka Okupacja: Królestwo Polskie i Kresy Wschodnie Pod Okupacją Mocarstw Centralnych 1914–1918*, ed. Grzegorz Kucharczyk (Warsaw: Instytut Historii PAN, 2019), 669–824. On the wider context of the emerging concepts of modern Belarusian statehood in Ober Ost, see Dorota Michaluk and Per Anders Rudling, "From the Grand Duchy of Lithuania to the Belarusian Democratic Republic: The Idea of Belarusian Statehood during the German Occupation of Belarusian Lands, 1915–1919," *Journal of Belarusian Studies* 7, no. 2 (2014): 3–36; Michaluk, *Białoruska Republika Ludowa*, 130–48; Rudling, *The Rise and Fall of Belarusian Nationalism*, 68–75.

German War Aims in Eastern Europe and Establishment of Ober Ost

Military actions on the European Eastern front started in 1914, but it was not until 1915 that the war reached the territories settled by the Belarusians. Over the course of the summer of 1915, the Russian army was forced to leave Poland, Kurland, Lithuania, Galicia, and parts of the Belarusian territories. On September 3, 1915, German armies took Hrodna, while Vil'nia was occupied by September 19. The offensive of 1915 in Eastern Europe continued until the end of September. For the following three years, the front stabilized along the Riga-Daugavpils-Baranaviči-Pinsk-Luts'k-Dubno line.[4] Throughout 1915, the western Belarusian areas (Vil'nia and Hrodna provinces, parts of Minsk province) were administered by the German occupation regime, while the eastern areas (parts of Minsk, Viciebsk, and Mahilioŭ provinces) remained within the Russian Empire. The occupied Belarusian-Lithuanian-Polish borderlands became a part of Ober Ost, officially established by the Germans as a new administrative unit on November 4, 1915, and spreading over contemporary Lithuania, as well as parts of Latvia, Poland, and Belarus.[5]

The German Empire entered the First World War without a well-defined plan concerning possible territorial gains in Eastern Europe. War aims changed depending on the situation at the fronts in different periods of time, but were united by a common feature of affirming the German Empire as a Great Power.[6] In September 1914, German chancellor Bethmann Hollweg made a statement regarding the chief objectives for the army, proclaiming that the German priority was to move Russia as far as possible from German borders and to end Russian rule over all of its non-Russian subject nationalities.[7] One of the approaches under consideration was the annexation of these lands and the expansion of the German Empire into the conquered territories. Alternatively, a different plan foresaw the creation of a belt of semi-autonomous formally independent states under German

---

[4]   Boris Khavkin, "Russland gegen Deutschland: Die Ostfront des Ersten Weltkrieges in den Jahren 1914 bis 1915," in *Die vergessene Front—der Osten 1914/15: Ereignis, Wirkung, Nachwirkung*, ed. Gerhard Paul Gross (Paderborn: Schöningh, 2006), 82; Presseabteilung Ober Ost, *Das Land Ober Ost: Deutsche Arbeit in den Verwaltungsgebieten Kurland, Litauen und Bialystok-Grodno* ([Kowno]: Verlag der Presseabteilung Ober Ost, 1917), 7–8.

[5]   Presseabteilung, *Das Land Ober Ost*, 307.

[6]   Richter, *Fragmentation in East Central Europe*, 17.

[7]   "Aufzeichnungen Bethmann Hollwegs über die Richtlinien der Politik beim Friedensschluss, Grosses Hauptquartier, den 9. September 1914," cited in Strazhas, *Deutsche Ostpolitik*, 108.

control. The latter strategy was at first oriented towards the establishment of monarchies to be ruled by German princes. However, from the very start, this plan appeared problematic due to tensions within the German nobility, who were concerned that the selection of monarchs for these states would disrupt the power balance within the empire.[8]

Development of a unified strategy towards Eastern Europe was further slowed down by the internal contradictions within the German government, as its decision-making was under the competing influence of the military command on the one hand, and the foreign ministry officials on the other. Eventually, civilian politicians failed to develop a sustainable long-term approach towards the territories in the East, ceding the decision to the military, where the hardline wing could always win the upper hand on important issues, as the growing influence of Paul von Hindenburg and Erich Ludendorff demonstrated.[9] The implementation of the project of installing pro-German puppet states was delayed until the fall of 1916, since early in the war Germany was still concerned that this plan would mean interference in the Austro-Hungarian sphere of influence, as was the case with the Polish state. German diplomacy also feared that the immediate establishment of pro-German semi-states could negatively influence potential separate peace negotiations with Russia. This hesitant stance in international politics directly benefited the German army command in its drive for annexation. In particular, the 3rd Supreme Command under Hindenburg and Ludendorff started promoting its own vision of a new order in the East, emphasizing military needs, security, and direct German control.[10] Annexation plans for Eastern Europe were also in line with the interests of German industrial elites, who supported an economic, military, and political expansion of power.[11]

In these circumstances, the predominance of military circles remained a defining feature of German policymaking in East-Central Europe. As Vejas Liulevicius argued, the war provided the German army with the possibility to engage in a unique, even utopian state-building project, relying on the instruments

---

[8]   Herfried Münkler, "Spiel mit dem Feuer: Die 'Politik der revolutionären Infektion' im Ersten Weltkrieg," *Osteuropa* 64, nos. 2–4 (February–April 2014): 120–21.

[9]   Joachim Tauber, "German Eastern Policy, 1917–1918," *Lithuanian Historical Studies* 13 (January 2008), Historical Abstracts with Full Text, EBSCOhost (Accessed April 9, 2015): 71; Münkler, "Spiel mit dem Feuer," 123.

[10]   Münkler, "Spiel mit dem Feuer," 120–22.

[11]   Karl-Heinz Gräfe, *Vom Donnerkreuz zum Hakenkreuz: Die baltischen Staaten zwischen Diktatur und Okkupation* (Berlin: Ed. Organon, 2010), 4.

of total control at its disposal.[12] The case of Ober Ost, established with the goal of keeping the Eastern European territories in the possession of Germany and affirming the German civilizing mission, can be viewed as a typical example of this trend. The chief role in conceptualizing and creating Ober Ost in this capacity is attributed to Hindenburg's deputy, General Erich Ludendorff, who has been described as a "war god" with his own visions of grandeur,[13] while Ober Ost itself was called his "private province."[14]

The close connection between the future of Ober Ost and German military aims was reflected in its name, which represented a shortened version of the official title of the German Supreme Commander in the East, Field Marshal Paul von Hindenburg.[15] All legislative, judicial, and executive power in Ober Ost belonged exclusively to the Supreme Commander, who was solely in charge of governance.[16] There was no option of establishing a civilian administration, as all governing institutions in Ober Ost were part of the army. Special departments, fulfilling the roles of ministries and subordinated to the headquarters of Ober Ost, were formed between November 1915 and May 1916. Administrative personnel were normally recruited from the German army ranks, unless there was a shortage of qualified candidates or they were needed for more urgent military tasks. Only in that case could locals be employed in the administration of Ober Ost.[17]

As a "mobile army formation," Ober Ost stood in stark contrast to the civil administrations set up by the Germans in other occupied territories, such as the

---

[12]   Liulevicius, *War Land on the Eastern Front*, 77.

[13]   Liulevicius, *War Land on the Eastern Front*, 55.

[14]   Strazhas, *Deutsche Ostpolitik*, 115.

[15]   Das Land des Oberbefehlshabers Ost—the Land of the Supreme Commander in the East; short version: Ober Ost.

[16]   The German authorities immediately introduced a number of changes in administration and governance, including the replacement of the Julian calendar used in the Russian Empire with the European Gregorian calendar. A corresponding order was signed by Hindenburg on May 25, 1915. German money was declared the official means of payment on the occupied lands in November 1915, with an exchange rate of 1.50 marks for 1 Russian ruble. The German authorities also established several monopolies as a form of economic control. In particular, the production of cigarettes and fine-cut tobacco was prohibited. The rights to import these articles belonged solely to the German Supreme Command. Monetary fines for the violation of this order ranged from 50 up to 50,000 marks. The production of brandy, compressed yeast, and vinegar was to be approved by the economics department of Ober Ost. The latter also had exclusive right to control the import and sale of alcohol. See LMAVB, RS, f. 23, b. 46/2, l. 23 r., l. 28r, l. 38, l. 55 r., l. 56.

[17]   Presseabteilung, *Das Land Ober Ost*, 85–86; Stephan Lehnstaedt, "Fluctuating between 'Utilisation' and Exploitation: Occupied East-Central Europe during the First World War," in Böhler et al, *Legacies of Violence*, 98.

General Governments of Belgium and Warsaw.[18] Military and security concerns determined the organization of everyday life for the local population in Ober Ost. All political activities of the local nationalities in the occupied territories were prohibited by Hindenburg's decree, signed on July 28, 1915.[19] Civilians were not allowed to leave the boundaries of their communities without permit papers.[20] According to Hindenburg's order signed on December 26, 1915, every person over ten years old had to obtain a passport from the new authorities. Failure to comply, as well as carrying false or invalid documents, was punishable with internment in a workhouse for a period of up to ten years. Passports were very detailed, with a photo of the owner at full height, a fingerprint of the right forefinger, and a detailed description of distinguishing marks.[21] Overall, the German authorities planned to issue about three million passports, thus covering the entire territory of Ober Ost. By 1917, about 1,800,000 persons had been photographed, registered, and issued official identifications.[22]

According to the German chancellor Bethmann Hollweg, the aim of the war was to secure German existence, both politically and economically, in the West and in the East.[23] Consequently, Ober Ost lands were treated primarily through the prism of their usefulness, while local interests and the concerns of the people who populated these lands were regarded as being of secondary importance.[24] In particular, paragraph six of the administrative regulations for Ober Ost stipulated that "the interests of the army and of the German Empire always precede the interests of the occupied land."[25] The priorities of the German authorities were clearly to take advantage of the territorial gains as much as was necessary for their own military progress. This attitude, along with intensive economic exploitation, remained the guiding principle of governance in the occupied territories.[26] The

---

18   Presseabteilung, *Das Land Ober Ost*, 86.

19   However, enforcement of this prohibition was not consistent, especially when Germany started to use the national factor in its anti-Russian politics in the region. See Edmundas Gimžauskas, *Bielaruski faktar pry farmavanni litoŭskaj dziaržavy ŭ 1915–1923 hh.* (Białystok: Bielaruskae histaryčnae tavarystva, 2012), 52.

20   LMAVB, RS, f. 23, b. 46/2, 51 r.

21   LMAVB, RS, f. 23, b. 46/1, l. 63, 63.

22   Presseabteilung, *Das Land Ober Ost*, 173, 176.

23   "Zu den Reichstagverhandlungen," *Zeitung der 10. Armee*, no. 3, December 14, 1915.

24   Presseabteilung, *Das Land Ober Ost*, 84.

25   Presseabteilung, *Das Land Ober Ost*, 85.

26   For instance, detailed instructions for flax cultivation foresaw that the sowing areas were to be considerably increased in 1916, as flax was to be exported to Germany for the needs of the textile industry and the production of flax oil. See Lietuvos Valstybės Istorijos Archyvas

financial documents concerning Ober Ost reveal that the Germans were able to extract economic gains from these lands. For instance, in January 1917 alone, the expenditures of the administration were assessed at 1,878,607 marks, while the income figure was valued at 2,912,236 marks. The surplus of 1,033,628 marks was appropriated by the German Empire.[27] During the entire period of the existence of Ober Ost the German authorities exported resources to the value of 338,606,000 marks, while the values of the imports were estimated to be at 77,308,000 marks.[28]

Along with the extraction of natural resources, the military administration of Ober Ost exploited its human capital. Throughout the course of the war, the Germans gradually came to an understanding that victory had to be achieved under the condition of a maximal mobilization of society. This attitude was transferred to the occupied territories, where it manifested itself in a more ruthless manner. In the fall of 1916, Ludendorff abandoned all reservations towards respecting international law and ordered forced labor recruitment in Ober Ost. Labor duty had existed from the start of the occupation, when the population was forced to do jobs locally if there was a need for it, yet by 1916 it had become a widely employed practice, often implying long-term work throughout the occupation zone. There were two major types of organized forced labor: civilian labor battalions (*Zivilarbeiterbataillonen*) and worker columns (*Arbeiterkolonnen*). The latter were usually put together for short-term assignments, while workers in the first category were interned in special camps, had to wear prison-style uniforms, and did not receive appropriate payment for their labor. These people were employed in agriculture, forestry, and road and railway construction, with a working day of ten to twelve hours.[29] By the fall of 1916, about 60,000 people had been forced to join civilian labor battalions in the Military Administration of Lithuania alone, with the districts of Hrodna and Białystok leading in this process. Worker columns were less numerous and numbered about 6,000 in the whole Ober Ost. According to Christian Westerhoff, in contrast to the General Government of Warsaw, the recruitment of the labor force in Ober Ost stood out due to its intensity, ruthlessness, and violence. Here, the German occupation

---

(hereafter LVIA), f. 641, ap. 1, b. 883a, l. 66. Another valuable resource extracted in Ober Ost was wood. Forests were massively cut down. The local population was forced to work for the Germans and assist them in transporting the lumber by railway and on the rivers. See LVIA, f. 641, ap. 1, b. 572, l. 12 r.

27   LVIA, f. 641, ap. 1, b. 697b, l. 5.

28   Liulevicius, *War Land on the Eastern Front*, 73.

29   Christian Westerhoff, *Zwangsarbeit im Ersten Weltkrieg: Deutsche Arbeitskräftepolitik im besetzten Polen und Litauen 1914–1918* (Paderborn: Schöningh Paderborn, 2012), 217–19.

administration was more prone to use violent methods, aiming to obtain a labor force immediately, instead of using forced recruitment as a tactic to push workers to sign up as volunteers for work in Germany. The arbitrariness and violence of the recruitment process, as well as unsatisfactory working conditions, soon resulted in growing popular dissatisfaction.[30]

The civilian population that was not mobilized for labor duty suffered from the army's presence on a daily basis. The privations of everyday life under the occupation are well portrayed in the reports filed by German district captains to the headquarters of Ober Ost. These documents were required for further decision-making and thus represent useful sources, unlikely to contain inaccurate or biased information. Administrative reports show that requisitions for the immediate needs of the army remained a heavy burden for the local population, while also threatening future German plans of exploiting the agricultural potential of Ober Ost.[31]

Ober Ost was defined by a military spirit throughout the whole occupation, but eventually the army failed to sustain the great ambitions Ludendorff had of creating an exemplary state order. The inefficient administration, changing wartime circumstances, and violence shattered the illusions of the generals, transforming them into an arbitrary military regime. Occupation policy thus drifted away from implementing utopian visions and veered towards the more practical needs of controlling the land and its peoples.[32] A German report compiled in 1917 revealed that two years of German rule had turned Vil'nia into a city plagued by hunger, disease, poverty, and growing mortality rates. The financing of local charities was neglected and funds were insufficient to cover the basic needs of the population. Exorbitantly high prices and inflation provoked open waves of discontent.[33] Problems were attributed to mistakes in food rationing, resulting in a lack of provisions in public kitchens. Ober Ost was not even able to guarantee an adequate bread supply for its population, as allocated rations were too small, and

---

30 Westerhoff, *Zwangsarbeit im Ersten Weltkrieg*, 222–23.

31 German district captain Geyer, who served in Kupiški (Kupiškis) in March of 1916, compiled his report with a specific emphasis on the revival of agriculture, livestock farming, and foodstuffs. The document heavily criticized army requisition squads that apparently acted in a ruthless way, even in the eyes of a German official. Peasants had to surrender to the army their last stocks of grain and potatoes, thus complicating the sowing season work. All available hay, straw, cattle, and horses were confiscated. See LVIA, f. 641, ap. 1, b. 572, l. 5–10.

32 Liulevicius, *War Land on the Eastern Front*, 81.

33 Bielaruski Dziaržaŭny Archiŭ-Muzej Litaratury i Mastactva (hereafter BDAMLIM), f. 3, vop. 1, spr. 126, ark. 92.

overpriced bread was smuggled into the German occupation zone. The provisions department was accused of corruption and criticized for its inadequate levels of contact with the local civilian institutions.[34]

According to the data collected by the charitable societies which provided assistance to war victims and the poor, in 1916 about 44,000 people, or 28% of the population of Vil'nia received aid in the form of food, clothing, school materials, and books.[35] German administrative reports from the Biržy (Biržai) district from the second quarter of 1917 noted that growing numbers of people from Vil'nia and its surroundings were about to become a "menace" for the provinces. The unemployment and lack of food forced them to leave the city and roam the neighboring districts in search of bread. The degree of desperation is evident from the fact that people disregarded strict regulations limiting the movements of the civilian population in Ober Ost, venturing on trips to the countryside without carrying proper travel permit papers.[36] In Hrodna, the situation was notably worse, as up until 1916 the population of the district remained dependent on German army food supplies, as the harvest had been destroyed by military actions.[37] To secure provisions, the German administration introduced a strict system of rationing.[38]

Popular dissatisfaction due to the continuing arbitrary requisitions and general labor duty further complicated the security situation in Ober Ost. Many people tried to avoid the latter by hiding in the woods where they joined fugitive POWs and their bands. According to a document issued by the Chief of Staff of the Eastern Front, Max Hoffmann, bands had gotten out of control by May 1917, seriously threatening the security of the occupied lands. The military was allowed to use weapons against both enemy soldiers and civilians suspected to be armed.[39] In July 1917, the Military Administration of Lithuania ordered all district captains to arrest every suspicious person who was without a proper form of identification.[40] Many inhabitants of the occupation zone started to believe that German rule would soon come to an end, as they heard about the attacks of

---

[34]   BDAMLIM, f. 3, vop. 1, spr. 126, ark. 92 adv.

[35]   *Homan*, no. 2, February 18, 1916, 4.

[36]   LVIA, f. 641, ap. 1, b. 52, l. 207 r.

[37]   Gerd Linde, *Die deutsche Politik in Litauen im Ersten Weltkrieg* (Wiesbaden: O. Harrassowitz, 1965), 53.

[38]   Kurt Klamrot and Ales' Smaliančuk, "Horadnia 1916 na staronkach Dzionnika rotmistra Kurta Klamrota," *Horad Sviatoha Huberta*, no. 6 (2012): 67.

[39]   LMAVB, RS, f. 23, b. 1/2, l. 309.

[40]   LMAVB, RS, f. 23, b. 1/1, l. 18.

Russian troops throughout 1916. Even German soldiers were becoming openly unenthusiastic about the war, avoiding confrontation with the armed forest bands.[41] All of these circumstances are important to keep in mind in order to avoid generalizations[42] regarding the German occupation regime in Ober Ost, especially when cultural and national policies are discussed.

German Encounters with the Ober Ost Nationalities

With a total area of 108,808 km², Ober Ost was the largest among all of the territories administered by the Germans in 1915. According to the compiled data for Ober Ost, based on the statistics taken from the Russian imperial census of 1897, the overall population numbers in the region were estimated to have dropped from 4,200,000 people living in these areas at the turn of the century to around 2,910,000 people during the war. Initially, the German occupation zone consisted of six major administrative areas: Kurland, Lithuania, Suwałki, Vil'nia, Białystok, and Hrodna. Through mergers in 1916 and 1917, three larger administrative units emerged: Military Administration Kurland (with its center in Mitau/Jelgava), Military Administration Białystok-Hrodna (Białystok), and Military Administration of Lithuania (Vil'nia). Lithuania was the most ethnically diverse territory in Ober Ost, inhabited by Lithuanians, Belarusians, Poles, Germans, Jews, and Latvians. The Latvian and German population dominated in Kurland, while Poles, Belarusians, and Jews were predominant in Białystok-Hrodna.[43] The military administration structures remained in place throughout the whole occupation, until finally transformed into civilian administrations by a decree of the German chancellor Max von Baden, signed a few days before the end of the First World War. In comparison to Kurland and Białystok-Hrodna, Military Administration of Lithuania was the largest in size, incorporating areas of the former Suwałki, Kaunas, and Vil'nia provinces with two thirds of the entire Ober Ost population residing there.[44]

The national distribution in Ober Ost was as follows: 1,550,315 Lithuanians (or 34.4% of the entire population), 936,067 Belarusians (20.8%), 468,946 Latvians (10.5%), 607,896 Jews (13.5%), and 534,102 Poles (11.8%).[45] The latter

41   Strazhas, *Deutsche Ostpolitik*, 66–67.
42   See for instance Rudling, *The Rise and Fall of Belarusian Nationalism*, 74.
43   Presseabteilung, *Das Land Ober Ost*, 89–91.
44   Liulevicius, *War Land on the Eastern Front*, 61–62; LMAVB, RS, f. 23, b. 1/2, l. 353.
45   Presseabteilung, *Das Land Ober Ost*, 433.

two groups comprised the majority of the urban population in this region.[46] Yet, this statistical data is useful only for a general overview of the demographic situation in the region, as it reflects only the pre-war situation and does not take into account mobilized soldiers, victims of military action, and streams of refugees, including both those who moved further east and those who came to Ober Ost fleeing military actions.

Within Ober Ost, the German authorities emphasized the restoration of order and winning the trust of the local population as one of their main tasks.[47] All nationalities had to act within the space defined by the Germans, who focused on the task of undermining the tsarist state and fostering anti-Russian sentiments through a controlled and limited toleration of local national movements.[48] However, in the early stages of the occupation, the Germans were only starting to make sense of the multicultural borderlands of the tsar's empire. The German army discovered that the conquered lands were inhabited by a multitude of ethnicities, each with their own language and culture.[49] The population was not easy to classify, as identities were often fluid or overlapping. This variety was confusing for German soldiers, who compared their experiences in Ober Ost to that of the German Empire. Convinced of their own civilizing mission in the East, they often dismissively treated locals as underdeveloped peoples.[50]

In an attempt to educate the soldiers, army newspapers started providing information on the different nationalities in Ober Ost. Lithuanians, Belarusians, Poles, and Jews were identified as major groups in the Vil'nia region. Cities were described as predominantly Polish and Jewish, while Lithuanians and Belarusians were presented as typical inhabitants of the countryside. The military newspaper *Zeitung der 10. Armee* informed German soldiers that both of the latter groups had weak feelings of national belonging, being under strong pressure to accept Polish culture. Nevertheless, it was noted that in the twenty years before the war these nationalities had started to follow common trends for East-Central Europe and were on the path of "regaining" their national consciousness.[51]

---

[46] Snyder, *The Reconstruction of Nations*, 54–56.

[47] Presseabteilung, *Das Land Ober Ost*, 307.

[48] Mark von Hagen, *War in a European Borderland: Occupations and Occupation Plans in Galicia and Ukraine, 1914–1918* (Seattle: Herbert J. Ellison Center for Russian, East European, and Central Asian Studies, University of Washington, 2007), 55.

[49] See, for example, Hermann Struck and Herbert Eulenberg, *Skizzen aus Litauen, Weissrussland und Kurland* (Berlin: George Stilke, 1916).

[50] Barthel, "Contesting the Russian Borderlands," 36–37; Strazhas, *Deutsche Ostpolitik*, 111; Liulevicius, *War Land on the Eastern Front*, 30.

[51] "Die Völker Litauens," *Liebesgabe zur Zeitung der 10. Armee*, no. 23, January 27, 1916.

In the occupied territories German soldiers also made the "discovery" of Eastern Jews (*Ostjuden*), who were different from the educated, prosperous, and assimilated Jews of the German Empire. For the Germans, this circumstance often evoked anti-Semitic images of smugglers, benefiting at the cost of others, preferring trade to physical work, and attempting to bribe officials. Stereotypes of Jewish filthiness, dishonesty, and haggling permeated among the German soldiers.[52] On the other hand, due to the linguistic closeness of Yiddish to German and their dissatisfaction with Russian rule, Jews were also considered to be potential partners for the German authorities in the task of establishing a system of governance in the occupied lands.[53] Moreover, the German administration made use of Jewish trade networks to extract food resources and raw materials, as indicated by the experiences of the Department of Military Resources in Hrodna in April 1916.[54] One concern here, however, was local anti-Semitism, as it was noted that Lithuanians often mistrusted Jews and that there was a danger that this mistrust might transfer further onto Germans too.[55]

In general, the occupying regime aimed to maintain balance in its relations with the Jews during the First World War. Jewish religious sentiments were to be respected. For instance, market days could not fall on Saturdays, while instruction at Jewish schools was left without any changes and interference.[56] Jews and Christians were not placed in the same units for labor duty, allowing Jews to follow their dietary rules and observe religious rites. However, the reason behind the latter decision was purely practical—Germans were primarily interested in achieving maximum labor efficiency from the exploited workers.[57] Despite these regulations, lower-level officials usually had anti-Semitic views and did not hesitate to demonstrate them in their reports, referring to Jews as a "cancer of the land," and as being engaged in suspicious speculative activities.[58]

Russia was consistently blamed for keeping its western provinces backward. It was presented as a barbaric power which "built an invisible wall," separating the non-Russian nationalities from the rest of Europe, where they rightfully belonged.[59]

[52]   Ismar Freund, "Ostjuden im Spiegel ihrer Religionsquellen," *Liebesgabe zur Zeitung der 10. Armee*, no. 23, January 27, 1916.
[53]   Barthel, "Contesting the Russian Borderlands," 115.
[54]   Klamrot, "Horadnia 1916," 66.
[55]   LMAVB, RS, f. 23, b. 1/2, l. 250.
[56]   LMAVB, RS, f. 23, b. 1/1, l. 89.
[57]   LMAVB, RS, f. 23, b. 1/1, l. 173, 173 r.
[58]   LVIA, f. 641, ap. 1, b. 52, l. 5, l. 15.
[59]   Presseabteilung, *Das Land Ober Ost*, 11.

The emphasis was placed on the history of the suppression of spiritual, religious, cultural, and economic development throughout the nineteenth century. Tensions between nationalities, in particular, Poles and Lithuanians, as well as between Poles and Jews, were attributed to the detrimental long-term effects of Russian rule, which was deemed responsible for cultural stagnation and the forceful conversion of churches and monasteries into Orthodox ones, while the years after 1863 were described as a time of "grueling persecution."[60]

Yet, German anti-Russian propaganda appears to have been more credible and successful when it turned to the more recent ruthless actions of the Russian authorities during the evacuation in 1915, rather than evoking images of past suffering. It made wide use of the fresh memories of officials departing in a hurry, taking all that was possible to move, while the army destroyed the harvest, burnt down buildings, and forcefully uprooted the population. In January and February of 1916, *Zeitung der 10. Armee* published a series of articles about Vil'nia during the Russian retreat, showing that the corrupt bureaucracy and the Russian government were responsible for moods of panic in the city, especially when all banks, businesses, enterprises, church bells, and state alcohol storage facilities, along with necessary military establishments and munitions, were moved east. More prosperous citizens rushed to leave the city, while workers and the poorer population with no means of securing overpriced train tickets were left behind. The Russian government was further accused of fostering "fears of German brutality" among the population during the evacuation.[61] Such a portrayal of an enemy power is not surprising, but it should not be necessarily dismissed as a biased one. The Russian army indeed pursued a "scorched earth" policy, moving all that was considered to be of importance and driving people away from their homes. The arbitrary behavior of the Russian generals, whose actions were often not coordinated with the Russian central government, contributed to the chaos and disorganization during the retreat.[62]

Anti-Russian rhetoric was soon complemented by the growing concerns over Polish nationalism in Ober Ost. By early 1916, German newspapers had already started to criticize the opening of Polish schools in Vil'nia, which were apparently financed not only by private organizations but also by municipal funds, thus depriving other nationalities, in particular, Lithuanians, Belarusians, and Jews, of

---

60   "Wilna und die Russen," *Zeitung der 10. Armee*, no. 16, January 11, 1916.

61   "Wilna im Kriege," *Zeitung der 10. Armee*, no. 35, February 24, 1916.

62   Gatrell, *A Whole Empire Walking*, 16, 33.

their fair share of support. With regard to schools in the provinces, it was noted that Vil'nia region did not have a significant Polish population, yet the majority of functioning schools were Polish,[63] despite the fact that German local authorities did not welcome them and even created obstacles to their establishment.[64] Growing German concerns over the strong Polish positions in the region prompted them to opt for a stronger Lithuanian component in Ober Ost. To a certain degree, this approach also benefited the Belarusian national movement, as the Germans could use it along with its Lithuanian counterpart as a tool to weaken the Poles.[65] Thus, the occupation authorities employed *divide et impera* methods in their interaction with the local nationalities. The following section will address the questions of how this tactic resulted in growing national competition in Ober Ost and what place the Belarusians occupied in the German discourse.

From "Weissrussland" to "Weissruthenien": Development of German Perceptions of Belarusians

Belarusian-populated areas of Ober Ost were located predominantly in former Vil'nia, Hrodna, and Białystok provinces, where, according to the German compilation of the data from the 1897 Russian imperial census, 936,067 Belarusians lived, comprising 20.8% of the entire population.[66] According to these statistics, Belarusians in Vil'nia province made up 42.0%, while their percentage among the urban population was only 4.2%. Districts under German occupation where the Belarusian population represented an overwhelming majority included Lida (73.2%), Vaŭkavysk (82.5%), Pružany (75.5%), Slonim (80.6%), and Sokółka (83.9%).[67]

One of the leading Belarusian national activists in Vil'nia during the First World War, Anton Luckievič, made an attempt to take the aspect of wartime population movements into account when he compiled an introductory summary report to the German authorities in late December 1915. He admitted that the actual numbers of Belarusians in German-administered lands were difficult to evaluate due to the war circumstances and the significant demographic changes caused by military actions and population displacement. Luckievič claimed that

---

[63]   *9. Liebesgabe zur Zeitung der 10. Armee*, no. 28, February 8, 1916.

[64]   LVIA, f. 641, ap. 1, b. 52, l. 35.

[65]   Strazhas, *Deutsche Ostpolitik*, 116; Rudling, *The Rise and Fall of Belarusian Nationalism*, 73.

[66]   Presseabteilung, *Das Land Ober Ost*, 433.

[67]   *Völker-Verteilung in West-Russland* (Kaunas: Verlag der Kownoer Zeitung, 1916), 8.

1.5 million ethnic Belarusians still inhabited this region during the First World War, a majority of whom (800,000) were native to the Hrodna province, while 300,000 to 400,000 Belarusians resided in the Vil'nia province. Further, Luckievič argued that the figure of 4.2% for the Belarusian population in the city of Vil'nia, recorded in the Russian census of 1897, was not correct. In his opinion, in contrast to the Russian population that had left the city en masse, Belarusians could not afford to move and had thus stayed. Moreover, people from the countryside had come to the city in search of employment, allegedly increasing the ethnic Belarusian population in Vil'nia to up to 10%.[68] Even if this optimistic assessment is taken into consideration, it should be noted that most of these people still did not possess a firm sense of national self-identification as Belarusians. The German census in Vil'nia, conducted in the early spring of 1916,[69] showed that the city population comprised 140,840 people, the majority of whom identified as Poles and Jews—70,629 persons (50.15%) and 61,265 (43.5%) respectively. Lithuanians with 3,699 persons (2.6%) and Belarusians with 1,917 persons (1.36%) were in the obvious minority.[70]

With all necessary caution both towards the quality of the data used by the German officials and Luckievič's optimistic estimates, both attest to the presence of Belarusians in Ober Ost and in particular in the Vil'nia region, if not in Vil'nia itself. The frequently cited passage from Ludendorff's memoirs states that initially Belarusians "did not come into consideration" for the high-ranking German authorities, who tended to see them as a "widespread, but extremely Polonized tribe."[71] Despite the numerical predominance of Belarusians in the Vil'nia region, they rarely received proper attention from the authorities, indicating that early in the war the occupation regime did not regard this group to be an important influence factor. Belarusians were often perceived as "too Russian."[72] Most likely,

---

[68]   BDAMLIM, f. 3, vop. 1, spr. 131, ark. 19, ark. 31.

[69]   Its results were extensively criticized by the Belarusian national activists, as apparently Poles conducted an extensive and aggressive national agitation, in order to raise the numbers of the Polish population. Moreover, German military officials, who conducted the census, claimed that they did not see any difference between Belarusian and Russian and usually addressed the people either in German or in Polish, thus involuntarily assisting the Poles in obtaining better statistics. See BDAMLIM, f. 3, vop. 1, spr. 134, ark. 16 adv.

[70]   Michał Brensztein, *Spisy ludności m. Wilna za okupacjji niemieckiej od d. 1 listopada 1915* (Warsaw: n. p., 1919), 21.

[71]   Erich Ludendorff, *Meine Kriegserinnerungen, 1914–1918, mit zahlreichen Skizzen und Plänen* (Berlin: E.S. Mittler und Sohn, 1919), 145.

[72]   Strazhas, *Deutsche Ostpolitik*, 112.

this concerned all Orthodox populations. Alternatively, the Germans classified Belarusians as Poles.[73] Such an approach prevailed even in cases when people consciously made a choice of adopting a Belarusian identity, as happened in an incident involving a student of the Belarusian teachers' courses, Jazep Salaviej. According to a complaint submitted by the Belarusian Committee for the Aid of War Victims[74] to the head of the German military administration in January 1916, Salaviej was trying to obtain his identification papers and was asked by a policeman about his nationality. After he told the officer that he was a Belarusian, he heard in reply that "we do not recognize Belarusians and Russians, it is possible to identify only as a Pole, a Lithuanian or a Jew." Salaviej protested and refused to be identified as a representative of any of the above-named nationalities, insisting that he was a Belarusian. The officer threatened him with arrest and inscribed Salaviej's nationality in his papers as Polish. The Belarusian Committee saw in this incident a violation of the rights of Belarusians and an attempt to manipulate demographic statistics in Vil'nia.[75]

The actions of the German official appear to have been in accordance with Hindenburg's decree on the introduction of obligatory passports for the Ober Ost population, signed in December 1915. The decree stipulated that identification documents were to be issued in two languages. One of them had to be German, the second language was to be the corresponding nationality's language. Among the latter, only Latvian, Lithuanian, Polish, and Yiddish were listed as acceptable choices.[76] Reluctance to treat Belarusians as a separate nationality, especially by the lower-level officials, persisted up until 1918. Similar to Salaviej, the case of Jazep Lickievič was documented two years later. He complained that the authorities in Vil'nia ignored the order of the Supreme Commander stipulating that every citizen could obtain a passport in his mother tongue. Apparently, passports in Vil'nia were issued exclusively in Polish. Lickievič complained that the official at the passport office refused to record him as Belarusian and recorded "Polish nationality" in the documents.[77]

---

[73] The reason was that many Belarusians who chose not to become refugees and stayed behind were mostly Roman Catholics, usually under pressure from the Catholic priests to adopt Polish identity, which often happened. See *Homan*, no. 74, September 14, 1917, 2.

[74] The Belarusian Committee for the Aid of War Victims (henceforth Belarusian Committee) united most of the Belarusian national elites in Ober Ost. As all political activities were prohibited by the German military authorities, national charities expanded their activities beyond the humanitarian sphere and acted as national representations.

[75] LCVA, f. 361, ap. 5, b. 14, l. 1.

[76] LMAVB, RS, f. 23, b. 46/1, l. 64.

[77] LCVA, f. 361, ap. 5, b. 14, l. 57.

Another point of contention between the Belarusian Committee in Vil'nia and the German occupation authorities was the public use of the Belarusian language. The Committee petitioned the Supreme Commander with a demand to introduce Belarusian on labels and in public spaces, justifying this request by the fact that all other languages of ethnic minorities, including Lithuanian, Latvian, and Polish, were widely used alongside German. The absence of Belarusian was interpreted as a refusal to recognize the full rights of the second-largest minority of Ober Ost. Further, concerning the forthcoming issue of Ober Ost currency, the so-called Ostrubles (*Darlehnskassenscheine*), the Committee asked for the inclusion of text and inscriptions in Belarusian on the new currency bills in order to ensure the equal treatment of all nationalities. Delegates of the Committee negotiated this issue with the German High Command, which appeared sympathetic. However, no visible results were achieved,[78] as none of the later official detailed descriptions of the Ober Ost currency contained information about the usage of text in the Belarusian language.[79]

Other examples of ignoring Belarusian are to be found in the public addresses to the local population in the Military Administration of Lithuania, where the German authorities mentioned Lithuanians, Poles, Belarusians, and Jews, yet posted these announcements only in the German, Lithuanian, Polish, and Yiddish languages.[80] The official newspaper *Verordnungsblatt der Deutschen Verwaltung für Litauen* contained all regulations both in German and Lithuanian, but not in Belarusian.[81] Supplements to the local *Białystoker Zeitung* and *Grodnoer Zeitung* appeared only in Polish and Yiddish.[82] In a detailed report addressed to the German authorities in late 1915, Anton Luckievič pointed out that the refusal of the German authorities to translate into Belarusian important announcements and orders, the ban on Belarusian radio messages, and the non-recognition of the Belarusian language in the Hrodna region contributed to growing resentment among the local population.[83] Popular reactions are difficult to evaluate here, but one thing is clear—this attitude of the German occupation authorities complicated the national mobilization work of the Belarusian activists.

---

[78] BDAMLIM, f. 3, vop. 1, spr. 132, ark. 12, 12 adv.

[79] See "Beschreibung der Darlehnskassenscheine der Darlehnskasse Ober Ost," *Anlage zum Befehls- und Verordnungsblatt*, no. 119, November 3, 1918, LMAVB, RS, f. 23, b. 46/2, l. 171.

[80] LMAVB, RS, f. 23, b. 1/1, l. 48.

[81] LVIA, f. 641, ap. 1, b. 883a, l. 134.

[82] Presseabteilung, *Das Land Ober Ost*, 137.

[83] BDAMLIM, f. 3, vop. 1, spr. 131, ark. 23.

Nevertheless, German treatment of Belarusian national demands was slightly modified over time. By 1917, Belarusians were reluctantly recognized by the German authorities as the second-largest ethnic group—for instance, this fact was stated in a book published by the Ober Ost press department, which described all aspects of the newly conquered territories and provided ample information on Ober Ost nationalities.[84] Two main factors determined this turn in German policy. Firstly, the Germans made an effort to develop a better distinction for Belarusians by separating them from Russians in order to maintain their positive image as protectors of all groups previously oppressed by the tsarist state. This trend was already evident in early 1916, when *Kownoer Zeitung* started to educate its readership about the peculiarities of Belarusian history. In particular, references were made to the Grand Duchy of Lithuania, described as a multinational state shared by Belarusians and Lithuanians. It was also noted that the first Slavic translation of the Bible had appeared in the Belarusian language.[85] The German military newspaper *Zeitung der 10. Armee* regularly published articles on Belarusian history and ethnography.[86] One of the activists of the Belarusian Committee, Julijana Menke, was employed by this newspaper as a translator, and also contributed articles to raise public awareness of the Belarusian question in Ober Ost. She cooperated with another staff member of the newspaper, German writer Walter Jäger, who later published a book about Belarus,[87] based on the materials that he and Menke provided for *Zeitung der 10. Armee*.[88]

The task of distinguishing Belarusians as a separate group was complicated by the linguistic closeness between the Slavic languages. While the use of Russian, as well as the Cyrillic script, was banned altogether in Ober Ost in January 1916,[89] signs of a more differentiated approach to Belarusian appeared later in the same year, when the use of Cyrillic characters was allowed along with the Latin script for the publication of the Belarusian newspaper *Homan*, in effect from September 1, 1916. However, all German district captains were specifically instructed to keep an eye on the distribution of this newspaper.[90] Cyrillic script for *Homan*

---

[84]   Presseabteilung, *Das Land Ober Ost*, 20.

[85]   Barthel, "Contesting the Russian Borderlands," 158–59.

[86]   See for instance "Die Völker Litauens," *Liebesgabe zur Zeitung der 10. Armee*, no. 23, January 27, 1916; "Aus Sitte und Aberglauben der Weißrussen," *Liebesgabe zur Armee-Zeitung*, no. 182, July 17, 1916.

[87]   Walter Jäger, *Weissruthenien: Land, Bewohner, Geschichte, Volkswirtschaft, Kultur, Dichtung* (Berlin: K. Curtius, 1919).

[88]   Vitan-Dubiejkaŭskaja, *Maje ŭspaminy*, 53.

[89]   LMAVB, RS, f. 23, b. 24/2, l. 37.

[90]   LMAVB, RS, f. 23, b. 1/1, l. 151.

remained the only exception, which did not concern other spheres of public life, as for instance postcards were allowed to be written in Belarusian only with the use of Latin characters.[91] Security reasons were the determinant in this case, but this policy also indirectly benefited the development of the Belarusian Latin script, which had been widely used in Ober Ost, in contrast to the eastern Belarusian provinces.

Second, and by far the most important factor resulting in the change in German attitudes towards Belarusians in Ober Ost, was connected to the reformatting of the German *Ostpolitik* in 1917. In the first two years of the war, German chancellor Bethmann Hollweg still believed in the possibility of a separate peace with Russia, which explained the cautious approach and lack of action of the German civilian authorities towards Ober Ost, especially in contrast to the ruthless plans of the military. However, as the possibility of peace negotiations waned, the positions of the German civilian and military authorities seemed to converge on the issue of the conquered territories.[92] Moreover, the proclamation of the Polish state in the Act of November 5, 1916 resulted in growing German frustrations due to the failure of this project to reinforce the Central Powers in the war. German military authorities adopted an anti-Polish stance, arguing for the economic exploitation of the territories in the East and curtailment of Polish ambitions.[93]

However, an outright annexation of the territories in the East was not an acceptable option, as it could have harmed the German image as a protector of oppressed nationalities, especially in light of the growing popularity of the concept of self-determination, which entered international politics after the February Revolution in Russia.[94] Another concern was the threat to the internal stability of the German Empire, already suffering from the war effort on two fronts. Consequently, the German leadership resorted to the approach of so-called "limited autonomy," which dated back to the early spring of 1917.[95] It marked the abandonment of the equal treatment of the Ober Ost nationalities by the Germans.

---

91   LMAVB, RS, f. 23, b. 46/1, l. 325 r., 326.

92   Herfried Münkler, "Spiel mit dem Feuer," 122; Gimžauskas, *Bielaruski faktar*, 62–63.

93   Piotr Stefan Wandycz, *The Lands of Partitioned Poland, 1795–1918* (Seattle: University of Washington Press, 1974), 354; Piotr Mikietyński, *Niemiecka droga ku Mitteleuropie: Polityka II Rzeszy wobec Królestwa Polskiego (1914–1916)* (Kraków: Towarzystwo Wydawnicze "Historia Iagellonica," 2009), 195–96, 244.

94   Borislav Chernev, *Twilight of Empire: The Brest-Litovsk Conference and the Remaking of East-Central Europe, 1917–1918* (Toronto: University of Toronto Press, 2019), 43–44.

95   Strazhas, *Deutsche Ostpolitik*, 171–73.

Aiming to keep strong Polish influences in Ober Ost under control, the German authorities started with the targeted support of other national groups, favoring Lithuanians and to a lesser degree Belarusians. This qualitative turn in German policy emerged in early 1917, when German policymakers started making statements about respecting the historical ties of Belarusians and Lithuanians.[96] In order to avoid misleading connotations which resulted in a "politically undesirable" image of Belarusians as a branch of the Russian nationality, an order of the Chief of the Military Administration of Lithuania signed on May 29, 1917, prohibited German authorities from using the names "Weissrussen" and "Weissrussland" to describe Belarusians and Belarus. New terms, "Weissruthenen" and "Weissruthenien," were introduced to emphasize the status of a separate nationality, different from Russians, and to promote the growth of national consciousness among the population.[97] Remarkably, Belarusian activists always used the latter combination in their official correspondence with the German authorities.[98]

In order to counterbalance the perceived and real dangers of Polish nationalism, German orders specifically emphasized the mother tongue criteria in determining nationality. For instance, this approach was implemented in Hindenburg's decree on the introduction of obligatory passports for the whole Ober Ost population. These documents contained information on the native language of the owner which was defined as the first language learned, "spoken by the parents of the passport owner during the time of his birth and childhood." It was specifically noted that in some cases people might speak Polish without belonging to this nation.[99] Germans identified the nationality of these peoples as Lithuanians and Belarusians, who "felt themselves Polish."[100]

Yet, it appears that the Germans had more confidence in the Lithuanian movement and expected that Polonized Lithuanians would return to their roots without any doubts. On the other hand, with regard to the Belarusian movement, it was unclear for the Germans whether at this stage it had the potential of overcoming the consequences of the Russification policies.[101] Eventually, the preference for using Lithuanians in the anti-Polish tactics determined all future relations of the German administration in Ober Ost towards the Belarusian national movement:

---

[96]   Strazhas, *Deutsche Ostpolitik*, 262.
[97]   LMAVB, RS, f. 23, b. 1/1, l. 307.
[98]   See for example BDAMLIM, f. 3, vop. 1, spr. 119, ark. 5.
[99]   LMAVB, RS, f. 23, b. 46/1, l. 62.
[100] "Die Völker Litauens," *Liebesgabe zur Zeitung der 10. Armee*, No. 23, January 27, 1916.
[101] Ibid.; Gimžauskas, *Bielaruski faktar*, 55–56.

the latter was tolerated as long as it suited the political interests of the occupation authorities, but it did not receive any significant support either in cultural or in political matters. It is evident that Belarusian national aspirations were taken into account only inasmuch as they were suitable for the German practical needs of controlling the occupied lands. Newspaper publications provided necessary background information, but hardly changed the common German perception of Belarusians. Outwardly friendly attitudes of high officials with assurances of support were of a superficial and inconsistent nature. They were often ignored at the lower levels of administration, as the cases involving nationality data in Ober Ost passports and the use of Belarusian in public spaces and on Ober Ost currency bills both clearly demonstrated.

Belarusian Committee for the Aid of War Victims in Vil'nia

How did Belarusians deal with the new opportunities for nation-building available from the new occupation powers? Were they able to advocate for the needs of their community and effectively advance national mobilization? During the First World War, Vil'nia remained the center of Belarusian life in Ober Ost, although the numbers of Belarusian activists who managed to stay in the city were low. Many fell victim to the forced evacuations of reservists during the retreat of the Russian army in 1915. According to Julijana Menke, who was closely affiliated with the Belarusian national movement and worked as a teacher and translator for Belarusian organizations, Polish nationalists sarcastically remarked that all Belarusian activists in Vil'nia would fit onto one couch.[102] Initially, most of them were working for the Belarusian Committee for the Aid of War Victims (henceforth the Belarusian Committee). Established in April 1915, the Belarusian Committee was able to revive its activities under the German administration in Ober Ost. Existing regulations limited its capabilities, as initially it was designed to provide assistance to all inhabitants of the Vil'nia, Hrodna, Minsk, Viciebsk, and Mahilioŭ provinces who suffered from the war. The Belarusian Committee in Ober Ost focused on setting up dining halls and residences for the refugees, supplying them with warm clothes and firewood, organizing medical care in areas which affected by the military conflict, and paying lump-sum allowances for foodstuffs and seeds.[103]

---

[102]   Vitan-Dubiejkaŭskaja, *Maje ŭspaminy*, 37.
[103]   LCVA, f. 361, ap. 5, b. 4, l. 2, l. 8.

In December 1915, the German authorities limited the activities of national charitable organizations. After receiving a number of applications for their creation, the occupation authorities proceeded with the issue of guidelines to regulate these activities. Most likely due to reasons of security, it was prohibited to open committees that spread their work simultaneously over several localities. The number of existing local national committees for the aid of war victims was controlled by the German High Command. It supervised all charities, making sure that their activities covered all those in need, Jews and Christians in equal manner. The latter regulation was connected to the fact that in the eyes of the German occupation powers Jews applied for too many charities.[104]

The Belarusian Committee was financed through membership fees, donations, and profits from charitable concerts, lectures, and theatrical performances.[105] Along with private donations, the Belarusian Committee was financially supported through funds received from international charities and the German authorities. For instance, in the period from June 1 to September 1, 1916, it received 300 marks from the municipality of Vil'nia, another 300 marks came through donations, and 4,000 marks were transferred from the General Relief Committee for the Victims of the War in Poland, located in Vevey, Switzerland.[106] Almost all of these funds were directed to the needs of schools and towards the payment of allowances for the poor, since estimates for school needs required about 1,000 marks monthly.[107]

It is evident that the Belarusian Committee was short of money and could not expand its work to reach every person in need. Its members worked for free in order to decrease the operational expenses.[108] International assistance was not a reliable source of income, as is clear from the tensions arising from the actions of the Polish Committee in Vil'nia, which was originally in charge of funds distribution. Apparently, the Polish Committee refused applications for assistance received from Belarusian speakers, despite having at its disposal considerable donations from the Polish General Relief Committee in Switzerland for the needs of the entire population of the occupied areas, including Poles, Lithuanians, and Belarusians.[109] When, in December 1915, the Polish Committee decided on the

---

104   LMAVB, RS, f. 23, b. 1/1, l. 89.

105   LCVA, f. 361, ap. 5, b. 4, l. 3 r.

106   For more on its activities, see Danuta Płygawko, *Sienkiewicz w Szwajcarii: Z dziejów akcji ratunkowej dla Polski w czasie pierwszej wojny światowej* (Poznań: Wydawnictwo Naukowe Uniwersytetu im. Adama Mickiewicza w Poznaniu, 1986).

107   BDAMLIM, f. 3, vop. 1, spr. 126, ark. 117, 117 adv.

108   "Try hady pracy Bielaruskaha Kamitetu," *Bielaruski Šliach*, no. 34, May 3, 1918, 1.

109   LCVA, f. 361, ap. 5, b. 7, l. 18. According to Belarusian historian Uladzimir Liachoŭski, these

distribution of the first part of the total of 300,000 marks received in donations from the General Relief Committee in Vevey, it agreed to transfer only the sum of 1,400 marks to the Belarusian Committee, while in the following year the amount was increased to about 3,000 marks, representing only a fraction of the donations.[110] Apparently, Vil'nia diocese administrator K. N. Michalkiewicz, who was put in charge of the funds distribution, directed the money primarily for the establishment and maintenance of Polish schools in the region as well as towards other initiatives in support of Polish nation-building, thereby neglecting the original humanitarian mission.[111]

According to the report of the General Relief Committee, published on December 2, 1917, in the Polish newspaper *Dziennik Polski*, the Polish Committee in Vil'nia received a total of over 800,000 francs between January 9, 1915, and March 31, 1917, which roughly equaled the same amount of money in marks. Out of this sum, only about 8,000 marks were assigned to the Belarusian Committee.[112] In 1916, *Homan* informed its readers that following complaints about the actions of the Polish Committee, the German High Command decided to take over the management of the funds from Switzerland. It attempted to oversee the distribution of money among all national charitable organizations in Ober Ost. In this way, the Belarusian Committee was at least able to continue its support for workshops and schools and provide financial aid for resettled refugees.[113]

The arrival of the Germans in September 1915 cut off all contacts with the eastern Belarusian areas, thus impacting communication between the Vil'nia and Minsk sections of the Committee, which continued to operate as two separate centers of charitable activities. The Minsk section struggled for its existence: by 1916, due to insufficient funding, it was forced to limit its activities to the operation of a single dining hall.[114] By contrast, the Vil'nia section of the Belarusian Committee for the Aid of War Victims still had more freedom in coordinating charitable projects, despite financial difficulties and the limitations imposed by the occupation powers. It supported and coordinated the work of primary schools,

---

funds were partly donated by the famous Polish writer Henryk Sienkiewicz, who died in 1916 and donated to the General Relief Committee for the Victims of the War in Poland a significant part of his Nobel Prize to be spent for the needs of the inhabitants of the former Grand Duchy of Lithuania. See Liachoŭski, *Škol'naja adukacyja*, 117.

[110] *Homan*, no. 41, July 4, 1916, 3.

[111] Strazhas, *Deutsche Ostpolitik*, 73.

[112] "U Wilni i wakolicach," *Homan*, no. 98, December 7, 1917, 2.

[113] *Homan*, no. 41, July 4, 1916, 3.

[114] Lapanovič, *Dzejnasc' dziaržaŭnych i hramadskich arhanizacyj*, 105.

orphanages, public kitchens, canteens, and dining halls. It also supervised the work of three workshops where woodwork, carving, sewing, and embroidery were taught.[115] The Committee also provided financial assistance to the refugees outside of Vil'nia. In the summer of 1916, resettled Belarusian peasants from Ašmiany and Svianciany (Švenčionys) districts, residing in Daŭgi (Daugai) south of Vil'nia, received 500 marks from the Committee. This sum was immediately spent on food and clothing.[116] In urgent circumstances, people could also apply for a one-time payment of special allowances. This was especially important for displaced persons, who fled from the war and settled in the city, such as the peasant Juljan Blažovič, originally from the village of Suraž (Lipniškė district). During the Russian retreat, his farm was burnt down and all cattle confiscated. Blažovič, his wife, and seven children ended up in Vil'nia with no means of survival. The Belarusian Committee helped the family to obtain temporary accommodations and provided them with some basic foodstuffs.[117]

Along with the humanitarian work, the Belarusian Committee acted in the capacity of a coordination center for national activism in Vil'nia. By October 1915 its representatives, including Vincent Sviatapolk-Mirski, Vaclaŭ Lastoŭski, and the brothers Ivan and Anton Luckievič, requested to be received by the Vil'nia governor Generalleutnant Wegener in an attempt to clarify "some issues regarding the origins of the Belarusian nation."[118] In May 1916, the Committee obtained permission from the German authorities for the organization of the Belarusian Club in Vil'nia. The main declared goal of the Club was the "promotion of the cultural and national unity of Belarusians" through the hosting of various talks, serving as a center for social gatherings, and providing entertainment and leisure activities. The Belarusian Club also proclaimed its intention to support Belarusian schools and the press, as well as to assist its members with childcare and parenting.[119] It housed and supported a library and a reading room. Finally, the Club became the base for the Belarusian Musical-Dramatic Group, organized by the Belarusian playwright Francišak Aliachnovič.[120] By December 1916, it organized concerts with the performances of a string quartet, a choir, and a children's choir. Its theatrical comedy shows gathered over 200 spectators.[121] Belarusians also made appearances

---

[115]   BDAMLIM, f. 3, vop. 1, spr. 124, ark. 102.
[116]   "Z usiaho kraju," *Homan*, no. 57, August 29, 1916, 3.
[117]   LCVA, f. 361, ap. 1, b. 7, l. 7.
[118]   BDAMLIM, f. 3, vop. 1, spr. 119, ark. 5.
[119]   BDAMLIM, f. 3, vop. 1, spr. 135, ark. 4.
[120]   BDAMLIM, f. 3, vop. 1, spr. 135, ark. 11–12 adv.
[121]   BDAMLIM, f. 3, vop. 1, spr. 15, ark. 1.

at various social events throughout the city: Sunday evenings in the Vil'nia Workers' Club were known for Polish, Lithuanian, and Belarusian performances, while one of the graduates of the Polish pedagogical courses recited Belarusian poems during the convocation ceremony.[122]

Other notable Belarusian organizations in Ober Ost were the Belarusian Society for Childcare *Zolak* led by Vincent Sviatapolk-Mirski, and the Cooperative Society *Rajnica* headed by Vaclaŭ Lastoŭski. Together with the Belarusian Society for the Aid of War Victims, the Belarusian Club, and the Musical-Dramatic Group, they became the founding members of the Belarusian Central Union of National Organizations, which aimed to coordinate, support, and develop Belarusian national work.[123] Designed to act as an umbrella organization, it did not manage to replace the Belarusian Committee as the most active body in the Belarusian community.

The Periodical Press in Ober Ost and the Belarusian Newspaper *Homan*

Ober Ost could boast a variety of periodicals in various languages. Initially, German front newspapers took care of delivering news to the army and raising the fighting spirit of the soldiers. The first military newspaper on the Eastern front, *Wacht im Osten*, was soon followed by eight different titles, covering the needs of the entire front. Furthermore, German authorities established local press organs, oriented towards the population of the occupied areas. Designed to maintain order and security, one of their chief tasks was to spread and strengthen popular respect for the new regime. Local newspapers appeared in the major cities of Ober Ost, including Liepāja (Libau), Jelgava (Mitau), Vil'nia, Hrodna, Suwałki, and Białystok, carrying the name of the respective city in their titles. Initially, these newspapers were published in German, yet in order to make them accessible and easy to read for the local population, it was decided to print them in the Latin font instead of the more commonly used Gothic letters. The average circulation of these newspapers was between 3,000 and 4,000 copies.[124]

The military administration produced such a flood of regulations and orders that even the lower-level district authorities complained about the amount of

---

122 "U Wilni i wakolicach," *Homan*, no. 68, October 6, 1916, 3.
123 BDAMLIM, f. 3, vop. 1, spr. 138, ark. 4.
124 Bundesarchiv (hereafter BArch), PH 30-III/5, 23.

paperwork. As the local population generally had a poor command of German, people often learned about new laws only when they were punished for violating them.[125] Jews were in a slightly better situation as they could understand German, but had trouble reading it well, since they were used to the Hebrew script. This problem was solved by the introduction of special supplements in Polish and Yiddish (however, not Belarusian) for newspapers appearing in Hrodna, Suwałki, and Białystok. With this step, the Germans hoped to reach substantial sections of the population which spoke these languages.[126] The newspapers informed their readers about economic, social, and administrative measures, in addition to providing censored information on the political and military situation. Finally, the local nationalities of Ober Ost, among them Latvians, Lithuanians, Poles, Jews, and Belarusians, received permission to publish their own newspapers: *Dzimtenes Ziņas, Dabartis, Dziennik Wileński, Letzte Nais,* and *Homan,* respectively.[127]

At first sight it appears that this step was in full accordance with the proclaimed German policy of equal treatment of the local nationalities. Yet, as in the previously described cases, security and military reasoning remained the guiding principles of German policy. All local newspapers were subjected to thorough military and political censorship, run by the press department of Ober Ost. They could not criticize German policies, while positive mentions of Russia were not tolerated. Moreover, all printed items, books, and maps were also censored, and their distribution was closely monitored. The importing of newspapers and journals, as well as their subsequent distribution, was allowed only for the German newspaper distribution units and official book sellers at the railway stations. Soldiers enjoyed preferential treatment, as they were allowed to subscribe to any periodicals through the military postal service.[128]

The occupying power diligently cultivated its image as the protector of nationalities' rights, and consistently presented the previous Russian administration as the main source of tensions in the region. According to the regulations for both German and local newspapers issued by the head of the press office in Vil'nia, the chief task for the periodical press in Ober Ost was to ensure that the public was aware that the "liberation from Russian rule serves their own [Ober Ost nationalities'] interests."[129] At the same time, the German authorities preferred to have total

---

[125] LVIA, f. 641, ap. 1, b. 572, l. 28.
[126] Presseabteilung, *Das Land Ober Ost,* 137.
[127] Presseabteilung, *Das Land Ober Ost,* 135–38.
[128] LVIA, f. 641, ap. 1, b. 883a, l. 75 r., l. 214.
[129] LCVA, f. 368, ap. 1, b. 17, l. 15.

control over the press designated for the local Ober Ost population; thus, for instance, they specifically prohibited the distribution of Lithuanian newspapers published in Germany.[130]

Considered to represent the biggest ethnic group, Lithuanians received their own newspaper almost immediately after the Germans entered East-Central Europe. The first issue of *Dabartis* (The Present) was already in print by September 1, 1915. The monthly journal *Ateitis* (The Future), which provided moralizing tales for youth, was published in Kaunas starting from June 1, 1916.[131] The head of the Military Administration of Lithuania, Prince Franz Joseph zu Isenburg-Birstein, encouraged cooperation between the German and Lithuanian authors of *Dabartis*, urging German officers to assist the newspaper with materials, including sketches on local issues, personal observations, and pieces on agriculture.[132] More concessions followed after German policy evolved, in late 1916 and early 1917, towards supporting the national aspirations of Lithuanians as a counterweight to Polish nationalism. A second Lithuanian newspaper, *Lietuvos Aidas* (Lithuanian Echo), was established in September 1917.[133] The district administration was obliged to subscribe to the Lithuanian newspapers, since according to the report from the district of Padbrodzie (in the vicinity of Švenčionis), individual subscriptions were rare, as only a fraction of the district population was able to understand Lithuanian.[134]

Belarusians were allowed to publish only one newspaper in Ober Ost. The first issue of *Homan* (The Clamor) appeared on February 15, 1916, although there had been several previous attempts to obtain permission for Belarusian periodical press projects. One of the early applications, submitted presumably in October 1915, was made by Uladzislaŭ Znamiaroŭski, requesting that the German High Command approve the publication of the daily newspaper *Naviny* and the weekly *Naša Chata*.[135] Yet, this attempt failed, as there is no evidence of a positive response to this application. Eventually *Homan*, in spirit the successor to *Naša Niva*, became the only Belarusian newspaper in Ober Ost, appearing twice weekly. The circulation of *Homan* was about 3,000 copies.[136] All editorial work was done by the Belarusian Committee, while the German authorities provided paper and

---

[130]   LMAVB, RS, f. 23, b. 36, l. 42.
[131]   Presseabteilung, *Das Land Ober Ost*, 452–53.
[132]   LMAVB, RS, f. 23, b. 36, l. 41.
[133]   Presseabteilung, *Das Land Ober Ost*, 138.
[134]   BArch, PH 30-III/3, 19.
[135]   BDAMLIM, f. 3, vop. 1, spr. 119, ark. 4.
[136]   Sukiennicki and Siekierski, *East Central Europe during World War I*, 156–57.

access to printing facilities. Vaclaŭ Lastoŭski served as the editor and brothers Ivan and Anton Luckievič were among the chief contributors to *Homan*.[137]

The Belarusian newspaper provided its readers with military and international news, usually supplied by the German press department. More importantly, it served as a good source for information on local life in Vil'nia, containing excerpts from other newspapers, tales and legends for entertainment purposes, correspondence from readers, advertisements, current prices, announcements of new initiatives of the Belarusian Committee, and social events for Belarusians. In this manner, the newspaper attempted to convince those still in doubt of their identity that the choice of being Belarusian was not connected to images of the backward peasant and that Belarusians in the city enjoyed equal rights with other nationalities. As a means of creating an "imagined community" of readers, it was similar to *Vol'naja Bielarus'* published in Minsk in 1917, yet it faced more limitations in terms of censorship and an enforced pro-German position.

The title of the newspaper reflected continuity with the origins of modern Belarusian identity, as it was named after the illegal periodical published in Minsk in 1884, which signaled the start of an organized national movement.[138] The new *Homan* in 1916 set the goal of uniting the forces of Belarusians and promoting national culture, thus laying the foundations for the growth of a nation.[139] Vaclaŭ Lastoŭski's editorial in the first issue of *Homan* stressed the importance of a newspaper in the mother tongue, designed "to know what is going on around us, to receive news from all over the world, . . . to be able to tell others what we need, what we are longing for. The newspaper . . . connects a human being with his nation, his homeland, and the whole world. It turns weak single voices of our homeland (*Kraj*) into a strong and powerful voice of a community."[140] Readers were reminded that only reliance on their own initiative could result in positive developments for the Belarusian nation. People were encouraged to rebuild schools and introduce Belarusian as the language of instruction instead of Russian, as well as to demand the introduction of their native language in church services, both Catholic and Orthodox.[141]

The overall rhetoric and mood of *Homan* was similar to other Ober Ost national newspapers. For instance, the new Polish newspaper, *Dziennik Wileński*, also called

---

[137] Vitan-Dubiejkaŭskaja, *Maje ŭspaminy*, 56.
[138] Turuk, *Belorusskoe dvizhenie*, 15.
[139] "Pieramieny," *Homan*, no. 2, February 18, 1916, 3.
[140] "Da čytačoŭ," *Homan*, no. 1, February 15, 1916, 1–2.
[141] "Pieramieny," *Homan*, no. 2, February 18, 1916, 3.

for the unified efforts of all Poles in rebuilding their national life. At the same time, it sounded more down-to-earth and less optimistic, noting the roadblocks of the difficult war circumstances, devastation, and extreme poverty. It urged readers to devote their energy to everyday work, primarily in the matter of popular education, with anticipated long-term benefits for nation-building.[142] Remarkably, Poles, who were also allowed only one newspaper in Ober Ost, did not welcome the publication of *Homan*, presenting it as an allegedly German-orchestrated project, initiated "with the goal of popularizing the so-called Belarusian movement"[143] and being a deliberate "action, directed against the Poles."[144]

Revival of the School System

Since the German occupation powers allowed all ethnicities in Ober Ost to establish their own schools, provided they could support them financially, it is interesting to see how the legal opportunity to receive education in the mother tongue influenced the processes of national mobilization in the Polish-Lithuanian-Belarusian borderlands. Along with the German policy of eliminating Russian influence in the region by satisfying some of the cultural demands of the nationalities, the establishment of schools also served the goal of maintaining order and control. As noted in the report of the German district captain in Retava (Rietavas), all Russian teachers had left the area at the start of the war. Children worked only on their parents' farms, growing up without proper attention and control from the authorities. This resulted in "a colossal lack of education and neglect of the youth."[145] Reports of German district captains indicated that during the winter of 1915, children of school age residing in the countryside often went to small privately organized schools, or they were taught by local women who did not have specialized pedagogical training. German authorities did not have confidence in these solutions,[146] since schools were viewed as basic institutions designed "to foster religious convictions, to accustom the youth to law obedience, respect for the German authority, its armed might as well as discipline and order."[147]

---

[142] "Od redakcyi," *Dziennik Wileński*, no. 1, February 2, 1916, 1–2.
[143] *Litwa za rządów ks. Isenburga* (Kraków: Nakł. Krakowskiego Oddziału Zjednoczenia Narodowego, 1919), 94.
[144] *Litwa za rządów ks. Isenburga*, 95.
[145] LVIA, f. 641, ap. 1, b. 360, l. 98.
[146] LVIA, f. 641, ap. 1, b. 572, l. 33, l. 13.
[147] LMAVB, RS, f. 23, b. 23/1, l. 94.

According to the *Fundamental Guidelines for the Revival of the School System* issued in January 1916, all educational initiatives in Ober Ost were placed under full German control. The opening and closing of schools and pedagogical courses, as well as the offering of private education and tutoring, first had to be approved by the head of the corresponding local administration. The Ober Ost department of education acted as the highest authority in school matters. It appointed school inspectors responsible for internal school affairs, approved curricula, and supervised the professional activities of all teachers. With an emphasis on security, schools were not allowed to host any meetings or gatherings which could contradict the policies of the German military administration. All teaching materials and textbooks were subject to official approval prior to their usage. While schools were emerging gradually, education at first remained a matter of choice for families, however, once a school was established, parents had to sign a paper, confirming the regular attendance of their children.[148]

The German authorities did not subsidize local schools. Rather, they were to be financed by the school tax collected by districts and municipalities. The accounting data for the entire Ober Ost for January 1917 indicates that the school system received subsidies only in the sum of 4,965 marks, while at the same time the subsidies for newspapers, including local national press organs, made up 63,946 marks.[149] Schools were also supported by voluntary donations and students' families. Later, public and national organizations stepped in, most prominent among them in the matter of school support were the Lithuanian Society *Rytas*, the Association for Education *Saule*, and the Polish Society for School Tuition.[150]

According to the official statistics, the following institutions were registered in Vil'nia in February 1916: seven high schools with 151 teachers and 1,150 students, eight pedagogical seminaries with 78 teachers and 770 students, 91 people's schools with 430 teachers and around 7,300 students, 14 specialized schools with 55 teachers and 620 students, 78 cheders and twelve Jewish religious schools with 1,500 students. Overall, more than 10,000 students were receiving education in various types of schools by early 1916.[151] The number of active students at this time was evaluated to have been equal to the pre-war period. It was also considered to be an improvement, since substantial numbers of Russian students accounted

---

[148]   LMAVB, RS, f. 23, b. 46/1, l. 52, 52 r.
[149]   LVIA, f. 641, ap. 1, b. 697b, l. 5.
[150]   LMAVB, RS, f. 23, b. 37, l. 12 r.; LMAVB, RS, f. 23, b. 11a, l. 69, l. 75.
[151]   According to the 1916 German-administered census, 140,840 people resided in Vil'nia. See Brensztein, *Spisy ludności m. Wilna*, 21.

for in the prewar statistics had left the city during the 1915 evacuation, and had been replaced by new students who came to the city during the war, resulting in overall higher numbers of those receiving education.[152] Teachers as well as students at the teachers' courses and seminaries had to be registered with the authorities for "military control," but they were freed from general labor duty and obligations to the German army.[153]

The German authorities stipulated that public schools were to accept students without discriminating against them by religion. Education was to be provided in the mother tongue of the students. The mother tongue in this case was defined as the language spoken by the parents in everyday life. The Russian language was banned as a language of instruction for all schools, and the same applied to all Russian books and teaching materials. By contrast, the number of German lessons had to be increased, with the goal of providing students with a good working command of the language after three compulsory years of schooling. German was also established as the main language of communication between teachers and school inspectors and was used in all school documentation.[154] German Interior Minister Max Wallraf was especially proud that the military administration of Ober Ost introduced German as only one of the subjects at schools, and not as the principal language of instruction, noting that under Russian rule only Russian was used in this capacity.[155]

Every nationality in Ober Ost proceeded with the establishment of schools where instruction was provided in the mother tongue of the students: German, Polish, Lithuanian, Latvian, Belarusian, Hebrew, and Yiddish. Polish educational activities stand out as a convincing case of how a rather strong national movement could make use of the new regulations. Without waiting for the official approval, Polish schools, often organized by enthusiasts, started to open as early as September 1915, immediately following the German takeover of the Russian borderlands. Poles had more qualified teachers and fully developed teaching methods in comparison to Belarusians and Lithuanians, offering better quality of instruction. A separate Polish Education Committee was established and put in charge of managing and overseeing educational activities. Designed to bridge political differences, it was to act in the general interests of the whole Polish nation.

---

152 "Szkoly ŭ Wilni," *Homan*, no. 7, March 7, 1916, 4.
153 BDAMLIM, f. 3, vop. 1, spr. 126, ark. 18 adv.
154 LMAVB, RS, f. 23, b. 46/1, l. 53.
155 "Reichstagsprotokolle, 13. Legislaturperiode, 181. Sitzung, 26. Juni 1918, 5687," http://www.reichstagsprotokolle.de/Blatt_k13_bsb00003417_00288.html (Accessed September 9, 2015).

As of January 1, 1916, there were already four Polish schools in Vil'nia with 815 students, eight municipal schools with 1,060 students, and thirty primary schools with 4,300 students. The overall number of those who received education in Polish exceeded 6,000 students. In addition, there were four vocational schools, several professional courses for adults and illiterate people as well as a public university named after Adam Mickiewicz.[156] However, the latter was a short-lived initiative, promptly closed by the Germans in February 1916. The occupation authorities were not eager to support higher education initiatives, as these would have interfered with the plans to Germanize local populations in the future.[157]

Following the incident with the Mickiewicz University, the German authorities issued a separate order, clarifying the *Fundamental Guidelines*. Due to the war circumstances, the opening of educational institutions and courses containing the word "university" in their title was prohibited. All existing academic courses and lecture series held outside of permitted schools were declared illegal. Special permits for single talks or lectures could be obtained only by direct application to the head of the German administration. Exceptions were made only for agricultural and purely technical courses, oriented toward skills acquisition.[158] Polish activities in the sphere of education did not wane, as the clergy sought more control over the schooling process. The Catholic Church actively applied for the establishment of its own schools in districts of Ober Ost along with those approved by the German administration.[159] According to a letter, forwarded to *Homan* and *Dziennik Wileński*, in the winter of 1915, Poles were very active in opening schools in the Vil'nia district. The local population, almost entirely comprised of Belarusians, was not happy with these schools, as their children were mostly Belarusian speakers in everyday life and had trouble with Polish as the language of instruction at school. Teachers were sent from Vil'nia and some of them had a good command of Belarusian, but they were prohibited from using Belarusian. However, this ban was not strictly enforced, since peasants submitted a complaint against one of the overzealous teachers to the authorities.[160] Evidently, Polish nationalism often opted for a more decisive and even confrontational approach and the occupation powers responded with suppression.

---

[156] "Komitet Edukacyjny," *Dziennik Wileński*, no. 1, February 2, 1916, 3–4.

[157] Liachoŭski, *Škol'naja adukacyja*, 81–82.

[158] LMAVB, RS, f. 23, b. 23/1, l. 78r.

[159] Hans Zemke, *Der Oberbefehlshaber Ost und die Schule im Verwaltungsbereich Litauen während des Weltkrieges* (Berlin: Junker und Dünnhaupt, 1936), 93.

[160] "U wiaskowych szkołach," *Homan*, no. 59, September 5, 1916, 2.

By 1917, the Germans turned to providing more support to the Lithuanians, who had also devoted special attention to education, along with charity work and the establishment of self-help organizations.[161] A letter written by the teacher Anton Giruliok, who worked in a Belarusian school for refugee children in Vil'nia, indicates this attitude of the German authorities. With an emphasis on the unequal educational opportunities available to Lithuanians and Belarusians, Giruliok described the situation of the refugee families who were living in former military barracks. Overall, the barracks housed about 4,000 people. Two schools, one Belarusian and one Lithuanian, operated there by 1918. Although the Lithuanian school enrolled all Lithuanian refugee children of school age, only 100 out of 300 Belarusian children had the opportunity to receive an education in the Belarusian school. The latter was obviously under-financed, neglected, and urgently required expansion and the hiring of a second teacher.[162]

The German preference for Lithuanian schooling is also evident from the following case: on August 20, 1917, a group of Belarusian teachers who had taught in the winter of 1916/1917 in the Polish schools submitted an application to the head of the Military Administration of Lithuania, Isenburg-Birstein, requesting the opening of schools with Belarusian as the principal language of instruction. The teachers referred to their recent experiences, noting that students often misinterpreted Polish and had trouble speaking the language. *Homan* intended to publish this collective request, but the entire article was rejected by the German censor and did not appear in print. Apparently, Isenburg-Birstein received a protest from Lithuanians who wanted the schools in the Vil'nia region to have instruction in Lithuanian.[163]

Belarusian Schools in Ober Ost: Accommodation, Toleration, or Instrumentalization?

The *Fundamental Guidelines for the Revival of the School System*, signed by Hindenburg on January 16, 1916, prohibited any use of Russian. This move was important for the Belarusian nation-building activities in Ober Ost. The *Guidelines* also pointed out that "the Belarusian language, which is not identical with Russian,

---

[161] "Z litoŭskaho žyccia," *Homan*, no. 1, February 15, 1916, 4.
[162] BDAMLIM, f. 3, vop. 1, spr. 140, ark. 133.
[163] LCVA, f. 368, ap. 1, b. 14, l. 7.

is allowed without any restrictions."[164] Belarusians thus could benefit from the opportunity to open and run schools in Ober Ost which were turning into tools of nation-building and the recruitment of national elites.[165]

The first Belarusian primary school in Ober Ost opened on November 13, 1915, in the Vil'nia city district of Lukiški (Lukiškės). The school was located in the building on 44 Georgenstrasse.[166] Alaiza Paškievič[167] was one of the most active members of the Belarusian Committee who contributed to its establishment, finding the space to rent, and providing the new school with all necessary teaching materials. Practical tasks also involved the active promotion of a new Belarusian initiative among the ethnic Belarusians in the city: going door-to-door, talking to people, and encouraging them to enroll their children in the new school.[168] Initially, thirty-six students signed up, while later the number grew to fifty.[169] The first teacher at this school was the former editor of the Christian Democratic newspaper *Biełarus*, Baliaslaŭ Pačobka. In the first months of its existence, the school provided only instruction, although later, students in need started receiving free lunches, textbooks, stationery, and clothing.[170]

By February 1916, five Belarusian primary schools were operating in Vil'nia, with the goal "of teaching Belarusian children in their mother tongue."[171] In April 1916, teacher Aliaksandr Hrykoŭski and his colleagues Stanislaŭ Kačynski and Vera Kraŭcevič managed to obtain permission for the opening of a Belarusian school in Hrodna.[172] Schools in Krynki[173] and several other localities in the Lida district soon followed. Despite the limited number of schools and their uneven

[164] LMAVB, RS, f. 23, b. 46/1, l. 53.
[165] Andrea Griffante, *Children, Poverty and Nationalism in Lithuania, 1900–1940* (Cham: Palgrave Macmillan, 2019), 54.
[166] Currently Gedimino prospektas, one of the major streets in Vilnius.
[167] Paškievič was a Belarusian poet and political activist, also known under the pseudonym Ciotka. She was married to the Lithuanian socialist Steponas Kairys.
[168] Vitan-Dubiejkaŭskaja, *Maje ŭspaminy*, 37–38.
[169] BDAMLIM, f. 3, vop. 1, spr. 126, ark. 118.
[170] "U Wilni i wakolicach," *Homan*, no. 81, November 21, 1916, 2.
[171] BDAMLIM, f. 3, vop. 1, spr. 124, ark. 10 adv.
[172] Andrej Čarniakievič, *Naradženne bielaruskaj Harodni: Z historyi nacyjanal'naha ruchu 1909–1939 hadoŭ* (Minsk: Januškievič, 2015), 18–19.
[173] It is likely that the early establishment of the school in Krynki had a long-term effect on the future of Belarusian national mobilization efforts in that area. According to the report of the Belarusian National Committee of the Hrodna region, by 1921 the youth organization in Krynki enjoyed widespread support and was known for its extensive cultural activities. NARB, f. 325, vop. 1, spr. 173, ark. 31.

territorial spread, Anton Luckievič optimistically hoped that these initiatives would lead to the establishment of a solid network of Belarusian primary schools in the region.[174]

Instruction was organized in Belarusian, with additional German and Polish lessons. The number of students who signed up was more than existing schools could accommodate. The Belarusian Committee planned to open another ten schools, yet municipal funding did not suffice, while the Committee itself was short on funds. As tuition was not charged, Belarusian activists struggled with securing funding for existing schools. Most likely, families also signed up their children for schools in order to alleviate difficult financial conditions, since most students were from poorer families who could not afford to feed them properly at home, whereas schools provided their students with lunches and often also operated as orphanages. Before the Belarusian Committee could organize free meals for students, children from the school on Antokal'skaja Street were known to have been frequent guests at the neighboring German barracks, where the soldiers shared their rations with them.[175] In November 1916, the Belarusian Committee took care of about 200 children in need, holding cultural events with charity lotteries to raise funds for their support.[176]

One of the chief problems at this stage was a lack of Belarusian textbooks. Despite the bans on Belarusian school education in the Russian Empire, several textbooks, including a Belarusian primer in both the Latin and Cyrillic scripts, already existed in the pre-war period,[177] but the limited number of titles was insufficient for the needs of existing schools. Anton Luckievič called on every Belarusian to contribute to this cause, "to put his or her own brick in this common construction project."[178] Gradually new textbooks appeared with the help from

---

[174] *Homan*, no. 56, August 25, 1916, 2.

[175] *Homan*, no. 1, February 15, 1916, 4.

[176] "U Wilni i wakolicach," *Homan*, no. 81, November 21, 1916, 2.

[177] For instance, Vaclaŭ Lastoŭski, *Karotkaja historyja Biełarusi: z 40 rysunkami* (Wilnia: Drukarnia Marcina Kuchty, 1910); Ciotka, *Pieršaje čytannie dlia dzietak-bielarusaŭ* (Pieciarburh: n. p., 1906). The first Belarusian primer *Biełaruski lementar abo pierszaja nawuka czytańnia* was published in 1906 in St. Petersburg. It appeared both in Latin and Cyrillic script; the first version was developed by Vaclaŭ Ivanoŭski, the second by Kazimir Kastravicki (literary pseudonym—Karuś Kahaniec). The decision to publish the primer in two versions simultaneously was most likely caused by the need to overcome the religious differences of the Belarusians and appeal in equal manner both to the Orthodox and Catholic populations, showing to both groups that they used the same language. For the detailed history of the first Belarusian primer, see Jury Turonak, *Madernaja historyja Bielarusi* (Vilnius: Instytut bielarusistyki, 2008), 34–38.

[178] *Homan*, no. 56, August 25, 1916, 2.

Homan. By mid-1917, German authorities issued an official permit for twelve Belarusian books to be used for teaching in schools,[179] among them were Belarusian grammars, readers, and religion and mathematics books. This number was almost on par with other nationalities, as by that time eighteen Lithuanian, fifteen Jewish, and twenty-five Polish textbooks had been approved as well.[180]

Yet, other issues were more pressing—first and foremost the establishment of schools required qualified professionals able to run them and teach. According to the official German statistics, only fifteen persons were officially listed and recognized as Belarusian teachers in Ober Ost in 1915.[181] Starting from December 15, 1915, the Belarusian Committee ran teachers' courses in Vil'nia. They were designed to last for three months but the German authorities ordered an extension of the study period for the certificates to be recognized.[182] The classes took place in the evenings, six days per week. Students were taught pedagogy, German, Belarusian, Polish, mathematics, physics, history, geography, as well as accounting and beekeeping.[183] Instructors included members of the Belarusian Committee, in particular, brothers Ivan and Anton Luckievič, Alaiza Paškievič, Vaclaŭ Lastoŭski, and Baliaslaŭ Pačobka.[184] Initially, twenty-three persons enrolled. The majority of the students were aged between 15 and 25 and were Roman Catholics, with the exception of two Orthodox and one Lutheran.[185] Sylwester Ascik, Oskar Kajrenius, Stanislava Kaminskaja, Andrej Korsak, Vincuk Lemieš, Stefanija Misiura, Zuzana Rusakievič, Hanna Savickaja, Adam Strelčunas, Aliaksandr Trot, and Andrej Trot successfully graduated in September of 1916 with the right to teach in the primary schools.[186]

Unfortunately, after the second set of students enrolled, the German authorities intervened and cancelled the courses. Another request of the Belarusian Committee

---

[179] LMAVB, RS, f. 23, b. 36, l. 27 r.

[180] LMAVB, RS, f. 23, b. 36, l. 26–27. For instance, among new Belarusian textbooks published in Ober Ost were the following: Anton Luckievič, *Jak pravil'na pisac pa-bielarusku* (Vil'nia: Homan, 1917); Šuster, *Karotkaja historyja sviataja* (Vil'nia: n. p., 1917), Vaclaŭ Lastoŭski, *Rodnyja ziarniaty: Knižka dlia škol'naga čytannia* (Vil'nia: Homan, 1916); G. Jurevič, *Zadačnik dlia pačatkovych škol* (Vil'nia: Homan, 1916).

[181] See Verzeichnis der Lehrer und Lehrerinnen, BDAMLIM, f. 3, vop. 1, spr. 124, ark. 14, 14 adv.

[182] BDAMLIM, f. 3, vop. 1, spr. 126, ark.119.

[183] Beekeeping was very popular among Belarusians in the early twentieth century. In the interwar period, a Belarusian cooperative association of beekeepers "Pčala" (The Bee) and a specialized journal *Bielaruskaja borc'* were established in Vil'nia. See Vieras, *Ja pomniu ŭsio*, 76–85.

[184] BDAMLIM, f. 3, vop. 1, spr. 124, ark. 14, 14 adv.

[185] BDAMLIM, f. 3, vop. 1, spr. 124, ark. 59.

[186] BDAMLIM, f. 3, vop. 1, spr. 124, ark. 7, ark. 60; BDAMLIM, f. 3, vop. 1, spr. 126, ark. 118.

for a Belarusian teachers' seminary in Vil'nia was refused without any additional explanations. It was hardly possible to expand the network of Belarusian schools in the provinces, given the insufficient number of teachers able to run them and the lack of a Belarusian pedagogical institution educating new staff.[187] By contrast, one Lithuanian and two Polish teachers' seminaries, with 92 and 69 students respectively, were approved to operate in Vil'nia.[188]

In October 1916, a new Belarusian teachers' seminary opened in Svislač (Vaŭkavysk district), located in the Military Administration Białystok-Hrodna. In contrast to the Belarusian teachers' courses in Vil'nia, it was an entirely German-orchestrated undertaking. In particular, the head of the Military Administration Białystok-Hrodna, Theodor von Heppe, was known for his support of a clear anti-Polish policy. He was convinced that the Poles demonstrated overzealous political activities and apparently used schools as a nationalist "weapon."[189] Therefore, the approval for the Belarusian teachers' seminary in Svislač was issued by the German authorities, most likely with the aim of creating a counterweight to the extensive Polish national activities in the region, which resulted in the now undesirable growth of Polish schools. Headed by the pro-German Pole Bendziecha, the seminary in Svislač operated until November of 1918. It was financed through the Ober Ost authorities and remained the only pedagogical institution within the German occupation zone which was authorized to prepare teachers for Belarusian schools. Studies at the seminary were open to both male and female students, and lasted for six months. German authorities encouraged the provincial district captains to cooperate with local school inspectors in order to secure higher enrolment numbers.[190]

Overall, 144 teachers graduated from the Svislač seminary during the two years of its operation. However, the quality of education was insufficient due to the inadequate qualifications of instructors employed at this institution. The Schooling Commission of the Belarusian Committee had no power in the matters related to the Svislač seminary. In order to enroll, prospective students had to contact the corresponding German district administration, instead of the Belarusian Committee. Moreover, the latter was not allowed to recommend students for tuition relief, had no control over the distribution of the graduates throughout the schools in the countryside, and did not even have detailed

---

[187]   Liachoŭski, Škol'naja adukacyja, 124.
[188]   LMAVB, RS, f. 23, b. 11a, l. 69–73.
[189]   Linde, Die deutsche Politik, 49–50.
[190]   LMAVB, RS, f.23, b. 15, l. 34 r.

information regarding the operation of these schools. Thus, the German authorities appropriated Belarusian schooling outside of Vil'nia and its surroundings for their own practical purposes of weakening Polish nationalism. This step allowed them to ignore the Belarusian national activists, effectively preventing the latter from playing any active role in education.[191]

In August 1917, the Schooling Commission of the Belarusian Committee made an attempt to regain its influence by establishing a central union of Belarusian teachers, designed to maintain contacts between all Belarusians employed as teaching staff in the Ober Ost area. Again, the German authorities refused the application, citing military reasons and restrictions on movement still in force.[192] Another factor, not mentioned in the official refusal letter, might have been reservations about giving too much leeway to the Belarusian movement, which could compromise close German-Lithuanian cooperation, which was in full swing by the summer of 1917.

A small network of Belarusian primary schools developed in the Hrodna region, including several schools in the Vil'nia region along with five primary schools in the city of Vil'nia and one in the Suwałki region. Between October 1916 and April 1918 they provided instruction in Belarusian to over 3,000 students.[193] In comparison to other Ober Ost nationalities, this number appears low: according to the official German statistics, the total number of primary school students in Ober Ost was recorded as 73,248 persons; of these 27,903 were Lithuanians, 17,503 Poles, 21,387 Jews, 2,698 Germans, and 3,266 Belarusians.[194] As of 1918, Belarusian high schools existed neither in Vil'nia nor elsewhere in Ober Ost, while among the ten high schools in Vil'nia, five were Polish with about 1,300 students, four were Jewish with 822 students, and one was Lithuanian with 276 students.[195] The first Belarusian high school (*himnazija*) opened in Vil'nia only in January 1919. In the interwar period, it made a significant contribution in the matter of educating future Belarusian national elites.[196]

The exact number of all Belarusian primary schools operating in the entire Ober Ost remains disputed. According to the Belarusian historian Uladzimir Liachoŭski, the most plausible number lies somewhere between 89 and 153.

---

[191] Liachoŭski, *Škol'naja adukacyja*, 130–32; "U Wilni i wakolicach," *Homan*, no. 2, January 5, 1917, 2.
[192] BDAMLIM, f. 3, vop. 1, spr. 126, ark. 86.
[193] BDAMLIM, f. 3, vop. 1, spr. 126, ark. 121.
[194] Zemke, *Der Oberbefehlshaber Ost und die Schule*, 102.
[195] LMAVB, RS, f. 23, b. 11a, l. 42, l. 42 r.–49, l. 51–67.
[196] Liachoŭski, *Škol'naja adukacyja*, 127.

The first figure was suggested by Hans Zemke's study on the school system in the Military Administration of Lithuania, based on German statistical documents,[197] while the latter was the rather plausible estimate of Anton Luckievič,[198] most likely based on the numbers of graduates of the Svislač teachers' seminary and available data on already existing schools. Belarusian Christian Democrat Adam Stankievič later stated that there were over 200 schools, while the Polish historian Marian Siemakowicz suggested the number as being 400.[199] Yet, these figures appear debatable. Jury Turonak and Uladzimir Liachoŭski dismiss claims of the existence of higher numbers of Belarusian schools in the area. Both researchers point out that such statements are not substantiated by any additional information on these schools, their locations, or the time period of their operation. Supposedly, the higher estimates were also based on unreliable sources, such as correspondence of the Belarusian national organizations with European governments and international organizations, aimed at justifying Belarusian national demands instead of prioritizing the presentation of verifiable facts.[200] Therefore, to maintain that "German administrators established Belarusian schools on a massive scale"[201] in this case would be a misleading conclusion, both in terms of quality and quantity.

Nevertheless, having been completely banned under Russian rule, the emergence of primary schools with Belarusian as the principal language of instruction represented a positive development for the promotion and strengthening of the Belarusian national cause among the wider population, especially compared to the regions of eastern Belarus, where such schools only started appearing in 1918. Belarusian teachers who shared their experiences with the Committee in Vil'nia were enthusiastic and hopeful. A postcard from Stanislaŭ Lachovič, a teacher from Augustów, sent to Anton Luckievič in December 1917 pointed out that children enjoyed going to the newly opened Belarusian school. In light of these successes, he was optimistically anticipating that Belarusians would be able to voice their national aspirations in the same manner as Poles and Lithuanians did, proving to the world that they were not a "stillborn" nation.[202]

---

[197] Zemke, *Der Oberbefehlshaber Ost und die Schule*, 101.

[198] BDAMLIM, f. 3, vop. 1, spr. 126, ark. 121.

[199] See Adam Stankievič, *Bielaruski hryscijanski ruch* (Vil'nia: n. p., 1939), 87; Marian Siemakowicz, "Polityka władz rosyjskich, niemieckich i polskich wobec szkolnictwa białoruskiego w latach 1903–1922," *Białoruskie Zeszyty Historyczne*, no. 7 (1997): 28.

[200] Turonak, *Madernaja historyja Bielarusi*, 522; Liachoŭski, *Škol'naja adukacyja*, 132–33.

[201] See Rudling, *The Rise and Fall of Belarusian Nationalism*, 74.

[202] BDAMLIM, f. 3, vop. 1, spr. 133, ark. 11.

Catholic Priests and Polish Nationalism

The process of establishing and running Belarusian primary schools in the provinces was not smooth and easy. The idealism of young Belarusian teachers could not match the intensity of the counteractions of Polish nationalists.[203] Polish initiatives in the provinces could count on the solid support of major landowners and the local Catholic clergy. The majority of provincial Catholic priests, in particular those from the Hrodna region, were known as ardent supporters of Polish culture. After the Revolution of 1905,[204] when it was possible to open primary schools with Polish as the language of instruction for the first time since 1863 (Belarusian schools were still out of the question), they actively engaged in the establishment of these Polish schools, often using their authority and power over their congregations to enforce the process.[205]

With the start of the First World War, the Catholic Church in the lands of Ober Ost was able to solidify its positions, since its priests did not abandon their congregations in the same manner as almost all of the Orthodox priests did, when they closed their churches and left the western provinces during the 1915 evacuation. About 500 Catholic priests continued to serve in the Vil'nia diocese, which encompassed the two provinces of Vil'nia and Hrodna.[206] They remained strongly dedicated to Polish culture and language. The local Polish nationalism benefited from the substitution of national identification with confessional belonging. For instance, in a letter addressed to the head of the Military Administration of Lithuania, the Belarusian Committee pointed out the regrettable fact that Belarusian Catholics were automatically considered to be Polish.[207]

---

[203] BDAMLIM, f. 3, vop. 1, spr. 126, ark. 120, 121.

[204] On the liberalization after the Revolution of 1905 and its implications for Polish culture in the Belarusian lands, see Andrzej Romanowski, "The Year 1905 and the Revival of Polish Culture between the Neman and the Dnepr," *Canadian Slavonic Papers/Revue Canadienne Des Slavistes* 41, no. 1 (1999): 45–67.

[205] The first notable exception in this intense Polonization trend was the Vil'nia Bishop Eduard von der Ropp, who was the first within the higher Roman Catholic circles to officially recognize the rights of the Belarusian language. In 1905 he stated that the Catholic Church did not harbor intentions to Polonize the Belarusian people and that religious instruction ought to use the native language that Belarusian children used at home, i.e., Belarusian. This attitude was confirmed by an official circular issued by von der Ropp in 1905 that allowed prayers, catechism, and religious history to be taught in the native languages of the population, including Polish, Lithuanian, and Belarusian. See Ales' Smaliančuk, *Pamiž krajovasciu i nacyjanalnaj idejaj: Polski ruch na bielaruskich i litoŭskich zemliach 1864–liuty 1917* (St. Petersburg: Neŭski prasciah, 2004), 209–10.

[206] Liachoŭski, *Škol'naja adukacyja*, 116.

[207] BDAMLIM, f. 3, vop. 1, spr. 133, ark. 18–19.

The establishment of Polish schools in Belarusian settlements was one of the examples of successful Polish national activities during the German occupation.[208] German administrative reports, compiled for the period of late 1917 and early 1918, documented strong Polish influences over the ethnically Belarusian population. They specifically warned about the Catholic clergy's dedication to the cause of promoting Polish schools in rural areas, where the ethnically Polish population was in the minority.[209] For instance, while the population of Ašmiany identified as Belarusian, Catholic priests there exclusively promoted and supported the opening of Polish schools.[210] In 1917, *Homan* described Belarusian Catholics from Hrodna region as taken "on lease" by the Poles.[211] Anton Luckievič noted that similar Polish nationalist trends were already present at the start of the German occupation. He noted that Poles dominating the municipal administration in Vil'nia boycotted everything connected to manifestations of Belarusianness in the city and started a massive campaign for Polish schools, encouraging the promotion of Polish identity among the Catholic population.[212]

The activities of pro-Polish Catholic priests represented one of the largest problems for Belarusian national activists, who were usually sent to the provinces in the capacity of teachers for the newly opened schools. For instance, the teacher Kačynski complained to Anton Luckievič in late 1917 that he was having a lot of trouble persuading people of the usefulness of his school, since the local Catholic priest from Navahrudak, who obviously had more leverage on the local people, denigrated his efforts and reportedly adopted militant anti-Belarusian positions. Initially, Kačynski was supposed to teach in Danilaviči (Dziatlava district), but he was not able to establish a school there. After waiting for one month in Dziatlava, he managed to open a school in the village of Chadaŭliany in October 1917.[213] Most likely, he received assistance from the occupation authorities, who were interested in weakening the Poles.

Teacher Anton Giruliok, who worked among Belarusian refugees from Vil'nia, mentioned the activities of a Catholic priest from a neighboring village. Apparently, his activities were not limited to only the spiritual sphere, as he actively promoted a Polish school, collected signatures, and submitted petitions

---

[208] BDAMLIM, f. 3, vop. 1, spr. 134, ark. 16, 17.
[209] BArch, PH 30-III/3, 19, 19 r.
[210] BDAMLIM, f. 3, vop. 1, spr. 131, ark. 23.
[211] "Chto vinavat," *Homan*, no. 74, September 14, 1917, 2.
[212] BDAMLIM, f. 3, vop. 1, spr. 131, ark. 23.
[213] BDAMLIM, f. 3, vop. 1, spr. 133, ark. 5 adv.

to the German authorities. Despite being an ethnic Lithuanian, the priest actively promoted the Polish national cause among Catholic Belarusian refugees.[214] The Belarusian primary school in Vasiliški (Lida district) had already been opened in November 1915, but its teacher Alena Ivanoŭskaja was not able to start teaching due to the obstacles created by a group of Polish chauvinists, organized around the local Citizens' Committee.[215]

Letters from Belarusian teachers who were sent to work in the provinces also indicated that the population was rather suspicious of the idea of Belarusian schools. The majority preferred the familiar option of Polish schools, especially as the local clergy actively campaigned for them.[216] A report submitted by one of the teachers in the Vil'nia area to the Belarusian Committee, most likely in 1918, indicated that Catholic priests were responsible for a school strike in the villages of Turgele, Biely Dvor, Slabada, and Rukojnie, located in the vicinity of Vil'nia. Attendance at all of the above-named schools dropped suddenly, when in 1917 the Belarusian school in Turgele had eighty-eight students, the one in Biely Dvor had fifty-nine, the one in Slabada thirty-two, and the school in Rukojnie sixty students. The local Catholic clergy, in particular Dean Szepecki from Turgele, the priest Hanuszewski from Rukojnie, and chaplain Sopotzko from Taburyčki, were identified as the primary instigators of the school strike. They were known for their negative attitudes toward the newly established schools with Belarusian as the primary language of instruction. Fearing their loss of authority and influence over the population, they discouraged the population from sending their children to Belarusian schools.[217]

There were in fact some Catholic priests who sympathized with the Belarusian movement, including Francišak Ramejka from Šerašava (Pružany district), Tamaš Siliuk from Kramianica (Vaŭkavysk district), Anton Šyško from Svislač (Vaŭkavysk district), and Henryk Beta and Janka Liaŭkovič from Janava (Sokółka district). But none of them initiated the opening of Belarusian schools due to concerns that Vil'nia diocese authorities might not welcome such steps.[218] By contrast, Lithuanian Catholic priests were known as active promoters of a Lithuanian national identity. The church of St. Mikalaj in Vil'nia had already introduced the use of the Lithuanian language for sermons and additional prayers by Christmas of 1901. The church

---

214   BDAMLIM, f. 3, vop. 1, spr. 140, ark. 133 adv.
215   Liachoŭski, *Škol'naja adukacyja*, 127.
216   BDAMLIM, f. 3, vop. 1, spr. 133, ark. 5 adv.
217   BDAMLIM, f. 3, vop. 1, spr. 126, ark. 105.
218   Liachoŭski, *Škol'naja adukacyja*, 129.

operated a Lithuanian primary school and served as a meeting place, used by both Lithuanian and Belarusian activists.[219] The clergy threatened to refuse communion to children if religion classes at Belarusian schools were not held in Polish, arguing that Belarusian was not previously used as an ecclesiastical language.[220] This trend changed only in 1918, when bishop Jury Matulevič, known for his friendly attitude towards Belarusians, was put in charge of the Vil'nia diocese. After his appointment, new Belarusian schools for the Catholic population started to appear in the provinces, followed by efforts to introduce the Belarusian language into additional church services, extending beyond the liturgies.[221]

Conclusion

The First World War on the Eastern front and German territorial gains in East-Central Europe resulted in the establishment of Ober Ost as an exemplary military-dominated state. Yet, Hindenburg and Ludendorff's illusions of total control waned as a series of ad hoc decisions benefitting only the interests of the German Empire turned Ober Ost into an arbitrarily ruled and poor occupation zone, devastated by the war, and exploited economically by the conquerors. The new administrative structures were set up and functioned with the single goal of maintaining security in the army rear and extracting resources.

At the same time, plans for an eventual German annexation of these territories were skillfully disguised with the attractive and popular slogans of supporting the struggle for freedom of the oppressed nationalities. With its relatively liberal treatment of non-Russian cultures, Ober Ost and its eclectic mix of ethnicities became a unique field for experimentation with the growing forces of nationalism. As the German Empire envisioned weakening Russia as its chief war aim, it was likely to find allies among the local national movements, as the latter harbored resentments towards the Russian Empire, which stifled rising nationalist movements in its western borderlands in the late nineteenth–early twentieth centuries through extensive Russification policies. In this context, even the limited concessions to the local national cultures within a larger framework of German international political interests can be regarded as being an improvement to the nationalities policy of the tsarist authorities.

---

[219] "Pamiatny dzień," *Homan*, no. 91, December 25, 1916, 2.
[220] Zemke, *Der Oberbefehlshaber Ost und die Schule*, 58.
[221] Liachoŭski, *Škol'naja adukacyja*, 129.

As Polish nationalism was the most developed in comparison to the Lithuanian and Belarusian movements, it was able to achieve significant successes, especially in the sphere of education, the promotion of national values among the Ober Ost population, and the presence of dedicated activists, while Belarusians were still in the process of recruiting their national elites. This trend was soon noted by the German authorities, who attempted to create a counterbalance to the strong position of the Poles by lending more support to the Lithuanians and partly also to the Belarusians. However, the Germans were not convinced that a Belarusian national movement could become a reliable partner. Despite the presence of a Belarusian population in the Vil'nia region, the occupation regime did not regard it as an important factor early in the war. Initially, Belarusians were perceived either as Poles or Russians. The number of activists in the underfinanced Belarusian Committee for the Aid of War Victims was low, schooling initiatives developed slowly and unevenly, and all the while the rural population was under pressure from the Catholic clergy to identify as Poles.

The demands of the few Belarusian nationalists were not taken seriously by the German authorities, as demonstrated by the fate of the requests to introduce the Belarusian language in the public sphere, in official identification papers, or on Ober Ost currency. Instead, Belarusian nationalism was instrumentalized by the occupying power in order to benefit German interests both in the region and internationally. In particular, it was used in efforts to weaken Polish influence, as is clear from the example of the German-sponsored project of a Belarusian teachers' seminary in Svislač. The occupation power was able to appropriate to a certain degree the initiative of national mobilization, while the Belarusian Committee for the Aid of War Victims in Vil'nia did not possess the leverage to reverse this process.

It is also evident that Belarusian activists in Ober Ost did not fare well in the national competition against the Poles and Lithuanians. The former were able to secure considerable popular support due to the developed nature and popular base of their national movement, while the latter were able to secure more German assistance with time. The Belarusian national movement in Ober Ost was merely tolerated and received half-hearted support only when its goals coincided with the German interests in the region. Nevertheless, the Belarusian cause in Ober Ost represented a remarkable contrast to the state of affairs in the eastern Belarusian provinces, which remained under Russian rule in 1915–1917. Even in the shadow of the Poles and Lithuanians, Belarusian activists in Ober Ost were able to achieve more in terms of nation-building than their counterparts on the eastern side of the front line. Despite financial difficulties, they legally opened schools with Belarusian as the primary language of instruction, published school textbooks, and educated teachers who went to the countryside to promote the Belarusian national project. None of these actions were possible in the eastern provinces which remained under Russian military rule. Yet, due to German restrictions on political activities, by 1917 the Belarusian national elites in Vil'nia lost the initiative to Minsk, which became the center of Belarusian politics after the February Revolution, hosting the All-Belarusian Congress in December 1917.

Chapter 3

"Common" Homeland of the Grand Duchy: National Politics in Ober Ost

Throughout the war Belarusian national activists in Ober Ost[1] developed their own visions of the future political organization of Belarus. This chapter focuses on the evolution of their political thinking in the wider context of German national politics in East-Central Europe between 1916 and 1918. Similarly to the Minsk-based Belarusian organizations that in 1917 supported the idea of autonomy within a future democratic Russia, Ober Ost Belarusians also focused on federal solutions, although their understanding of federalism departed from Russia-oriented thinking and was rooted in a specific form of a regional collective identity known as *krajovasc*.[2] Appealing to common historical memory, it centered around the idea of close cooperation between the nations of the former Grand Duchy of Lithuania (GDL).[3]

The main questions addressed here deal with the interplay of regional and national interests in the Belarusian-Lithuanian-Polish borderlands immediately before the start of the First World War, and again during the German occupation, reflecting

---

[1]   Incidentally, Ober Ost included a significant part of the core region where Belarusian national mobilization was concentrated in the early twentieth century. Most of the national activists and intelligentsia were natives to the Vil'nia, Ašmiany, Vilejka, Minsk, and Sluck districts, where the highest numbers of correspondents of *Naša Niva* resided. The contemporary literary Belarusian language is also based on the dialects common to this region. See Tereshkovich, *Etnicheskaia istoriia Belarusi*, 178.

[2]   In Polish this term is known as *krajowość*.

[3]   The Grand Duchy of Lithuania, Ruś, and Samogitia—a multiethnic state, often described as a joint Belarusian-Lithuanian polity. It included contemporary territories of Belarus and Lithuania from the 1230s up to the late eighteenth century, since 1569 in a federation with Poland, known as the Polish-Lithuanian Commonwealth (Rzeczpospolita). At the time of its maximal territorial expansion in the mid-fifteenth century, this state stretched over territories 12 times larger than the ethnic Lithuanian lands. With the rise of the modern nationalist movements in the late nineteenth and the early twentieth centuries, the legacy of the Grand Duchy became an issue of contention, with no consensus reached by the historians from Belarus, Lithuania, Poland, and Ukraine up until the present time. See Vital' Silitski and Jan Zaprudnik, *Historical Dictionary of Belarus* (Lanham, MD: Scarecrow Press, 2007), 137–39.

on the failures and victories of the concepts of civic and ethnic nationalism, respectively. These competing concepts also influenced the development of political
thought within the Belarusian national milieu. Therefore, particular attention
will be dedicated here to the attractiveness of *krajovasc'* for Belarusians, and its
incorporation into the political programs of other national movements in the
lands of the former Grand Duchy. Why did federalism, rather than a nation-state
concept, enjoy popularity among the Belarusian activists at that time, both in
Ober Ost and on the eastern side of the front? What practical steps did the Vil'nia
Belarusians undertake to secure their vision of a post-war state organization, and
what were the results?

The following discussion will be placed within the larger context of international politics and rivalries in East-Central Europe in the last two years of the
First World War. In this period, the German Empire moved on from a *divide
et impera* approach in its national politics in the East to more resolute actions
directed towards utilizing national aspirations in the region, backed up by the
rhetoric of national-self-determination, in vogue since the February Revolution in
1917. Lithuanian national activists did not hesitate to take advantage of the new
German *Ostpolitik*, seizing the opportunity to construct their own nation-state,
while Belarusians found themselves between German imperialism and Lithuanian
nationalism.

Belarusian elites in Vil'nia attempted to secure the post-war settlement
that would best suit the needs of their nation-building project and benefit the
interests of the Belarusian people. Initially, they hoped to achieve these goals by
supporting federative state-building strategies within the framework of a revived
Grand Duchy of Lithuania, which they envisioned as a democratic multinational
state, guaranteeing equal national rights for each nationality. These initiatives were
short-lived, as Belarusian activists moved on to the idea of establishing a separate
Belarusian state and uniting all ethnically Belarusian territories divided by the
front line. The issue of securing territorial integrity for the Belarusian territories
became even more pressing with the commencement of the Brest-Litovsk peace
negotiations between Soviet Russia and the Central Powers in late 1917.
A summary of the peace talks will conclude this chapter, with particular attention to
the question of how the concept of national self-determination was (mis)used by
both the Central Powers and Soviet Russia to ensure dominance in East-Central
Europe, where military power was instrumental in establishing a new order in the
early months of 1918.

Regional and National Identities on the Eve of the First World War

The phenomenon of *krajovasc'* refers to a specific regional identity which emerged in the early twentieth century among the Lithuanian and Belarusian Poles, or, in other words, the antecedents of Belarusians and Lithuanians, native to the lands of the former Grand Duchy of Lithuania. Over the centuries that had passed since the decline of the GDL in the late seventeenth century, they accepted Polish culture in order to improve their social standing in society.[4] By the turn of the century, they were represented by the gentry, landowners, and intellectuals, who played major social, economic, and cultural roles, despite being a minority in the Belarusian-Lithuanian region. After the Revolution of 1905, concerns of being isolated due to the growing levels of local nationalism, in particular that of the Lithuanians, forced the Poles in historic Lithuania, as well as in the Vil'nia intelligentsia circles, to develop a new political approach to ensure Polish predominance in the region in the face of growing local nationalisms. Based on the perceptions of common political, social, cultural, and economic interests among the nations of the former Grand Duchy, encompassing contemporary Belarusian and Lithuanian territories, they developed a separate identity from the Poles native to the Kingdom of Poland.[5] Instead of focusing on ethnic and religious differences, the emphasis shifted to the territorial and cultural unity of historic Lithuania, or the *Kraj* (Homeland), as these territories were usually described. The *krajovasc'* approach was based on the principle of equality between the Lithuanian and Belarusian people, the need for peaceful coexistence, and mutual efforts to secure the well-being of the common homeland. An essential feature was the primacy of the interests of the whole *Kraj* over the interests of its separate nationalities.[6]

In the broad definition of *krajovasc'*, suggested by the Belarusian historian Aliaksandr Smaliančuk, this phenomenon is interpreted as a concept referring

---

4   Leon Wasilewski, *Litwa i Białoruś: Przeszłość, teraźniejszość, tendencje rozwojowe* (Kraków: Książka, 1912), 65–70.

5   Rimantas Miknys and Darius Staliūnas, "The 'Old' and 'New' Lithuanians: Collective Identity Types in Lithuania at the Turn of the Nineteenth and Twentieth Centuries," in *Forgotten Pages in Baltic History: Diversity and Inclusion*, ed. Martyn Housden and David J. Smitt (Amsterdam, New York: Rodopi, 2011), 38.

6   Jan Savicki, "Michał Römer wobec problemów narodowościowych ziem Litewsko-białoruskich na początku XX wieku," in *Krajowość—tradycje zgody narodów w dobie nacjonalizmu: Materiały z międzynarodowej konferencji naukowej w Insytucie Historii UAM w Poznaniu (11–12 maja 1998)*, ed. Jan Jurkiewicz (Poznań: Instytut Historii UAM, 1999), 75; Juliusz Bardach, *O dawnej i niedawnej Litwie* (Poznań: Wydawnictwo Naukowe Uniwersytetu im. Adama Mickiewicza w Poznaniu, 1988), 262, 265.

to the idea, movement, or ideology promoting the legacy of the peoples native to historic Lithuania. Described as a "reconciliation of particular local or national interests to common interests," it represented a form of local supra-national patriotism.[7] *Krajovasc'* essentially dismissed any forms of chauvinism and imperialism along with the notions of political, cultural, or military hegemony.[8] Originating from the reaction of the old political and cultural elites to modernization and the growth of national movements, *krajovasc'* offered a vision of a historical compromise, based on a democratic polity, equality, and the leveling of national conflicts. It was designed to prevent any further politicization of the Lithuanian movement and to overcome the threats of aggressive nationalism.[9] *Krajovasc'* centered around the idea of a civic nation, to be built around patriotic feelings of belonging to the former Grand Duchy.[10]

The broad interpretation of the *krajovasc'* concept caused a lack of consensus on the question of what groups in fact had belonged to the *Kraj*. Initially, only Lithuanian Poles, Belarusians, and Lithuanians were recognized as its main constituent nations. Others, Russians and Jews in particular, were treated as "foreign." Kanstancyja Skirmunt,[11] known as one of the most important contributors to the ideology of *krajovasc'*, denied the Russians the right of belonging to the community of the *Kraj* citizens, seeing in them representatives of a repressive civilization that contradicted the very notion of unhindered national coexistence.[12] However, with time, *krajovasc'* evolved towards the acceptance and inclusion of those groups with apparently weaker ties to the *Kraj*. Another prominent *krajovasc'* supporter, Michał Römer, advocated the extension of *krajovasc'* to include Jews. Römer pointed out that Jews formed an isolated and

---

[7]   Aliaksandr Smaliančuk, "Krajovaść vis-à-vis Belarusian and Lithuanian National Movements in the Early 20th Century," in *Belarus and Its Neighbors: Historical Perceptions and Political Constructs; International Conference Papers*, ed. Ales' Lahvinec and Taciana Čulickaja (Warsaw: Uczelnia Łazarskiego, 2013), 71.

[8]   Rimantas Miknys, "Michał Römer, krajowcy a idea zjednoczenia Europy w pierwszej połowie XX wieku," in *O nowy kształt Europy: XX-wieczne koncepcje federalistyczne w Europie Środkowo-Wschodniej i ich implikacje dla dyskusji o przyszłości Europy*, ed. Jerzy Kłoczowski and Sławomir Łukasiewicz (Lublin: Instytut Europy Środkowo-Wschodniej, 2003), 96.

[9]   Maria Zadencka, "Krajowość a strategie elit wobec emancypacji narodowej ludu w końcu XIX i początku XX wieku: Litwa i Białorus, prowincje Bałtyckie, Finlandia," in Jurkiewicz, *Krajowość—tradycje zgody narodow*, 51.

[10] Smaliančuk, *Pamiž krajovasciu i nacyjanalnaj idejaj*, 125.

[11] On her political thinking, see Dariusz Szpoper, *Gente Lithuana, Natione Lithuana: Myśl polityczna i działalność Konstancji Skirmuntt (1851–1934)* (Gdańsk: Arche, 2009).

[12] Smaliančuk, *Pamiž krajovasciu i nacyjanalnaj idejaj*, 242.

closed community in Belarusian-Lithuanian lands, determined to keep their cultural and religious distance. They were not assimilated by either of the groups, despite the fact that the Jewish intelligentsia widely used the Russian language. The trend towards isolation was typical for the lands of historic Lithuania, being even more pronounced than in Poland. This, combined with the insufficient contacts with other *Kraj* nationalities, accelerated the formation of a Jewish national identity. The lack of assimilation processes among the Jewish community thus caused the Jews to lose feelings of connection to the *Kraj*, resulting in insufficient interest on their part to questions regarding potential statehood organization. Nevertheless, Römer was hopeful that Jews would eventually join the *Kraj* (*ukrajowic się*) without giving up their own national differences.[13]

In addition to the flexible and open interpretations of belonging, *krajovasc'* was represented by an array of different political currents and groups, ranging from conservatives to liberal democrats. Each offered their own approach to the solution of the national question. Liberal democrats with Michał Römer strove for mutual understanding and cooperation between Belarusians and Lithuanians, which was realized through the economic and cultural organizations of various nationalities in Vil'nia, common publishing projects (*Kurjer Krajowy*), and the existence of masonic lodges. Another liberal democratic group led by Ludwik Abramowicz adopted a more pragmatic approach, moving towards treating *krajovasc'* as a means of securing the interests of the Lithuanian Poles in the region, who were primarily viewed as members of the Polish nation. In contrast to Römer, Abramowicz and his supporters saw in the Belarusian national movement a government-sponsored anti-Polish intrigue. Finally, the conservative-liberal wing of *krajovasc'*, with I. Korwin-Milewski at its helm, gradually gravitated towards the positions of the Polish National Democrats. They were cautious of the radical socialist component, a characteristic of both the Belarusian and Lithuanian movements, convinced that it represented a threat to Polish national interests. Yet, political positions within this current varied greatly, ranging from the resolute dismissal of national movements to cooperation with them. For instance, landowner Raman Skirmunt sympathized with the Belarusian movement. In 1917, he became the head of the newly created Belarusian National Committee in Minsk. Another prominent *krajovasc'* supporter, Kanstancyja Skirmunt, was known for her consistent opposition to escalation of the Polish-Lithuanian conflict, while Princess Magdalena Radzivil provided financial assistance to the Belarusian and Lithuanian initiatives.[14]

13   Savicki, "Michał Römer," in Jurkiewicz, *Krajowość—tradycje zgody narodow*, 79–80.
14   Smaliančuk, *Pamiž krajovasciu i nacyjanalnaj idejaj*, 341, 359–60.

The framework of *krajovasc'* represented a convenient strategy, which was particularly suitable for the needs of Belarusian national activists. Their weaker national movement, lagging behind in its phase of active national activities, readily accepted the main tenets of this ideology, treating it as a transitory stage, in the hope of gaining time to develop unhindered by the competing neighboring national movements. In this regard, the activities of the brothers Ivan and Anton Luckievič, known as the most outspoken proponents of *krajovasc'* ideals within the Belarusian national milieu in the early twentieth century, are of particular interest.

The Luckievičes' political thinking was typical for the liberal democratic wing of *krajovasc'*, supporting universal humanitarian values and the ideals of freedom, equality, and peaceful coexistence. Anton Luckievič viewed *krajovasc'* as the exact opposite of the limited worldview offered by nationalism, which he described as a "sick aberration" which took hold among the Poles, Jews, and Lithuanians, with Belarusians being next in line. Aggressive nationalism was criticized for blinding people to the confines of their own nation and forcing them to ignore the plight of their neighbors. Luckievič contrasted it to *krajovasc'*, which he recognized as a different and better option of uniting all democratic elements within local nations in order to create a viable and successful political force.[15] At the same time, Luckievič made a distinction between destructive aggressive nationalism and the constructive forces of national revival, supporting the latter as one of the preconditions for *krajovasc'* to succeed. In his opinion, the fate of the *Kraj* was to be decided not by single individuals, but by its constituent nations, among which he counted nationally-conscious Belarusians and Lithuanians.[16]

On the eve of the First World War, the Luckievič brothers were involved in the publishing of the newspapers *Kurjer Krajowy* and *Vecherniaia Gazeta*. Both periodicals were published in Vil'nia starting from 1912. *Kurjer Krajowy* appeared until the middle of 1914 with a circulation of between 3,000 and 4,000 copies, while *Vecherniaia Gazeta* appeared with 10,000 copies and was published until the end of June 1915. The Luckievičes' initiative followed the *krajovasc'* tradition, established in the periodic press by *Gazeta Wileńska* in 1906. Oriented towards a broader Russian- and Polish-speaking public as well as "denationalized Belarusians," both newspapers promoted universal democratic values, state decentralization, the "rebirth" of the Belarusian people, and cooperation between the nations.[17] The Luckievič brothers deliberately concealed their involvement with both *Kurjer*

---

[15]   Luckievič, *Da historyi bielaruskaha ruchu*, 64–66.

[16]   "Paznajmo svajo imia," *Homan*, no. 23, May 2, 1916, 2.

[17]   BDAMLIM, f. 3, vop. 1, spr. 131, ark. 22 adv.; See also Sidarevič, *Pra Ivana Luckieviča*, 19.

Krajowy and *Vecherniaia Gazeta*, never signing articles with their real names and avoiding acting as official editors. As a Russian-language democratic periodical, *Vecherniaia Gazeta* was designed to weaken the influence of the Russian far right, who were particularly active in the Belarusian provinces during the election campaign for the Fourth Duma in 1912. According to Aliaksandr Smaliančuk, *Vecherniaia Gazeta* should also be given credit for the creation of "Russian democracy with a clear *krajovasc'* orientation" in Vil'nia.[18]

Kurjer Krajowy was designed as a democratic newspaper for the Polish *krajovasc'*-friendly circles. As the Luckievič brothers preferred to stay in the background, Juliusz Sumorok was appointed as its official editor, while their friend Józef Mańkowski took over the actual editing position. While *Vecherniaia Gazeta* attacked the Russian far right and the Black Hundred hordes, *Kurjer Krajowy* surprisingly caused discord among the Vil'nia democratic establishment, as it encountered competition from *Przegląd Wileński*, established in 1911 and headed by Ludwik Abramowicz. Since both newspapers had an identical orientation, Ivan and Anton Luckievič offered to the publishers of the *Przegląd Wileński* to unite their efforts in a common project, yet the latter hesitated and reacted in a reserved manner. According to Michał Römer, who was among the few supporters of the joint editorship, cooperation failed due to a lack of confidence on the side of the *Przegląd* publishers, who did not trust Belarusians and wanted to see the democratic periodical only in Polish hands.[19] This incident foreshadowed the inability of *krajovasc'* to counteract the growing national sentiments, which would result in its crisis and eventual decline during the First World War.

Attempts at Political Cooperation among the Ober Ost Nationalities

The early period of the First World War saw a number of *krajovasc'*-inspired political initiatives emerging in the German-administered Ober Ost between 1915 and 1916. References to the legacy of the Grand Duchy remained particularly attractive within the Belarusian and Lithuanian national milieus.[20]

[18] Smaliančuk, *Pamiž krajovasciu i nacyjanalnaj idejaj*, 264, 268.
[19] Zbigniew Solak, *Między Polską a Litwą. Życie i działalność Michała Römera, 1880–1920* (Kraków: Wydawnictwo Arcana, 2004), 194–95.
[20] For instance, in 1916, Vil'nia Belarusians and Lithuanians demonstrated their fascination with the legacies of the GDL by the wearing in public of badges with the GDL coat of arms, depicting a white knight on a horse (*Pahonia* in Belarusian, *Vytis* in Lithuanian). See *Homan*, no. 51, August 8, 1916, 2.

Local Poles initially participated in common political projects too, but their support was not wholehearted and waned as the vision of an independent Poland forced them to abandon *krajovasc'* ideas. As stated in a joint declaration of the Polish representatives, addressed to the head of the Military Administration of Lithuania, Isenburg-Birstein, in May 1917, Lithuanian Poles at that time had already positioned themselves as an "inseparable part of the great Polish nation."[21]

Generally, during the First World War, Poles of all political associations started to treat Belarusians and Lithuanians from positions of Polish cultural supremacy. For instance, Józef Piłsudski, incidentally a native to the Vil'nia region, did not recognize in Belarusians the potential to become a full-fledged sovereign nation. He assigned them either to Polish or Russian spheres of influence, and did not view the Belarusian question as a strong factor in the region. By contrast, Poles were considered to be the driving force in the dismantling of the Russian Empire. In line with this logic, Polish socialists supported Belarusian, Lithuanian, and Ukrainian national movements only inasmuch as all of them could be used as instruments of the anti-Russian struggle.[22] The Polish Socialist Party (*Polska Partia Socjalistyczna*, PPS) had already expressed such leadership ambitions in the Belarusian-Lithuanian lands earlier in the twentieth century. From 1902–1903, the PPS facilitated the publication of socialist brochures in the Belarusian language. However, the sole aim was to dominate the socialist initiatives of various nationalities. The same pragmatic reasoning determined the failed attempts to create a unified territorial socialist party of Lithuania to be subordinated to the PPS.[23]

Józef Piłsudski and Polish socialists from the PPS were also known for their concept of federalism, originating from the *krajovasc'* tradition. As already mentioned, the Vil'nia democratic circles were never able to reach an organizational unity. During 1915–1917, they were gradually divided into two different currents. The first remained faithful to *krajovasc'*, supporting the notion of independent historical Lithuania and recognizing the distinct identity of Lithuanian Poles. More importantly, it continued to emphasize the equal rights of Lithuanian Poles,

---

[21]   Bardach, *O dawnej i niedawnej Litwie*, 236.

[22]   Krystyna Gomółka, *Między Polską a Rosją: Białoruś w koncepcjach polskich ugrupowań politycznych 1918–1922* (Warsaw: Gryf, 1994), 17–18; Eugeniusz Mironowicz, *Białorusini i Ukraińcy w polityce obozu piłsudczykowskiego* (Białystok: Wydawnictwo Uniwersyteckie Trans Humana, 2007), 10.

[23]   Smaliančuk, *Pamiž krajovasciu i nacyjanalnaj idejaj*, 190–91, 194. Another representative of the socialist bloc was the SDKPiL (Social Democracy of the Kingdom of Poland and Lithuania), yet this party was Marxist in character and did not belong to the Polish movement. Subordinated to RSDRP (Russian Social Democratic Labor Party), it did not support a national agenda, turning instead to class struggle. Ibid., 188–89.

Belarusians, and Lithuanians to decide on the future of their common homeland. The second current was composed of Polish federalists, who assigned a special role in the future state-building process to the Polish nation. In contrast to the incorporation aspirations of the Polish National Democrats, Piłsudski and Polish socialists[24] still supported close ties for the former Grand Duchy with the revived Polish state, yet they clearly shifted their emphasis towards the leading role of the Polish element, instead of supporting the notion of the equal rights of various nationalities. This approach inspired Piłsudski's project of a federal Intermarium (*Międzymorze*) and the "Central Lithuania" military affair of Lucjan Żeligowski in the fall of 1920.[25]

On the other side of the political spectrum stood the Polish National Democrats, reflecting the growing appeal of modern nationalism. They had abandoned the old Commonwealth-inspired slogan of fighting "for our freedom and yours," drawing a clear distinction between Poles and non-Poles, including among the latter all non-Polish successors of the Polish-Lithuanian Commonwealth.[26] Their leaders, Roman Dmowski and Jan Ludwik Popławski, were even less likely than the socialists to recognize the notion of political rights for Belarusians, dismissively treating them as a passive by-product of the Polish-Russian existential struggle. In terms of the territorial organization of the future Polish state, Dmowski did not exclude the possibility of the eventual incorporation of some eastern territories settled by Poles, yet he resolutely departed from the idea of restoring the pre-1772 borders of the old Polish-Lithuanian Commonwealth. The positions of the Vil'nia National Democrats towards the Belarusian question were identical: one of their representatives, Jan Bułhak, considered the Belarusian language to be a "coarse dialect," and suggested that Belarusians should not waste time in establishing their own culture when they had the option of taking advantage of the old and fully developed cultures, be those Polish or Russian.[27]

The confrontational stance of the National Democrats towards the Belarusian and Lithuanian movements was already noticeable by 1915. This can be attributed not only to the expanded independent national activities, but also to the relatively

---

24   See more on Polish socialist federalism in Snyder, *The Reconstruction of Nations*, 58.

25   Bardach, *O dawnej i niedawnej Litwie*, 235–37, 272; Tomas Balkelis, "A Dirty War: The Armed Polish-Lithuanian Conflict and Its Impact on Nation-Making in Lithuania, 1919–23," *Acta Poloniae Historica* 121 (August 2020): 248.

26   Brian Porter, *When Nationalism Began to Hate: Imagining Modern Politics in Nineteenth-Century Poland* (New York: Oxford University Press, 2000), 213.

27   Gomółka, *Między Polską a Rosją*, 15–16.

higher degree of cultural freedoms allowed by the German occupation regime, enabling these national movements to increase their public visibility. Later, the German Empire also instrumentalized local nationalisms as a tool of its anti-Polish policies. The result was that almost all political orientations within the Polish milieu became hostile to the Belarusian and Lithuanian movements. Poles started assuming that historical Lithuania would be able to exist only under the protection of the Polish nation-state.[28]

One of the attempts at cooperation between the nationalities of the former GDL early in the war reveals this sudden crisis of *krajovasc'* attitudes. It preceded the German occupation of Vil'nia and revolved around the revitalization of the local City Council. After the departure of Russian officials, the Council barely existed, as half of its members had left the city during the evacuation process, thus making it highly unlikely for the remaining half, consisting exclusively of Poles, to be recognized by the Germans as a legitimate institution to represent the interests of the population. In an attempt to reorganize the municipal self-government of Vil'nia, local democratic circles formed an initiative group that proposed the introduction of Belarusian, Lithuanian, and Jewish elements into the City Council. Giving representation to different nationalities should have democratized the City Council, preparing a legitimate platform for future interactions of the multinational region with the new authorities. Initially, Ivan Luckievič and Vincent Sviatapolk-Mirski were listed as candidates to represent Belarusians in the renewed version of the City Council. Yet, local Poles were unwilling to share power and deliberately slowed down decision-making on the issue, hoping to secure and maintain a dominant Polish position in the city.[29] This strategy failed, as well as the entire new City Council concept, since the German Supreme Command meticulously solidified the occupation administration in 1915, and did not hesitate to dismiss all local institutions, transferring all powers in Vil'nia into the hands of the German mayor. The City Council was reduced to a "municipal advisory body," while its former members were only allowed to assist in the implementation of German orders.[30]

The Vil'nia-Koŭna Citizens' Committee was another initiative in the spirit of *krajovasc'*, designed to represent the interests of all local nationalities with the German authorities. According to Anton Luckievič's memoirs, Polish

---

[28] Smaliančuk, *Pamiž krajovasciu i nacyjanalnaj idejaj*, 360.
[29] Luckievič, *Da historyi bielaruskaha ruchu*, 96.
[30] "U Wilni i wakolicach," *Homan*, no. 3, February 22, 1916, 3.

leadership ambitions stood in the way here too, as local Poles agreed to include other nationalities into this body on unfair conditions, keeping about half of the positions for themselves.[31] Twelve Poles, representing various political currents, from right to left, joined the Citizens' Committee. Lithuanian conservatives did not want to join an institution where they did not have a majority, but the left-wing politicians delegated Steponas Kairys, Jonas Kymantas, Vladas Stašinskas, Jurgis Šaulys, and Jonas Vileišis. They were joined by Belarusians Anton and Ivan Luckievič, Vaclaŭ Lastoŭski, and Aliaksandr Zaštaŭt, as well as four Jewish members. German authorities tolerated the existence of the Committee during the first months of the occupation, using it to establish a functioning administration and for maintaining contacts with the local population. Yet, its dissolution was inevitable, especially after its Polish members became involved in an incident concerning the unfair distribution of donations received from the Swiss-based General Relief Committee for the Victims of the War in Poland.[32] Former member and deputy chair Vileišis pointed out in his open letter to the committee chair Kognowicki and the second deputy chair Boguszewski that these funds were sent to the Citizens' Committee for the needs of all Ober Ost nationalities, yet were promptly redirected, implying that the money was used to assist only the Polish population.[33]

It is likely that in the case of the Vil'nia-Koŭna Citizens' Committee, the Poles hoped to create an image of the most loyal nationality, anticipating that the German authorities would give them more powers,[34] and acting as if they already had them. Yet, this behavior only prevented the Citizens' Committee from becoming a truly functional institution. Eventually Polish calculations failed, as the Germans conducted their occupation policy in a pragmatic manner, preferring to play one nationality against the other, instead of stating clear preferences.[35] By March 1916, the Citizens' Committee had not held any meetings for several months and gradually fell apart, as both its Belarusian and Lithuanian members resigned.[36]

---

[31] Luckievič, *Da historyi bielaruskaha ruchu*, 96.

[32] Sukiennicki and Siekierski, *East Central Europe during World War I*, 128–30.

[33] *Homan*, no. 19, April 18, 1916, 3. See also Chapter 5.

[34] At the start of the occupation Poles, along with Russians, were the most known nationality for Germans in this part of East-Central Europe. In September 1915, the notoriously famous address of Graf Joachim von Pfeil to the residents of Vil'nia referred to the city as "the pearl of the Polish kingdom." See Edmundas Gimžauskas, ed., *Lietuva vokiečių okupacijoje Pirmojo pasaulinio karo metais, 1915–1918: Lietuvos nepriklausomos valstybės geneze: Dokumentų rinkinys* (Vilnius: Lietuvos istorijos instituto leidykla, 2006), 62.

[35] "Pamiaci Ivana Luckieviča ŭ pieršyja uhodki s'mierci Jaho (20.08.1919–20.08.1920)," in *Pra Ivana Luckieviča: Uspaminy, sviedčanni*, ed. Anatol' Sidarevič (Minsk: Knihazbor, 2007), 21–22.

[36] "U Wilni i wakolicach," *Homan*, no. 11, March 21, 1916, 3.

They were followed by the Jews and the representatives of workers and Polish democrats.[37] In May 1916, the only example of effective cooperation between all the nations of Ober Ost was to be found in the humanitarian sphere, where the Association of Medical and Food Aid still kept Belarusians, Lithuanians, Poles, and Jews working together in charitable projects providing relief to children.[38]

Towards a New Grand Duchy? Federalism as a State-Building Strategy

Despite the fact that in 1915 Ober Ost covered only a part the former Grand Duchy territories, references to this state were abundant in the contemporary Ober Ost press. The Belarusian newspaper *Homan* evoked an image of separate ancient lands, known among its population as the *Kraj*, a common home to Lithuanians and Belarusians who lived there side by side, united in their experiences of suffering under Russian rule, which deliberately kept these territories economically and culturally backward.[39] This image lies at the foundation of another political project, designed after *krajovasc'*-inspired patterns—the Confederation of the Grand Duchy of Lithuania. This initiative is attributed to an anonymous group of Belarusian, Lithuanian, Polish, and Jewish representatives from the liberal democratic circles, who proclaimed their intentions in the *Universal Act of the GDL Confederation*, issued on December 10, 1915. The document called for a common state of Lithuania and Belarus on the lands under German occupation. All other nations and organizations were invited to join in the Confederation, being assured of guarantees for minority rights.[40] Among the Belarusians, Ivan and Anton Luckievič were known as the most ardent supporters of the Confederation project, with the authorship of the *Universal Act* attributed to Ivan Luckievič.[41]

---

[37]   "U Wilni i wakolicach," *Homan*, no. 17, April 11, 1916, 3.

[38]   *Homan*, no. 25, May 9, 1916, 3. The Association of Medical and Food Aid stood out in contrast to the Citizens' Committee by its principled approach in the issue of distributing donations. In 1916, it received substantial funds from the Jewish organizations in Germany. However, the Association decided to extend its assistance (in particular, this concerned the provision of milk and medical services) to all babies and sick children of Vil'nia, irrespective of their nationality and religion. See *Homan*, no. 14, March 31, 1916, 3.

[39]   "Zabrany Kraj," *Homan*, no. 3, February 22, 1916, 2.

[40]   "Universal Konfederacii Vialikaho Kniaz'stva Litoŭskaho," in Aliaksandr Smaliančuk, *Vol'nyja muliary u˘bielaruskaj historyi: Kaniec XVIII–pačatak XX st.* (Vilnius: Gudas, 2005), 184.

[41]   Vitan-Dubiejkaŭskaja, *Maje ŭspaminy*, 45. According to Anton Luckievič, his brother Ivan was the author of the text of the *Universal Act*, while the Lithuanian Jurgis Šaulys wrote the second

The proclamation of the Temporary Council of the GDL Confederation followed in February 1916. Commonly known under the title "Citizens!," it was the second and the last commonly coordinated document related to the re-creation of the GDL. The Luckievič brothers, Vaclaŭ Lastoŭski, and Daminik Siamaška signed the proclamation on behalf of Belarusians, while Jurgis Šaulys and Jonas Vileišis represented the Lithuanians. Local Poles had already abandoned the GDL Confederation by this point. The document reiterated the idea of an indivisible and independent GDL, focusing on the wish of its constituent nations to part from Russia.[42] The project of the new state was limited to the lands of ethnographic Lithuania and western Belarus; however, a possible shift of its borders to the east was not excluded, as the proclamation contained provisions for the future state to include "at least those lands currently occupied by the German army."[43] Anton Luckievič noted that this wording was ambiguous and left territorial issues open to interpretation, reflecting the differing political intentions of both Belarusians and Lithuanians. The latter tended to favor the concept of "ethnographic" Lithuania, which in their opinion, had to include the Belarusian-populated former Vil'nia and Hrodna provinces.[44] In other words, the re-creation of the GDL within the German occupation zone suited the Lithuanian vision of the eventual construction of a nation-state, while Belarusians interpreted the proclamation in broader terms of striving for greater historical Lithuania with the eventual inclusion of eastern Belarusian areas.[45]

On the eve of the Third Conference of Nationalities in Lausanne in June 1916, Belarusian positions remained faithful to the principles of *krajovasc'*, declaring solidarity with those Lithuanians, Poles, and Jews who identified as citizens of a common Homeland and who supported "the true masters of these lands—Belarusian and Lithuanian people" in the task of securing "the highest degree of cultural and economic development." The local nations were called upon to secure such a system of governance in the *Kraj*, which would protect them from

---

proclamation, issued in February 1916. See "Sobstvennoruchnye pokazaniia A. I. Lutskevicha," in Luckievič, *Da historyi bielaruskaha ruchu*, 191.

[42]   Gimžauskas, *Bielaruski faktar*, 55; Zenowiusz Ponarski, "Konfederacja Wielkiego Księstwa Litewskiego 1915–1916," *Białoruskie Zeszyty Historyczne*, no. 10 (1998): 59.

[43]   Anton Luckievič, "Palityčnyja liozungi Bielaruskaha ruchu," in Luckievič, *Da historyi bielaruskaha ruchu*, 80.

[44]   In this instance Lithuanian nationalists conveniently substituted historical Lithuania with ethnic Lithuania.

[45]   Luckievič, "Palityčnyja liozungi Bielaruskaha ruchu," 81.

the "appetites" of their neighbors.[46] Yet, the project of the re-creation of the Grand Duchy posed the problem of divided lands for the Ober Ost Belarusians, who had not yet developed a coherent approach for how to advocate for unified Belarusian interests on both sides of the front. As argued by Anton Luckievič, the general starting point was the idea of "free existence" for the whole of the Belarusian lands. From this premise, he envisioned a closer regional cooperation of nations, including Lithuanians, Latvians, Belarusians, and Ukrainians in the space between the Baltic and the Black seas.[47]

The ambitious yet unsuccessful idea of reviving the Grand Duchy as a democratic multinational state demonstrated the limits of *krajovasc'* as well as its susceptibility to the growing nationalisms in the region. Lithuanians were sympathetic to the GDL Confederation only in the beginning, and soon switched towards support for an exclusively Lithuanian nation-state due to the gradual Lithuanian pull towards Germany, while Jews did not display any firm beliefs at all in connecting their future with the peoples of the former GDL. This can be explained by the fact that under the tsarist rule, Jews tended to gravitate somewhat more towards Russian culture, even if superficially, while their ties with Belarusian or Lithuanian cultures remained minimal.[48]

Local Poles were even less receptive towards the idea of reviving the GDL than the Lithuanians, feeling more confident about the re-establishment of the Polish state with its center in Warsaw.[49] The progressive ideals of civic nationalism, embodied in *krajovasc'*, were ahead of their time, succumbing to the divisive forces of nationalism.

The prospect of the creation of a Polish state during the First World War in fact had a two-fold effect, not only contributing to the decline of *krajovasc'*, but also leading to the rapprochement of various political divisions within Polish politics. The prominent representative of the democratic current of *krajovasc'*, Michał Römer, had already observed this trend early on in the war, during his service in Piłsudski's legions. Römer noted with regret that both ordinary legionnaires and Polish national elites lacked any interest in the revival of the joint Polish-Lithuanian polity as a union of equals, including Poland, Lithuania, and Belarus. Neither group understood the notion of historic Lithuania, displaying interest in

---

[46]   "Na zjezd u Losanni," *Homan*, no. 36, June 16, 1916, 2.

[47]   "Na zjezd u Losanni," *Homan*, no. 36, June 16, 1916, 2.

[48]   Vladas Sirutavičius, Darius Staliūnas, and Jurgita Šiaučiūnaitė-Verbickienė, *The History of Jews in Lithuania: From the Middle Ages to the 1990s* (Paderborn: Ferdinand Schöningh, 2020), 89.

[49]   Smiarčuk, *Vol'nyja muliary u bielaruskaj historyi*, 54.

this region only because of their concerns to secure the rights of Poles who resided there. A clear aim towards the establishment of an independent Poland was the mutual ground for understanding among all Poles.[50]

In this respect, the dedication of Belarusians to *krajovasc'* ideals can partly be explained by the belated development of the modern Belarusian national movement, which was the last one to abandon the idea of re-creating the multinational Grand Duchy of Lithuania in favor of the establishment of a nation-state. This explanation needs to be examined in a broader context, because it is likely that Belarusian activists were well aware of their chief weaknesses, in particular, the unsatisfactory state of national mobilization in the provinces, aggravated by the division of the Belarusian territories by the front line. This division effectively terminated all personal and political contacts, both horizontal, within the national elites, and vertical, between the elites and the population. The numbers of Belarusian national activists in Ober Ost were limited, while most of their organizations and initiatives were based in Vil'nia, lacking equally developed national organizations and support outside the city, which complicated cultural and educational activities,[51] not to mention the challenges that it created for political advocacy and the practical tasks of state-building.

Therefore, by advocating for equal status within a federation, the Belarusian national movement hoped to buy itself some time to catch up with the promotion of the national idea among the broader population and expand the activists' ranks. Last but not least, Belarusian elites realized the negative implications of losing Vil'nia to the Lithuanians, as apart from being a large economic and cultural center of the region, the city also served as a base of Belarusian national activism, full of ideological and cultural connotations of historical Lithuania, which could be successfully used to nurture Belarusian national identity.[52]

As pointed out by Anatol' Sidarevič, a federative state solution was also a rational and realistic tactic, based on the potential economic advantages of a common Belarusian-Lithuanian state.[53] Statements made by the Belarusian activists as late

---

[50] Solak, *Między Polską a Litwą*, 291.

[51] See Chapter 5.

[52] Zachar Šybeka, "Z historyi bielaruskich maraŭ pra Vil'niu: Peryjad niameckaj akupacyi, 1915–1918 hh.," in *Harady Bielarusi ŭ kanteksce palityki, ekanomiki, kul'tury: Zbornik navukovych artykulaŭ,* ed. I. P. Kren' and I. V. Sorkina (Hrodna: HrDU, 2007), 176; Darius Staliūnas, "Making a National Capital out of a Multiethnic City: Lithuanians and Vilnius in Late Imperial Russia," *Ab Imperio*, no 1 (2014): 166.

[53] Anatol' Sidarevič, "Anton Luckievič: Ad krajovas'ci da niezaležnictva (1916–1918)," *ARCHE*, nos. 1–2 (2006): 86.

as September 1917 confirm this thesis, as it is evident that they address Belarusian-Lithuanian areas not only as a cornerstone for the restoration of the former Grand Duchy, but also as a common legal and economic construct. A form of statehood uniting Lithuanian and Belarusian territories with eventual access to the Baltic Sea was regarded as a guarantee of free, stable, and balanced development.[54] *Homan* correctly pointed out that the Belarusian people would have to face a very difficult situation after the eventual end of the war. An essential feature of a successful post-war economic recovery would have been access to the sea and Baltic ports. Consequently, the newspaper stated that the wishes of all nationally conscious Belarusians were to see the eastern and western parts of their homeland united and tied through a federation to Lithuania and Kurland, identified as the most suitable possible partners due to their similar economic interests.[55] Anton Luckievič noted that all political currents within the Belarusian movement had to aim for the establishment of "a free Belarus, in a federation with the two free neighboring nations, forming a so-called 'united states' from the Baltic to the Black Sea."[56]

The preference for a federative state-building strategy by the Belarusians in Ober Ost echoed the political reasoning of the Belarusian activists in eastern Belarus. Throughout 1917, leading Belarusian national forces on the other side of the front line were known for their support of Belarusian autonomy, albeit in this case, within a future Russian democratic state, envisioned as a voluntary federal union of separate nations. A common government was to be formed by the consent of the constituent republics, and its tasks were to be limited to guaranteeing state security, serving as an intermediary in judicial matters, and securing minority rights.[57] For instance, such an approach was characteristic for the leading Belarusian political party, the Belarusian Socialist Hramada (BSH). Its representatives regarded federative governance as an essential feature for the strength and stability of the state.[58] The Belarusian People's Party of Socialists, more moderate in comparison to the BSH, also supported the idea of Belarusian territorial and national autonomy within a future federative Russian state, emphasizing the need of having separate Belarusian legislative and executive organs.[59] Only the violent dispersion of the All-Belarusian Congress in December 1917 and

---

[54]   BDAMLIM, f. 3, vop. 1, spr. 131, ark. 38, 39.
[55]   *Homan*, September 28, 1917, 1.
[56]   LMAVB, RS, f. 21, b. 276, l. 6 r.
[57]   "Na što nam federacyja," *Vol'naja Bielarus'*, no. 31, November 23, 1917, 2.
[58]   "Rezalucyja rabočych-bielarusaŭ Narvskaha rajena ŭ Pietragradzi," *Vol'naja Bielarus'*, no. 4, June 24, 1917, 4.
[59]   LMAVB, RS, f. 21, b. 2213, l. 2, 3.

the ruthless actions of the Bolshevik authorities clearly signaled the turn towards abandoning federative concepts of state organization.[60]

Debut of Belarusian Diplomacy

In order to legitimize its rule over East-Central Europe in the early stages of the war, the German imperial government oriented its policies towards the exploitation of various national movements among the former Russian subject nationalities. Internationally this approach was promoted by the German-sponsored *Liga der Fremdvölker Russlands* (League of Non-Russian Nationalities), an organization presenting the German Empire as the defender of the rights of small nations.[61] The League focused on spreading anti-Russian propaganda and uniting all of the already extant émigré organizations of non-Russian peoples in Europe. Officially established in the spring of 1916, it was headed by the Baltic German Friedrich von der Ropp, and financed by the German foreign ministry. In June 1916, the League acted as the organizer of the Third Conference of Nationalities in Lausanne. Supposedly politically neutral, the conference nevertheless aimed to demonstrate that the Entente powers disregarded the aspirations of the stateless nationalities, contrasting this attitude to the positively evaluated German involvement in the matter of securing nationalities' rights.[62]

Belarusian representatives took part in the Lausanne Conference, bringing the issue of the political and cultural rights of Belarusians to an international level for the first time.[63] Ivan Luckievič and Vaclaŭ Lastoŭski attended the conference and spoke on behalf of the Belarusian people.[64] Apparently, the German authorities issued travel permits, anticipating from the Belarusians demonstrations of loyalty, as Ivan Luckievič was even offered financial support for his trip (which he declined).[65] According to his brother, Luckievič's Belarusian-Lithuanian "independent stance" at the conference interfered with German plans to stage the creation of Lithuania on the narrow basis of the already existing Military Administration of Lithuania,

---

[60]   See Chapter 5 for a detailed discussion of this aspect.

[61]   Seppo Zetterberg, *Die Liga der Fremdvölker Russlands, 1916–1918: Ein Beitrag zu Deutschlands antirussischem Propagandakrieg unter den Fremdvölkern Russlands im ersten Weltkrieg* (Helsinki: Finnische Historische Gesellschaft, 1978), 15.

[62]   Zetterberg, *Die Liga der Fremdvölker Russlands*, 106–7.

[63]   BDAMLIM, f. 3, vop. 1, spr. 193, ark. 59–60.

[64]   "Sobstvennoruchnye pokazaniia A. I. Lutskevicha," in Luckievič, *Da historyi bielaruskaha ruchu*, 192.

[65]   Vitan-Dubiejkaŭskaja, *Maje ŭspaminy*, 58.

which meant that the future state was to be composed of mostly Lithuanian ethnic territories, inclusive of the Belarusian-populated Vil'nia and Hrodna regions.[66]

To ensure the articulation of their positions and national interests, Belarusian delegates went to Lausanne with an extensive report regarding the so-called "triple union," which advocated the creation of a vast federation from the Black to the Baltic seas, to be comprised of Belarus, Lithuania, and Ukraine, with the eventual inclusion of Latvia. In their opinion, such a union was justified by reasons both economic (variety of resources) and strategic (geographical location). Obviously, this did not suit German interests in the region, as it could potentially pose a threat to German domination in Eastern Europe. This concern eventually decided the fate of the report. It never reached the conference, as it was confiscated at the old German-Russian border and forwarded to the Ober Ost authorities, who chose not to return it.[67] This incident also prompted the German authorities to keep a closer eye on Belarusian activities in Vil'nia. After his return from Lausanne, Ivan Luckievič discovered that a German censor, Edmund Susemihl, had moved into the *Homan* editorial office to oversee the newspaper publication process.[68]

The memorandum of the Belarusian delegation presented at the Lausanne Conference represented a summary of the confiscated report, with an emphasis on the federation plans in the region. It was composed from a Belarusian-centered point of view, offering a synopsis of Belarusian history followed by the presentation of the former Grand Duchy of Lithuania as a strong state formation[69] and a common polity of Belarusians and Lithuanians, with an emphasis on the leading roles of Belarusians. It specifically pointed out that old Belarusian served as the only official language in the Grand Duchy, used in governance, administration, and the courts. The following historical overview featured an extensive account of repressive Russian policies in the nineteenth century, citing as examples the forced conversions of the Uniates into Orthodoxy, bans on Belarusian publishing, and Russian colonization measures. The memorandum expressed the hope that after the war, the cultural and political (listed in that particular order) rights of the Belarusian people would be guaranteed by the international community. It is evident that the Belarusian delegation referred to the period of the Grand Duchy as the "golden age" in an attempt to claim its legacy.[70]

---

66   "Pamiaci Ivana Luckieviča," 23.

67   I. M., "Uvaskrossy prajekt," *Sialianskaja Praŭda*, no. 10, October 22, 1924, 1.

68   Vitan-Dubiejkaŭskaja, *Maje ŭspaminy*, 61; "Pamiaci Ivana Luckieviča," 23. For more on Susemihl, see Ales' Paškievič and Andrej Čarniakievič, "Stary niamecki ahent ci bac'ka radzimickaha narodu?," *ARCHE*, no. 4 (2005): 147–65.

69   "Relacja ab zjezdzi u Losannie," *Homan*, no. 52, August 11, 1916, 2.

70   Ibid., 2–3; *Homan*, no. 53, August 15, 1916, 3.

Yet, despite appealing to the international community for the support of Belarusians in the post-war settlements,[71] the memorandum focused primarily on historical facts, be those preferred forms of governance or the accounts of national oppression. It failed to point out any practical characteristics of the Belarusian question relevant for the political situation of 1916, which could have benefited its international image and increased the interest of major powers in the region. Moreover, while emphasis on cultural development and national revival appeared logical from the viewpoint of the Belarusian national activists, it rendered their demands less credible in the international arena, as no realistic political plan was offered.

By contrast, the Lithuanian and Ukrainian national activists possessed more experience by this time, since they had already been actively engaged in émigré national politics. Even though the Ukrainian question did not feature in the German *Ostpolitik* until later in the war, the authorities in Berlin were kept informed about Ukrainian national ambitions and their readiness to cooperate with the Central Powers to achieve separation from Russia. Ukrainian political immigrants in Germany and Austria-Hungary acted through the Union for the Liberation of Ukraine (*Soiuz vyzvolennia Ukraïny*, or SVU). Established with the outbreak of the war in 1914, it was known for conducting national activities among the Ukrainian POWs.[72] The Ukrainian theme was even more prominently featured in the German public sphere, where the Ukrainian Press Bureau, run by Dmytro Dontsov,[73] contributed to raising awareness of the Ukrainian question, which was often used to the benefit of anti-Russian wartime rhetoric. For instance, Paul Rohrbach, a Baltic German by origin, regularly published analytical pieces on Ukraine, with specific attention to its economic potential, presenting it as a tool to achieve the war goals of weakening Russia and even exercising pressure on Poland.[74]

Within the Lithuanian political immigrant circles, Juozas Gabrys represented a good example of a national activist with a developed set of political advocacy skills. In 1911, Gabrys established the Lithuanian Information Bureau in Paris. With the extensive promotion of public knowledge about Lithuania, he became a

---

71   *Homan*, no. 53, August 15, 1916, 3.

72   Frank Grelka, *Die ukrainische Nationalbewegung unter deutscher Besatzungsherrschaft 1918 und 1941/42* (Wiesbaden: Harrassowitz Verlag, 2005), 86.

73   Dontsov was one of the chief ideologists of Ukrainian nationalism. He served as the main source of inspiration for the Bandera faction of the Organization of Ukrainian Nationalists in the 1930s. See Zenon E. Kohut, Bohdan Y. Nebesio, and Myroslav Yurkevich, *Historical Dictionary of Ukraine* (Lanham, MD: Scarecrow Press, 2005), 137; Serhii Kvit, *Dmytro Dontsov: Ideolohichnyi portret* (Lviv: Halyts'ka vydavnycha spilka, 2013), 26–31.

74   Grelka, *Die ukrainische Nationalbewegung*, 88–89.

rather famous figure within European political circles, expanding contacts and cooperating with other oppressed nationalities, who were struggling for their rights (Balkan Slavs, Latvians, Irish, Armenians, etc.). These activities resulted in the creation of the *Union des Nationalités*, which held the First Nationalities Congress in June 1912.[75] Its press organ was a monthly journal, *Annales des Nationalités*, initially focusing on the Balkans and the Baltics. By 1914, it switched to active anti-Polish propaganda, criticizing Polonization measures directed against Lithuanians, Latvians, Ukrainians, and also Belarusians.[76]

During the war, Gabrys was approached by German diplomats, who skillfully used him to conceal the anti-Russian character of the Third Nationalities Conference in Lausanne, as the Entente powers were not entirely sure of his ties to Germany. The German connections of Gabrys are not disputed in the research literature; however, it is also stressed that he was a "Lithuanophile" in the full sense of this word, prioritizing the interests of his nation first and foremost.[77] Gabrys and his activities illustrate that knowledge of the international situation and the use of *Realpolitik* for disseminating knowledge about national demands were essential skills for national activists, which allowed them to promote their cause internationally and gain valuable diplomatic experience. At this point in time, Belarusian national elites possessed neither any patriotic émigré structures nor sufficient resources to act in a similar manner and coherently present their demands. Belarusians gradually started establishing their visibility on the European political scene only after the appearance at the Third Nationalities Conference in Lausanne.

Following the Lausanne Conference in June 1916, another congress of the non-Russian subject nationalities was planned for February 1917 in Stockholm. The delegation from Vil'nia was composed of the Lithuanians Šaulys, Smetona, and Kairys, with only one Belarusian representative—Anton Luckievič. The news about the cancellation of the congress due to the revolutionary events in Russia reached the entire delegation when it was en route to Sweden in Berlin. With the assistance of Baron von der Ropp, who headed the League of Non-Russian Nationalities, the Lithuanians managed to meet and negotiate with the German Foreign Minister Arthur Zimmermann. The latter seemed sympathetic to their argumentation in support of the Lithuanian national idea. The Lithuanian memorandum stated that the German occupation zone was inhabited solely by Lithuanians, who merely happened to speak different languages, among them

---

[75]   Demm, *Ostpolitik und Propaganda*, 148.
[76]   Demm, *Ostpolitik und Propaganda*, 153.
[77]   Demm, *Ostpolitik und Propaganda*, 169; Sukiennicki, *East Central Europe*, 224.

Lithuanian, Belarusian, and Polish. At the same time, the very existence of Belarusian Catholics in Ober Ost was denied.[78]

Upon learning the news of the February Revolution, Belarusian representative Anton Luckievič decided to leave for Vil'nia immediately, while the Lithuanian members of the delegation remained in Berlin for a few days. They managed to arrange a meeting with the German chancellor Bethman Hollweg, presenting him a detailed plan for the Lithuanian state, to be based on the ethnic principle. Before his departure, Luckievič attempted to counterbalance Lithuanian actions and compiled a separate memorandum to be forwarded to the German chancellor, where he requested equal rights for Belarusians in the future Lithuanian state. However, it remains unknown whether this document ever reached its addressee.[79] It is highly unlikely that Luckievič's presence in Vil'nia at this time was more important than the missed opportunity to present and argue the case for Belarusian interests to the highest German authorities in person. In this particular instance, Luckievič failed to demonstrate to the German authorities that Belarusian demands also had to be taken into consideration as another factor in Ober Ost. The lack of political advocacy diminished their value, especially in contrast to the persuasiveness of the Lithuanian delegation, which already had specific and well-developed plans, conveniently coinciding with the German interests in the region.

Lithuanian Turn of the German *Ostpolitik*

Ambitious federation plans finally fell victim not only to the growing forces of local nationalisms, but also, to a greater degree, to the changes in the German Eastern policy. Until the early spring of 1917, one of the tenets of the German occupation in Ober Ost had been a more or less equal approach to all local nationalities, with an enforced ban on all political activities. German chancellor Bethmann Hollweg still cherished hopes for a separate peace with Russia and preferred to keep these territories ready for trade. As Russia remained unresponsive, annexation of the conquered territories became a more attractive option for Germany by the late fall of 1916.[80] Moreover, after the February Revolution in Russia, the

---

[78]   Gimžauskas, *Bielaruski faktar*, 62.

[79]   "Sobstvennoruchnye pokazaniia A. I. Lutskevicha," in Luckievič, *Da historyi bielaruskaha ruchu*, 192–93.

[80]   See Herfried Münkler, "Spiel mit dem Feuer: Die 'Politik der revolutionären Infektion' im Ersten Weltkrieg," *Osteuropa* 64, nos. 2–4 (February–April 2014): 122; Gimžauskas, *Bielaruski faktar*, 62–63.

slogans of national self-determination found their way into international politics and diplomacy. The Central Powers soon recognized their potential for the achievement of their war aims of weakening Russia and ruling over its former western territories. According to the Foreign Minister of Austria-Hungary, Ottokar Czernin, the non-Russian nationalities in this region had the right to decide on their state allegiance, while at the same time benefiting from political and economic protection from the Central Powers.[81]

The turn from annexationist plans to the instrumentalization of national self-determination processes in East-Central Europe was also connected to the need to secure the internal stability of the German Empire, which was threatened by a prolonged war on two fronts, growing war-weariness among the German soldiers, and the privations of the population, which caused strikes in a number of German cities. A continuation of the war with Russia only for the sake of keeping conquered territories in the East was not feasible, as it was associated with the aggravation of social and political tensions within German society. Thus, in addition to the shifted emphasis in international politics, fears of internal problems prompted the German leadership to develop the concept of so-called "limited autonomy,"[82] which became the basis for German policies in Ober Ost from early 1917 onwards. In May 1917, Bethmann Hollweg explained this approach as "imitating independent states which would have internal self-rule, but in a military, political, and economic sense would be subordinate to us."[83]

The option of orchestrating an "independent" Lithuania had been present in German foreign policy since late 1916, especially when faced with the consequences of the Act of November 5, 1916 proclaiming the establishment of a Polish state. While German civilian authorities connected the decision of establishing a Polish state to potential post-war benefits within the *Mitteleuropa*[84] concept, in particular, envisioning economic exploitation and security for the eastern borders of the German Empire, the German military command viewed it primarily in terms of immediate army needs, as a source of recruitment for the weakened German army after its high losses in the battle of Verdun. The German

---

[81]   Chernev, *Twilight of Empire*, 51–52.

[82]   Strazhas, *Deutsche Ostpolitik*, 171–73.

[83]   Cited in Joachim Tauber, "German Eastern Policy, 1917–1918," *Lithuanian Historical Studies* 13 (January 2008): 72.

[84]   The *Mitteleuropa* concept was developed by Friedrich Naumann in 1915, arguing for the creation of an extensive union under German leadership on the territories located between the Baltic Sea and the Alps. See Friedrich Naumann, *Mitteleuropa* (Berlin: G. Reimer, 1916), 3–4.

High Command was especially disappointed and adopted a clear anti-Polish stance, as the failure of the strategy to reinforce the Central Powers at the cost of Poland soon became apparent. Ludendorff in particular proposed the increased economic exploitation of Poland and significant territorial cuts.[85]

The German-inspired project of instrumentalizing Lithuanian self-determination ambitions dates back to a meeting of the German General Headquarters in Bingen on July 31, 1917, which decided to create a so-called Lithuanian Council of Trust (*Vertrauensrat*), consisting of twenty persons to be appointed by the German authorities. German officials also contemplated the eventual inclusion of some Belarusians into this Council. However, this project failed, as all prominent Lithuanian national activists declared their lack of confidence in the occupation powers and refused to join this institution. This step had a certain symbolic meaning, benefiting the political image of the Lithuanian movement in the international arena. The alternative solution to the Council of Trust— the Lithuanian Council (*Lietuvos Taryba*)—was hardly an independent project. Officially established at the Lithuanian Conference in September 1917, Taryba was conceptualized as a representative organ, in contrast to being appointed by the German authorities. However, the supposedly new façade could not change the underlying principle on which Taryba was allowed to exist: its members were only those trusted and approved by the occupation powers.[86]

German officials treated Taryba from positions of superiority and power. For instance, statements made by the chief of the Military Administration of Lithuania, Theodor von Heppe, reveal that the authorities did not regard it as an equal partner even by 1918, privately referring to the Taryba members as "coffeehouse politicians and adventurers," who were not able to contribute anything in the sphere of practical governance. Another German official, responsible for maintaining communication with Taryba, often called it a "circus."[87] Max Hoffmann, the Chief of Staff of the Eastern Front, was known for his opinion of the Lithuanian state as a utopian undertaking.[88]

---

[85]   Piotr Stefan Wandycz, *The Lands of Partitioned Poland, 1795–1918* (Seattle: University of Washington Press, 1974), 354; Piotr Mikietyński, *Niemiecka droga ku Mitteleuropie: Polityka II Rzeszy wobec Królestwa Polskiego (1914–1916)* (Kraków: Towarzystwo Wydawnicze "Historia Iagellonica," 2009), 195–96, 244; on the German disillusionment with state-building in Poland, see also Richter, *Fragmentation in East Central Europe*, 22–23.

[86]   Strazhas, *Deutsche Ostpolitik*, 176–77, 180–81.

[87]   Joachim Tauber, "The View from the Top: German Soldiers and Lithuania in the Two World Wars," in *Forgotten Pages in Baltic History: Diversity and Inclusion*, ed. Martyn Housden and David J. Smith (Amsterdam, New York: Rodopi, 2011), 225–26.

[88]   Linde, *Die deutsche Politik*, 84.

The German dominance of Lithuanian politics is also evident from the events surrounding the proclamation of Lithuanian independence. On December 1, 1917, the Taryba delegation negotiated with the new German chancellor, Georg von Hertling, over the question of establishing a sovereign Lithuanian state. As expected, its official recognition was connected to the condition of maintaining close union-like ties to the German Empire. A corresponding agreement was ratified by Taryba in Vil'nia on December 11, 1917. However, two months later, on February 16, 1918, Taryba unilaterally proclaimed Lithuanian independence without reference to the previous arrangements with the German Empire. This was rejected by the German chancellor, who insisted on the subordinated position of Lithuania and its ties to the German Empire. The December agreement with the Lithuanians was used as another tool against Soviet territorial claims in the peace talks, underway in Brest-Litovsk between December 1917 and March 1918, while in Lithuania itself its publication and dissemination was not allowed.[89] After the signing of the Brest-Litovsk peace treaty, where Lithuanians were not even invited to negotiate, they were effectively deprived of their freedom of action and had to accept recognition on German terms on March 23, 1918, thus succumbing to the initial German plan of ruling over Lithuania as a semi-vassal state.[90]

Taryba proceeded to invite the Duke of Württemberg, Wilhelm von Urach, to become the king of Lithuania. In July 1918, it started referring to itself as the State Council, and in August von Urach was officially pronounced Lithuanian king under the name of Mindaugas II. German military authorities opposed these actions of Taryba and placed its president, Antanas Smetona, under pressure to reverse these decisions. Eventually Smetona abandoned the State Council title for Taryba, yet refused to make concessions in the case of von Urach. Tensions continued throughout 1918, and only when the German collapse became evident in October 1918 did the Lithuanian delegation in Berlin manage to receive assurances of Lithuanian independence from the German chancellor Max von Baden. Yet, the German defeat also meant that the Lithuanians found themselves in a precarious situation by the end of the First World War, having lost the only protection they had against both the Poles and the Bolsheviks.[91]

---

[89]   Demm, *Ostpolitik und Propaganda*, 322.
[90]   Demm, *Ostpolitik und Propaganda*, 136.
[91]   Alfred Erich Senn, *The Emergence of Modern Lithuania* (New York: Columbia University Press, 1959), 37–41.

Parting of Ways: Belarusian versus Lithuanian Demands in 1917

German interest and involvement in Lithuanian politics along with the regime change in Russia after the February Revolution raised the hopes of Ober Ost Belarusians of reuniting Belarusian territories on both sides of the front line, and contributed to the growing discord among the Belarusian and Lithuanian activists throughout the summer of 1917. Political statements of the Luckievič brothers became more radical, designating the city of Vil'nia the role of the future capital. The sensitive question over contested Vil'nia prompted the Lithuanians to respond with claims of being the sole heir of the historical legacy of the Grand Duchy. Their memorandum to the German authorities, submitted in July 1917, contained claims on ethnically Belarusian territories and presented the Belarusian language as "Polish-Russian jargon."[92] One of the members of the Organization Committee organizing the Lithuanian Conference, Petras Klimas, reported on relations with the Belarusians on August 1, 1917, pointing out that all contact had ceased as soon as the Lithuanians stated their intentions to build a nation-state within the Lithuanian ethnographic borders, inclusive of the disputed Vil'nia province.[93] Belarusian territories to the east of the front line were considered an undesirable addition, since in that case the Belarusian population would have represented a liability by outnumbering the ethnic Lithuanians in the future state.[94]

This ambition towards claiming the historical legacy of the Grand Duchy already distinguished the Lithuanian activists after the January 1863 Uprising. The obvious result of this trend was the eventual appropriation of Vil'nia, which was to become Vilnius, by the Lithuanians in the twentieth century. Their vision of Vil'nia as the future capital dates back to 1905. Despite being in a distinct minority, both in the city and in the surrounding region, the Lithuanian national movement sought an independent state with Vil'nia at its center.[95] Apart from being an economic and cultural center of the region, the city was a valuable asset for the Lithuanian national movement, since it served as the main link between the historical legacy of the Grand Duchy and modern Lithuania.[96] With the advantage of being several decades ahead of its Belarusian counterpart, the Lithuanian national movement could develop well-articulated interpretations of

92 Šybeka, "Z historyi bielaruskich maraŭ pra Vil'niu," 173.
93 Gimžauskas, *Bielaruski faktar*, 64.
94 Ponarski, "Konfederacja Wielkiego Księstwa Litewskiego," 58.
95 Staliūnas, "Making a National Capital," 158.
96 Staliūnas, "Making a National Capital," 160.

the ancient Lithuanian character of the Grand Duchy, while Belarusian activists in this period were still far from the claims of modern nationalism, focusing instead on the multinational and democratic traditions of the Grand Duchy.[97]

The meeting of the Belarusian Club on September 8, 1917, demonstrated this way of thinking, as it suggested another solution, based on a common state of Belarus and Lithuania, where both nations were promised clearly delineated autonomies with equal national rights. National belonging was to be defined using the criterion of the native language of the population.[98] It is evident that in this case Lithuanians would not have obtained the Vil'nia region, which was predominantly settled by a Belarusian-speaking population. Moreover, by 1917 Belarusian activists had also started to stress the indivisibility of the Belarusian territories, referring to the broad notion of historical Lithuania and envisioning the eventual inclusion in the future state of all of the ethnically Belarusian territories of Vil'nia, Kaunas, Suwałki, Hrodna, Viciebsk, Mahilioŭ, and Minsk provinces. The emergence of this "national conception," as opposed to earlier federative projects, is attributed to the Union for the Independence and Indivisibility of Belarus (*Suviaz' Niezaležnasci i Niepadzel'nasci Bielarusi*), championed by Vaclaŭ Lastoŭski, Vincent Sviatapolk-Mirski, and Kazimir Šafnagel'. It was the first organization that moved away from the idea of a joint Belarusian-Lithuanian state in favor of an independent Belarusian state with its capital in Vil'nia.[99]

Highly patriotic leaflets issued in the name of the Union for the Independence and Indivisibility of Belarus reveal that this organization was founded on June 2, 1917, in order to counteract the possible loss of Belarusian territories by their inclusion into other states, as well as to prevent the merger of temporarily divided western Belarusian territories with Lithuania. Resolutions of the Union called for the unification of all ethnically Belarusian territories to create the basis for an independent nation-state, to be organized as a republic, with guarantees of all national rights and needs of Belarusians as well as those of the national minorities. At the same time, the Union also admitted that an independent Belarus could secure its existence through federative ties to its closest neighbors. However, possible federation partners remained unnamed and were to be determined later by the democratically elected Belarusian Constituent Assembly.[100]

---

[97]   Snyder, *The Reconstruction of Nations*, 45.

[98]   BDAMLIM, f. 3, vop. 1, spr. 140, ark. 87.

[99]   Šybeka, "Z historyi bielaruskich maraŭ pra Vil'niu," 174; Michaluk and Rudling, "From the Grand Duchy of Lithuania," 12.

[100]   LMAVB, RS, f. 21, b. 871, l. 1.

The vague definition of future federation plans presented by the Union for Independence might have suited the interests of the German authorities, since they benefited most from the existence of several political currents within the Belarusian community, each offering different visions of state organization. The continued efforts for creating a joint Belarusian-Lithuanian state, supported by the Luckievič brothers, were not attractive for German policy in the region, as they evoked the image of a former historical entity and could potentially result in Polish ambitions to recreate the Commonwealth. Finally, in April 1917, the German High Command was delegated the authority to determine the eastern borders of the formal pro-German states that were planned in East-Central Europe, and needed more options to be able either to foster internal discord within the national movements in Ober Ost, or to play them more effectively against each other. In this regard, the existence of various political interest groups was perceived as instrumental to German interest in the region.[101]

Polish historian Dorota Michaluk suggests that Lastoŭski had already founded the Union for Independence and Indivisibility in April 1916, as apparently he had sent out correspondence in its name, but at that time the independence-oriented program was not yet fully supported by other Belarusian organizations in Ober Ost, which were dominated by the Luckievič brothers and their federalist concepts.[102] However, it appears more likely that Lastoŭski's own leadership ambitions within the Belarusian movement and his competition with the Luckieviches prompted the emergence of his more radical program, which eventually took shape in the summer of 1917, facilitated by the growing rift between Belarusians and Lithuanians. According to Anton Luckievič, the German authorities might have used Lastoŭski to divide Belarusian national forces from within.[103] Neither a socialist nor a revolutionary, Lastoŭski made attempts to advance his political career by creating his own political movement in the form of a conservative party, as a counterweight to the socialist-oriented initiatives led by the Luckievič brothers.[104] Nevertheless, Lastoŭski's initiative within the Union for Independence and Indivisibility for the first time brought forth the idea of the unification of all ethnically Belarusian lands in an independent nation-state.

[101] Gimžauskas, *Bielaruski faktar*, 66.

[102] Michaluk, *Białoruska Republika Ludowa, 1918–1920,* 147.

[103] See for instance Document No. 0283 "List Antona Luckieviča (Vil'nia) Jazepu Varonku i Ramanu Skirmuntu (Miensk) za 24.04.1918," in Šupa, *Archivy Bielaruskaj Narodnaj Respubliki,* 123.

[104] Luckievič, *Da historyi bielaruskaha ruchu,* 164; "Pamiaci Ivana Luckieviča," 24; Vitan-Dubiejkaŭskaja, *Maje ŭspaminy,* 94–95.

The Belarusian Conference and Creation of the Great Belarusian Rada in Vil'nia

The Lithuanian Taryba excluded the possibility of Belarusian membership on an equal basis and was ready to negotiate Belarusian participation only as a representation of a national minority. The cooptation of the minority members was fixed not to exceed one quarter of the entire membership of Taryba, in order to secure a Lithuanian majority in the decision-making. Among all Ober Ost nationalities, Belarusians remained the only available option for national minority representation in Taryba, as by 1917 Poles completely ignored Lithuanian affairs, while the Jewish population increasingly connected their future with Russia. In October 1917, the first contacts of Lithuanians and Belarusians were limited to meetings with the group around Lastoŭski, since Lithuanians hoped that it would be more likely to cooperate than the Luckievičs-led majority of the Belarusian National Committee. However, these negotiations were soon stalled due to Lastoŭski's intentions to include ethnic Belarusian areas in the east in the future state, as he had articulated in the Union for the Independence and Indivisibility of Belarus.[105]

The Belarusian community in Vil'nia interpreted the plans for their inclusion as minority representatives in Taryba as an outright offence, issuing a protest resolution at a rally held at the Vil'nia Workers' Club by a number of socialist and democratic Belarusian, Polish, Lithuanian, and Jewish organizations on September 16, 1917.[106] Belarusian delegates who gave speeches at the rally also condemned Lithuanian cooperation with the Germans.[107] Following the official creation of Taryba on September 23, a general meeting was held in the Belarusian Club on September 30, 1917. This initiative was not welcomed by the German authorities. Despite issuing a permit for the meeting, the dissemination of information on its decisions was suppressed, as the German political censor did not allow the resolutions prepared for publication in *Homan* to reach the public.[108]

The meeting was unanimous that the appointment of Taryba was in violation of the principles of popular representation in Ober Ost, and infringed on the historical rights of the Belarusian people to their lands. All those present at the meeting (according to *Homan*, about 200 people) demanded guarantees for Belarusian

---

[105] Tomaš Blaščak, *Bielarusy ŭ Litoŭskaj Respublicy (1918–1940)* (Smolensk: Inbelkult, 2022), 56–57, 100–101.
[106] "U Wilni i wakolicach," *Homan*, no. 75, September 18, 1917, 3.
[107] "Pamiaci Ivana Luckieviča," 24; Vitan-Dubiejkaŭskaja, *Maje ŭspaminy*, 94–95.
[108] LCVA, f. 368, ap. 1, b. 14, l. 5.

interests on the following basis: all Belarusian lands under German occupation had to be united in a single administrative unit. In practice, this translated into a request to merge the existing military administrations of Białystok-Hrodna and Lithuania. Secondly, the meeting demanded the proportional representation of Belarusians in the Regional Council for all occupied Belarusian-Lithuanian lands, as opposed to the proposition of Taryba to include merely a representation for the Belarusian minority. Finally, the meeting stated that Belarusian participation in Taryba was impossible, due to the latter's unfair organization, thereby declaring their intention to start preparations for a Belarusian Conference in Vil'nia. Its purpose was to gather Belarusians from the occupied lands in order to ensure their effective and fair participation in the provisional organization of governance.[109]

In an attempt to create a counterweight to Taryba, the Organization Committee for the Convocation of the Belarusian Conference had already started its daily meetings by November 1917. Anton Luckievič chaired it, with Vincent Sviatapolk-Mirski and Kazimir Šafnagel' serving as his deputies, while Vaclaŭ Lastoŭski was assigned secretary duties. Among the board members were Jazep Lickievič, Jazep Salaviej, Daminik Siamaška, Janka Stankievič, and Jazep Turkievič, as well as representatives of the Belarusian Catholic clergy, Jan Siemaškievič and Uladzislaŭ Taločka, and Orthodox archpriest Michail Golenkievič. With the principal aim of unifying "all circles and political directions of the Belarusian community for the sake of the all-national cause of calling the All-Belarusian National Conference," the board established a coalition editing body for *Homan.*[110] As is evident from its composition, the preparations for the Belarusian Conference overshadowed the competition between the socialist and more moderate right-leaning currents within Belarusian politics, represented by the Luckievič brothers and Lastoŭski, respectively. In essence, the positions of Lastoŭski's Union and the Luckievičes-led faction were converging by the fall of 1917, as the latter had also started emphasizing the need to include the eastern Belarusian lands into the future federative state with the Lithuanians.

The political program of the Organization Committee focused on the independence of all Belarusian-Lithuanian lands under German occupation, with provisions for the eventual inclusion of eastern Belarusian territories. The future state was envisioned as a federation of two fully autonomous units with borders delineated according to the ethnographic principle, guaranteeing equal rights

---

[109]   LCVA, f. 368, ap. 1, b. 14, l. 5.
[110]   "Od redakcyi," *Homan*, no. 91, November 13, 1917, 1.

for all nationalities and confessions. The role of the Belarusian language received special attention, as it was noted that it had to be used in governmental and public institutions, schools, and in Orthodox and Catholic churches along with Lithuanian.[111]

In late January 1918, the German authorities finally granted permission for the convocation of the Belarusian Conference, most likely due to the need to keep in check the increased independent activities of Taryba, in addition to the unclear situation caused by a break in the Brest-Litovsk peace negotiations.[112] The Belarusian Conference gathered between January 25 and 28, 1918, in Vil'nia, declaring its intention to solve "important political and cultural-national tasks."[113] It was conceived as a common platform of cooperation for all Belarusian activists from the German zone of occupation who had to coordinate their positions on the political situation. The second goal was the establishment of a Belarusian national representation, which had to prepare for the organization of the Constituent *Sejm* in the Belarusian and Lithuanian lands, authorized to decide on the future form of state organization. Meanwhile, the national representation had to take over the leading role in Belarusian politics in Ober Ost, protecting and guaranteeing the interests of the Belarusian people in the process of potential state building in the region.[114] In accordance with these tasks, the Belarusian Conference elected the Great Belarusian Rada in Vil'nia[115] to act as the highest national authority of Belarusians in the occupied lands. The Presidium of the Rada consisted of Anton Luckievič, Ivan Luckievič, Kazimir Šafnagel', Uladzislaŭ Taločka, and Daminik Siamaška.[116] Although designed to include twenty Belarusian representatives from all areas of Ober Ost, the initial membership of the Rada was limited to fourteen persons, due to the absence of the representatives from the Białystok and Hrodna regions. They were not able to reach Vil'nia to attend the conference, as the German authorities refused to issue travel permits for them.[117]

With reference to self-determination principles, conference delegates demanded an independent sovereign democratic state, consisting of two principal autonomous territories, Belarusian and Lithuanian, maintaining close links with

---

[111]   LCVA, f. 368, ap. 1, b. 16, l. 4.

[112]   Gimžauskas, *Bielaruski faktar*, 69.

[113]   "Biełaruskaja Konferencija," *Homan*, no. 8, January 25, 1918, 1.

[114]   Ibid.

[115]   Not to be confused with the Great Belarusian Rada in Minsk, which was created in October 1917, acting as one of the chief organizers of the All-Belarusian Congress.

[116]   BDAMLIM, f. 3, vop. 1, spr. 140, ark. 31.

[117]   BDAMLIM, f. 3, vop. 1, spr. 140, ark. 124 adv.

Kurland. The borders between the Belarusian and Lithuanian autonomies were to be drawn according to the native language of the population. The Belarusian language was to be guaranteed equal official rights in the government, judicial system, schools, and churches. The Belarusian Conference stressed the indivisible territorial rights of the Belarusian people on both sides of the front. Its delegates specifically noted that they did not recognize the legitimacy of Taryba as a representative of the Ober Ost people.[118] Finally, the Conference expressed a wish for Belarus to be freed from any kind of "guardians," demanding the removal from its territories of all foreign Russian and Polish armies and announcing the plan to create a Belarusian army or militia instead.[119]

These resolutions indicate that even by early 1918, *krajovasc'*-inspired approaches still prevailed in Belarusian political thinking, yet the idea of the unification of all Belarusian territories and the establishment of autonomy based on the ethnic principle implied that the future state would have a strong Belarusian component, due to the numerical predominance of an ethnically Belarusian population. Thus, national activists signaled their potential leadership ambitions, which were unacceptable for the Lithuanians, who could easily proceed with the creation of their own nation-state with guaranteed German support.

On February 18, 1918, when the German armies started their offensive on the Eastern front, advancing further east, the Belarusian Rada in Vil'nia issued a call to the German Empire, as well as to all other states that supported the right to self-determination, reminding them of the decisions of the Belarusian Conference in Vil'nia and the resolutions of the All-Belarusian Congress in Minsk. It requested assistance in the reconstruction of the independence of the common Lithuanian-Belarusian state (Grand Duchy) without taking into consideration the division of the Belarusian territories by the front line, arguing for the indivisibility of Belarusian lands.[120] Similar concerns regarding the need to prevent further territorial divisions and to secure Belarusian autonomy with the inclusion of the occupied territories settled by the Belarusian population also dominated the agenda of the Executive Committee formed by the Council of the All-Belarusian Congress. It operated unofficially in Minsk after the dispersal of the All-Belarusian Congress on December 18 (N.S. December 31), 1917, and made an attempt to argue this issue at the peace talks in Brest-Litovsk.[121]

---

[118] LCVA, f. 368, ap. 1, b. 14, l. 15–16.

[119] LCVA, f. 368, ap. 1, b. 14, l. 16.

[120] BDAMLIM, f. 3, vop. 1, spr. 140, ark. 37 adv.

[121] See Document No. 0072 "Deklaracyja bielaruskaj delehacyi na mirnych pieramovach u Bierasci za 19.01.1918," in Šupa, *Archivy Bielaruskaj Narodnaj Respubliki*, 40–42.

Peace Negotiations in Brest-Litovsk

In February 1918, Germany and Soviet Russia were involved in peace negotiations in Brest-Litovsk, which started after the signing of the ceasefire on December 15 (O.S. December 2), 1917. The new Soviet power entered the negotiations with a program based on its earlier decree on peace, proclaimed on November 8 (O.S. October 26), 1917. The emphasis on the peace program received full support from Lenin, as it was vital for the new Soviet government in its efforts to preserve power. With the signing of the armistice it acquired stable support among the soldiers, and was no longer facing the threat of popular opposition, as had been the case with the Russian Provisional Government, which had refused to take Russia out of the war.[122] The Bolshevik peace program resolutely renounced forced annexations and indemnities, demanding the immediate liberation of the occupied lands and self-determination rights for nationalities.[123] The German diplomats interpreted this program in a different light, seeing no contradiction in the detachment of Poland, Lithuania, Kurland, and parts of Estonia and Livonia from Russia, since it was presented not as an annexation, but as a free expression of the popular will.[124] These differing views on the principle of national self-determination concerned the future borders between Soviet Russia and the Central Powers, and thus became the major issue of contention between the peace talk parties.

For instance, during the discussion of territorial questions on January 12, 1918, both sides expressed their positions on the contested former Russian borderland regions. As the Soviet delegation argued, the new Russian state was not attempting to hold former territories of the Russian Empire by force. Instead, it was dedicating itself to "safeguarding real freedom of self-determination."[125] Yet, it refused to recognize the separation of Poland, Lithuania, and Kurland, as apparently none of them possessed genuine "democratically elected organs" to express the popular will.[126] Responding to that, General Hoffmann pointed out in a blunt manner that constant Soviet appeals to national self-determination rights did not conform in any way to the recent Bolshevik actions, citing as examples

---

[122] Rex A. Wade, *The Russian Revolution, 1917* (Cambridge: Cambridge University Press, 2005), 259–60.
[123] Chernev, *Twilight of Empire*, 47–48.
[124] Chernev, *Twilight of Empire*, 17; *Proceedings of the Brest-Litovsk Peace Conference: The Peace Negotiations Between Russia and the Central Powers, 21 November, 1917–3 March, 1918* (Washington: U.S. G.P.O., 1918), 44–45.
[125] *Proceedings of the Brest-Litovsk Peace Conference*, 81.
[126] *Proceedings of the Brest-Litovsk Peace Conference*, 80.

the violent dispersal of the All-Belarusian Congress in December 1917 and the Bolshevik ultimatum to Ukraine, which led to an armed conflict. Criticizing the inconsistencies of the Soviet approach, Hoffmann noted the seemingly more democratic German policies, which were apparently taking into account popular will in the occupied territories by calling into life local representative assemblies and supporting their wishes to part from Russia.[127]

In addition to these misunderstandings, the proclaimed Soviet commitment to peace was accompanied by the hesitant stance of the Soviet delegation. Its head, Lev Trotsky, mostly known for his "neither war, nor peace" approach, was sent to Brest-Litovsk with the task of stalling the negotiation process, as the Bolshevik authorities awaited the "inevitable" outbreak of the proletarian revolution in Europe.[128] By contrast, the German Empire was anxious to secure a prompt solution on the Eastern front. Signing a separate peace with Soviet Russia allowed for the concentration of more forces on the Western front to start a new victorious offensive there. In this regard, the interests of the German military command played a significant role in influencing diplomacy throughout the negotiations. Ludendorff in particular was confident of German progress in the war and wanted to complete the negotiations in Brest-Litovsk as soon as possible.[129]

Equally important for the imperial government at this stage of the war was the need to secure material support of the German war effort through the economic exploitation of Eastern Europe, which explains the growing role of the Ukrainian factor in German Eastern policy by the latter stages of 1917. By January 1918, both Ludendorff and the German diplomats had already played with the idea of "creating a Ukrainian state," just they had done in the Baltics. This sudden interest in Ukraine by the end of the war was determined mostly by the practical considerations of possible economic benefits, including the extraction of resources, foodstuffs, grain, and cattle.[130] On the eve of the First World War, the Ukrainian share of the world production of grain was estimated to be nearly 10% (250 million tons), accounting for 80% of the entire Russian grain exports.[131] Further, German involvement in Ukraine was perceived as a reinforcement of the anti-Polish policy. Finally, the German emperor, Wilhelm II, was convinced that Ukraine was the

---

[127] *Proceedings of the Brest-Litovsk Peace Conference*, 82.

[128] Winfried Baumgart, *Deutsche Ostpolitik 1918* (Vienna: Oldenbourg, 1966), 21.

[129] Baumgart, *Deutsche Ostpolitik 1918*, 18.

[130] Grelka, *Die ukrainische Nationalbewegung*, 80.

[131] Stephan M. Horak, *The First Treaty of World War I: Ukraine's Treaty with the Central Powers of February 9, 1918* (Boulder: East European Monographs, 1988), 4.

main supplier of food to Russia. Thus, control over Ukraine could turn it into a tool exerting pressure against Russia, and serve as another guarantee of security for the German Empire, especially in light of the unpredictable situation after the Bolshevik takeover of power.[132]

Within Ukraine, the Central Rada acted as a representative for the political aspirations of Ukrainians after the February Revolution. Its demands were similar to those of the Belarusians throughout 1917, as they focused on achieving autonomy within a future democratic Russian federation. However, Ukrainian political parties had a stronger support base among the population, securing 80% of votes in the elections to the All-Russian Constituent Assembly in November 1917, while the Bolsheviks managed to get only 10%. By that time, the Central Rada had already proclaimed Ukrainian autonomy in the First Universal on June 23 (O.S. June 10), 1917. The Ukrainian National Republic, with acknowledgement of its federative ties to the Russian republic, was declared in the Third Universal on November 20 (O.S. November 7), 1917.[133] The Soviet government did not hesitate to resort to violence in order to regain control over Ukraine, and demanded freedom of action for the Ukrainian Bolsheviks in an ultimatum issued on December 17 (O.S. December 4) 1917, threatening military actions if Ukraine would not give up its demands for autonomy. After the Central Rada rejected the ultimatum, the Ukrainian Bolsheviks proclaimed the Ukrainian Soviet Socialist Republic on December 25 (O.S. December 12) in Kharkiv, while the Red Guard units under the command of Antonov-Ovseenko advanced on Kyiv.[134] One day before the ultimatum, the Central Rada had already made its first contact with the representatives of the German government in Brest, who recognized the potential effect of using Ukraine as a "Trojan horse."[135]

The delegation representing the Ukrainian Central Rada faced some obstacles on its way to Brest, as the Bolsheviks at first refused it the right to cross the front line under the false excuse that the delegation would not arrive in Brest in time. The Bolsheviks did not want to share their role of representing the whole of Russia's nationalities, despite formally granting the latter the rights to self-determination, preferring a controlled and directed form of national self-determination.[136]

---

[132]   Grelka, *Die ukrainische Nationalbewegung*, 80–81.
[133]   Horak, *The First Treaty of World War I*, 19, 30; III Universal Ukrain'skoi Tsentral'noi Radi, http://gska2.rada.gov.ua/site/const/universal-3.html (Accessed October 26, 2015).
[134]   Paul Robert Magosci, *A History of Ukraine* (Toronto: University of Toronto Press, 2010), 511–12.
[135]   Horak, *The First Treaty of World War I*, 31; Grelka, *Die ukrainische Nationalbewegung*, 78, 83.
[136]   Horak, *The First Treaty of World War I*, 30.

The actions of the Ukrainian Central Rada, similar to those of the All-Belarusian Congress with its critical positions towards the usurpation of power by the Bolsheviks, did not fit into this specific interpretation.

Initially, the Ukrainian delegation joined the Brest-Litovsk peace talks with consultative rights only. However, by January 4, 1918, the Germans had already officially started separate negotiations with the Ukrainians. At this time, the Central Rada merely aimed to receive a confirmation of state sovereignty from the new Russian government, as declared in the Third Universal on November 20, 1917. The struggle for recognition of the Ukrainian state was still accompanied by the hopes of possible participation in the construction of a future federal democratic Russian state. Being aware of the precarious economic situation of the Central Powers, the Ukrainians even boldly threatened to leave the negotiations if the Ukrainian state was not recognized. On January 12, 1918, Germany and Austria-Hungary made the first step towards a separate peace with Ukraine by recognizing the Central Rada as the legitimate Ukrainian government.[137] As the Bolsheviks protracted the negotiations, separate talks between the Central Powers and the Ukrainian delegation benefited both parties. The former gained access to much-needed resources, while the Ukrainian Central Rada could count on support in its struggle against the Bolsheviks.[138]

In contrast to Ukraine, the issue of Belarusian autonomy was not discussed in Brest. The lack of German interest can be explained by the fact that Belarus did not possess such vast and strategic resources as did Ukraine, while the Soviet delegation was even less likely to tolerate another group which could interfere in its manipulative games with the principle of national self-determination, and result in further territorial losses. Nevertheless, the Executive Committee of the Council of the All-Belarusian Congress managed to send an unofficial delegation to the peace talks. It consisted of Symon Rak-Michajloŭski, Aliaksandr Cvikievič, and Ivan Sierada. Belarusian delegates were detained by the Bolsheviks, and could reach Brest only through Ukraine. Trotsky did not agree to Belarusian participation in the negotiations, as Soviet Russia did not recognize Belarusian autonomy. The Belarusian representatives were able to take part in the negotiations only as observers from the Ukrainian side, and thus failed to articulate their interests in an effective

---

[137] Grelka, *Die ukrainische Nationalbewegung*, 79–81. For a detailed discussion of the Brest-Litovsk treaty and Ukraine, see Chernev, *Twilight of Empire*, 120–57.

[138] Aleksandr Shubin, "The Treaty of Brest-Litovsk: Russia and Ukraine," *Lithuanian Historical Studies* 13 (January 2008): 91.

manner.[139] According to the declaration that the Belarusian delegation brought to Brest, the delegates' chief aim was to prevent further divisions of Belarusian territories. Yet, similarly to the Ukrainians, the Belarusian representatives arrived in Brest with their beliefs intact in the possibility of constructing a democratic federation with the Russian republic.[140]

On January 18, 1918, an impasse was reached in the German-Soviet talks, when General Max Hoffmann presented the Soviet delegation with a map displaying the German vision of the future borders of Eastern Europe, excluding Poland, Lithuania, and Kurland from the Russian-controlled sphere. Trotsky protested against the detachment of the former Russian imperial possessions of Poland and Lithuania, as well as lands settled by Ukrainians, Belarusians, and Estonians. He requested a ten-day long break in the work of the political commission and left for Petrograd for consultations.[141] The Bolshevik Central Committee was not unified in its views, as Lenin supported peace in order to keep the socialist state intact at all costs, even sacrificing some of the rhetoric of self-determination; the circle around Bukharin supported the concept of a "revolutionary war" against Germany in the hope that the German army would be infected with revolutionary slogans, while the rest agreed with Trotsky's strategy of "neither war, nor peace." The meeting of the Bolshevik Central Committee eventually re-confirmed Trotsky's approach as the negotiation strategy.[142]

After the talks in Brest-Litovsk were resumed on January 29, it was too late for the Soviet state to interfere in the progress of the German-Ukrainian talks. As Russia failed to guarantee Ukrainian autonomy, the Central Rada finally gave up its long-lived hopes for a Ukrainian future within a Russian democratic federation, and reoriented itself towards the new ally which it found in Germany. After the proclamation of independence on January 22, 1918, in the Fourth Universal, the Ukrainian government received full authority to conduct its international relations, which led to the signing of a separate peace with the Central Powers on

---

[139] Rak-Michajloŭski and Cvikievič managed to establish some contact with the German delegation in Brest, as they submitted a short report, covering the history of the Belarusian movement and the state of Belarusian politics on February 25, 1918. However, the timing of this report suggests that the Germans might have been interested in this information only for the practical reason of establishing an efficient occupation regime, as on this day they entered Minsk. See Document No. 0090 "Karotkaja daviedka ab historyi bielaruskaha ruchu i ab stanovišču bielaruskaha pytannia da 1–13 liutaha 1918," in Šupa, *Archivy Bielaruskaj Narodnaj Respubliki*, 49.

[140] Michaluk, *Białoruska Republika Ludowa*, 218–19; Turuk, *Belorusskoe dvizhenie*, 40.

[141] *Proceedings of the Brest-Litovsk Peace Conference*, 115–16.

[142] Baumgart, *Deutsche Ostpolitik*, 21–22.

February 9, 1918. In light of the Bolshevik offensive on Kyiv, the Germans used Ukrainian vulnerability to dictate their own peace terms.[143]

On February 10, 1918, Trotsky delivered a passionate speech against imperialism, announcing that Russia had ordered the demobilization of its troops. He refused to accept the peace conditions of the Central Powers, stating that they represented a "permanent threat" for the Russian people and that they violated the interests of the peoples of Poland, Ukraine, Lithuania, Kurland, and Estonia. Trotsky declared Russian withdrawal from the war, yet refused to sign the peace treaty, as in his opinion, it was annexationist in character.[144] German Foreign Minister von Kühlmann noted that a one-sided termination of the state of war and demobilization of the Russian army did not automatically lead to peace. Since the only purpose of the December armistice was the signing of peace and this goal was not achieved, Germany intended to resume military action. In regard to Trotsky's statement on the termination of the war, Kühlmann requested to confirm the borders of Russia. In response, Trotsky refused to continue negotiations and announced his departure to Petrograd.[145]

Germany now had the full freedom to decide whether to interpret the new circumstances as a continuation of war or as peace. Kühlmann was inclined towards keeping the state of war, yet at the same time he also did not want to terminate the armistice. The German Foreign Minister realized that the unclear situation in the East benefited Germany most, and feared possible serious internal repercussions in war-weary German society should military action be resumed. His tactic was thus oriented towards "peace of mutual exhaustion."[146] The German Supreme Command, on the contrary, could not accept an unfinished state of affairs on the Eastern front. Ludendorff and Hindenburg supported taking immediate and resolute military actions, fearing that the Bolsheviks would soon gain control over Ukraine and deprive Germany of much-needed grain. Eventually, tensions between the military circles and the Foreign Ministry diplomats resulted in an inconsistent compromise as a solution, where the German Empire opted for a military advance, yet gave up the idea of an offensive against Petrograd, taking into account some of Kühlmann's reservations. As the peace treaty was not signed, Germany commenced military action against Soviet Russia on February 18, 1918,

---

[143]   Grelka, *Die ukrainische Nationalbewegung*, 83–84.
[144]   *Proceedings of the Brest-Litovsk Peace Conference*, 172.
[145]   *Proceedings of the Brest-Litovsk Peace Conference*, 170–71.
[146]   John W. Wheeler-Bennett, *Brest-Litovsk: The Forgotten Peace, March 1918* (New York: Norton Library, 1971), 103.

easily advancing further east.[147] The Bolshevik government declared its readiness to sign the peace treaty on German terms in an urgent wireless message. As the German military command refused to recognize it as an official document, a few more days passed before the talks could be resumed.[148] The negotiations ended with the signing of the Brest-Litovsk peace treaty on March 3, 1918, entirely on German-dictated terms. As Borislav Chernev argued recently, from a perspective of decolonization, the Brest-Litovsk treaty officially marked the collapse and transformation of imperial Russia.[149]

The issue of national self-determination dominated the Brest-Litovsk peace talks, but in a rather unconventional way, as the representatives of the Central Powers and Soviet Russia constantly referred to it, yet hardly took into account the actual concerns of the nations in the contested regions, withholding from them the right to negotiate peace solutions. The peace negotiations between Soviet Russia and imperial Germany represented a mockery of the idealistic Fourteen Points peace program[150] of the American President Woodrow Wilson, made public on January 8, 1918, right before the second phase of the negotiations in Brest commenced.

The participation of the Ukrainian delegation, which was able to secure a separate peace treaty with the Central Powers, was the only exception. This special treatment of Ukraine is primarily explained by the pragmatic German interest in its vast economic resources, increasingly important for the war-exhausted Central Powers. Another reason was the opportunity to use Ukraine as political leverage against both Poland and Soviet Russia, including it as a link in the belt of pro-German semi-states, designed to increase the security of the German Empire.[151] By contrast, the Belarusian issue remained marginal, as it could not offer the Central Powers anything useful in terms of strategic resources. Eventually, the failed Soviet strategy to stall the Brest-Litovsk negotiations along with the ongoing demobilization of the Russian army made it easy for the German army to advance

---

[147] Baumgart, *Deutsche Ostpolitik*, 24–26.
[148] *Proceedings of the Brest-Litovsk Peace Conference*, 175–76.
[149] Chernev, *Twilight of Empire*, 215.
[150] Wilson's Fourteen Points represent a good example of political idealism. He offered a general vision of peaceful cooperation in the postwar world, emphasizing the democratic rights of various peoples. With regard to the former western borderlands of Russia, he only stressed the need for the evacuation of the Russian territories and opportunities for the "independent determination of her own political development." See Christian Rust "Self-Determination at the Beginning of 1918 and the German Reaction," *Lithuanian Historical Studies* 13 (January 2008): 49.
[151] Grelka, *Die ukrainische Nationalbewegung*, 80.

east and occupy almost all of the Belarusian territories by March 3, 1918. For a while, it seemed that the German Empire had become the undisputed ruler of East-Central Europe.

Conclusion

On the eve of the First World War, a new form of a regional identity emerged in the lands of the former Grand Duchy of Lithuania. Loosely based on the patriotic feelings and loyalty towards the old multinational polity of the Grand Duchy, *krajovasc'* represented a broad and inclusive concept. Due to its tolerant and democratic character, it became a popular trend in the pre-war years. *Krajovasc'* inspired the emergence of federative state-building solutions within the framework of projects designed to revive the Grand Duchy as an equal union of all nations in the lands of historic Lithuania, including Lithuanian Poles, Belarusians, Lithuanians, and eventually Jews and other minorities. Yet, its fortunes changed drastically throughout the course of the war, due to the growing intensity of Polish and Lithuanian "national egoisms" in the region.

The Belarusian national movement stood aside in this respect. Remaining the last faithful supporter of *krajovasc'*-based political thinking, it actively participated in the various attempts at political cooperation among the Ober Ost nationalities. Yet, while Belarusian activists sought support amongst their neighbors, the Grand Duchy Confederation projects were in rapid decline by 1916. The failure of all these initiatives demonstrated the limits of *krajovasc'*, as it entered an uneven competition with the radicalizing and growing national sentiments in the region. In particular, the rise of Polish national aspirations during the First World War soon prompted the Lithuanian Poles to abandon *krajovasc'* in favor of an independent Poland. Consequently, Polish-centered visions of federalism replaced *krajovasc'*-based approaches to state-building in the region. The essential difference of the Polish version entailed the primacy of the independent Polish state to lead all union-building initiatives on the lands of the former Grand Duchy, departing from the notion of the equal roles of nationalities. This approach dominated Polish policies in the region up until 1921. Lithuanians were the next in line to develop their own form of "national egoism." They abandoned the projects of a joint state with Belarusians as soon as the German authorities indicated their plans to use the Military Administration of Lithuania as a basis for the creation of a loyal German-dependent Lithuanian semi-state. This prospect caused a crisis in all joint Belarusian-Lithuanian political initiatives.

Belarusians continued to emphasize federative solutions, yet their demands gradually radicalized too, especially when they started claiming rights to the city of Vil'nia as their future capital, and adopted the idea of the indivisibility of all Belarusian territories, thus advocating their eventual reunification with eastern Belarus. This approach contradicted the vision of the Lithuanians, who rejected the broad notion of a Belarusian-Lithuanian state, instead aspiring to create their own nation-state. It was to encompass only the ethnically Lithuanian territories, but with the important addition of the Vil'nia and Hrodna regions, where the Belarusian population comprised a majority. In this way, the Lithuanians wanted to secure the core regions of the former Grand Duchy and make sure that the ethnic Lithuanians would not be outnumbered by the Belarusians in the future state. Finally, the Lithuanian national movement also chose to claim to be the sole heir of the old multinational Grand Duchy, which contradicted the convictions of Belarusian national activists about the centrality of the Belarusian component in the latter's legacy.

Based on the progressive principles of civic nationalism, *krajovasc'* essentially placed Belarusian nation-building in the background during the initial period of the German occupation. The attractiveness of federative solutions in the Belarusian case is explained by two main factors. Firstly, it could buy time to complete the phase of active national agitation and the promotion of the Belarusian national idea among wider circles of the population. Secondly, sustainable post-war development and security were tied to the economic potential and resources that were easier to attain through a federative state. Therefore, it is not surprising that the Belarusian elites, both in Ober Ost and in eastern Belarus, preferred this type of state organization. Only in the final year of the war did Belarusian political thought in Ober Ost gradually evolve from federalist concepts towards accepting the need of their own statehood formed on an ethnic basis and uniting all of the Belarusian territories divided by the front line.

Eventually, external political factors delivered a decisive blow to all federation projects in the region. As the possibility of the conclusion of a separate peace with Russia waned by early 1917, German foreign policy abandoned its *divide et impera* nationalities policy in Ober Ost, opting to expand its spheres of influence. The annexation drive was disguised by the popular principle of national self-determination, which was misused by the Germans with the primary aims of weakening Russia and counteracting Polish ambitions in the region. Resource deficits motivated the German authorities towards further experiments with nationalism, causing a gradual shift of priorities in East-Central Europe. By late

1917, the German imperial government started expressing interest in Ukraine, which had more to offer in terms of strategic resources and pressures on Russia than the Belarusian region. The signing of the Brest-Litovsk peace treaty on March 3, 1918, resulted in the expansion of German dominance in Eastern Europe. Almost all Belarusian territories were now under German occupation, yet the new power refrained from guaranteeing their territorial indivisibility in the future.

Chapter 4

The Political Organization of the Belarusian Movement in the Non-Occupied Territories in 1917

The liberalization of political life in the wake of the February Revolution facilitated the rise of national movements in the former Russian Empire. At the same time, the Provisional Government neglected the issue of nationalism in the peripheries in favor of rallying the population around the war cause and maintaining order. Autonomy was recognized only for Finland and Poland, while the modest demands of other nations were ignored or postponed until the convocation of the Constituent Assembly. The Provisional Government underestimated the growing power of nationalism and failed to maintain a clearly defined position on the national issue, radicalizing national movements, especially in a situation of wartime deprivations and the diminishing authority of the central power in the peripheries.[1] National elites were confronted with a variety of tasks in the attempts to consolidate and strengthen their national movements. Since all repressive restrictions imposed by the tsarist authorities with the start of the First World War were lifted after the February Revolution, territories to the east of the front line experienced an "explosion" of political activities.[2]

The unexpected liberalization caught Belarusian national activists by surprise. During the war they were scattered across Russia and the unoccupied Belarusian provinces, where political activities were severely restricted and could only act through refugee committees or war relief societies, which were allowed to function as philanthropic organizations. After the revolution, Belarusian patriots faced two chief sets of obstacles. Firstly, legacies of the imperial Russification policies of the second half of the nineteenth century exercised a decisive influence on the promotion of a separate Belarusian national project, portraying it as an unattractive choice. Secondly, activists lacked a strong and structured previously existing organization, which often prevented them from reaching agreements or

---

[1]   Andreas Kappeler, *The Russian Empire: A Multiethnic History* (Harlow: Longman, 2001), 355–56.
[2]   Piotr Wróbel, *Kształtowanie się białoruskiej świadomości narodowej a Polska* (Warsaw: Wydawnictwo Uniwersytetu Warszawskiego, 1990), 36.

taking decisive actions required during a revolution. A high degree of idealism also did not allow them to correctly evaluate their influence and their position in relation to other competing political forces, in particular, the socialists. The latter were able to gain the sympathies of the peasants, who were primarily concerned with social rather than national issues.

In the first months following the February Revolution, Belarusian national activists managed to reorganize their forces on territories not occupied by Germany (Minsk, Mahilioŭ, Viciebsk, and parts of Vil'nia provinces). This chapter analyzes the challenges they faced in their interaction with other political actors with particular attention to the evolution of thinking in national terms and reactions to the revolutionary changes. It follows the course of Belarusian national politics throughout 1917, which eventually led to the convocation of the First All-Belarusian Congress in December 1917.

Legacies of the Nineteenth-Century Russification Policy

In order to understand the challenges that the Belarusian national project faced in this period, some background information on Russian imperial legacies is essential, in particular, on the Russification policy, which in the Belarusian case clearly pursued assimilation goals. In the eyes of the tsarist officials, all Eastern Slavic people were essentially Russian. Russian imperial authorities wanted to proceed with assimilation for those ethnic groups that they believed could be assimilated. The Russian Empire did not perceive Belarusians and Ukrainians as separate nationalities, and in line with this logic they had to be merged into the Great Russian nation.[3] This view crucially influenced all imperial policies in the Belarusian provinces, which were designed in the first place to "bring back" Belarusians to the allegedly closely knit East Slavic family by way of eradicating all influences considered to be Polish or perceived as such.

Imperial Russian policies towards different ethnic groups varied, depending on pragmatic reasons. While de-Polonization measures were vigorously pursued in the North-Western[4] provinces, this was not the case for the Polish provinces, since Russian authorities did not think that they could realistically assimilate

---

[3]   Staliūnas, *Making Russians*, 303. See also Theodore Weeks, "'Us' or 'Them'? Belarusians and Official Russia, 1863–1914," *Nationalities Papers* 31, no. 2 (June 2003): 213; A. I. Miller, *The Romanov Empire and Nationalism: Essays in the Methodology of Historical Research* (Budapest–New York: CEU Press, 2008), 57.

[4]   Vil'nia, Minsk, Koŭna, Hrodna, Mahilioŭ, and Viciebsk provinces.

all Poles. Therefore, with regard to the Poles from the Kingdom of Poland, only segregation measures were implemented.[5] In contrast, Belarusian territories, along with the Lithuanian lands, were seen as the place of an essential confrontation of Russian and Polish interests. Since the Russian imperial administration considered Belarusian territories to be inherently Russian, it attempted to purify them of their Polish component, particularly by emphasizing the de-Polonization aspect of the new policy for the North-Western provinces in reaction to the uprising of 1863–1864. The principal measures concerned administration, the judicial system, and education, where they were most consistently implemented. Restrictions on occupying official positions for persons of Polish descent resulted in the removal of those officials who by the nature of their duties were in constant contact with the peasant population.[6] They were replaced with a Russian bureaucracy and the Orthodox clergy which became the main tools of the new Russian policies in the region. Moreover, officials of Russian origin could count on additional income and benefits if they agreed to assume posts in the North-Western provinces.[7]

De-Polonization also included the gradual elimination of Polish landowner-ship in the region,[8] along with an increase in discrimination against Catholics, thus gradually introducing the concept of equating religious affiliation with nationality.[9] However, in order to determine the nationalities of its subjects in the North-Western provinces, the Russian imperial government used a mixture of criteria. Religion as a factor of national identification was suggested by the statistician R. Erkert, who also admitted the importance of self-identification.[10] In contrast, Pavel Bobrovskii, who did some research on Hrodna province, considered linguistic and cultural aspects to be the decisive determinants, while self-identifications did not matter much. As both Erkert and Bobrovskii were recognized as experts by the Russian officials, both their criteria sets were used interchangeably, depending on the desired result. Religion as a national marker was used in designing measures against the nobility, whose Catholicism was interpreted as a sign of their Polishness, yet at the same time the Belarusian Catholic peasantry was described to be "Belorussian"[11] and therefore potentially subject to assimilation.

---

[5] Staliūnas, *Making Russians*, 301. See also Dolbilov and Miller, *Zapadnye okrainy*, 209.

[6] Miller, *The Romanov Empire*, 58; Dolbilov, *Zapadnye okrainy*, 211.

[7] Aleksandr Kravtsevich, Aleksandr Smolenchuk, and Sergei Tokt', *Belorusy: Natsiia Pogranich'ia* (Vilnius: EGU, 2011), 153.

[8] Staliūnas, *Making Russians*, 71.

[9] Staliūnas, *Making Russians*, 127.

[10] Kravtsevich, *Belorusy: Natsiia Pogranich'ia*, 154.

[11] Kravtsevich, *Belorusy: Natsiia Pogranich'ia*, 156.

The intention of the Russian Empire to assimilate Belarusians faced one obstacle: in order to assimilate an entire ethnic group, it first had to be recognized as such. The Russian ethnographic discovery of Belarus after 1863 was a part of this attempt, primarily designed to prove the existence of unbreakable ties between all East Slavic peoples, allegedly united by a common history, religion, and blood. Eventually, these efforts led to the emergence of the ideology of West-Russism.[12] Belarusian identification was to remain strictly regional, subordinated to the larger All-Russian project.[13] Nevertheless, even this orchestrated recognition of national identity in a colonial context contributed to the development of modern Belarusian nationalism, as it allowed people to "imagine" Belarus in a completely new way.[14]

By the early twentieth century, West-Russism had taken firm hold in the eastern Belarusian regions, often serving as an encouragement and an excuse for radical rightists, whose behavior caused the indignation of the local intelligentsia.[15] After the February Revolution, West-Russism was notable for presenting itself under the guise of Belarusian organizations, as was the case in 1917 with the Belarusian National Union in Viciebsk or the Homiel'-based Union of Belarusian Democracy. These organizations belonged to the right-wing, conservative current within West-Russism, denying a separate Belarusian nation. However, over time West-Russism also proved to be capable of evolving. In particular, its second current was more socialistic in character. It displayed less chauvinism, admitted the existence of ethnic and cultural characteristics specific to Belarusians, and eventually supported the creation of a separate administrative unit for all ethnically Belarusian territories. Although it was not yet a demand for autonomy, this approach nevertheless foresaw a certain degree of economic self-sufficiency and self-administration.[16] A typical representative of this current was the Belarusian Oblast' Committee, formed by Belarusians within the Executive Committee of the All-Russian Soviet of the Peasants' Deputies after the October Revolution. Along with the Great Belarusian Rada, it was among the organizers of the All-Belarusian Congress in December 1917.[17]

---

[12] Bulgakov, *Istoriiia belorusskogo natsionalizma*, 151.
[13] Dolbilov, *Russkii krai, chuzhaia vera*, 195.
[14] Tereshkovich, *Etnicheskaia istoriia Belarusi*, 187.
[15] LCVA, f. 368, ap. 1, b. 10, l. 110.
[16] Stanisłaŭ Rudovič, "Zachodnierusizm va ŭmovach revalucyi 1917 hoda: Pamiž imperskasciu i bielaruskaj idejaj," *Białoruskie Zeszyty Historyczne*, no. 16 (2001): 63–64.
[17] Rudovič, "Zachodnierusizm va ŭmovach revalucyi 1917 hoda," 65.

Russian imperial authorities interpreted Belarusian language as merely another manifestation of Polish influences. This perception resulted in restrictive linguistic policies in the nineteenth century which coincided with the development of the modern literary Belarusian language. The first publications in Belarusian appeared in the 1840s and 1850s and used the Latin alphabet, since their authors usually belonged to the local Catholic nobility. Vincent Dunin-Marcinkievič, who wrote plays in Belarusian and translated Adam Mickiewicz's *Pan Tadeusz* into Belarusian in 1859, noted that the use of the Latin alphabet made more sense, since there were more literate peasants who could read the Latin alphabet than those who were able to read Cyrillic.[18] This was a valid observation, as literacy rates among the Catholics were almost three times higher by the end of the nineteenth century than among the Orthodox.[19]

However, Russian imperial authorities decided to ban the use of the Latin alphabet both for Belarusian and Ukrainian printed works in 1859, alarmed by the spread of Ukrainian language publications.[20] The prohibition of publications in Belarusian was enforced after the January Uprising in 1863, stalling early attempts to develop a modern form of the Belarusian language in the nineteenth century. Overall, between 1863 and 1900, only nine Belarusian books were published in the Russian Empire, amounting to some 160 small format pages of content of moralizing stories or folk tales.[21] The content of these publications predetermined the image of the Belarusian language as a peasant vernacular. The weak resilience of the language, which only started to develop its modern literary form in the nineteenth century, contributed to its marginalization. In lieu of a unified linguistic norm, people often used a variety of different dialects, especially in the borderland areas. Moreover, its linguistic closeness to other Slavic languages—Russian, Polish, and Ukrainian—prevented the perception of Belarusian as a unique language.[22]

---

[18] Jan Zaprudnik, *Belarus: At a Crossroads in History* (Boulder: Westview Press, 1993), 54–55.

[19] Tereshkovich, *Etnicheskaia istoriia Belarusi*, 172.

[20] For a detailed description of the development of the Latin alphabet in the Belarusian and Ukrainian cases in the nineteenth century and a comparison of their usage, see Alexei Miller and Oksana Ostapchuk, "The Latin and Cyrillic Alphabets in Ukrainian National Discourse and in the Language Policy of Empires," in *A Laboratory of Transnational History: Ukraine and Recent Ukrainian Historiography*, ed. Heorhii Kasianov and Philipp Ther (Budapest–New York: CEU Press, 2009), 178–81. See also Staliūnas, *Making Russians*, 285.

[21] Sergei Tokt', "Latinitsa ili kirillitsa: Problema vybora alfavita v belorusskom natsional'nom dvizhenii vo vtoroi polovine XIX-nachale XX veka," *Ab Imperio: Studies of New Imperial History and Nationalism in the Post-Soviet Space*, no. 2 (2005): 301.

[22] Timothy Snyder actually pointed out the advantages of the Lithuanian language in this context: belonging to the Baltic language family, it was different from Slavic languages and had more

In the early twentieth century, the tsarist bureaucracy maintained its denigration of the Belarusian language, deeply convinced of its inferiority and describing it as a "dialect."[23] At the turn of the century, the language continued to be used primarily by rural populations, who constituted the majority of ethnic Belarusians. Official reports rarely even mentioned them by their nationality, referring to them only as "peasants."[24] Social mobility was connected to learning either Russian or Polish, which were considered to be markers of belonging to the elites. Since the use of Belarusian signaled the existence of class differences, the majority of the population did not hesitate to abandon it even without extensive outside pressures.[25] For instance, the newspaper *Biełarus* complained in 1914 that the majority of the young people who left for the towns in search of education immediately turned away from their native language. The newspaper linked this phenomenon to an insufficient understanding of the national cause and relations between the Belarusian-speaking peasantry and the Russian- or Polish-speaking elites, who enjoyed the respectability of a higher social class.[26] Consequently, peasants associated assimilation to another culture, be it Polish or Russian, with social advancement rather than with a conscious national choice.

Belarusian national identification in the nineteenth century failed to turn into an attractive option, as the constructed image of a Belarusian at that time was closely linked to the peasant world. The Belarusian idea thus failed to incorporate higher social circles, as, for instance, in the literature of that period only peasants spoke Belarusian, in contrast to the landowners, who were mostly presented as Polish-speaking. This focus on the peasant aspects of national identity eventually failed to create an inclusive community attractive for all social circles, and especially for the most active ones with high hopes of social mobility.[27] In this context, educated people, who opted for Belarusian national identification, grew more aware of social differences[28] and by 1917 this had resulted in clearly articulated socialist backgrounds for the majority of Belarusian national activists.

Integrating Belarusian language into the national project and increasing its symbolic value proved to be a difficult task for activists themselves as well. Often,

---

practical value for the peasantry there, who often could not understand Russian and Polish, unlike their counterparts on the Belarusian side. See Snyder, *The Reconstruction of Nations*, 47.

23   Weeks, "'Us' or 'Them,'" 216.
24   Weeks, "'Us' or 'Them,'" 213.
25   Radzik, *Vytoki sučasnaj bielaruskasci*, 214–15.
26   "Kirunak naszaj adukacyi," *Biełarus*, nos. 29–30, July 25, 1914, 1.
27   Radzik, *Vytoki sučasnaj bielaruskasci*, 320.
28   Radzik, *Vytoki sučasnaj bielaruskasci*, 178.

they tried to construct a positive image of the language by linking it to more distant historical traditions.[29] Practical challenges that activists encountered in expanding the use of Belarusian language in the public sphere are also evident from the documents of the Mahilioŭ Belarusian National Committee from 1917. Its protocols reveal that most of its members had Russified backgrounds and despite their sincere efforts, they had trouble communicating in Belarusian. Yet, at the same time, these documents reveal their determination to change the situation: while written almost exclusively in Russian, they also have a tendency to gradually introduce more Belarusian expressions throughout 1917, while at times still adhering to the Russian orthography.[30]

Fortunately for the Belarusian national movement, a consistent and full implementation of the assimilation program of Belarusians was limited by a shortage of funding in the Russian Empire.[31] Overall, even on the eve of the First World War, the Russian Empire still conceived Russification policies to be an integral part of de-Polonization measures, seeing Belarusians as passive subjects. Russian officials did not even think of the possibility that they might come up with their own national idea. In rare cases when they mentioned it, they invariably connected it to "Polish intrigues."[32]

The February Revolution and Revival of Political Life

The February Revolution in the Belarusian provinces followed the general pattern that was typical in most of the Russian provinces. It can be summarized in three main stages, which in essence followed the course of the revolution in Petrograd, with the only exception being that mass street demonstrations usually took place after the establishment of the new governing authorities. First, the liberal forces of society, most often members of zemstvos or public organizations, formed a public

---

[29] Lizaveta Kasmach, "Between Local and National: The Case of Eastern Belarus in 1917," *Journal of Belarusian Studies*, no. 2 (2017): 17.

[30] See for example "Protocol from April 12, 1917," BDAMLIM, f. 3, vop. 1, spr. 136, ark. 20.

[31] Staliūnas, *Making Russians*, 303; see also Theodore Weeks, *Nation and State in Late Imperial Russia: Nationalism and Russification on the Western Frontier, 1863–1914* (DeKalb, IL: Northern Illinois University Press, 1996), 12.

[32] Weeks, "'Us' or 'Them,'" 220–21. The theme of "Polish intrigue" in fact outlived the Russian Empire. This is exactly what was repeated in 1917, but this time not by the governing circles but by the opponents of the Belarusian national movement, who presented it as the idea of Polish landowners trying to enslave the Belarusian peasantry. See Cvikievič, *Kratkii ocherk*, 7; Turuk, *Belorusskoe dvizhenie*, 33.

committee, followed by the establishment of local soviets of workers', soldiers', or peasants' deputies by the Socialist-Revolutionary and Social Democratic forces. These two institutions usually worked in contact with each other. The final stage included public demonstrations in support of the revolutionary gains.[33] Patriotism, equality, fairness, justice, and dedication to the revolution became common slogans in early 1917.[34] The news about the revolution in Petrograd reached the Belarusian provinces quickly. The Minsk Committee of Public Safety and the Minsk Soviet were created already in early March 1917. Their support of the Provisional Government depended on the implementation of promised democratic reforms. The executive committee of the Minsk Soviet was chaired by the social democrat Boris Pozern.[35] One of the distinctive features of all Belarusian soviets was that they were predominantly created by the soldiers.[36]

Revolutionary changes and the liberalization of society affected party activities as well. The overall number of political parties active on Belarusian territories between March and November 1917 reached twenty-six. Their political programs ranged from conservative to revolutionary-democratic. Fourteen parties were of Belarusian origin, while the rest represented Jewish and All-Russian parties. Most notable among the All-Russian parties active in eastern Belarus were the Constitutional Democrats (Kadets), also known as the Party of People's Freedom, the Socialist Revolutionaries, and the Social Democrats (Bolsheviks and Mensheviks).[37] Despite their ideological differences, their positions in regard to national politics and the right to self-determination of nations were similar. As Stanislaŭ Rudovič demonstrated, both the governing circles and an overwhelming majority of the All-Russian political parties, including conservatives, liberals, and all varieties of socialists, were united by their disregard of national demands and their firm intentions to maintain the territorial integrity of Russia.[38] They could not abandon the idea of a Great Russian state, despite this contradicting the common revolutionary democratic slogans. Often this attitude was concealed under the notion of postponing the solution to the national question until the convocation of the Constituent Assembly.

---

[33]   Wade, *The Russian Revolution*, 49–50.

[34]   Gatrell, *Russia's First World War*, 200–201.

[35]   Stanislaŭ Rudovič, *Čas vybaru: Prablema samavyznačennia Bielarusi ŭ 1917 hodzie* (Minsk: Technalohija, 2001), 36.

[36]   Zachar Šybeka, *Narys historyi Bielarusi, 1795–2002* (Minsk: Encyklapedyks, 2003), 179.

[37]   U. F. Ladyseŭ and P. I. Bryhadzin, *Pamiž Uschodam i Zachadam: Stanaŭlienne dziaržaŭnasci i terytaryjalnaj celasnasci Bielarusi (1917–1939)* (Minsk: BDU 2003), 10.

[38]   Rudovič, *Čas vybaru*, 84.

The Party of People's Freedom (Kadets), which dominated the Provisional Government in early 1917, clearly prioritized the preservation of the Russian state, strongly opposing secession and the creation of any sovereign and independent units.[39] In practice, this thinking in terms of "Russia, one and indivisible" meant that they gradually lost the confidence of national minorities, as the latter's demands for autonomy rights grew. Throughout 1917, the Kadets displayed some flexibility as the new coalition government in July 1917 declared its readiness to accept solutions entailing autonomy. According to the statement of the Kadet party representative Samoilo during the Congress of Belarusian organizations in July 1917, the project of Belarusian autonomy could potentially be discussed by the Constituent Assembly. The news was met with such enthusiasm that Samoilo specifically had to warn the Congress to be more cautious and to consider the interests of Russia first and foremost.[40] Obviously, the government's reluctant approach to autonomy contrasted with the priority of this issue for the nations of the former Russian Empire.

Other political parties used the national question to their own advantage. For instance, the Bolsheviks recognized the right of nations to self-determination, distinguishing between regressive and progressive nationalism. In Lenin's view, the nationalism of repressed minorities had to be separated from the nationalism of oppressor nations. Therefore, granting the former the right to self-determination was intended to eliminate the mistrust of the working classes and ensure that small nations would not in fact seek secession, as oppression would vanish.[41] Thus, class interests remained a dogmatic priority, while the right to secession was open to wide interpretations, suitable for the Bolsheviks. They recognized the practical use of nationalist movements in the short-term, which allowed them to increase the numbers of their supporters. In reality, the Bolsheviks were convinced that nationalism would be soon rendered obsolete by the advance of socialism.[42] Generally, all Social Democrats leaned towards the centralist concept of a state. The Mensheviks supported the Austro-Marxist vision of extra-territorial national autonomy, developed by Otto Bauer and Karl Renner. It recognized the existence

[39] Robert Paul Browder and Aleksandr Fyodorovich Kerensky, *The Russian Provisional Government, 1917: Documents*, vol. 1 (Stanford, CA: Stanford University Press, 1961), 317.

[40] *Vol'naja Bielarus'*, no. 12, August 8, 1917, 4.

[41] Jeremy Smith, *The Bolsheviks and the National Question, 1917–23* (New York: St. Martin's Press, 1999), 16. Terry Martin terms it Greatest-Danger Principle, see Terry Martin, *The Affirmative Action Empire: Nations and Nationalism in the Soviet Union, 1923–1939* (Ithaca: Cornell University Press, 2001), 7.

[42] Wade, *The Russian Revolution*, 151.

of national differences and suggested accommodating them within a strong centralized state, which was obliged to guarantee cultural and linguistic rights to the national minorities.[43]

Austro-Marxism in essence advocated that the administrative division of the state should not necessarily coincide with its national division; however, nationalities were allowed to determine cultural policies through special elected bodies comprised of the members of the respective national groups. Since 1901, this approach was also incorporated into the political program of the Bund (General Jewish Workers' Union in Lithuania, Poland, and Russia), which was active in Belarusian territories. Since the Belarusian provinces were located within the borders of the Pale of Settlement, a significant segment of its urban population was Jewish.[44] In the early twentieth century, Minsk became one of the main centers of Jewish socialism. The Bund and the Jewish Social Democratic Labor Party Poalei Zion enjoyed significant influence in the Minsk region and in the city, respectively.[45]

While Poalei Zion combined Zionism and Marxism, favoring national and political autonomy for the Jewish minority with the ideal of their own territory in Palestine, the Bund had a different position in 1917, supporting a cultural autonomy program for the Jewish minority. With regard to the Belarusian situation, the Bund also supported Belarusian cultural autonomy within Russia.[46] Jewish national awakening followed the same trends as the national movements of their neighbors in Eastern Europe. For instance, the attempts to elevate the role of Yiddish as the language of high culture in the Jewish community[47] faced similar obstacles as the efforts of Belarusian activists to promote the use of Belarusian. During the revolution, Jews showed understanding for the Belarusian demands, while Jewish and Belarusian socialists even formed a bloc during the municipal elections in the summer of 1917.[48] However, there were also opponents, and the

---

[43]   Smith, *The Bolsheviks and the National Question*, 10–11.

[44]   According to the data from the 1897 Russian census, about 14% of the population in the Belarusian provinces was Jewish. There were no conflicts in their relations with the Belarusians, and some Jews even participated in the Belarusian national movement. See Tereshkovich, *Etnicheskaia istoriia Belarusi*, 146–47.

[45]   Elissa Bemporad, *Becoming Soviet Jews: The Bolshevik Experiment in Minsk* (Bloomington, IN: Indiana University Press, 2013), 22–23.

[46]   Ladyseŭ and Bryhadzin, *Pamiž Uschodam i Zachadam*, 33–34.

[47]   Delphine Bechtel, "The Russian Jewish Intelligentsia and Modern Yiddish Culture," in *Nationalism, Zionism and Ethnic Mobilization of the Jews in 1900 and Beyond*, ed. Michael Berkowitz (Leiden: Brill, 2004), 214.

[48]   *Vol'naja Bielarus'*, no. 13, August 11, 1917, 2.

majority of them supported the internationalist idea that nations were destined to become superfluous. Some Jews without party affiliations were also against the national self-determination of Belarus or Ukraine, because they feared further dispersion of the Jewish nation, as it was already divided between different nations.[49]

Belarusian National Parties and Organizations

Changes in the political situation in 1917 influenced the status of Vil'nia and Minsk as centers of Belarusian national activities. By early 1917, the Belarusian national movement had developed in parallel form, but not with equal intensity, in both cities. The First World War and German occupation gradually changed the status of Vil'nia as the leading center of Belarusian activism. Although it became more prominent in cultural and educational matters due to the nature of the occupation regime, which allowed more freedoms in these spheres, political activities remained restricted by the German authorities. In these circumstances, Minsk gradually assumed the role of a political center during 1917.[50]

In 1917, Belarusian philanthropic organizations entered the political scene in a new capacity. After the February Revolution, the Minsk section of the Belarusian Committee for the Aid of War Victims declared itself a National Committee and became involved in political activities. Initially, there was a possibility for its potential cooperation with the Minsk Soviet of Workers' and Peasants' Deputies; however, this failed almost immediately.[51] At that moment, most socialists considered the national question to be an anachronistic remnant of the past and therefore showed no sympathy for Belarusian national ambitions, represented by the National Committee.

One of the most influential Belarusian political parties—the Belarusian Socialist Hramada (BSH)—was revived in March 1917 after nearly a decade of non-existence. In an official declaration announcing the resumption of its legal activities on March 25, 1917, its representatives expressed their support of the Provisional Government and an intention to continue the war, which was interpreted as a just war of revolutionary Russia against German militarism, aiming to protect freedom

---

[49]   Z. Biadulia, *Żydy na Bielarusi: Bytavyja štrychi* (Minsk: Drukarnia Ja. A. Hrynbliata, 1918), 28–29.

[50]   Cvikievič, *Kratkii ocherk*, 7.

[51]   Rudovič, *Čas vybaru*, 78–79.

and fighting for peace without annexations and indemnities. The BSH prioritized preparations for the convocation of the Constituent Assembly, with an emphasis on federal republican forms of governance and Belarusian autonomy. It also called for social justice, an eight-hour working day, the equality of all citizens, equal political, economic and civic rights for all nationalities, the nationalization of the school system, and the development of national culture and self-government. The land question was to be solved by turning over all land to those who worked it without the use of hired labor. At the same time, the BSH warned the peasantry against unorganized actions, condemning voluntary land seizures.[52]

The BSH stressed the right of the Belarusian people to develop their national consciousness and to form a separate unit in the Russian democratic state. The latter was understood as a voluntary union of separate nations. This structure was interpreted as an essential feature for the strength and stability of the state. The BSH activists noted that dangers came from two directions. First, the counteractions of local Polish nationalists, landowners, and clergy had to be taken into account. Second, the identified group of political adversaries included Russian "Black-Hundreds" and their local collaborators, who were ready to treat the Belarusian national project as a threat to Russian unity through alleged German intrigues.[53]

Within a short time, BSH organizations were established in Petrograd, Moscow, Minsk, Saratov, Viciebsk, Babrujsk, and in various cities across Siberia and Ukraine. According to the party activist Zmicier Žylunovič, by the end of April the party had about 1,000 supporters in Petrograd alone.[54] In the spring of 1917, the BSH numbered up to 5,000 members and published the party newspaper *Hramada* between April and June 1917. The second party congress of the BSH in the summer of 1917 showed more tendencies towards radicalization,

52   NARB, f. 325, vop. 1, spr. 2, ark. 5, 6.
53   "Rezalucyja rabočych-bielarusaŭ Narvskaha rajena ŭ Pietragradzi," *Vol'naja Bielarus'*, no. 4, June 24, 1917, 4.
54   Z. Žylunovič, "Liuty—Kastryčnik u bielaruskim nacyjanalnym ruchu," in *Bielarus': Narysy historyi, ekanomiki, kul'turnaha i revoliucyjnaha ruchu*, ed. A. Stašeŭski, Z. Žylunovič, U. Ihnatoŭski (Minsk: Vydannie Centralnaha Komitetu Bielaruskae Savieckae Socyjalistyčnae Respubliki, 1924), 184–85. By comparison, the representation of Ukrainian parties and organizations in Petrograd was more impressive. The Ukrainian National Rada was organized there after the February Revolution, in an attempt to consolidate and engage politically almost 100,000 Ukrainians of Petrograd. By March 1917, they had organized a demonstration on Nevskii prospekt (the central street of Petrograd), attended by some 20,000 people. The Ukrainian National Rada in Petrograd also played a key role in making itself heard by the Provisional Government, thus serving as a link between the Provisional Government and the Central Rada in Kyiv, actively promoting the issue of Ukrainian autonomy. See Volodymyr Serhiichuk, "Mykhailo Hrushevs'kyi i ukrainstvo Petrohradu," *Ukrains'kyi Istoryk* 34, no. 1/4 (April 1997): 187–89.

which is attributed to the place where the congress took place (Petrograd) and the social composition of its participants, many of whom had refugee, military, or worker backgrounds.[55] The shift of the party to more leftist positions helped it to recruit more supporters, but at the same time it lost the sympathies of the political center and the right.[56] At this time, the BSH was also reluctant to support the idea of creating a national army and did not approve of Belarusians joining Polish or Lithuanian regiments.[57]

The Belarusian People's Party of Socialists (*Bielaruskaja Narodnaja Partyja Sacyjalistaŭ*, BNPS) was more moderate in comparison to the BSH. It was organized in May 1917, and among its members were Viktar Čavusaŭ, Paviel Aliaksiuk, General Kandratovič, and Raman Skirmunt. The People's Socialists declared that their main goal was to promote national culture and to develop the national question, based on the interests of working people.[58] The party supported Belarusian territorial and national autonomy within a Russian federative democratic republic with its own legislative organ—*Bielaruskaja Krajovaja Rada*. The land question received a lot of attention in the BNPS program, according to which all land had to become public property. A national land fund was to be formed from church, state, and partly from landowners' possessions, while uncontrolled land seizures were not encouraged. A more comprehensive solution to the agrarian question was postponed until the convocation of the Constituent Assembly.[59]

Not all parties with Belarusian roots can be automatically regarded as supporters of the Belarusian national project. Often their only connection to the latter were the words "Belarusian" and "national" in the organization's name, creating confusion and often discrediting the Belarusian movement, as in the case of the notorious Belarusian National Union from Viciebsk, established in early May 1917 by conservative bureaucrats, Orthodox clergy, and government officials, who were on the far right even in the time of the Russian Empire. They covertly opposed democratization and were known for expressing chauvinist and anti-Semitic views in public, despite their reluctant recognition of the Provisional Government.[60] The political program of the National Union did not differ much

---

55 Latyšonak, *Žaŭnery BNR*, 38.
56 Šybeka, *Narys historyi Bielarusi*, 183.
57 Latyšonak, *Žaŭnery BNR*, 41.
58 LMAVB, RS, f. 21, b. 2213, l. 1.
59 LMAVB, RS, f. 21, b. 2213, l. 2, 3.
60 Rudovič, *Čas vybaru*, 95.

from programs of other organizations: it declared the goal to unite all Belarusians of Viciebsk province, aiming to support democratic reforms and to create a separate economic administrative unit on Belarusian territories.[61] In reality, the actions of the National Union revealed other allegiances. During a gathering of public organizations in Viciebsk on June 25 and 26, 1917, it declared its unanimous support of resolutions from teachers' and peasants'[62] congresses condemning the "separatist and chauvinistic desires of a small group of the Belarusian population."[63] It should be noted that all "separatist desires" at that point in time were limited to the modest wishes of autonomy. According to the National Union, Belarusian territories were inseparable from the Russian state, and Russian was considered to be the native language of the population. While the existence of Belarusian culture was not denied completely, the Union from Viciebsk suggested that schools had to prioritize the study of the history of West Russian principalities,[64] implying the alleged connections of all East Slavic tribes in the tradition of West-Russian ideology. During the Congress of the Belarusian Party and Public Organizations in July 1917, the delegates of the Viciebsk Belarusian National Union Zbitkoŭski and Piatuchoŭ were the only ones who were against the decision to send a telegram of support to the Ukrainian Central Rada and even left the Congress in protest.[65]

While the pro-Russian Belarusian National Union established its structures, Belarusian national life in the city of Viciebsk suffered from a lack of activists, as the report of the representative of the Viciebsk section of the BSH, Mialeška, showed. Most activists were students, who could not form a serious opposition to the National Union, led by old "Black-Hundreds" with vast financial resources.[66] The position of the Belarusian movement in Viciebsk province remained precarious throughout 1917. According to a report in the newspaper *Vitebskoe Slovo*, when local socialists decided to contribute to the interaction of various nationalities in Viciebsk and organized an evening of national songs, Belarusians were not represented there. The program featured performances of Polish, Lithuanian, Ukrainian, and Jewish groups and was very popular with the public. The author

---

[61] LMAVB, RS, f. 21, b. 2225, l. 1–2.

[62] See section *The Belarusian National Committee (March–July 1917)* below for the discussion of the peasant organizations dominated by the Bolshevik forces.

[63] LMAVB, RS, f. 21, b. 2225, l. 3.

[64] LMAVB, RS, f. 21, b. 2225, l. 3.

[65] "Zjezd delehataŭ ad bielaruskich partyjnych i hramadskich arhanizacyj 8–10 lipnia ŭ Minsku," *Vol'naja Bielarus'*, no. 8, July 21, 1917, 2–3.

[66] "Zjezd delehataŭ ad bielaruskich partyjnych i hramadskich arhanizacyj 8–10 lipnia ŭ Minsku," *Vol'naja Bielarus'*, no. 9, July 26, 1917, 2–3.

of the report regretted that planned performances of Belarusian and Latvian groups did not take place,[67] implying that these nationalities did not have enough human resources. Viciebsk province remained heavily Russified, and the fact that in this situation the Belarusian National Union posed as a genuine Belarusian organization, following the radical right program at the same time, was especially dangerous for and detrimental to the national mobilization of Belarusians.[68]

Another example of a "blackhundred-spirited" organization was the Union of Belarusian Democracy in Homieľ, which was established by "Russifiers,"[69] mostly state officials, teachers, and bureaucrats, who were evacuated from Viľnia at the start of the First World War. The Homieľ Union of Belarusian Democracy was active between April and November 1917 and was chaired by P. Karankievič. It opposed appeals for the autonomy and nationalization of schooling in cooperation with reactionary organizations of peasants and teachers who were hostile to the Belarusian national movement. It is also noteworthy that the Union ran separately from the democratic bloc in the elections to the Homieľ City Duma.[70] It demanded the full integration of Belarus with the rest of Russia and like the Belarusian National Union from Viciebsk, it also advocated for schooling in the Russian language, claiming that all Belarusians would understand it.[71]

These circumstances indicate that the enormous task of promoting the idea of a modern Belarusian nation within a very limited time faced serious competition from other political forces which were active in eastern Belarus, especially in Viciebsk and Homieľ, often creating confusion among the population. Another obstacle was the territorial dispersion of Belarusian activists: Belarusian parties and organizations were often operating from Russia, where a lot of refugees remained. This led to a lack of coordination between them on the one hand, and insufficient communication between them and the wider population on the other. In addition, All-Russian parties were ready to step in and to implement their own agenda on Belarusian territories. In particular, they developed their own vision of the future state structure, reflected in the idea of the creation of the Western oblasť as a separate administrative unit, in contrast to the demands of Belarusian autonomy. Socialist Revolutionaries, Bolsheviks, Kadets, and the Bund supported

---

[67] "Vecher natsionalnykh pesen," *Vitebskoe Slovo*, no. 1, October 6, 1917, 4.
[68] Rudovič, *Čas vybaru*, 96.
[69] Žylunovič, "Liuty—Kastryčnik," 188.
[70] Mikalaj Siamenčyk, "Sajuz Bielaruskaj Demakratyi," in *Encyklapedyja Historyi Bielarusi*, vol. 6 (Minsk: Bielaruskaja Encyklapedyja imia Pietrusia Broŭki, 1994), 248.
[71] Žylunovič, "Liuty—Kastryčnik," 188; Rudovič, *Čas vybaru*, 102.

this idea, as they established their oblast'-level organizations, encompassing Belarus and the Western front. This concept also had its supporters among the delegates from the Belarusian provinces attending the peasants' congresses in Russia and active in the Executive Committee of the All-Russian Soviet of the Peasants' Deputies. After the October Revolution, these delegates formed the Belarusian Oblast' Committee, uniting Belarusians with pro-Russian sentiments on positions of West-Russian ideology, known as *oblastniki*.[72]

Finally, revolutionary events radicalized the entire society, which was reflected in local politics.[73] Often it complicated national work and had a negative impact on the basic functions of political institutions. According to an eyewitness account from an unoccupied part of Vil'nia province in 1917, the district zemstvo in that particular district was elected in a revolutionary mood, under the slogan "daloŭ i davaj,"[74] which left no room for compromises. Even the impoverished village teachers were labeled as bourgeois counterrevolutionaries and had no chance to be elected. All attempts to establish order were "washed away by the waves of Soviets."[75] Inefficiency and radicalism were gradually eliminated only by 1918, when some of the local landowners, rural teachers, former bureaucrats native to the area, and some of the elders were re-elected to a new zemstvo.[76]

The First Congress of Belarusian National Organizations

The promotion of the Belarusian national idea was complicated by the influence of All-Russian political parties, which knew how to use social tensions to their own advantage, while national activists did not want to give up their idealistic faith in the revolutionary gains. This became evident as early as March 1917, during

---

[72] Rudovič, "Zachodnierusizm va ŭmovach revalucyi 1917 hoda," 66.
[73] For instance, mob law was a common occurrence in 1917. According to a report from Viciebsk, a youth was attacked there by a crowd after it found out that he was wearing a false military uniform. He was beaten and dragged away by the militia, while the crowd was still raging and trying to kill him. In Smolensk a thief was discovered at the train station. People tried to kill him right on the platform. See *Vitebskoe Slovo*, no. 1, October 6, 1917, 2. Although crime rates soared in Belarus starting from the summer of 1917, violence was characteristic in the former Russian Empire on the whole in 1917. For instance, in Siberia crowds lynched suspected thieves, while in the Baltics, the population was constantly terrorized by armed bands. Joshua Sanborn termed this phenomenon the "decentralization of legitimate violence." See Sanborn, *Imperial Apocalypse*, 224.
[74] In English: "Down with and we want."
[75] *Bielaruski Šliach*, no. 30, April 27, 1918, 1.
[76] *Bielaruski Šliach*, no. 30, April 27, 1918, 1.

one of the first large events in Belarusian national life—the First Congress of Belarusian National Organizations. It demonstrated contradictory approaches to the Belarusian question between the nationally oriented activists and the far more numerous followers of the All-Russian parties. The congress opened in Minsk on March 25, 1917, with the objectives of estimating the power of the Belarusian movement, establishing its main aims, determining the level of popular support, and finally "show[ing] its face to the world."[77] About 150 civilian and military representatives attended the congress. Most of them had already been involved in national work and felt that the moment was right to make significant progress. One of the delegates, Zmicier Žylunovič, described the general mood as excessively optimistic.[78]

Activists demonstrated enthusiasm for the national cause and had high expectations. However, there was no unity among the participants of the congress, which reflects general problems which plagued the Belarusian national movement in 1917—including intolerance and an unwillingness to regard Belarusians as a separate nation resulting from the predominance and influence of the All-Russian parties. In the unofficial conversations before the start of the Congress, some delegates had covertly expressed their skepticism about the Belarusian language and ridiculed the idea of the Belarusian nation. So-called "scientific" explanations of the inexpedience of the national Belarusian revival were expressed more openly.[79] This particular theme was not unique for this congress alone and it would dominate public discussions of the Belarusian national project throughout the revolutionary year.

The congress opened as a solemn occasion: on the first day a presidium was elected and delegates started to deliver welcoming speeches, sharing reports from their respective localities.[80] However, the day ended unexpectedly with a heated discussion, which was involuntarily started by a comment made by a certain Ivan Metlin, who had been elected to the presidium as a deputy chair. Zmicier Žylunovič recalled that at that time, Metlin used to serve as an aide to the Provisional Government's Provincial Commissar and sympathized with the views of the right wing of the SR party. Metlin's exact words, which provoked the incident, were as follows: "it is not the right time to raise the national question.

---

[77] Z. Ž., "Zjezd bielaruskich nacyjanalnych arhanizacyj 25 sakavika 1917 h.," *Polymia*, No. 6 (1925): 202.

[78] Z. Ž., "Zjezd bielaruskich nacyjanalnych," 203.

[79] Z. Ž., "Zjezd bielaruskich nacyjanalnych," 203.

[80] NARB, f. 325, vop. 1, spr. 21, ark. 5.

We need to strengthen the freedom that we have gained by uniting in the matter of calling the Constituent Assembly. The Belarusian movement is not natural, because it lacks a firm foundation among the masses."[81]

This statement sparked a chain of fiery protests. Liavon Zajac pointed out that Russia would not be able to survive as a state if it refused autonomous rights to its peoples. Ivan Kraskoŭski, representing Belarusians from Ukraine, fervently urged the congress not to follow people who were still afraid of "scary" words, such as free nation or federalism.[82] Lawyer Viktar Čavusaŭ from Minsk also opposed Metlin, noting that Belarusians deserved the right to national self-awareness. Paviel Aliaksiuk remarked in a very emotional fashion that Metlin was a foreigner, a Great Russian, who was unable to understand the feelings of the Belarusians present at the congress. Metlin was forced to resign from his position of deputy chair and left, but his departure did not calm down the situation. Apparently, several of the delegates shared his feelings and tried to start a fight with Burbis from the BSH, while a certain P. Karatkievič demonstrated immature behavior by running around and deliberately making fun of Taraškievič's linguistic research and the Belarusian language.[83]

According to the memoirs of Zos'ka Vieras,[84] the protocols of the congress described the incident in a rather "delicate" fashion, since Metlin had been deliberately rude and had referred to the Belarusian flag as a "rag." There were even more responses from other delegates who were not in the presidium. One of them, an older peasant, knelt and kissed the flag in protest. Vieras said that this act impressed the audience more than all the discussions, providing an adequate response to the sweeping statements about the unpopularity and artificiality of the Belarusian movement.[85]

The congress demonstrated ambiguities in Belarusian society with regard to the national cause immediately after the overthrow of the monarchy. The chauvinistic nature of Metlin's remarks caused such an outrage amongst most of the congress participants because they associated this kind of rhetoric with the oppressive Russification policies of the tsarist state, but not yet with the policies of the socialist circles.[86] The Belarusian delegates at the congress were under

---

[81]   NARB, f. 325, vop. 1, spr. 21, ark. 5.
[82]   NARB, f. 325, vop. 1, spr. 21, ark. 5.
[83]   Z. Ž., "Zjezd bielaruskich nacyjanalnych arhanizacyj," 205.
[84]   Pseudonym of Ludvika Sivickaja.
[85]   Vieras, *Ja pomniu ŭsio*, 54.
[86]   Z. Ž., "Zjezd bielaruskich nacyjanalnych arhanizacyj," 204.

the influence of the liberal achievements of the revolution and were guided by their beliefs in democratic ideals. They supported the idea of Belarusian autonomy within a federation with democratic Russia as a preferred form of governance, failing to realize that the political establishment of the new Russia would be unwilling to abandon the principle of a "one and indivisible" state. The congress also revealed mutual intolerance and excessively emotional reactions, which would remain characteristic for the political process throughout 1917, often hindering discussions, debates, and political decisions.

In connection with the Metlin incident, the significance of the SR party on Belarusian territories has to be noted separately, since it had numerous supporters among the peasantry, government officials, and soldiers of the Western front. A distinctive feature of the SR organizations on Belarusian territories, which numbered up to 30,000 members in 1917, was their popularity with the officer corps and government officials. While this can be explained by their pragmatic behavior and career concerns, it also indicates that they leaned more towards the right-wing of the party and were more conservative in their actions than could normally be expected from the SR.[87] Therefore, the activities of the SR party in Belarus were not always fully in accordance with the main program of the party, as can be demonstrated by the national question. In particular, the SR organization of the Western front did not support the autonomy of Belarus and regarded the latter solely as a part of Russia, despite the party program, where a federation with territorial autonomy for Ukraine, Belarus, Lithuania, Latvia, Estonia, Georgia, and others was seen as the most suitable form of government for Russia.[88]

The SR party managed to establish and maintain strong party structures in the rear of the Western front, where it had virtually no competitors: the positions of Belarusian nationalists were still marginal in rural areas, due to the weak positions of the Belarusian national cause among the peasants. The latter often had no permanent contacts outside their traditional communities; even the news of the revolution reached the villages later, often in the form of rumors only. For instance, a correspondent of *Vol'naja Bielarus'* from the village of Karpilaŭka in Vilejka district reported in August 1917 that despite the revolution, life in the village remained unchanged. Peasants showed interest in the land question, only insofar as it concerned their local interests. The village did not have any Belarusian activists or even a school, and showed no initiative to reopen the one that had

---

[87]   Rudovič, *Čas vybaru*, 56.

[88]   Ladyseŭ and Bryhadzin, *Pamiž Uschodam i Zachadam*, 32; Rudovič, *Čas vybaru*, 58.

been used before the war. Subscriptions to newspapers or reading books were not popular either.[89] In this situation, the SR had a better chance of gaining the sympathies of the peasants, while the widespread network of SR organizations guaranteed that they could be effective too. This explains why peasant congresses on local levels and later the Soviets of Peasants' Deputies were organized and dominated by the All-Russian socialist parties.[90]

The popularity of the All-Russian parties can also be explained by the changes in the demographic situation of the Belarusian territories during the First World War, when significant numbers of ethnic Belarusians, who might have been more responsive to the nationalist cause, became refugees and were resettled.[91] In contrast to areas under German occupation, the eastern Belarusian provinces were overpopulated.[92] The influx of soldiers, refugees, workers, and administrative personnel to the cities further disrupted the ethnic composition of the population, which even initially did not favor the growth of Belarusian nationalism.

According to the memoirs of Kanstancin Ezavitaŭ, the population of Minsk in 1917 consisted of local Jews who dominated in industries, trade, and the press, and numerous representatives of Russian military organizations as well as various offices of the All-Russian Union of Zemstvos and Towns. It was difficult to notice the Belarusian movement, especially if newcomers and strangers were not interested in local national life.[93] The first congress of the delegates of the Western front, which took place in Minsk in April 1917, confirms this, since it declared its support for the Provisional Government without even mentioning Belarus.[94] Furthermore, soldiers were known for their increased political activity throughout

---

[89] "Pa Bielarusi," *Vol'naja Bielarus'*, no. 14, August 17, 1917, 2. According to the data of the Russian Imperial Census, conducted in 1897, literacy among the Belarusians, aged from 10 to 49 and residing in provinces of Vil'nia, Viciebsk, Hrodna, Minsk, and Mahilioŭ was 22.4%. In comparison, the literacy rate among the non-Belarusian population in these five provinces was at 51.5%. Literacy rates among Belarusians were the highest in the western regions: Vil'nia province, 34.7%; Hrodna province, 34.0%; Viciebsk province, 18.8%; Mahilioŭ province, 17.7%; and Minsk province, 16.2%. Literacy was higher in towns than in rural areas. See Steven L. Guthier, *The Belorussians: National Identification and Assimilation, 1897–1970* (Ann Arbor, MI: Center for Russian and East European Studies, University of Michigan, 1977), 46–47.

[90] Rudovič, *Čas vybaru*, 43.

[91] National activists in Ukraine also complained about the similar situation, noting the "denationalization" of cities. In the Ukrainian case urban centers became more Bolshevik in character. See Gatrell, *A Whole Empire Walking*, 184.

[92] Helena Głogowska, *Białoruś 1914–1929: Kultura pod presją polityki* (Białystok: Białoruskie Towarzystwo Historyczne, 1996), 24.

[93] Kanstancin Jezavitaŭ, "Pieršy Üsebielaruski Kanhres," *Bielaruskaja Minuŭščyna*, no. 1 (1993), 26.

[94] Šybeka, *Narys historyi Bielarusi*, 182.

1917, since they were among the main initiators of creating the soviets in Belarus, both on the fronts and in the cities. The majority of them supported the SR party.[95]

The municipal elections in Mahilioŭ and Minsk in the summer of 1917 demonstrate to what degree political life on Belarusian territories was influenced by the military on the one hand, and All-Russian parties on the other. Belarusian life in Mahilioŭ cannot be described as particularly vibrant, but the Mahilioŭ Belarusian Committee was established on March 31, 1917, aiming to unite the Belarusian population of the Mahilioŭ province in support of the Provisional Government's efforts to reform Russia as a democratic republic. It also intended to defend Belarusian interests at the Constituent Assembly and to promote the economic and cultural development of Belarus.[96] Yet, even with these broadly defined aims, the Mahilioŭ Belarusian Committee experienced competition from the very first days of its existence, forced to confront a strong Kadet party and a number of All-Russian revolutionary parties. According to the memoirs of one of its members, Michail Kachanovič, who later became the Committee's chair, it also had to conduct the municipal election campaign in a city full of military-related organizations and soldiers, whose presence influenced the results of local elections.[97] The Committee gained 2,082 votes out of 22,005 votes in the Mahilioŭ municipal election on August 13, 1917, winning six places out of sixty-four in the City Duma.[98] While this could still count as a good result for a new political force, it also demonstrated the difficult conditions for the national mobilization of Belarusians in the city where the Supreme Headquarters of the Russian army (Stavka) had been located since 1915.

Municipal elections in Minsk took place in similar settings. According to the newspaper *Vol'naja Bielarus'*, Minsk was full of soldiers and refugees at that time; hence, among those elected to the City Duma were many non-local people who were expected to leave Minsk once the war was over.[99] Elections in Minsk also showed that socialists disregarded the national issue. The Minsk Soviet of Workers' and Peasants' Deputies was one of the most vocal supporters of the socialists, yet its electoral campaign did not mention the electoral list number twelve, under which the BSH (Belarusian Socialist Hramada) ran together with one Lithuanian,

---

[95]   Latyšonak, *Žaŭnery BNR*, 37.

[96]   BDAMLIM, f. 3, vop. 1, spr. 137, ark. 20, 20 adv.

[97]   Michail Kachanovič, "Mahilioŭcy i niezaležnasc' Bielarusi (Maje ŭspaminy)," *Spadčyna*, no. 6 (1997): 4.

[98]   *Vol'naja Bielarus'*, no. 16, August 28, 1917, 4.

[99]   *Vol'naja Bielarus'*, no. 13, August 11, 1917, 2.

two Ukrainian, and two Jewish socialist parties. The SR party won the majority of votes, gaining 67 seats out of 102 in the Minsk City Duma, while the BSH won only two seats (for Arkadz' Smolič and Liavon Zajac). While here, too, it was regarded as a relatively good start for the Belarusian parties, which were making their entrance into politics, the regrettable behavior of the Minsk Soviet was noted separately. The latter was accused of contributing to the delusions of the city electorate about the actual political platform of the parties represented in the electoral list number twelve.[100]

In this context, the incident of Metlin's speech at the Congress of Belarusian National Organizations in March 1917 can be viewed not as an exception, but rather as typical behavior of a government official and a representative of the SRs. It also demonstrated that the All-Russian parties did not intend to concede any autonomy to Belarusians in 1917. This was in line with the official position taken by the higher governing circles. When the Belarusian delegation visited Petrograd in early October 1917 in order to participate in the work of the Pre-Parliament of the Provisional Government, it joined the United Organization of National Minorities. When the latter demanded a place in the Pre-Parliament Presidium for its representatives, the only answer they received was that "it is not an ethnographic museum here."[101] Furthermore, when the Organization of National Minorities expressed the wish to at least read its declarations, the Pre-Parliament Presidium offered them the opportunity to do so during the break, when no one was present to hear.[102]

The Belarusian National Committee (March–July 1917)

The Congress of Belarusian National Organizations established the Belarusian National Committee (*Bielaruski Nacyjanal'ny Kamitet*, BNK), which consisted of eighteen delegates [103] and was chaired by Raman Skirmunt. Paviel Aliaksiuk, Usievalad Falski, Liavon Zajac, and Branislaŭ Taraškievič were elected as the presidium

---

[100] *Vol'naja Bielarus'*, no. 13, August 11, 1917, 2.
[101] LMAVB, RS, f. 21, b. 2077, l. 15, l. 16.
[102] LMAVB, RS, f. 21, b. 2077, l. 15, l. 16.
[103] The full list of the BNK members included Raman Skirmunt, Arkadz' Smolič, Paviel Aliaksiuk, Liavon Zajac, Edvard Budz'ka, Usievalad Falski, Branislaŭ Taraškievič, Vincent Hadleŭski, Jaŭsiej Kančar, Ivan Kraskoŭski, Ales' Burbis, Kazimir Kastravicki, Jazep Babarykin, Fabian Šantyr, Michail Kachanovič, Vaclaŭ Ivanoŭski, Liavon Dubiejkaŭski, and Zmicier Žylunovič. See "Pratakol druhoha dnia Zjezdu," *Spadčyna*, no. 4 (1990): 33.

members. The BNK announced that its aims were "to organize Belarus in contact with the Provisional Government," to prepare elections to the *Bielaruskaja Krajovaja Rada*,[104] and to publicize elections to the Russian Constituent Assembly, based on the principle of a federal democratic republic. The BNK declared itself open to cooperation with representatives of the Orthodox and Catholic clergy as well as the delegates of peasant and other Belarusian national organizations.[105]

The BNK chair, Skirmunt,[106] was an experienced politician: a landowner and successful entrepreneur and native of the Pinsk area, he was elected to the First Duma from Minsk province in 1906, where he established a so-called "Territorial Circle," uniting the representatives of the Lithuanian and Belarusian provinces, who supported local patriotism, commonly known as *krajovasc'*.[107] Skirmunt's unusual choice in favor of the Belarusian movement (the majority of *krajoŭcy* switched to supporting the Polish national project) and his career choice of becoming a Belarusian politician date back to January 1917, when he started to serve as the head of the Minsk section of the Belarusian Committee for the Aid of War Victims. His active involvement in the Belarusian national cause continued after the February Revolution. Skirmunt was among the organizers of the Day of the Belarusian Badge on March 12, 1917. His speeches were noted for always being carefully prepared, in contrast to the empty slogans of his opponents, and oriented towards specifically promoting Belarusian interests.[108] With such a background, Skirmunt appeared to have been a suitable candidate to lead the BNK. Contemporaries also emphasized that he possessed an established authority and had experience in Russian politics, which was regarded as an important asset for negotiations with the Provisional Government.[109]

It should be noted that not everyone supported the election of Raman Skirmunt as the BNK chair. In particular, Aliaksandr Cvikievič considered Skirmunt, as a landowner, to be unpopular among the peasant population and therefore easy to manipulate by the opponents of the Belarusian movement who represented the Belarusian national cause as an intrigue of Polish landowners.

---

[104] In English: "Belarusian Regional Council."

[105] "Pratakol druhoha dnia Zjezdu," *Spadčyna*, no. 4 (1990): 33.

[106] On Skirmunt, see Aliaksandr Smalinačuk, *Raman Skirmunt (1868–1939): Žycciapis hramadzianina Kraju* (Minsk: Vydavec Zmicier Kolas, 2018).

[107] Stanislaŭ Rudovič, "Bielaruski dzejač z vialikich panoŭ: Epizody palityčnaj bijahrafii Ramana Skirmunta," in *Histaryčny almanach* (Hrodna: Bielaruskae histaryčnaje tavarystva, 1999), 18.

[108] Rudovič, "Bielaruski dzejač z vialikich panoŭ," 21–22.

[109] Vincent Hadleŭski, "Z bielaruskaha palityčnaha žyccia ŭ Miensku ŭ 1917–18 hh.," *Spadčyna*, no. 5 (1997): 22.

Allegedly, Skirmunt was one of them, and conspired to separate Belarus from Russia with the subsequent goal of enslaving Belarusian peasants to the Polish landowners.[110] Cvikievič pointed out that despite the absurdity of such an interpretation, by connecting the autonomy of Belarus to the "landowners' intrigue," it managed to dominate public opinion for a while and initially led to near disastrous consequences for national mobilization. The land question became an important argument in the competition for influence over the peasantry, which was in full swing by March 1917. At that time, the Bolshevik M. V. Frunze (also known as M. A. Mikhailov), who was in charge of the city militia, chaired the newly formed Minsk Province Peasant Committee. It attempted to organize the peasantry on provincial and district levels, in contrast to the intentions of the national consolidation of the peasantry envisioned by the BNK.[111]

The weaknesses of Belarusian activists became evident during peasant congresses, which were led by non-Belarusian forces under the slogan of the Bolshevik struggle for the land. These peasant congresses displayed irreconcilable hostility towards the Belarusian intelligentsia. Personal insults and even acts of violence against the representatives of Belarusian national elites were commonplace.[112] The Bolshevik Mikhailov, who chaired the Peasant Congress of Minsk and Vil'nia provinces on April 22, 1917, was known for his statements which explicitly associated the BNK with the "landowners' intrigue" and accused the BSH of having these connections as well. This news even reached Belarusians in Russia's Kazan, who sent their unanimous protest, condemning the "Russificatory" nature of the resolutions passed by the Minsk Peasant Congress.[113]

The influence of pro-Bolshevik forces was a significant factor, and Belarusian national activists faced serious obstacles in competing with them for popular support, as demonstrated by a report from Sluck district published in *Vol'naja Belarus*. It describes how a group of national activists observed the activities of the SRs, the Bolsheviks, and representatives of the Minsk Peasant Soviet in the countryside who directed their propaganda against the BNK and Skirmunt personally, followed by the denigration of the BSH and accusations of its bourgeois sympathies. This caused a lot of confusion in the villages. Asvencimski, the author

---

[110] Cvikievič, *Kratkii ocherk*, 7; Turuk, *Belorusskoe dvizhenie*, 33.
[111] Rudovič, *Čas vybaru*, 85, 87.
[112] Cvikievič, *Kratkii ocherk*, 7–8.
[113] "List u redakcyju," *Vol'naja Bielarus'*, no. 1, May 28, 1917, 4.

of the report, and his colleagues, who were meeting with peasants too, chose a very cautious course of action and did not even use the Belarusian language all the time, switching to Russian or to Polish, if they felt the need to facilitate communication. Eventually, they managed to gather an audience exceeding 500 people. According to Asvencimski, the activists had to provide detailed explanations of the plans of the Bolsheviks, and compare them with the program of the BSH, which previously had been presented to the peasants as a plan of the landowners. People did not react favorably to the Bolsheviks; however, the growth of sympathy towards the BNK was explained by the strong position that Belarusian activists held in this area since 1905, rather than its political program. This case also revealed that the BNK needed to be more active in establishing and maintaining connections to peasant communities.[114]

Skirmunt's attempts to recruit other landowners like himself to the Belarusian cause also made it easier for his enemies to continue labeling BNK activities as a "landowners' intrigue." However, from a pragmatic perspective, his actions can be interpreted as a means of gaining broader social support for the Belarusian movement, and thus giving it greater stability. Initially, there were some favorable responses. Landowners from Barysaŭ district even expressed some understanding of and sympathies for the Belarusian movement.[115] Princess Magdalena Radzivil is an example of a philanthropist and patron of Belarusian initiatives. She established Belarusian schools on her estates as early as the summer of 1917, when the question of Belarusian schooling was only discussed in theory, but had not yet been implemented anywhere in the eastern Belarusian areas.[116] Princess Radzivil also provided financial support for Belarusian publishing initiatives both in St. Petersburg and Vil'nia before the start of the First World War, and helped Belarusian priests by supporting the activities of the Belarusian Society at the Petrograd Roman Catholic Theological Academy.[117] She also showed an interest in the idea of a revival of the Uniate Church, recognizing its potential to represent the "popular faith" of the Belarusians.[118]

[114] "Zjezd delehataŭ ad bielaruskich partyjnych i hramadskich arhanizacyj 8–10 lipnia ŭ Minsku," *Vol'naja Bielarus'*, no. 9, July 26, 1917, 2–3.
[115] "Pa Bielarusi," *Vol'naja Bielarus'*, no. 14, August 17, 1917, 2–3.
[116] Paŭlina Miadziolka, *Sciežkami žyccia* (Minsk: Mastackaja litaratura, 1974), 96.
[117] Aliaksandar Nadsan, *Kniahinia Radzivil i sprava adradžennia Unii ŭ Bielarusi* (Minsk: Biblijateka časopisa Bielaruski Histaryčny Ahliad, 2006), 11–13, 19.
[118] Hanna Chadasievič, "Magdalena Radzivil—patryjotka nacyjanalnaha i relihijnaha adradžennia," in *Bielarus' i Hermanija: Historyja i sučasnasc': Materyjaly mižnarodnaj navukovaj kanferencyi*, Vypusk 7, Kniha 1, ed. A. Kavalienia (Minsk: MDLU, 2009), 80–81.

In addition to her cultural activities, Magdalena Radzivil attended the regular session of the BNK from May 13 to 15, 1917, along with the Minsk politician Edvard Vajnilovič and Prince Drucka-Liubecki. However, aside from this, there is no further evidence of her active involvement in political matters.[119] There were only indirect indications that landowners and the nobility could potentially embrace new Belarusian identities. Yet, the undisguised radicalism of other BNK members with socialist backgrounds had scared them away. Eventually, only Raman Skirmunt continued his involvement in Belarusian politics, while Princess Radzivil provided some financial support.[120]

Given the dominant position of the socialists in the Belarusian national milieu, Skirmunt's more balanced and realistic approach did not result in any political gains. The hopes of using his political skills and experience in the negotiations with the Provisional Government were not realized[121] and contributed to his political demise. Also, Skirmunt did not have enough time, since the BNK turned out to be a short-lived initiative. It was replaced by the socialist-dominated Central Rada of Belarusian Organizations in July 1917 following the Congress of the delegates of the Belarusian party and public organizations. Among other issues, it revealed rather modest BNK achievements. According to the report of the BNK member Usievalad Falski, the organization was forced to operate under "incredibly difficult" political and financial circumstances. It still managed to keep track of existing and new Belarusian organizations and to hold a fundraiser for national needs. Paviel Aliaksiuk, another BNK member, remarked that its achievements were meagre due to the lack of human resources. Another reason mentioned was that national self-awareness started to manifest itself only when people were away from their homes in foreign lands and tried to find a community there.[122]

Other political objectives of the BNK included establishing contacts with the Provisional Government. However, the achievements of the delegation's visit to Petrograd were not very promising. The Ministry of the Interior immediately inquired as to which real political force the delegation represented. Aliaksiuk's statement about the great moral authority supporting Belarusians sounded neither convincing nor impressive.[123] Belarusian national activists were unable to prove

---

[119]   Vieras, *Ja pomniu ŭsio*, 47.
[120]   Hadleŭski, "Z bielaruskaha palityčnaha žyccia," 22–23.
[121]   LMAVB, RS, f. 21, b. 2077, l. 15.
[122]   "Zjezd delehataŭ ad bielaruskich partyjnych i hramadskich arhanizacyj 8–10 lipnia ŭ Minsku," *Vol'naja Bielarus'*, no. 8, July 21, 1917, 2–3.
[123]   Ibid.

in these first crucial months after the February Revolution that they should be regarded as a consolidated and powerful force to be reckoned with. Claims of moral authority clearly could not be as convincing as practical demonstrations of activities directed towards gaining political autonomy. Unfortunately, the Belarusian movement had still not realized this in 1917 and failed to make a corresponding statement to the Provisional Government. This is especially evident from the contrasting examples of Belarusian neighbors to the west and to the south. The cases involving the Lithuanians and the Ukrainians, presented below, show potential courses of action, which were available under the circumstances of 1917.

Most of the Lithuanian territories were still under German occupation in 1917, and a significant number of Lithuanians were scattered across Russia as refugees. Their sense of national belonging became stronger, as their refugee experiences set them apart from Russians. This was reinforced by significant differences in language and religion. In this situation it was easier for the Lithuanian national activists to set up national refugee relief organizations.[124] These efforts resulted in more coordinated actions throughout 1917, when all leading Lithuanian parties and organizations came together in Petrograd in March and established the Lithuanian National Council in Russia which issued a call for political autonomy.[125] On May 27, 1917, it called a Lithuanian Sejm, which gathered about 330 representatives of various parties in Petrograd. Delegates were elected from all Lithuanian communities across Russia. Similarly to the Belarusian case, unity was also hard to achieve, as the tensions between the left and right were so intense that the Sejm was in danger of falling apart. The main debates here revolved around the question of autonomy versus independence, which led to sharp divisions. However, even in a situation of intense confrontation between the different political forces, the final resolution of the Sejm called for independence.[126] The Provisional Government interpreted all of these actions as separatist, and recognized them as a threat, because it anticipated the internationalization of the Lithuanian question, similarly to the Polish case. The Russian Foreign Ministry warned about the dangers of the expanded territorial ambitions of Lithuanians and strongly resented the fact that the Lithuanian Constituent Assembly was preferred by Lithuanians to the Russian Constituent Assembly.[127]

---

[124]   Gatrell, *A Whole Empire Walking*, 161.
[125]   Strazhas, *Deutsche Ostpolitik*, 159.
[126]   Strazhas, *Deutsche Ostpolitik*, 160–61.
[127]   Raimundas Lopata, "The Lithuanian Card in Russian Policy, 1914–1917," *Jahrbücher für Geschichte Osteuropas*, no. 3 (1994): 353.

Ukrainian demands after the February Revolution echoed the Belarusian ones and were also initially limited to an appeal for autonomy in a democratic federal Russian state. Another common feature was the rapid revival of party activities and their drift to the left during 1917. However, the Ukrainian national movement was at a more advanced stage, compared to its Belarusian counterpart. First, it was more organized and possessed different dynamics, relying on solid popular support. Ukrainian identity was already rooted in the consciousness of a significant number of people, as the example of the massive demonstration in support of autonomy in April 1917 in Kyiv indicated. Nevertheless, the national cause also had more success in combination with social and land issues.[128] Political actions were more resolute in comparison with the vacillating activities of the BNK. The latter's Ukrainian equivalent in early 1917 was the Central Rada, which consisted of more than 600 members, uniting the intelligentsia, representatives of various parties, including delegates from the All-Ukrainian National Congress, and representatives from military, workers', and peasants' congresses. In contrast to the Belarusian scenario, since the Provisional Government failed to address the Ukrainian demands for autonomy, the Central Rada took the initiative and proclaimed autonomy in the First Universal on June 23, 1917. It proceeded with the establishment of a General Secretariat, which started acting in the capacity of an executive authority. The Provisional Government did not have the resources to reverse this maneuver and was forced to recognize the new Ukrainian government.[129]

Ukrainians were also at the forefront of actively promoting the idea of a federative Russian republic in the summer of 1917, attempting to coordinate the efforts of all national movements of the former Russian Empire. The Congress of Nationalities of Russia was organized by the Ukrainian Central Rada and was held in Kyiv from September 8 to 15, 1917. It gathered together 84 delegates, among them Ukrainians, Belarusians, Georgians, Estonians, Latvians, Jews, Moldovans, Tatars, and Azerbaijanis. The majority supported the idea of a democratic republic uniting autonomous units within a federation, with the exception of the Poles and Lithuanians, who stated their intentions of pursuing full independence.[130] All participants agreed on the need to call local constituent assemblies along with

[128] Serhy Yekelchyk, *Ukraine: Birth of a Modern Nation* (Oxford: Oxford University Press, 2007), 69–70.
[129] Yekelchyk, *Ukraine: Birth of a Modern Nation*, 70.
[130] V. I. Holovchenko and V. F. Soldatenko, *Ukrains'ke pytannia v roky Pershoi svitovoi viiny* (Kyiv: Parlaments'ke vydavnytstvo, 2009), 118–19.

the general Russian Constituent Assembly, in order to determine the forms of internal governance for each nation and to delineate future relations within the federation.[131] A separate resolution regarding Belarus pointed out the dangers of the existing territorial division, since a significant portion of Belarusian territories still remained under German occupation and were separated from the eastern regions. The resolution urged the Provisional Government to announce Belarusian autonomy, acknowledging the ethnographic borders of Belarusian settlement.[132]

While the resolutions of the Kyiv congress reflected the strong aspirations of small nations towards a federative form of governance, they did not succeed in changing the policies of the Provisional Government. This became evident at the All-Russian Democratic Conference held on from September 14 to 22 in Petrograd. Jazep Varonka, who spoke on behalf of the Belarusian delegation, specifically referred to the unwillingness of the Provisional Government to take steps towards granting Belarusian autonomy under conditions of its territorial division, remarking that it accepted the self-determination of Poland under similar conditions, at a time when it was not even a part of Russia. However, the Provisional Government continued to ignore Belarusian demands.[133]

Central Rada of Belarusian Organizations

Different forms of possible autonomy continued to dominate the debates at the Congress of Belarusian Public and Party Organizations, which took place in Minsk from July 8 to 10, 1917. Cvikievič, at that time representing the Belarusian People's Hramada in Moscow, still did not consider political autonomy a necessary step, preferring autonomy only in economic matters. Smolič dismissed this proposition on the grounds that the Moscow organization did not have an adequate picture of Belarusian national life and was thus threatening its development in Minsk. Raman Skirmunt interpreted Cvikievič's words in a similar way—as a suggestion to accept zemstvo self-government with slightly widened authority, preserving the old centralist order. Further, in his passionate response to Cvikievič, he dismissed his remarks about the allegedly existing unity of the nations of Russia, pointing out that such a unity had to be kept in place by force. Skirmunt stressed that "people now

---

[131]   Holovchenko and Soldatenko, *Ukrains'ke pytannia*, 120.

[132]   Holovchenko and Soldatenko, *Ukrains'ke pytannia*, 229; Ladyseŭ and Bryhadzin, *Pamiž Uschodam i Zachadam*, 38–39.

[133]   Ladyseŭ and Bryhadzin, *Pamiž Uschodam i Zachadam*, 39.

cannot and should not endure the old centralist order. Our well-being and the well-being of Russia are founded on the wide political autonomy of lands and peoples. The term 'political autonomy' does not necessarily imply one's own army, money, or customs borders. These can be common. However, we cannot and should not give up our genuine needs."[134] For Skirmunt these needs were similar to those of the Ukrainians, as he considered the actions of the Ukrainian Central Rada to be elaborate and mature, with a clear understanding of its own people's interests.[135]

The majority of the delegates remained uncertain as to the new organization to replace the BNK. Delegate Sušynski, representing the Belarusian People's Party of Socialists, remarked that people were already familiar with the BNK and its activities; therefore, it made no sense to establish new organs at every congress, which could be a source of confusion.[136] Two possible options were discussed: establishment of the Belarusian Central Rada as a central representation of the Belarusian people or more cautious representation for Belarusian organizations. Michail Kachanovič, along with Jazep Dyla and Paviel Aliaksiuk, emphasized the latter option, stressing the need to work with people, instead of getting involved in power struggles and being accused of power usurpation.[137] In this way, he wanted to make it clear that the new central authority would be uniting only various organizational structures, without any ambitions to represent the whole of Belarus.

The resolution of the Congress turned over control of the BNK to the Executive Committee of the Congress, which was entrusted with the task of calling a meeting of delegates from Belarusian organizations in August 1917. The cultural responsibilities of the BNK were transferred to the Society of Belarusian Culture.[138] This was an attempt to revive the national cause in light of the slow activities of the BNK, which was replaced by a new organization—the Central Rada of Belarusian Organizations and Parties. Its structure allowed for the incorporation of representatives from towns, villages, refugee, and military organizations, provided that they recognized the need for the self-government of Belarus and supported its language and culture. However, they were allowed to send only one delegate, while Belarusian political organizations could send one delegate for every hundred members.[139] This uneven representation scheme

---

[134]   *Vol'naja Bielarus'*, no. 11, August 3, 1917, 2.
[135]   *Vol'naja Bielarus'*, no. 11, August 3, 1917.
[136]   *Vol'naja Bielarus'*, no. 11, August 3, 1917, 3.
[137]   *Vol'naja Bielarus'*, no. 11, August 3, 1917, 2–3.
[138]   *Vol'naja Bielarus'*, no. 12, August 8, 1917, 4.
[139]   Document No. 0030 "Pratakoly pieršaj sesii Central'naj Rady Bielaruskich Arhanizacyjaŭ u

emphasized that this new structure was interested in the political coordination of Belarusian organizations. Politically, it was dominated by the BSH, which considered it to be a better option for reflecting the radicalizing popular moods during the summer of 1917.[140] Left-wing moods were dictated by revolutionary logic, as people turned to socialism as the only viable strategy for the future. This also explains why a wide variety of parties had the word "socialist" in their titles. Two major Belarusian socialist parties—the BSH and the BNPS (Belarusian People's Party of Socialists)—were in essence parties of Belarusian patriots, yet the former had a stronger socialist component.[141]

The establishment of the new leading organization within the Belarusian national milieu did not run smoothly and revealed disagreements between the BSH and the BNPS. The political struggle had a negative impact on the national movement, which no longer appeared to be a priority for the majority of delegates at the Congress of Belarusian Party and Public Organizations, as some of them specifically pointed out that the national cause was neglected for the sake of party politics and did not appear to interest anyone at that point.[142] A crisis broke out on July 9, 1917, during the elections of the Executive Committee of the Congress, as the BSH and the BNPS were unable to agree. The BSH preferred the majority method, which was criticized as undemocratic and unfair by other delegates. It tried to defend its position by suggesting a coalition list, including representatives of other parties and non-party delegates. According to Badunova, the BSH was trying to prevent the election of people who would harm its work in the future. Aliaksiuk did not agree with such an approach and accused the BSH of manipulating the electoral process, trying to get elected only those people who were convenient for the party's interests, while a true coalition implied that each party could nominate its own candidates independently, instead of agreeing to the BSH's suggestions. Eventually, the BSH agreed to proportional elections. The new Executive Committee consisted of Liosik, Badunova, and Falski from the BSH list and Aliaksiuk and Anton Liavicki (also known as Belarusian writer Jadzvihin Š.) from the BNPS list.[143]

Nevertheless, on July 10, the rift between the BSH and the BNPS deepened. Dyla from the BSH suddenly made a proposition to hold a re-election of the

---

Miensku, 5–6.08.1917," in Šupa, *Archivy Bielaruskaj Narodnaj Respubliki*, 11.

[140]   Varonko, *Bielaruski ruch*, 4.

[141]   Hadleŭski, "Z bielaruskaha palityčnaha žyccia," 29.

[142]   *Vol'naja Bielarus'*, no. 13, August 11, 1917, 3.

[143]   *Vol'naja Bielarus'*, no. 13, August 11, 1917, 3.

Executive Committee of the Congress, as in his opinion the results of the previous elections had been unfair. His party colleague Žylunovič joined him, stating that the elections took place in haste and parties did not have enough time to agree on the candidates. Smolič was more cautious, stating that the elections were fair, but at the same time admitting that the elected Executive Committee would have trouble working effectively. The BNPS took a stand and defended the results of the elections, pointing out that requests of separate groups or parties were not a valid reason for new elections.[144] Finally, it turned out that the BSH delegates were opposed to the election of Aliaksiuk to the Executive Committee. This confession caused the BNPS delegates Aliaksiuk, Sušynski, and Stul'ba to leave the congress. Budz'ka joined them, explaining that the withdrawal of the BNPS made the congress lose its all-Belarusian character. The congress nevertheless decided to hold new elections according to a majority system, as only the BSH and non-party delegates remained. The new Executive Committee as of July 10, 1917, included Liosik, Liavicki, Smolič, Falski, and Halubok. Subsequently, the BNPS submitted an official protest against the actions of the BSH, denouncing its political methods and protesting against violations of the rights of party minorities.[145]

The first session of the Central Rada of Belarusian Organizations, which took place on August 5 and 6, 1917, revealed the predominance of the socialists[146] and new priorities, as was evident from the exchange of opinions between Vanda Liavickaja and Paluta Badunova during the first day of the session. As the participants were delivering reports from various localities, Liavickaja remarked that the delegates did not pay enough attention to the nation in their speeches. Badunova immediately responded that socialism had to go before the interests of the nation.[147]

The voting on the statute of the Central Rada of Belarusian Organizations was another indication of its leftist leanings. Delegates who voted against it pointed out the changes in political orientation. In particular, Liavicki was disappointed that the congress had been called on national foundations, yet had ended with the

---

[144] *Vol'naja Bielarus'*, no. 13, August 11, 1917, 2.

[145] *Vol'naja Bielarus'*, no. 13, August 11, 1917, 3.

[146] The new Statute determined that the Executive Committee of the Central Rada of Belarusian Organizations should consist of nine members. The following persons were elected: Liosik, Dyla, Astroŭski, Halavač, Šantyr, Smolič, Kurčevič-Siaŭruk, Badunova, and Žylunovič. All of them were members of the BSH. See Document No. 0030 "Pratakoly pieršaj sesii Central'naj Rady Bielaruskich Arhanizacyjaŭ u Miensku, 5–6.08.1917," in Šupa, *Archivy Bielaruskaj Narodnaj Respubliki*, 12.

[147] Šupa, *Archivy Bielaruskaj Narodnaj Respubliki*, 9.

acceptance of socialist resolutions. Paŭlina Miadziolka voiced similar reservations. She explained her unwillingness to vote for the proposed statute by stating her concern that the Kyiv Organization of Belarusians would not agree, as it united people of various political views, despite the predominance of socialists.[148]

Conclusion

Tensions within the Belarusian movement, which was dominated by socialists, left it internally fractured and weakened. More importantly, the movement failed to establish a strong organization representing the national interests of Belarusians in 1917. The Minsk Committee for the Aid of War Victims in eastern Belarus managed to transform into the Belarusian National Committee. However, from early 1917 onward, it faced strong competition from All-Russian parties and organizations, which enjoyed popularity in eastern Belarus due to the presence there of numerous Russian government officials and large numbers of non-Belarusian soldiers from the Western front. The BNK could not demonstrate any significant achievements during the three months of its existence. The Central Rada of Belarusian Organizations replaced it in July 1917, opting for a more socialist program to the detriment of national development. The trend towards socialist dominance alienated potential moderate members of the national movement. Moreover, there was no unity among socialist organizations: some, like the Moscow People's Hramada, started to compete for influence, instead of cooperating.

What all national organizations lacked in 1917 were time and resources, both human and financial. People were often willing to engage in the activities of stronger Russian or Polish structures, considering them to have more potential and prospects for the future.[149] Financial problems were also evident from the inability of the BNK to set up national organizations throughout eastern Belarus or to even reach out to the population and disseminate information about its goals and eliminate the competition of the all-Russian parties. This was a part of a larger problem, namely, the lack of communication. On one level, organizations in Belarus did not have sufficient contact and coordination with organizations of Belarusians in Russia. There was also no connection to the western parts of Minsk and Vil'nia provinces, which were under German occupation at that time.

---

[148] Šupa, *Archivy Bielaruskaj Narodnaj Respubliki*, 11–12.

[149] *Vol'naja Bielarus'*, no. 26, October 26, 1917, 4.

These areas were not as heavily Russified and did not experience such dramatic demographic changes as in eastern Belarus, and potentially could have become a more solid base for national work. In sum, the required work was unable to take place, and Belarusian nation-building efforts lagged behind that of the surrounding nations.

Chapter 5

The First All-Belarusian Congress

Focusing on the preparation and the convocation of the First All-Belarusian Congress on December 5–17 (N.S. 18–31), 1917 in Minsk, this chapter addresses the consolidation attempts of the Belarusian national forces in the second half of 1917. The first notable development within the national milieu at this time was the effort of the newly formed Central Belarusian Military Rada to establish Belarusian army units. Simultaneously, the ineffective organization of the Belarusian movement in Minsk was rejuvenated by the creation of the Great Belarusian Rada, which was more inclusive in character than its predecessor, the Central Rada of Belarusian Organizations, and oriented towards a broader program of national integration. Its main competitor for political leadership was the Belarusian Oblast' Committee, which originated from the All-Russian Soviet of Peasants' Deputies in Petrograd in November 1917 and prioritized close ties to Russia. Despite the fundamental differences in their programs, these two rival centers emerged as the main co-organizers of the All-Belarusian Congress. Often described by contemporaries as a Belarusian version of a constituent assembly,[1] the Congress was one of the key events of 1917 in Belarusian national life. Its outcomes marked an important transition in the political positions of Belarusian activists, convincing them to abandon aspirations to the status of an autonomous unit within a federative Russian republic, an attitude prevalent throughout 1917. Yet, while some researchers point to the secessionist moods of the Congress participants,[2] it was not the Congress per se but rather the consequences of its violent dissolution by the Minsk Bolshevik authorities which marked the turning point in the political outlook of the Belarusian national movement.

While Belarusian historiography has produced a number of studies incorporating an analysis of the First All-Belarusian Congress within the broader context

---

[1]   Varonko, *Bielaruski ruch*, 7; Cvikievič, *Kratkii ocherk*, 8.

[2]   Nicholas P. Vakar, *Belorussia: The Making of a Nation—A Case Study* (Cambridge: Harvard University Press, 1956), 100; Jury Vesialkoŭski, *Bielarus' u Pieršaj Susvietnaj vajne: Histaryčny narys* (Białystok-London: n. p., 1996), 124; Rudling, *The Rise and Fall of Belarusian Nationalism*, 77.

of the revolutionary period,[3] English-language research does not yet offer detailed accounts of this event. Apart from the most obvious explanation—the unpopular and rather marginal position of Belarusian studies in the West[4]—this particular omission can also be explained by the scattered and incomplete documentation pertaining to the Congress. Full archival records of the proceedings were not preserved, while the fate of many important documents, including the shorthand records, remains unknown.[5] According to the memoirs of Kanstancin Jezavitaŭ,[6] the Congress produced a lot of materials, including the resolutions of separate sections, reports, summaries, and speeches. All of these documents were submitted to the Presidium of the Congress. Tamaš Hryb, in his capacity of secretary, was put in charge of keeping the official archives. He immediately declared his intention to prepare a publication of selected materials, yet the traces of the Congress archives are lost after 1918.[7] The Bolsheviks were also partly to blame, as they destroyed the documentation of some commissions during the violent dispersal of the Congress.[8]

Preserved official Congress materials are scarce, unsystematized, and scattered across different archival holdings.[9] Reports on the Congress proceedings were also available in the press in 1917. *Vol'naja Bielarus'* and *Belorusskaia Rada* provided coverage,

---

3   Ladyseŭ and Bryhadzin, *Pamiž Uschodam i Zachadam*; Rudovič, *Čas vybaru*; M. Ja. Siamenčyk, *Hramadska-palityčnae žyccio na Bielarusi ŭ peryjad Liutaŭskaj i Kastryčnickaj revaliucyi: sakavik 1917–sakavik 1918 hh.* (Minsk: Bielaruski dziaržaŭny pedahahičny universitet imia Maksima Tanka, 2001).

4   See for instance David Marples, "Belarusian Studies in the West," *Belarusian Review* 27, no. 1 (Spring 2015): 2–3, M. Paula Survilla, "Retrospective Positions and Introspective Critiques: A Belarusist in the Academic Trenches," *Belarusian Review* 27, no. 1 (Spring 2015): 11–16.

5   Vital' Skalaban, "Usiebielaruski Zjezd 1917 hoda: Perspektyvy vyvučennia," *Białoruskie Zeszyty Historyczne* no. 15 (2001): 69.

6   Kanstancin Jezavitaŭ (1893–1946), a native of Dzvinsk (Daugavpils), was a graduate of Viciebsk Teachers' College, earning a reputation as a prominent Belarusian national activist in the Russian army during the First World War. As the deputy chair of the Central Belarusian Military Rada in 1917, he supported the creation of the Belarusian army and participated in the First All-Belarusian Congress. In 1918, Jezavitaŭ served as the minister of defense in the government of the Belarusian Democratic Republic and later as its official representative to Latvia and Estonia. Between 1921 and 1944 he lived in Latvia, promoting Belarusian cultural initiatives and schooling. Arrested by the Soviets in 1945, he died in prison under unclear circumstances. See Zaprudnik, *Historical Dictionary of Belarus*, 165–66. For more on Jezavitaŭ's activities in Belarus, see Latyšonak, *Žaŭnery BNR*, 44–63, 77–81, 132–36; in Latvia—Eriks Jekabsons, "Belorusy v Latvii v 1918–1940 godakh," in *Bielaruskaja dyjaspara jak pasrednica ŭ dyjalohu cyvilizacyj: Materyjaly III Mižnarodnaha kanhresa bielarusistaŭ* (Minsk: Bielaruski knihazbor, 2001), 47–71.

7   Jezavitaŭ, "Pieršy Ŭsiebielaruski Kanhres," 29.

8   "Bielaruski Konhres," *Bielaruski Šliach*, no. 25, April 22, 1918, 1.

9   See, for instance, f. 325 at NARB and f. 582 at LCVA.

while *Bielaruski Šliach* published some statistical data and summaries in 1918.[10] *Belorusskaia Rada* in particular is a valuable primary source, as it published a series of detailed records of the Congress proceedings compiled by Captain Jaruševič.[11] Moreover, memoirs of the participants, as well as early attempts of historical analyses made by the contemporaries, offer an additional perspective for research.[12]

The Struggle for the Belarusian National Army during 1917

Given its spread over the whole region of eastern Belarus, the Western front represented a considerable political factor during 1917. By February 1917, the 2nd, 3rd, and 10th Armies of the Western front altogether numbered more than 1.6 million soldiers, officers, and military personnel, most of whom were of non-Belarusian origin and therefore not likely to care about local politics and concerns.[13] By contrast, the Belarusian movement was well-known and supported on the distant Romanian front, where many ethnic Belarusians served.[14] After the February Revolution, encouraged by the Petrograd Soviet, soldiers started electing soldiers' committees. The democratization of the former imperial army was enthusiastically welcomed by the rank-and-file. By September 1917, the number of soldiers' committees on the Western front reached more than 7,000.[15] The central organization was formed earlier, in April, when military representatives of the Western front and its rear gathered in Minsk and formed the Executive Committee of the Western Front (also known as the Front Committee); it was to become one of the leading political organizations on the Western front.[16]

The Russian army command at first adopted a cautious approach to national organizations of soldiers. However, as the year 1917 progressed, this idea gained

---

[10]   See, for instance, "Usiebielaruski Zjezd (Ahliad)," *Vol'naja Bielarus'*, no. 36, December 31, 1917, 1; "Bielaruski Konhres," *Bielaruski Šliach*, no. 26, April 23, 1918, 1.

[11]   Due to the efforts of the archivist Vital' Skalaban, who traced the rare issues of this newspaper, protocols were published in *Bielaruski histaryčny časopis*. See issues nos. 1–4 for 1993.

[12]   Jezavitaŭ, "Pieršy Ŭsebielaruski Kanhres," 25–29; Makar Kraŭcoŭ, "Razhon: Uspamin," *Bielaruskae žyccio*, March 18, 1920; Evsevii Kancher, "Iz istorii Grazhdanskoi voiny v Belorussii v 1917–1920 gg.: Fragmenty 5-oi glavy," *Bielaruskaja Dumka*, no. 1 (2010): 92–97.

[13]   Rudovič, *Čas vybaru*, 40.

[14]   NARB, f. 325, vop. 1, spr. 21, ark. 52.

[15]   I. M. Ignatenko and G. V. Shtykhov, *Istoriia Belorusskoi SSR* (Minsk: Nauka i tekhnika, 1977), 231.

[16]   Later the Executive Committee of the Western front fell under Bolshevik influence and in line with the primacy of class over nation, started to oppose national divisions and the creation of national organizations within the army. See Rudovič, *Čas vybaru*, 42.

more popularity, under the assumption that national-territorial units would revitalize the army, foster discipline, and increase fighting efficiency.[17] For instance, the command of the Romanian front supported the creation of national units in order to compete with the growing popularity of the Bolsheviks.[18] The changing approaches of the Russian military command to nationalization in the army are also illustrated by the case of the Polish units on the Western front. In June 1917, Poles who served in the Russian army held a general congress and decided on the formation of a Polish army. Initially, their efforts were fruitless, since Kerensky, who was the war minister at that time, did not support the idea of dividing the army along national lines. Permission to create Polish army units was granted by General Kornilov only in late July. After establishing their headquarters in Minsk, General Józef Dowbór-Muśnicki proceeded with the organization of the First Polish Corps.[19]

Initially, Polish military units within the Russian army took the position of non-interference in Russian politics. Their main concern was their eventual return to Poland. Yet, both Stavka and the soviets closely observed the actions of the Polish Corps, worried about the reluctance of the latter to follow orders for democratization in the army.[20] Dowbór-Muśnicki and his Corps were stationed on Belarusian territories and became one of the external players in Belarusian politics after the October Revolution. At the time of the Bolshevik takeover of power in Minsk in late October 1917, Polish troops declared neutrality; however, they also promised to protect the population of the city if needed.[21] Later they confronted the Bolsheviks, in protest against the arrest of the commander of the Western front, General Baluev.[22] It is obvious that the Corps was gradually abandoning its declared neutral attitude. More importantly, Polish soldiers felt compelled to interfere to protect the interests of the Polish population in eastern Belarus, as the estates of many local landowners were pillaged and destroyed.[23] In November 1917, the Polish Corps headquarters were moved away from Minsk to the east, to the area encompassing the triangle of Rahačoŭ–Žlobin–Babrujsk.[24] In an

---

[17]   Rudovič, *Čas vybaru*, 139.

[18]   Latyšonak, *Žaŭnery BNR*, 54.

[19]   Sukiennicki and Siekierski, *East Central Europe during World War I*, 330.

[20]   Siamenčyk, *Hramadska-palityčnae žyccio*, 89.

[21]   "U Minsku," *Vol'naja Bielarus'*, no. 29, November 14, 1917, 4.

[22]   Sukiennicki and Siekierski, *East Central Europe during World War I*, 465.

[23]   Józef Dowbór-Muśnicki, *Krótki szkic do historji I-go Polskiego Korpusu*. Cz. 2 (Warsaw: Placówka, 1919), 68–71, cited in Sukiennicki and Siekierski, *East Central Europe during World War I*, 465.

[24]   Siamenčyk, *Hramadska-palityčnae žyccio*, 89.

attempt to boost its numbers, it actively recruited soldiers of the Western front. In particular, nationally indifferent Belarusian Catholics often chose to identify with the Polish national cause and joined the Corps.[25] Often they were not aware of the alternatives, as Belarusian national activism in the army, not to mention the issue of national units, was still in the making and could not demonstrate comparable levels of recognition and appeal as did the Polish Corps. Polish military units would remain a factor to consider later in winter, when the Bolsheviks fled from Minsk in February of 1918.

The first organization of Belarusian soldiers emerged on May 8, 1917, in Riga, due to the efforts of Jazep Mamon'ka, who had been active in the national movement before the war and during his service in the 12th Army on the Northern front. The Belarusian Military Organization in Minsk followed on May 15, 1917. Yet, at that time, the need for establishing a Belarusian army was not addressed at all. Initially, the goals and demands of these groups were only cultural and social in character.[26] This can be explained by the fact that in 1917, Belarusian political actors preferred to assume the continued existence of the Russian state, renewed as a democratic federation. An intention to establish a national army in these circumstances would have automatically signaled separatist tendencies. However, such a cautious approach did not enjoy unanimous support in the Belarusian national milieu. For instance, delegate Sušynski, representing the Belarusian People's Party of Socialists (BNPS) at the Congress of Belarusian Public and Party Organizations on July 8–10, 1917, criticized national activists for thinking of the future with only Russia in mind, while forgetting about the priority to take care of the Belarusian people and to consolidate all national forces. Sušynski specifically emphasized the need to organize activists in the military.[27]

However, as Sušynski's party, the BNPS, was defeated in the political struggle with the BSH in July 1917, it also lost the ability to influence the decision-making process. The BSH became the dominant voice in the Central Rada of Belarusian Organizations, established as the leading organ of the Belarusian movement in July 1917. It retained a reluctant attitude towards the creation of Belarusian army units. For instance, this is evident from the official approval of the regulations for establishing Belarusian groups in the army, adopted on August 5, 1917. These groups were to be subordinated to the Rada, while their primary goals were

---

[25]   Latyšonak, *Žaŭnery BNR*, 43.
[26]   Latyšonak, *Žaŭnery BNR*, 40–41.
[27]   *Vol'naja Bielarus'*, no. 11, August 3, 1917, 3.

defined to be cultural and educational in character. Soldiers could not establish Belarusian regiments without the explicit consent of the Rada.[28]

Yet, the voices of the soldiers from already existing organizations indicated the opposite, namely, that there was a genuine need for Belarusian regiments among the rank-and-file soldiers. They pointed out that the masses of nationally indifferent Belarusian soldiers urgently needed strong leadership, which would motivate them by setting an example and would advance the national cause. For instance, in June 1917 a group of Belarusian soldiers from Veliž (Viciebsk province) sent a collective letter to the Belarusian National Committee, expressing their gratitude for the BSH newspaper *Hramada*. They mentioned that both the newspaper and the proclamations of the Belarusian National Committee were very popular, as all copies were very quickly distributed. The leader of the group, Andrej Kaliadka, also shared his experiences of organizing a Belarusian group. He noted that it was a slow process, mostly due to the fact that the soldiers in his regiment were "downtrodden people"[29] en masse. Apparently, ordinary soldiers felt ashamed to join the Belarusian group and communicate in Belarusian, as they experienced strong peer pressure from Russians, who outnumbered them in the regiment. These feelings had roots in the legacies of the Russification policies, and the resulting image of the Belarusian language as a backward "peasant dialect." Among other major obstacles, Kaliadka identified the lack of Belarusian officers, especially compared to the much stronger army organizations of the Ukrainians. Soldiers from Veliž suggested the creation of exclusively Belarusian regiments, yet they realistically noted the lack of a central organization which could enforce such a decision.[30]

A different example, this time from the Northern front, shows that the presence of dedicated activists and stronger organizational structures were crucial to spearheading soldiers' involvement in national affairs. In July 1917, Belarusian soldiers from the 12th Army created a temporary committee uniting about 1,000 members in its ranks.[31] Its executive committee, consisting of twenty members, including Jazep Mamon'ka, decided to establish contacts with the central Belarusian organizations immediately. They also intended to start strengthening national self-consciousness among Belarusians serving in the army.[32] Similarly to

[28] See Prilozhenie No. 11 "Statut Bielaruskich Nacyanalnych Kul'turna-Pras'vetnych Hurtkoŭ u Vojsku," in Turuk, *Belorusskoe dvizhenie*, 94.

[29] "Bielaruskamu Nacyanalnomy Kamitetu ŭ h. Minsku," *Vol'naja Bielarus'*, no. 3, June 20, 1917, 4.

[30] Ibid.

[31] Latyšonak, *Žaŭnery BNR*, 41.

[32] NARB, f. 325, vop. 1, spr. 21, ark. 10.

the soldiers serving in Veliž, their counterparts from the Northern front were also under pressure to identify as Russians. Assembly proceedings of the 12th Army indicate high levels of assimilation: soldiers decided to hold the meetings and keep the protocols in Russian due to the insufficient knowledge of Belarusian by the majority of participants. Remarkably, they also made a conscious choice to overcome and reverse the assimilation process, as they opted to keep all correspondence with the central national organizations exclusively in Belarusian, welcomed the attempts to speak Belarusian during the meetings, and planned to change to literary Belarusian completely in due course.[33]

Belarusian soldiers' organizations were able to move forward from cultural to political demands as the political situation radicalized during the summer of 1917, and it became clear that the Russian state was falling apart along with its army. Another factor was the unwillingness of Kerensky to consider Belarusian requests for national military units, while similar requests had been granted to Ukrainians, Poles, and Latvians. Jazep Varonka interpreted this discriminatory position of the Provisional Government as an obstacle for the "most necessary and vital manifestation of the national movement."[34] By the fall of 1917, the considerations of the Provisional Government were cast aside and it was decided to act in "a revolutionary way."[35] The Belarusian national movement in the army "exploded suddenly and spontaneously."[36] According to a report from the 10th Army (South-Western front), soldiers enthusiastically decided to proceed with the organization of Belarusian groups, elected a delegation for the front congress in Kyiv, and voiced a clear demand for a Belarusian army.[37]

Disillusionment with the authorities contributed to the growing feeling among the soldiers to take matters into their own hands. One of the sources of dissatisfaction with the government was its neglect in keeping the promise of the right to national self-determination. Soldiers from the 12th Army were disappointed that the Russian central government was depriving nationalities of even those rights which the latter received through the revolution, noting that throughout the revolutionary year Belarusians always supported Russian democracy, in the hope that the rights of all nations, including the smallest ones, would be guaranteed. Soldiers were embittered that national self-determination

33   NARB, f. 325, vop. 1, spr. 21, ark. 8.
34   Varonko, *Bielaruski ruch*, 5.
35   LMAVB, RS, f. 21, b. 2077, l. 15.
36   "Dopisy," *Vol'naja Bielarus'*, no. 32, November 30, 1917, 3.
37   Ibid.

had to be achieved through struggle and that the first Belarusian regiments in Minsk and Viciebsk, which were emerging spontaneously in "a revolutionary manner," faced severe restrictions from the army command.[38]

Central Belarusian Military Rada

A crucial event for the national organization in the army was the Congress of Belarusian Soldiers of the Western Front, which met in Minsk from October 18 to 24, 1917. The 12th Army of the Northern front, the Baltic fleet, and the Romanian front also sent their representatives to this congress. All participants agreed that the creation of a Belarusian army was a necessary and urgent matter. In an attempt to coordinate the work of all Belarusian organizations in the army, the congress established the Central Belarusian Military Rada (*Central'naja Bielaruskaja Vajskovaja Rada*, CBVR) in charge of organizing Belarusian army units.[39] The CBVR closely cooperated with the Central Rada of Belarusian Organizations, which at this time was transformed into the Great Belarusian Rada.[40]

One of the main initiators of the army congress on the Western front was Symon Rak-Michajloŭski, who was in many ways a typical example of a national activist. He started his career as a teacher in the Svianciany (Švenčionys) and Vilejka districts, where he collected local folklore and became involved in local politics. In 1906, he distributed revolutionary proclamations of the BSH and travelled to St. Petersburg to the State Duma in the capacity of a peasant petitioner. The Russian authorities treated him as a politically unreliable person. Later this forced him to seek higher education opportunities far away from home, in Feodosiia. Nevertheless, Rak-Michajloŭski maintained strong patriotic feelings, subscribed to *Naša Niva* and *Biełarus*, and even named his children after Rahvalod and Rahnieda (the legendary Polack ruler and his daughter who lived in the ninth century). With the start of the First World War, he was mobilized into the Russian army and sent to the Western front. Immediately after the February Revolution, Rak-Michajloŭski was active both in promoting Belarusian national schooling and in advocating for the national cause of the Belarusian army.[41]

---

38   *Biulleten' Belorusskoi Rady XII armii*, no. 1, December 18, 1917, 1.
39   NARB, f. 325, vop. 1, spr. 2, ark. 40.
40   LMAVB, RS, f. 21, b. 2077, l. 15.
41   Ales' Paškievič, "Symon Rak-Michajloŭski: staronki žyccia i dzejnasci," *Kuferak Vilenščyny* 12, no. 1 (2007): 6–7.

It is a lesser known fact that Rak-Michajloŭski was not able to supervise the organization of the Congress of Belarusian Soldiers of the Western Front personally, as he could not voluntarily leave his regiment stationed near Maladzečna. All technicalities became the responsibility of Zos'ka Vieras,[42] who was later known as the only woman present at the congress. According to her memoirs, she was treated in the same manner as any other participant.[43] Following the example set by the overwhelming majority of the congress participants, she also entered her name in the lists for future Belarusian regiments.[44]

The core of the CBVR formed on October 20, 1917, and consisted of fifteen persons. On October 24, Rak-Michajloŭski was elected as the head of the temporary Executive Committee of the CBVR, while Jazep Mamon'ka and Kanstancin Jezavitaŭ acted as his deputies. Viačaslaŭ Adamovič, Vasil' Zacharka, Ihnat Dvarčanin, and Fabian Šantyr were all counted among the notable activists of the Western front.[45] On November 25, 1917, the CBVR started publishing its own newspaper, *Belorusskaia Rada*, edited by Captain Jarušević. It promoted the All-Belarusian Congress and closely followed its proceedings.[46] The CBVR also organized separate Belarusian congresses of the Northern, South-Western, and Romanian fronts in Viciebsk, Kyiv, and Odesa, respectively, in order to consolidate

---

[42] Zos'ka Vieras (real name Ludvika Sivickaja) was known as a public figure, a writer, and a translator. During 1917 she worked for the Minsk branch of the Belarusian Society for the Aid of War Victims and the Belarusian National Committee. She was actively engaged in national politics and served as a secretary for the majority of Belarusian congresses in 1917. See I. U. Salamievič, "Vieras," in *Encyklapedyja history Bielarusi*, ed. M. V. Bič, vol. 2 (Minsk: Bielaruskaja Encyklapedyja imia Pietrusia Broŭki, 1994), 246.

[43] The contributions of women to the Belarusian national movement were recognized and valued by their contemporaries, who also noted that the amount of work in already existing national organizations prevented women from organizing women's national groups. Women in turn considered the creation of their own national organization to be a more private and less urgent matter, which could wait until better times. See A. Vilejski, "Žanočy ruch," *Bielarus'*, no. 22 (49), November 14, 1919, 1. The same attitude regarding the question of women as a part of a larger project persisted in the interwar period, when they were perceived as a part of a class in Soviet Belarus and as a part of a nation in the eyes of Belarusian activists in the Second Polish Republic. As Elena Gapova has argued, in both cases it was assumed that the success of the larger project would result in liberation for women too. See Elena Gapova, "The Woman Question and National Projects in Soviet Byelorussia and Western Belarus (1921–1939)," in *Zwischen Kriegen: Nationen, Nationalismen und Geschlechterverhältnisse in Mittel- und Osteuropa, 1918–1939*, ed. Johanna Gehmacher, Elizabeth Harvey, and Sophia Kemlein (Osnabrück: Fibre, 2004), 128.

[44] Vieras, *Ja pomniu ŭsio*, 55–56.

[45] Latyšonak, *Žaŭnery BNR*, 42, 44; Cvikievič, *Kratkii ocherk*, 8.

[46] Siamenčyk, *Hramadska-palityčnae žyccio*, 101.

support at these fronts for the CBVR as the central military organization.[47] All congresses delegated their representatives to the CBVR, which by January 1918, numbered over one hundred delegates working in Minsk, its surroundings, and on the fronts.[48]

The front congresses of Belarusian soldiers served the dual purpose of political organization along with promotion of the national cause. The latter aspect was sometimes even more distinctly expressed. According to a report from the South-Western front, many of the delegates showed up at the front congress without any previous knowledge of the Belarusian movement, while some delegates were even in opposition to it, fearing separatism.[49] Yet, the majority of them also cared deeply about the future of their homeland, and agreed that the fate of Belarus had to be decided upon by Belarusians themselves. The congress demanded Belarusian autonomy together with the organization of a Belarusian army to protect the country from chaos, while the resolutions were dominated by the theme of "Belarusian People's Power."[50]

By late October 1917, the situation became favorable to implement resolutions concerning Belarusian army units. By that time General Kipryjan Kandratovič had drafted a plan, which was to be presented to the Supreme Commander-in-Chief. However, the timing of this request was rather unfortunate, coinciding with the October Revolution.[51] The Bolsheviks were busy securing their grip on power and promptly began reorganizing the army.[52] Despite the popularity of the Decree on Peace among the soldiers, the Bolsheviks still had to assert themselves against the old Russian military command, the officer corps, and the generals at the Stavka in Mahilioŭ, who in an attempt to preserve the army, adopted a "wait-and-see" approach after the October Revolution, hoping that the Bolsheviks would not last long in power.[53]

The days of the old General Headquarters (Stavka) were numbered, when Lenin ordered the Commander-in-Chief, General Nikolai Dukhonin, to start negotiating a separate peace with the Germans. Dukhonin faced a dilemma, since by

[47] NARB, f. 325, vop. 1, spr. 21, ark. 36.
[48] Kanstancin Jezavitaŭ, "Bielaruskaja Vajskovaja Rada," *Kryvič*, no. 9, 1925, 89.
[49] "Zjezd voinaŭ-bielarusaŭ paudz.-zachod. frontu ŭ h. Kievi," *Vol'naja Bielarus'*, no. 36, December 31, 1917, 4.
[50] Ibid.
[51] NARB, f. 325, vop. 1, spr. 21, ark. 35.
[52] John Erickson, *The Soviet High Command: A Military-Political History, 1918–1941* (London: Frank Cass, 2001), 12; Sanborn, *Imperial Apocalypse*, 227.
[53] Wade, *The Russian Revolution*, 264–65.

obeying this order he would have recognized Bolshevik power, while ignoring it would have increased his unpopularity among the soldiers. The general hesitated, which only resulted in his removal from the position of Commander-in-Chief. His replacement was a former ensign, Bolshevik Nikolai Krylenko, who immediately went to Mahilioŭ to take charge of Stavka, accompanied by a group of Baltic sailors.[54] The army was split, as the Northern front and some parts of the Western front recognized the command of Krylenko, while the Romanian and South-Western fronts and other parts of the Western front still remained formally under the command of Dukhonin, who was desperately trying to retain some semblance of control over the disintegrating military structures.[55]

Under these circumstances, the issue of a future Belarusian army was not among the top priorities for either side in the Russian Revolution. Therefore, to maximize their efforts, Belarusian representatives petitioned both Dukhonin and Krylenko, seeking support for the Belarusian regiments. By that time, General Kandratovič had already developed a plan for the establishment of a Belarusian regiment in Minsk and a Belarusian Corps on the Western front, but hesitated to implement it independently. As any loyal officer would, he was still patiently waiting for an official order from Stavka.[56] In late October, a delegation from the Western front, consisting of Symon Rak-Michajloŭski, General Kandratovič, Jarušević, and Ščerba went to Mahilioŭ to see Dukhonin, who kept them waiting for a week, eventually refusing to give a conclusive and straightforward answer.[57] Distracted by the Bolshevik takeover of power, Dukhonin ignored Belarusian matters and limited his actions to allowing the formation of the First Belarusian Regiment in Minsk.[58]

A second delegation, with Kanstancin Jezavitaŭ, was sent to the Bolshevik authorities by the Congress of Belarusian Soldiers of the Northern Front. The Belarusians managed to meet Krylenko in his railway carriage in Viciebsk on November 19, 1917, while he and his sailors were en route to Mahilioŭ to advance on Stavka.[59] The Belarusian delegation requested permission for the formation of the first Belarusian regiment, and in contrast to the modest results achieved by the first delegation in negotiating with Dukhonin, this request was granted. Another

---

[54] Erickson, *The Soviet High Command*, 14–15.
[55] NARB, f. 325, vop. 1, spr. 21, ark. 35.
[56] Latyšonak, *Žaŭnery BNR*, 45; Šybeka, *Narys historyi Bielarusi*, 187.
[57] NARB, f. 325, vop. 1, spr. 21, ark. 35.
[58] Kanstancin Jezavitaŭ, "Bielaruskaja Vajskovaja Rada," *Kryvič*, no. 1 (7), 1924, 40.
[59] Latyšonak, *Žaŭnery BNR*, 46. See also Jezavitaŭ's report: NARB, f. 325, vop. 1, spr. 21, ark. 36.

request for the Belarusian Corps, following the scheme of the Polish Corps, did not meet any obstacles; however, in this instance the delegation was asked to present a detailed plan for examination and approval.[60]

By the time Krylenko arrived at Stavka, the Mahilioŭ Military-Revolutionary Committee had proclaimed itself as the highest authority in the city.[61] After Dukhonin's murder by an angry mob on November 20, the resolution on the Belarusian regiments was forwarded to the main headquarters of the Western front, which prepared a draft of the corresponding order. It had been signed by the commander of the Western front Aleksandr Miasnikov (Miasnikian) and even sent to the press to be published. However, when the Military-Revolutionary Committee of the Western Front learned about this, it urged Krylenko to withdraw his approval, whereupon the latter used this as an excuse to postpone the decision on the Belarusian regiments until the convocation of the All-Belarusian Congress. He also suspended the formation of the unit, which already numbered 350 soldiers, while his initial order was not released from the printing house.[62]

According to Kanstancin Jezavitaŭ, people from the rear and the fronts were unaware of these rapid developments and continued to arrive in Minsk in hopes of joining the national army. The CBVR managed to obtain a permit to send volunteers to one of the Minsk-based regiments (289th Reserve Infantry Regiment), cherishing the secret hope of making it a de facto Belarusian regiment, bypassing the lack of an official order.[63] After the Bolsheviks discovered the growing Belarusian presence in the 289th Reserve Infantry Regiment, they attempted to remove it from Minsk by promising the soldiers lucrative work in bread convoys.[64] As the CBVR could not apparently afford to secure the soldiers' provisions, the regiment was spread out along the railway lines connecting Minsk with Viciebsk, Smolensk, and Orel. Later it disintegrated from within, as soldiers decided to abandon the regiment and return home in the absence of a strong leadership.[65] With regard to the events of December 1917, this meant that there would be no loyal Belarusian soldiers in Minsk to guard and protect the All-Belarusian Congress.

---

60   NARB, f. 325, vop. 1, spr. 21, ark. 37.
61   A. I. Azarov, ed., *Iz istorii ustanovleniia sovetskoi vlasti v Belorussii i obrazovaniia BSSR: Dokumenty i materialy po istorii Belorussii*, vol. 4 (Minsk: Izdatel'stvo Akademii Nauk BSSR, 1954), 279.
62   NARB, f. 325, vop. 1, spr. 21, ark. 37.
63   NARB, f. 325, vop. 1, spr. 21, ark. 38.
64   NARB, f. 325, vop. 1, spr. 21, ark. 43.
65   Latyšonak, *Žaŭnery BNR*, 54.

Further attempts to organize the Belarusian army were stopped by the Bolsheviks, whose conflict with the Ukrainian Rada caused them to reconsider their position on national regiments.[66] Already by December 8, 1917, Krylenko ordered a halt in the nationalization process in the army, prohibited national congresses in the front zones, stopped the Ukrainization process, and issued an order to the Polish armed forces requiring absolute subordination.[67] In this context, it was unlikely that the CBVR delegation would have been able to achieve any progress with the Bolsheviks regarding the official permission for national units. Ivan Sierada and Kanstancin Jezavitaŭ still managed to see Krylenko, who promised them he would issue a new order for the Belarusian army and suggested establishing contact with the commander of the Western front, Miasnikov. Yet, for Jezavitaŭ, it was also evident that both Krylenko and Miasnikov were manipulating them, as he saw that in reality the Bolsheviks were using various excuses to prevent the organization of the Belarusian army.[68] For instance, when Miasnikov appointed a special commission to deal with the issue of Belarusian regiments, he deliberately chose such members who were paralyzing its work.[69]

Despite support for national units among the rank-and-file soldiers in the army, an official decision authorizing the creation of Belarusian regiments was delayed until late 1917, when political circumstances were rather unfavorable. Unfortunate timing was reinforced by the marginal influence of Belarusian political organizations on internal Russian politics, and a lack of effective leverage on the decision-making process. Moreover, the cautious actions of the Belarusian officers in charge of national units indicated that they were still reluctant to assume the responsibility of speaking in the name of a nation, failing to realize that revolutionary times required and, most importantly, justified more resolute steps.

"To All Belarusian People": The Great Belarusian Rada in Minsk

By October 1917, Belarusian national activists of various political backgrounds realized the growing dangers of being sidelined by external political forces. The idea of calling a country-wide congress was circulating in the Belarusian national milieu even in the early months of 1917, but only the political radicalization later in

---

[66] Siamenčyk, *Hramadska-palityčnae žyccio*, 89.
[67] NARB, f. 325, vop. 1, spr. 21, ark. 42.
[68] NARB, f. 325, vop. 1, spr. 21, ark. 52.
[69] NARB, f. 325, vop. 1, spr. 21, ark. 43.

the year prompted more resolute actions, initiated simultaneously by at least four different centers. Among them were the Great Belarusian Rada from Minsk, the Belarusian Oblast' Committee from Petrograd, the Belarusian People's Hramada from Moscow, and the Regional Organizational Bureau, consisting of peasants' deputies from Minsk and Vil'nia provinces and rightist teachers' unions. None of these organizations strove for cooperation—on the contrary, they all preferred to act independently in the matter of the convocation of the All-Belarusian Congress in December 1917, which resulted in misunderstandings. For instance, there was confusion concerning the dates of the Congress's opening, as two different days— December 5 and 15—were suggested and advertised.[70] On a larger scale, this was a reflection of the competition between the two centers which emerged as the leading organizers of the Congress: the Great Belarusian Rada, which represented a broad coalition of national activists in Minsk, and the Belarusian Oblast' Committee, comprised of Belarusians of the All-Russian Soviet of Peasants' Deputies in Petrograd who were West-Russist in their ideological outlook.

Belarusian national activists tried to consolidate their forces politically in the Great Belarusian Rada, created in October 1917 as an upgraded replacement for the short-lived and ineffective Central Rada of Belarusian Organizations. The latter existed briefly for several months, from July until October 1917, and only caused further structural weakening of the Belarusian movement by privileging the political views of the BSH. The emphasis on the socialist program, along with the intensification of class rhetoric to the detriment of national consolidation, alienated some of the moderate national activists. Consequently, the Central Rada was perceived as a leftist organization, which prevented it from becoming a truly unifying structure.[71] Finally, the BSH could not claim large bases of support outside of the Minsk province. Existing organizations in the Mahilioŭ and Viciebsk provinces leaned towards West-Russism and were not always enthusiastic about including the same amount of Belarusian national rhetoric in their programs as the BSH had.[72] According to Jazep Dyla, Minsk remained the only likely choice as the center of Belarusian politics, since Viciebsk apparently was "a nest of former Black Hundreds," Mahilioŭ was "sleepy," while so-called "democrats" from Homiel' almost beat up the Central Rada representative from Minsk.[73]

---

[70]   Cvikievič, *Kratkii ocherk*, 8–9; Rudovič, *Čas vybaru*, 167–68; Skalaban, "Usiebielaruski Zjezd," 68.

[71]   See Chapter 4.

[72]   Siamenčyk, *Hramadska-palityčnae žyccio*, 167.

[73]   "II-ja sesija Central'naje Rady Bielaruskich Arhanizacyj," *Vol'naja Bielarus'*, no. 26, October 26, 1917, 4.

With the internal weaknesses of the BSH, the need for a stronger, more authoritative organization able to unify and direct national mobilization efforts was obvious. A major structural change to the Central Rada was agreed upon on October 17, 1917, when a general meeting approved its transformation into the Great Belarusian Rada (*Vialikaja Bielaruskaja Rada*, VBR).[74] One of its first steps was to send some of its members, including Jazep Varonka, to Petrograd to ensure that the interests of Belarusians were represented. On October 27, the VBR issued a "Letter to the Belarusian People," signed by a broad coalition, including the CBVR, the Belarusian Executive Committee of the Western Front, the BSH, and the BNPS. The unification of Belarusians into one big family around the VBR was proclaimed to be the main goal.[75]

The VBR viewed Belarus as a single entity, consisting of Vil'nia, Viciebsk, Hrodna, Minsk, and Mahilioŭ provinces. Belarusians, regardless of their religious affiliations, were addressed as members of one nation, united by a common language and history.[76] The so-called "brotherly ties" to the Russian federative republic were not left out of the declaration, but the emphasis was clearly shifting due to the circumstances, forcing Belarusians to rely only on their own forces to protect their freedom and secure their national future.[77] The overall tone of the VBR declaration "To All Belarusian People" suggests that the new organization defined its tasks in terms of the unity of the Belarusian nation. The VBR appealed to the right of Belarusians to remain together, inseparable as a nation, and viewed the formation of the national army units as one of the indispensable guarantees of this unity. Further, it promised fair and free-of-charge redistribution of the land to the people, protection of the existing resources of the country, and a prohibition on requisitions in all of Belarus (which was especially important for the population living in the devastated regions near the front). These tasks were entrusted exclusively to the local power elected by the Belarusian people. In practical terms, this issue was to be resolved at the congress of the nation's representatives, scheduled to take place on December 5, 1917, in Minsk.[78]

---

74   *Vol'naja Bielarus'*, no. 27, October 30, 1917, 1.
75   See Prilozhenie No. 12 "Hramata da Bielaruskaho Narodu," in Turuk, *Belorusskoe dvizhenie*, 95–96; *Belorusskaia Rada*, no. 12, December 21, 1917, reprinted in "Usiebielaruski Zjezd 1917 hoda: svedčannie sučasnika," *Bielaruski histaryčny časopis*, no. 4 (1993): 51.
76   NARB, f. 325, vop. 1, spr. 2, ark. 58.
77   Prilozhenie No. 13 "Ko vsemu Narodu Belorusskomu," in Turuk, *Belorusskoe dvizhenie*, 97.
78   Ibid., 99.

On November 18, 1917, the VBR forwarded the information on the convocation of the All-Belarusian Congress to the provinces, inviting their delegates to Minsk. The creation of local Belarusian democratic power and the protection of the interests of the Belarusian people who "could and would not remain indifferent to their own fate" were defined as its main goals.[79] Instructions received by the delegates from their constituencies reflected a popular acceptance of the VBR program. For instance, the Mahilioŭ National Committee prioritized international politics, including the representation of Belarusian interests at the peace negotiations, the establishment of Belarusian autonomy, and the immediate organization of national army units in order to ensure the preservation of the remaining national wealth and guarantee the right of Belarusians to self-determination.[80] Similar moods prevailed among the Belarusians in Smolensk province, as demonstrated by the elections of the delegates to the Congress by Belarusians of the Minsk military district and the civilian Belarusian population of that province. The resolution on autonomy was adopted unanimously with only one abstention.[81]

The VBR endorsed political dialogue and cooperation with other parties, including the BNPS and the Christian Democrats, despite the continuing predominance of the BSH representatives in the Executive Committee,[82] chaired by Viačaslaŭ Adamovič, with Aliaksandr Prušynski[83] and Arkadz' Smolič as his deputies.[84] The Rada appeared to be a timely attempt to consolidate national forces, yet the balance was still fragile, as became clear at the 3rd Congress of the BSH, held from October 14 to 25, 1917. Aside from the party split, some of the members did not completely agree with the reorientation of the BSH towards a broad national platform.[85] The BSH had not yet overcome its internal crisis, since its leadership regarded the VBR to be a step in the wrong direction, leading away from a purely socialist program. In protest, Žylunovič even left the newly elected Executive Committee of the BSH.[86] All these contradictions are indicative

---

[79]   LMAVB, RS, f. 21, b. 2224, l. 1.

[80]   LMAVB, RS, f. 21, b. 2218, l. 38, 39.

[81]   LMAVB, RS, f. 21, b. 2209, l. 5.

[82]   The Executive Committee consisted of twenty-four members, the majority of whom were politically affiliated with the BSH, Christian Democrats were represented by Edvard Budz'ka, and the BNPS by Anton Liavicki and Paviel Aliaksiuk. See Michaluk, *Białoruska Republika Ludowa*, 177.

[83]   Belarusian poet Ales' Harun.

[84]   Šybeka, *Narys historyi Bielarusi*, 185.

[85]   Žylunovič, "Liuty—Kastryčnik," 193.

[86]   Ladyseŭ and Bryhadzin, *Pamiž Uschodam i Zachadam*, 42–43.

of a highly unstable situation within the national forces camp.[87] Stanislaŭ Rudovič is correct in criticizing its excessive idealization, pointing out that the Great Belarusian Rada remained a phenomenon of local politics, albeit with the potential to become a full-fledged political actor of its own under the condition of winning over to the patriotic program a considerable number of the adherents of West-Russism. However, the latter were still undecided on autonomy, as opposed to the creation of an administrative unit within the future Russian republic.[88]

Belarusian Oblast' Committee in Petrograd

A typical case of the West-Russist current was embodied by the representatives of the Belarusian peasantry in the All-Russian Soviet of Peasants' Deputies in Petrograd. Supporting closer cooperation and maintenance of links with Russia, they formed the Belarusian Oblast' Committee (*Belorusskii Oblastnoi Komitet*, BOK) in November 1917.[89] Members of the BOK are also known in the research literature as the *oblastniki*.[90] In contrast to the VBR, the *oblastniki* recognized all governing structures established by the Bolsheviks. Ideologically, they were also close to the Bolshevik leadership—the Russian Council of the People's Commissars (Sovnarkom) and the People's Commissariat for Nationalities under Stalin. These structures sympathized with the BOK and lent it financial support.[91]

Politically, this organization was built around the idea of an oblast'-level organization of the Belarusian lands with a clear pro-Russian orientation.[92] The BOK regretted that Russia let Lithuania and Ukraine go their separate ways, and expressed concern that it might be too weak to keep Belarus under its protection. The common fear, completely in line with the West-Russist worldview, was that Russia would have to give up Belarus, which would be "torn to pieces" at once.[93]

[87] In this regard the statement of Nicholas Vakar, describing the VBR, the CBVR, and the Executive Committee of the Western Front as anti-Soviet organizations which attempted "to organize national resistance" appears to be far-fetched. See Vakar, *Belorussia: The Making of a Nation*, 98.

[88] Rudovič, *Čas vybaru*, 141.

[89] Rudovič, "Zachodnierusizm va ŭmovach revalucyi 1917 hoda," 66.

[90] Another variant is the Belarusian-derived *ablasniki*. However, in this case transliteration from Russian appears more logical in order to illustrate the pro-Russian character of this organization.

[91] Anatol' Hryckievič, *Vybranaje* (Minsk: Knihazbor, 2012), 33.

[92] Turuk, *Belorusskoe dvizhenie*, 36.

[93] Prilozhenie No. 14 "Deklaratsiia Belorusskogo Oblastnogo Komiteta pri Vserossiiskom Sovete Krest'ianskikh Deputatov," in Turuk, *Belorusskoe dvizhenie*, 104.

"Monarchic Poland" was demonized as the principal danger to the Belarusian lands, threatening immediate destruction of the revolutionary achievements.[94]

According to Jazep Varonka, who was representing the VBR in Petrograd in November 1917, the *oblastniki* were shocked to learn about the establishment of the Great Rada in Minsk, as they still cherished hopes of asserting their own supremacy in Belarusian politics without any serious local competition.[95] The BOK essentially started to act as a counterweight to the VBR. Claiming that they would organize Belarusian statehood according to the wishes of the working classes, the *oblastniki* hoped to overpower the national activists in Minsk.[96] With this agenda and an emphasis on peasant interests, the BOK made clear its ambitions to determine the fate of the Belarusian territories, and emerged as a contender for leadership in the Belarusian milieu.

The missing nationalist component in the BOK rhetoric was compensated for by a deliberate and straightforward focus on class inequalities. The *oblastniki* noted the increasing influence of the VBR and the CBVR among refugees, soldiers, and workers, and thought that they were in a better position to address the peasants. Even if the BOK was mistakenly placing too much hope in the peasants, it was nevertheless well aware of the fact that the rural population tended to refrain from the political process, preferring to take a neutral stance for the time being. From another perspective, the focus of the BOK on the peasantry could also have a positive meaning, since it can be interpreted as the politicization of the nationally indifferent population through the connection of everyday economic interests to the broader issues of future state-organization.[97]

Yet, by placing their hopes on the Bolsheviks to assert domination in Belarusian politics, the *oblastniki* were unconsciously acting as tools in the hands of the new Russian authorities. While discussing the issue of the organization of power in Belarus in December 1917, the chair of the BOK, Jaŭsiej Kančar, mentioned the possibility of a Belarusian People's Soviet Republic during his negotiations with Lenin and Stalin. In response, the Bolshevik leaders admitted that they were in need of "a serious support and elimination of current defects," therefore, the BOK was promised assistance in exchange for their complete loyalty to Soviet power.[98] In other words, the *oblastniki* made a deal and agreed to ensure

[94]   Turuk, *Belorusskoe dvizhenie*, 103.
[95]   NARB, f. 325, vop. 1, spr. 2, ark. 90.
[96]   Kancher, "Iz istorii Grazhdanskoi voiny," 93.
[97]   Rudovič, *Čas vybaru*, 170–71.
[98]   Vital' Skalaban, "Jaŭsiej Kančar—palityk, historyk, memuaryst," *Bielaruskaja Dumka*, no. 1 (2010):

the deliberate weakening of the VBR, which in the eyes of the Bolsheviks was the leading bourgeois national structure in Belarus.

Several members of the BOK supported Kančar in his intentions to proclaim a Soviet republic in Belarus, but eventually they all agreed that further consultations with Lenin and Stalin were necessary.[99] Stalin, in his capacity as the Commissar of Nationalities, approved the convocation of the country-wide Belarusian congress,[100] which theoretically was in line with the Bolshevik *Declaration of the Rights of the People of Russia* issued on November 2, 1917, guaranteeing the equality of all nations and granting them the right to free self-determination and even secession from Russia.[101] However, it was implied that the Belarusian congress should not deviate from the principle of Soviet power, and ought to maintain very close ideological, economic, and cultural ties with Russia.[102] Aiming to prevent uncontrolled national self-determination, the Bolsheviks used the *oblastniki* as a convenient cover to obscure their primary objective to divide and subdue the Belarusian organizations in Minsk. Yet, they did not trust the BOK completely, despite the latter's solemn promises of loyalty. Alerted by the activities of the VBR and its attempts to establish national army units, the central government sent a telegram to the Minsk Bolsheviks urging them to "take all measures to paralyze the convocation of the Congress."[103]

The close contacts of the BOK with the Bolshevik government and the possibility of a shift of the political center away from Minsk to the east contributed to the tensions between the *oblastniki* and the VBR.[104] In his letter from Petrograd, dated November 26, 1917, Jazep Varonka warned his colleagues in the Rada—Dyla, Rak-Michajloŭski, Mucha, Prušynski, Kraskoŭski, Dvarčanin, and Mamon'ka—to be "diplomatic" in negotiations with the BOK delegates.[105] Varonka pointed to the existence of so-called "prejudiced elements" among the *oblastniki*, who were hostile to the BSH in particular, and to the Rada in general.[106]

90, citing Russian State Archive of Literature and Arts (hereafter RGALI), f. 1345, op. 5, d. 21, l. 17, l. 18.

[99] Kancher, "Iz istorii Grazhdanskoi voiny," 92.

[100] Skalaban, "Jaŭsiej Kančar," 90, citing RGALI, f. 1345, op. 5, d. 21, l. 17, l. 18.

[101] Declaration of the Rights of the People of Russia, https://www.marxists.org/history/ussr/government/1917/11/02.htm (Accessed February 10, 2015).

[102] Skalaban, "Jaŭsiej Kančar," 90, citing RGALI, f. 1345, op. 5, d. 21, l. 17, l. 18.

[103] "Bielaruski Konhres," *Bielaruski Šliach*, no. 26, April 23, 1918, 1.

[104] Ibid.

[105] NARB, f. 325, vop. 1, spr. 2, ark. 91.

[106] NARB, f. 325, vop. 1, spr. 2, ark. 90.

Another warning concerned Bolshevik hypocrisy and their far-reaching promises, including the assurances of Lunacharskii to re-open the Vil'nia university. Fully aware of Bolshevik political flexibility, Varonka noted that Stalin, who had earlier openly proclaimed guarantees for the self-determination of nations, was in no hurry to implement all his declarations in practice.[107]

The political struggle between the VBR and the BOK resulted in confusion around the dates and venues for the Congress. With the approval and financial support of the Sovnarkom, the BOK intended to hold the Congress around December 15, 1917. Kančar's memoirs indicate that the BOK vision for the All-Belarusian Congress of Soviets prioritized the unification of revolutionary soviet democracy in a single oblast' organization, a discussion of the political future of Belarus, and preparations for the autonomy of the Belarusian soviets. The venue was not firmly decided upon, as several cities were named as possibilities, among them Minsk, Rahačoŭ, Homieĺ, Sluck, and Mahilioŭ. The BOK cautiously stated that the final choice depended on the political situation.[108] It is obvious that the *oblasniki* were uncomfortable with the thought of having the Congress in Minsk, where the VBR had more influence as compared to Mahilioŭ province, with its traditionally stronger West-Russist attitudes.

The BOK lacked a consolidated, unified position regarding the future Congress, while the meeting of its members on November 11, 1917, revealed serious divisions. Eventually, a more inclusive approach prevailed, and the majority of the BOK supported the participation of the VBR and the Moscow-based Belarusian People's Hramada in the future Congress.[109] In this way, the risk of having two simultaneous congresses gave way to a fragile political balance and the possibility of dialogue. Moreover, according to the observations of Jazep Varonka, who was representing the VBR in Petrograd, some *oblastniki* who used to be hostile to the idea of Belarusian autonomy started to change their minds, reacting favorably to the resolutions of the military congresses and the VBR.[110]

Despite the general agreement of the VBR and the BOK to cooperate in the matters of organizing the All-Belarusian Congress, each side still continued attempts to enforce their own agendas. In particular, the BOK was keen on scheduling the Congress on a later date and preferred to move it away from Minsk, preferably to

---

[107]   NARB, f. 325, vop. 1, spr. 2, ark. 91.
[108]   Kancher, "Iz istorii Grazhdanskoi voiny," 92. See also Jezavitaŭ, "Pieršy Ŭsebielaruski Kanhres," 27.
[109]   Jezavitaŭ, "Pieršy Ŭsebielaruski Kanhres," 27.
[110]   NARB, f. 325, vop. 1, spr. 2, ark. 90.

Rahačoŭ,[111] while the VBR intended to start sooner and insisted on Minsk as the congress venue. Acting in the name of the VBR, Varonka and Mamon'ka conducted negotiations with the BOK on November 22 and 23, specifically pointing out that the Rada in its role as the main organizer intended to hold the congress in Minsk on December 5. While there was still some flexibility with the date, Varonka's handwritten note at the end of his letter to his colleagues in the VBR specifically urged them "not to let Minsk out of their hands."[112]

The Bolsheviks and the October Revolution in Belarus

In contrast to the February Revolution, the spread and pace of the October Revolution outside Petrograd followed a variety of patterns. Taking into account the pre-existing political situation, social structures of the major cities, presence of the military, personalities of the local leaders, and nationality conflicts, Rex Wade delineated the three most common scenarios for the Bolshevik takeover of power. In the first case, the Bolsheviks did not meet significant obstacles and were able to assert their authority quickly. This was a common occurrence in the cities, where their positions were already strong and where they did not encounter significant resistance. In the second type of scenario, the power takeover process extended over a week and was accompanied by confrontation, sometimes resulting in armed clashes. Finally, the third type extended beyond the initial consolidation of power, and involved a prolonged political struggle between the Bolsheviks and other socialist forces, which had their own interpretations of Soviet power principles. Often, this went hand in hand with the struggle for national self-determination.[113]

The revolution in Minsk combined elements of the second and third scenarios. Power consolidation of the new regime went along with the resolute establishment of pro-Bolshevik governing structures against a broad socialist coalition, while the subsequent political struggle culminated in the violent dispersal of the All-Belarusian Congress in December of 1917. As the Bolsheviks were well aware of the strategic geographical location and military importance of the Belarusian territories, they hurried to secure their positions here.

---

[111] Kancher, "Iz istorii Grazhdanskoi voiny," 92; Vasil' Zacharka, "Haloŭnyja momanty bielaruskaha ruchu," *Zapisy*, no. 24 (1999): 24–26.

[112] NARB, f. 325, vop. 1, spr. 2, ark. 91 adv.

[113] Wade, *The Russian Revolution*, 251–52, 260.

In the spring of 1917, the Minsk Bolsheviks were still a marginal group, which managed to organize a Temporary Bureau of the Bolshevik party, headed by the Armenian Aleksandr Miasnikov (Miasnikian), an ambitious newcomer to politics. His career as a Bolshevik had started only after the February Revolution, when he left his army unit stationed at the Western front and found himself in Minsk.[114] The Bolsheviks were able to increase their public presence and boost their party membership from about forty members in June 1917 to more than 28,000 in October.[115] The re-election of the Minsk Soviet in late September resulted in a Bolshevik majority for the first time with 184 deputies out of a total of 337, while other large factions included the Socialist-Revolutionaries (18%), Mensheviks (6%), the Bund (6%), and an unaffiliated faction (14%).[116] On October 25, the Executive Committee of the Minsk Soviet, chaired by the Bolshevik Karl Lander, issued Order No. 1 which announced the takeover of power in the city.[117] Bolshevik members of the Minsk Soviet formed the core of the Military-Revolutionary Committee of the Western Front, formally established on October 26.[118] Soldiers at the Western front were promptly informed of the Bolshevik decrees concerning peace and land, and asked for their support.[119]

On that same day, the non-Bolshevik members of the Minsk Soviet protested against these unilateral actions. The Executive Committee of the Western Front, the Minsk City Duma, and peasant and national organizations united together in the Committee for the Salvation of the Revolution of the Western Front. All demanded the representation of a broad leftist bloc in power.[120] At this early stage of the revolution, neither the Minsk Soviet nor the Committee for the Salvation of the Revolution was strong enough to maintain their claims to power. Both sides signed an agreement, stipulating that the committee would not send government-loyal troops from the Western front to suppress the revolution in Petrograd and to defend the Provisional Government. In exchange the Minsk Soviet recognized the authority

---

[114] Wacław Solski and S. N. Khomich, *1917 god v Zapadnoi oblasti i na Zapadnom fronte* (Minsk: Tesei, 2004), 42, 74.

[115] Lubachko, *Belorussia under Soviet Rule*, 14, 16.

[116] Stanislav Rudovich, "Rozhdenie Soveta," in V. I. Adamushko, ed., *Minskii gorodskoi Sovet deputatov: 1917–2012: Dokumenty i materialy* (Minsk: Belorusskii dom pechati, 2012), 8.

[117] Document No. 25 "Prikaz No. 1 Minskogo Soveta o perekhode vlasti v g. Minske v ruki Soveta," in Adamushko, *Minskii gorodskoi Sovet deputatov*, 37–38.

[118] Rudovich, "Rozhdenie Soveta," 8.

[119] Document No. 26 "Radiogramma Minskogo Sovet voiskam Zapadnogo fronta s prizyvom podderzhivat sovetskoe pravitel'stvo," in Adamushko, *Minskii gorodskoi Sovet deputatov*, 38.

[120] Ignatenko, *Istoriia Belorusskoi SSR*, 235; Rudovich, "Rozhdenie Soveta," 8.

of the Committee in the city.[121] While the latter attempted to maintain neutrality, it had no authority outside Minsk and could not prevent the transportation of army units to Petrograd from other fronts, which in the eyes of the Bolsheviks could have affected the terms of the agreement. The Committee also chose not to confront the Bolsheviks directly, due to their concerns of unleashing violence in the city should the Bolsheviks decide to summon to Minsk army units from the front, where they enjoyed growing popularity. In other words, the left bloc coalition admitted its own powerlessness in the belief that the crisis would soon be over and that only the Committee for the Salvation of the Revolution could emerge as a stable basis for an authoritative and qualified organ to organize power in the city.[122]

The Bolsheviks were not as patient, and had already confronted the Committee for the Salvation of the Revolution by October 27, seizing arms in Minsk and threatening to use artillery weapons against the city in response to the Committee's request to disarm.[123] A stalemate situation lasted for about a week, until November 2, when the balance of forces changed with the arrival in Minsk of pro-Bolshevik military units and an armored train from the Western front.[124] The Committee for the Salvation of the Revolution tried to prevent the train from entering the city, as even the rumors of its existence caused panic among the population. However, the Bolsheviks in the Minsk Soviet were more resolute in their actions and immediately arrested the representative of the Committee, Kolotukhin, who had tried to intervene in their plans.[125] Even though the situation in Minsk did not reach the point of open confrontation, the Bolsheviks still felt insecure, since not all army units went over to their side. On November 13, they panicked and even had to interrupt a session of the Minsk Soviet, due to the arrival in the city of a battalion of soldiers who opposed them.[126] Martial law and a curfew were declared in Minsk on November 30, 1917.[127]

After the newly elected Provincial Commissar I. Metlin[128] and his cabinet resigned on November 6, the Minsk province was deprived of a civilian administration

[121] Ignatenko, *Istoriia Belorusskoi SSR*, 236.
[122] "Minskaja Horadskaja Duma," *Vol'naja Bielarus'*, no. 29, November 14, 1917, 4.
[123] Ibid.
[124] Šybeka, *Narys historyi Bielarusi*, 186.
[125] "Minskaja Horadskaja Duma," *Vol'naja Bielarus'*, no. 29, November 14, 1917, 4.
[126] See Document No. 28 "Informatsiia v gazete 'Zvezda' o zasedanii Minskogo Soveta," in Adamushko, *Minskii gorodskoi Sovet deputatov*, 40.
[127] See *Vol'naja Bielarus'*, no. 33, December 8, 1917, 3.
[128] Metlin was infamous in the Belarusian milieu due to his derogatory comments during the First Congress of Belarusian National Organizations on March 25–27, 1917.

and was left at the mercy of the local Bolsheviks, who started to expand their own political structures.[129] The Military-Revolutionary Committee of the Western Front started to act as the highest authority both on the unoccupied Belarusian territories and at the front. Miasnikov became Commander-in-Chief of the Western front.[130] The imposition and extension of military administration structures into civilian life became a specific feature of the Bolshevik regime in Belarus. In order to legitimize their claims to power, the Bolsheviks held three large congresses between November 18 and 25 in Minsk.[131]

The Military-Revolutionary Committee of the Western Front approved the resolutions of all three pro-Bolshevik congresses and proceeded with the organization of a single power in the Western oblast'[132] and over the region of the Western front. Each of the congresses formed their own executive committees, which then merged into the Oblast' Executive Committee of the Soviets of Workers', Soldiers', and Peasants' Deputies of the Western Oblast' and Front, more commonly known as Obliskomzap.[133] It declared itself to be the major power over the whole area of the Western front as well as Minsk, Mahilioŭ, Viciebsk, and parts of Vil'nia provinces. Ironically, there was not a single Belarusian in the Presidium of the Obliskomzap.[134] Representation was skewed in favor of the Western military front. It was chaired by M. Rogozinkii, with P. Kozlov and N. Krivoshein as his deputies. In order to exercise executive power in the provinces where the Western front was located, Obliskomzap formed the Soviet of People's Commissars of the Western Oblast' and Front, led by Karl Lander. In practical terms, this meant

---

[129] "U Minsku," *Vol'naja Bielarus'*, no. 29, November 14, 1917, 4.
[130] Latyšonak, *Žaŭnery BNR*, 47.
[131] The Congress of the Soviets of the Workers' and Soldiers' Deputies of the Western Oblast', the 3rd Congress of the Peasant Deputies of Minsk and Vil'nia Provinces, and the 2nd Congress of the Armies of the Western Front. See Rudovič, *Čas vybaru*, 148; Šybeka, *Narys historyi Bielarusi*, 188.
[132] The Western oblast' as an administrative unit was established at the Congress of Soviets of Minsk, Vil'nia and Mahilioŭ provinces in June 1917 as a temporary merger of provinces in order to centralize the local Soviets' operations. After the October Revolution it included Viciebsk, Mahilioŭ, and the unoccupied parts of Vil'nia and Minsk provinces, yet its borders remained fluid and ambiguous, since Obliskomzap dedicated all its efforts towards building up its military potential to protect the revolution, instead of taking care of its territorial administration. After the majority of Belarusian lands were occupied by the German army in February 1918, the center of the Western oblast' was moved to Smolensk and included Smolensk province. In September 1918, the Western oblast' was renamed the Western Commune. It ceased to exist on January 1, 1919, due to the proclamation of the Belarusian Soviet state. See Petr Ambrosovich, "K 90-letiiu Vsebelorusskogo siezda," *Białoruskie Zeszyty Historyczne*, no. 29 (2008): 229–30.
[133] Abbreviation of the Oblastnoi Ispolnitel'nyi Komitet Sovetov Rabochikh, Soldatskikh i Krest'ianskikh Deputatov Zapadnoj Oblasti i Fronta.
[134] Ignatenko and Shtykhov, *Istoriia Belorusskoi SSR*, 239.

that front organizations representing soldiers instead of the local population were claiming power in the name of that same population.[135] The actual merger of the administrative unit of the Western oblast' with the structures of the front was a unique mix of military and civilian powers, which took hostile positions towards Belarusian self-determination, treating the demands of the national organizations as counterrevolutionary activities.[136]

These hectic activities of the Bolsheviks in establishing their own administrative structures can be regarded as a response to the efforts of the VBR and the BOK to initiate the All-Belarusian Congress. However, even in spite of the organization of the pro-Bolshevik congresses in November of 1917, Obliskomzap lacked legitimation, as it was composed primarily of military representatives of non-Belarusian origin. The Soviet of People's Commissars of the Western Oblast' and Front did not have a single department in charge of Belarusian national matters. The effective authority of the Obliskomzap also left a lot to be desired, as it extended only over the Minsk province and parts of the Vil'nia province, while Viciebsk and Mahilioŭ provinces still remained under the temporary command of local Military-Revolutionary Committees.[137]

In a similar manner, the Bolsheviks attempted to take control over the local civilian administrations. Sluck District Commissar Astroŭski, in a telegram to the VBR, outlined the common Bolshevik strategy of forcing out locals from the Sluck Soviet of Peasants' and Workers' Deputies and replacing them with loyal persons. The Bolsheviks then proceeded with a hastily organized peasant congress, apparently modeled after the larger pro-Bolshevik gathering of the peasant deputies of Minsk and Vil'nia provinces in November 1917. Events in Sluck demonstrated that the removal of political opponents along with the legitimization of the takeover of power were equally important goals for the new authorities. The local congress there was forced to approve the arrest of BSH sympathizers, while the arrival in the area of so-called "alien elements from Vologda, Viatka, and Kostroma" was to secure Bolshevik positions. As news of looting and the disruptive behavior of Bolshevik supporters came in from different localities across all of eastern Belarus,[138] Astroŭski urged the VBR to take responsibility and enter the contest for power in order to protect the country from further destruction.[139]

---

[135] I. Ihnacenka, "Kastryčnicki etap revalucyi," in *Historyja Bielarusi ŭ šasci tamach*, vol. 5, ed. Michail P. Kasciuk (Minsk: VP Ekaperspektyva, 2005), 41.

[136] Ambrosovich, "K 90-letiiu Vsebelorusskogo siezda": 231.

[137] Siamenčyk, *Hramadska-palityčnae žyccio*, 100.

[138] *Vol'naja Bielarus'*, no. 30, November 19, 1917, 4.

[139] "Poklič da Bielaruskae Rady," *Vol'naja Bielarus'*, no. 30, November 19, 1917, 4.

The Bolsheviks were not to be underestimated, as they proved able to improve their image significantly due to the progressive character of their decrees, promising people immediate peace and land redistribution.[140] An extensive campaign among the battle-weary soldiers of the Western front highlighted these aspects, resulting in an overwhelming success for the Bolshevik party in the elections to the Constituent Assembly. It managed to win around 653,000 soldiers' votes out of a total 976,000 at the Western front, while the SR party could boast only 180,000.[141] Leading in the Minsk district and in the city itself, the Bolsheviks turned out to be the second most popular party after the Jewish bloc.[142]

By contrast, the Belarusian national parties failed to achieve any success in these elections, mostly because their priorities had shifted towards the organization of the All-Belarusian Congress to the detriment of the electoral campaign for the All-Russian Constituent Assembly, which in the end damaged their public image.[143] The Belarusian parties could not even agree on the formation of electoral coalitions.[144] In this regard, the electoral strategy disagreement between the BSH and the Moscow-based Belarusian People's Hramada is one of the most telling cases, demonstrating an essential lack of trust within the Belarusian national milieu, where every center tried to achieve dominance at the cost of the others.

Relations between the Belarusian national organizations from Minsk and the People's Hramada were not as strained as with the *oblastniki* in Petrograd, but still left a lot to be desired. Edvard Budz'ka, who attended the People's Hramada meeting on November 19, 1917, reported that it recognized the VBR and was

---

[140] "Padzei apošniaho času," *Vol'naja Bielarus'*, no. 30, November 19, 1917, 1.

[141] Oliver Radkey explains the overwhelming Bolshevik popularity on the Western front as a result of its closeness to the center of the revolution in Petrograd. In contrast, SR influence increased gradually from the Western to the Southwestern, then to the Romanian, and finally to the Caucasian front, where they overpowered the Bolsheviks by a ratio of five to one. See Oliver H. Radkey, *Russia Goes to the Polls: The Election to the All-Russian Constituent Assembly, 1917* (Ithaca: Cornell University Press, 1990), 38–39.

[142] Due to high absenteeism, the total number of voters who participated in the elections to the Constituent Assembly in Minsk was 35,651, representing only about 40% of the entire population eligible to vote. The Jewish bloc emerged as the most popular party with 12,624 votes, followed by the Bolsheviks with 9,521 votes, and the Polish bloc with 4,261 votes. The SR had 977 votes and the BSH was able to win only 161 votes. See "Pa Bielarusi," *Vol'naja Bielarus'*, no. 33, December 8, 1917, 3.

[143] Rudovič, *Čas vybaru*, 164.

[144] By contrast, the Ukrainians showed more enthusiasm and consolidation by winning around five million votes using various methods, including agreements on joint lists and the formation of electoral blocs. See Radkey, *Russia Goes to the Polls*, 20.

eager to send its delegates to the All-Belarusian Congress.[145] In addition, Varonka pointed out that by that time, some of the Moscow-based activists, among them Cvikievič, Vasilevič, and Zajcaŭ, were more likely to make concessions and become cooperative partners of the VBR, but he also considered it necessary to warn his Minsk colleagues that complete trust was out of question.[146] In practice, this attitude resulted in a political failure for the Belarusian national parties during the elections to the Constituent Assembly. The People's Hramada negotiated with the Russian Socialist-Revolutionaries for the inclusion of Belarusian representatives into the SR electoral lists. After the BSH found out, it immediately accused the People's Hramada of an allegedly lenient West-Russist position and refused to form a bloc with the Hramada in the electoral campaign. Yet later, the BSH made an unsuccessful attempt to independently negotiate the same agreement with the Russian SR party.[147] It is obvious that on the eve of the All-Belarusian Congress, none of the major Belarusian political actors—the BSH in Minsk, the People's Hramada in Moscow, and the Belarusian Oblast' Committee in Petrograd— could overcome their mutual distrust. Their minor disagreements and personal squabbles weakened their appeal for a population prone to falling under the spell of Bolshevik demagogy, which promised an end to war privations and a satisfying solution to all burning social issues.

Opening of the All-Belarusian Congress

The evening of December 5, 1917 was a busy one in the Minsk city theatre. A mixed crowd of delegates from various localities and organizations, along with guests, sympathizers, and undercover provocateurs waited for the opening of the All-Belarusian Congress. At 7.30 pm, Symon Rak-Michajloŭski, the chair of the Executive Committee of the CBVR, declared on behalf of the congress organizers that 300 delegates with voting rights out of an expected total of 900 were present at the Congress.[148] Delays in the arrival of the delegates were caused by the uncoordinated actions of the VBR in Minsk and the BOK in Petrograd, as the former had invited delegates for December 5 and the latter had insisted on the date of December 15 and even sent out corresponding invitations. After

---

[145] NARB, f. 325, vop. 1, spr. 2, ark. 90 adv.
[146] NARB, f. 325, vop. 1, spr. 2, ark. 91.
[147] Rudovič, *Čas vybaru*, 163–64.
[148] "Usiebielaruski Zjezd (Ahliad)," *Vol'naja Bielarus'*, no. 36, December 31, 1917, 1.

the official opening of the Congress on December 7, the *oblastniki* were forced to conform and urged their delegates to join as soon as possible.[149]

While waiting for the arrival of the participants, Rak-Michajloŭski suggested proceeding in a conference format on December 5. Attending participants elected a temporary Council of the Congress.[150] Its composition reflected a wide representation, with twenty-three delegates from all major political organizations, including the Belarusian Oblast' Committee, the BSH, the BNPS, the Belarusian People's Hramada, the Central Belarusian Military Rada, the VBR, refugee organizations, the Soviet of the Workers' and Soldiers' Deputies, professional organizations of railway workers, teachers, and district zemstvos of Minsk, Mahilioŭ, and Viciebsk provinces, soviets of peasant deputies, municipal self-governments, and cooperatives.[151] On the same evening, the general meeting elected a temporary presidium and formed eight thematic panels. The political situation and the future of Belarus featured as key points on the agenda.[152]

While delegates of the Congress continued to arrive, the proceedings of December 6 revolved primarily around secondary technical issues of representation in the Council of the Congress, as not every group was content with its allotted numbers. In particular, peasants from Vil'nia and Hrodna provinces demanded the same representation in the Council as the peasantry from the non-occupied provinces. This proposition was supported, contrary to the indignant reaction of the many delegates who had been provoked by a similar request from Fabian Šantyr, who demanded representation for his left wing of the BSH.[153] Šantyr, known for his increasingly pro-Bolshevik leanings, was obviously not a popular figure at the Congress from the very start: when, on December 5, he demanded the right to hold a speech, most delegates voted against it. Such an attitude also hinted at the ongoing tensions within the BSH, which had arisen at its recent party congress in October 1917. Šantyr's former party colleagues tried to downplay his activities and denied the fact of a BSH split, pointing out that an expelled party

[149]   Document No. 0057 "Pratakol No. 13 pasiedžannia Rady Ŭsiebielaruskaha Zjezdu ŭ Mensku 8.12.1917," in Šupa, *Archivy Bielaruskaj Narodnaj Respubliki*, 29.
[150]   It was also known as the Council of the Elders. See protocols of the Congress from *Belorusskaia Rada*, no. 6, December 8, 1917, reprinted in *Bielaruski histaryčny časopis*, no. 1 (1993): 66–67.
[151]   Document No. 0045 "Pratakol pryvatnae narady siabroŭ Usiebielaruskaha Zjezdu ŭ Mensku 5.12.1917," in Šupa, *Archivy Bielaruskaj Narodnaj Respubliki*, 15–16.
[152]   *Belorusskaia Rada*, no. 6, December 8, 1917, 66–67.
[153]   *Belorusskaia Rada*, no. 6, December 8, 1917, 67.

member could not speak on its behalf.[154] Eventually, the Council of the Congress ruled democratically and granted representation to the left wing of the BSH.[155]

The biggest concern for the Council was the issue of the powers of the Congress, as not every delegate was present. According to the credentials commission, 383 delegates with voting rights representing both the civilian population and the army had arrived by December 6. After long debates, the Council decided to open the Congress on the next day and to send additional telegrams to the localities, asking the delegates to join the Congress as soon as possible. In particular, this concerned the BOK in Petrograd, which, as mentioned earlier, initially planned the Congress for December 15.[156] The general meeting on December 6 showed that the overwhelming majority of the delegates were in favor of the prompt opening of the Congress, except for some twenty persons who voted against. Mamon'ka from the 12th Army encouraged the Congress to establish power over Belarusian territories, pointing to the recent example of the Bolsheviks, who unscrupulously took power in Petrograd without even bothering to obtain legitimation from a country-wide congress. Cvikievič, representing Belarusian refugees in Russia, had a similar opinion and openly criticized the cynical Bolshevik understanding of self-determination. Even Šantyr, on behalf of the Belarusian Bolsheviks, spoke in favor of self-determination and a Belarusian revolution, which he contrasted with hypocritical Russian demagogy. Generally, the delegates agreed that the Congress was authorized to establish power over Belarusian territories.[157]

The formal ceremony of the opening of the All-Belarusian Congress took place in the Minsk city theatre on the evening of December 7, 1917. Rak-Michajloŭski delivered the opening speech, addressing all Belarusian people and their representatives at the Congress with a call to serve the interests of the entire nation. A military orchestra played a Belarusian version of the Marseillaise.[158]

---

[154] *Belorusskaia Rada*, no. 6, December 8, 1917, 65.

[155] Document No. 0050 "Pratakol No. 4 pasiedžannia Rady Ŭsiebielaruskaha Zjezdu ŭ Mensku 6.12.1917," in Šupa, *Archivy Bielaruskaj Narodnaj Respubliki*, 20.

[156] Document No. 0050 "Pratakol No. 4 pasiedžannia Rady Ŭsiebielaruskaha Zjezdu ŭ Mensku 6.12.1917," in Šupa, *Archivy Bielaruskaj Narodnaj Respubliki*, 20. See also "Bielaruski Konhres," *Bielaruski Šliach*, no. 26, April 23, 1918, 1.

[157] *Belorusskaia Rada*, no. 7, December 10, 1917, reprinted in "Pieršy Usiebielaruski Zjezd. Pratakoly," *Bielaruski histaryčny časopis*, no. 1 (1993): 69. See also "Usiebielaruski Zjezd (Ahliad)," *Vol'naja Bielarus'*, no. 36, December 31, 1917, 1.

[158] The song is also known under the title "Ad vieku my spali" (We Have Been Sleeping for Centuries), lyrics written by Aliaksandr Michalčyk.

The choir, dressed in national costumes, continued with a performance of revolutionary songs, which were enthusiastically received by the audience. The official part of the evening continued with a series of welcoming speeches: Aliaksiuk addressed the delegates on behalf of the VBR, followed by a number of greetings to the Congress delivered by the representatives of various fronts, refugees, teachers, parties, and professional unions.[159]

One incident, however, darkened the overall mood on the first evening, as the representative of the Latvian section of the Russian Social Democrats, Rezausskii,[160] provocatively stated that in his opinion any national divisions were useless. In an even more confrontational manner, he pointed to the Belarusian national flag hanging over the Presidium and demanded that it should be thrown out. This caused protests among all who were present in the hall, offended by such impudence. After the removal of Rezausskii from the premises, even the pro-Bolshevik Šantyr expressed his indignation at such an insulting attitude to the national aspirations of Belarusians.[161] This incident was in many ways reminiscent of the similar statement made by the Russian Socialist-Revolutionary Metlin at the first Congress of Belarusian Organizations in March 1917,[162] except that in this case the Bolsheviks had to be taken into account as more ruthless opponents. After Rezausskii was forced to leave and his covert comrades failed to disrupt the work of the Congress in the following days, the Bolsheviks most likely realized their failure to control and direct it.

Other ill omens preceding the Rezausskii incident on December 7 were the arrests of the chair of the Minsk Soviet of Peasants' Deputies, Makarjeŭ, and three Ukrainian representatives of the Front Committee,[163] which also indicated a possible Bolshevik plan of action. Kanstancin Jezavitaŭ pointed to the deliberate campaign of the Bolsheviks to breed discord among the congress delegates from the very first days. In particular, he was concerned about the weak position of the Belarusian movement among the peasants.[164] Jezavitaŭ's point

---

[159] *Belorusskaia Rada*, no. 8, December 12, 1917, reprinted in "Usiebielaruski Zjezd 1917 hoda: svedčannie sučasnika," *Bielaruski histaryčny časopis*, no. 2 (1993): 47–49.

[160] Rezausskii would later be among the Bolsheviks who commanded the dispersal of the Congress. See *Belorusskaia Rada*, no.1, January 13, 1918; LMAVB, RS, f. 21, b. 2283, l. 95.

[161] Document No. 0065 "Pratakol No. 12 adkryccia pasiedžannia Ŭsiebielaruskaha Zjezdu ŭ Mensku 7.12.1917," in Šupa, *Archivy Bielaruskaj Narodnaj Respubliki*, 27.

[162] See Chapter 2.

[163] Document No. 0065 "Pratakol No. 12 adkryccia pasiedžannia Ŭsiebielaruskaha Zjezdu ŭ Mensku 7.12.1917," in Šupa, *Archivy Bielaruskaj Narodnaj Respubliki*, 26, 28.

[164] NARB, f. 325, vop. 1, spr. 6, ark. 14, 15.

about the insufficient political experience of the broader population was proved by a representative of the Mahilioŭ province peasantry, who noted the following: "Bolsheviks are bullied here. There should not be any parties and splits. We will support everyone."[165]

Presumably, this statement could also refer to the need to achieve unity among the delegates, especially considering that a group of *oblastniki* represented an internal obstacle to the work of the Congress. As the Congress continued, and the temporary Council was replaced by a full Presidium, the *oblastniki* were joined by some similarly minded delegates from the Mahilioŭ province, who protested against the election of the Presidium, as apparently they were concerned about being underrepresented at the Congress. Nevertheless, a permanent Presidium of the Congress was elected on December 9 by the two largest factions at the Congress: the leftist group and the socialist bloc. The latter also incorporated the unaffiliated delegates. Both factions were comparable in size, as 169 votes were submitted for Presidium candidates from the list of the left faction, while the socialist list won 173 votes. The Presidium was chaired by Rak-Michajloŭski and consisted of eight persons. In addition, each province was allowed to have one representative, thus raising the number of Presidium members to thirteen.[166]

By December 14, it became clear that disagreements between various groupings and factions at the Congress were increasing. Jazep Dyla hinted at the ongoing attempts of the Bolsheviks to disrupt the Congress and noted the special position of the BOK members, who were not popular among the delegates.[167] According to the memoirs of the congress participant Vasil' Zacharka,[168] representatives of the BOK divided their activities between engaging in "awful demagogical agitation against the national organizations and their leaders" and covertly trying to win over the unaffiliated delegates to attain the leadership role in the Congress. Seeing the dissatisfaction among the delegates due to the

---

[165] *Belorusskaia Rada*, no. 7, December 10, 1917, reprinted in "Usiebielaruski Zjezd 1917 hoda: svedčannie sučasnika," *Bielaruski histaryčny časopis*, no. 2 (1993): 51.

[166] *Belorusskaia Rada*, no. 8, December 12, 1917, reprinted in ibid., 51–52; Document No. 0063 "Pratakol No. 18 ahul'naha pasiedžannia Ŭsiebielaruskaha Zjezdu ŭ Mensku 9.12.1917," in Šupa, *Archivy Bielaruskaj Narodnaj Respubliki*, 34–35.

[167] *Belorusskaia Rada*, no. 10, December 16, 1917, reprinted in "Usiebielaruski Zjezd 1917 hoda: svedčannie sučasnika," *Bielaruski histaryčny časopis*, no. 3 (1993): 63.

[168] In 1918, Vasil' Zacharka worked for the government of the Belarusian Democratic Republic. After the First World War was over, he emigrated to Prague and in 1928 became the president of the Council of the Belarusian Democratic Republic in Exile, serving in this capacity until 1943. See Zaprudnik, *Historical Dictionary of Belarus*, 316.

prolonged debates, representatives of the Belarusian Military Rada threatened the most disruptive *oblastniki* with arrest and refused to allow the Bolsheviks from Obliskomzap access to the Congress meetings.[169]

In order to avoid further political splits, representatives of all groups and factions approved structural changes to the Presidium, which was to be assigned more technical functions, instead of serving as a representation of separate groups. It was to be incorporated in full into the revived Council of the Congress, now designed as a broader representation of all factions.[170] Ivan Sierada[171] was elected as the new chair of the Congress Presidium, while Aliaksandr Vazila[172] and Aliaksandr Prušynski served as his deputies. The approved membership of the Council of the Congress consisted of the representatives from twenty-seven different groups, including political organizations, parties, councils of peasants' and soldiers' deputies, city municipalities, districts, land committees, cooperatives, professional unions, and fronts.[173]

Self-Determination Debates in the Congress

The Congress worked in separate sections, responsible for political, national, agrarian, financial, social, and cultural issues, as well as for setting up a local administration and a national army.[174] Overall, twelve sections were formed, each of which was divided

---

[169]   Zacharka, "Haloŭnyja momanty bielaruskaha ruchu," 25–26.

[170]   *Belorusskaia Rada*, no. 10, December 16, 1917, reprinted in "Usiebielaruski Zjezd 1917 hoda: svedčannie sučasnika," *Bielaruski histaryčny časopis*, no. 3 (1993): 63.

[171]   Ivan (Janka) Sierada, member of the BSH, in 1917 and 1918 chaired the Presidium of the All-Belarusian Congress and the Rada of the Belarusian Democratic Republic (BDR), respectively, and in 1919–1920 was a member of the Supreme Rada of the BDR. He decided to remain in Soviet Belarus in the 1920s, choosing an academic career in veterinary sciences and agriculture. Sierada was arrested in 1930 on charges of belonging to the "Union for the Liberation of Belarus," and sent to Siberia. His fate after 1943 remains unknown. See Jurka Vasileŭski, "Sierada," in *Encyklapedyja historyi Bielarusi*, ed. M. V. Bič, vol. 6 (Minsk: Bielaruskaja Encyklapedyja imia Pietrusia Broŭki, 2001), 291.

[172]   Aliaksandr Vazila was also known under the pseudonyms Alek De-Vazilini, Klim Zlobič, Praŭdaliub, and Anton Chatynia. A native of Mahilioŭ province, in 1917, Vazila was a convinced Social Democrat. Despite abandoning political activities after 1918, he was persecuted by the Soviet authorities and his fate remains unknown. See V. U. Skalaban, "Vazila," in *Encyklapedyja historyi Bielarusi*, ed. M. V. Bič, vol. 2 (Minsk: Bielaruskaja Encyklapedyja imia Pietrusia Broŭki, 1994), 185.

[173]   *Belorusskaia Rada*, no. 10, December 16, 1917, reprinted in "Usiebielaruski Zjezd 1917 hoda: svedčannie sučasnika," *Bielaruski histaryčny časopis*, no. 3 (1993): 65.

[174]   Document No. 0049 "Pratakol No. 5 pryvatnae narady siabroŭ Usiebielaruskaha Zjezdu ŭ

into special commissions to deal with separate problems. With ten different sub-commissions, the section on education and culture was one of the most numerous at the Congress, reflecting the need to advocate for the national cause. The Belarusian state-building section was also popular and usually attracted a lot of attention from all factions of the Congress. All section sessions were open, i.e., every member of the Congress who wanted to make a contribution could participate in their work. Some sessions gathered big audiences of several hundred delegates, thus also serving educational and national mobilization purposes[175] and repeating the patterns of the army and refugee congresses held earlier in 1917.

The general meeting on December 12 attempted to sum up the preliminary results of the Congress. The international situation, in particular, the possible repercussions of the planned peace negotiations in Brest-Litovsk, emerged as an area of common concern. Varonka addressed the issue of maintaining the territorial integrity of Belarus, hinting at the danger of a Lithuanian takeover of the Vil'nia and Hrodna provinces. Professor Jaŭchim Karski shared the same concerns and pointed out that the demographic situation was disadvantageous for the Belarusians in those areas due to the high numbers of refugees who had left en masse in 1915. Assuming that Germany could force the remaining population to recognize Lithuanian authority, Karski urged the Congress to make inquiries with Trotsky concerning the matter of peace negotiations. In response, Cvikievič pessimistically noted that the Bolsheviks did not take Belarusians into account, admitting that the question of a Belarusian presence at the peace negotiations could be resolved only by Germany, which he did not consider possible.[176]

This was a realistic evaluation, as German foreign policy in Eastern Europe was oriented first and foremost toward the expansion of German influence in the region, prioritizing strategic military interests and the exploitation of resources. It was to be achieved indirectly, through supporting select national movements and their aspirations for statehood, rather than by means of a straightforward conquest. Using its image as the protector of the rights of the oppressed nationalities,[177] along with a skillful manipulation of the concept of self-determination, Germany

---

Mensku 6.12.1917," in Šupa, *Archivy Bielaruskaj Narodnaj Respubliki*, 18–19.

[175] Jezavitaŭ, "Pieršy Ŭsiebielaruski Kanhres," 27.

[176] *Belorusskaia Rada*, no. 9, December 14, 1917, reprinted in "Usiebielaruski Zjezd 1917 hoda: svedčannie sučasnika," *Bielaruski histaryčny časopis*, no. 3 (1993): 62.

[177] On the evolution of German interpretations of occupation and new forms of control throughout the First World War, see Jonathan E. Gumz, "Losing Control: The Norm of Occupation in Eastern Europe during the First World War," in Böhler et al., *Legacies of Violence*, 83.

intended to weaken the Russian state as much as possible. This attitude explained the increased German support for Lithuanian state-building ambitions starting in early 1917. Yet, Belarus did not feature in any of the German plans for the East.[178] In practical terms, the support of Belarusians did not offer Germans anything useful in return. The invisibility of Belarusian national aspirations at the start of the First World War, especially when contrasted against Polish or Lithuanian ambitions, predetermined the attitudes of the Germans, who saw that in terms of resources and influence they did not gain anything from providing support to the Belarusians.[179]

The Bolsheviks were even less delicate in obscuring their intentions, as in practice they did not display any semblance of respect for their progressive slogans in regard to the rights of nationalities. Rather, they appropriated the right of representing all the peoples of Russia at the negotiations in Brest-Litovsk, signing an armistice with Germany on December 15, 1917. By refusing to allow the Ukrainian delegation to cross over the front line to reach Brest in time to join the negotiations, the Bolshevik government blatantly ignored its own assurances of national self-determination. Notably, compared to the Belarusian case, Ukraine at that time demonstrated more progress on the path towards establishing its own statehood, as the Ukrainian National Republic had already been declared on November 20, 1917, in the Third Universal.[180] Apparently, being aware of the developments in Ukraine, delegate Sušynski boldly suggested to the All-Belarusian Congress to proclaim a Belarusian Republic immediately and enter the peace negotiations in the capacity of a subject of international politics. Some delegates expressed enthusiasm at this possibility, but the voting revealed that the majority was more reserved in their expectations. They agreed only on authorizing the Presidium to establish contact with Trotsky. Depending on the outcome of this mission, delegates were then to be sent to Petrograd and to the peace talks.[181]

The issue of Belarusian self-determination featured prominently in Jazep Varonka's speech to the Congress. He stressed the leading role of the VBR in protecting the interests of the Belarusian people, noting that the BSH

---

[178] Joachim Tauber, "German Eastern Policy, 1917–1918," *Lithuanian Historical Studies* 13 (January 2008), 72.

[179] By contrast, in early 1918, German foreign policy focused on the economic potential of Ukraine, contemplating to sponsor the "creation" of a Ukrainian state. See Grelka, *Die ukrainische Nationalbewegung*, 80.

[180] Horak, *The First Treaty of World War I*, 30–31.

[181] *Belorusskaia Rada*, no. 9, December 14, 1917, reprinted in "Usiebielaruski Zjezd 1917 hoda: svedčannie sučasnika," *Bielaruski histaryčny časopis*, no. 3 (1993): 62.

representatives voiced these intentions on August 17 in Moscow, and later reiterated them at the All-Russian Democratic Conference on September 17 in Petrograd. In both instances, these requests were typical for 1917, and were limited to an autonomous solution for Belarus within a Russian federative democratic republic which was to guarantee the rights of minority nationalities. Nevertheless, the Russian Provisional Government ignored these demands completely, while the similar but more resolute statements of Ukrainian representatives were met with direct protests by Kerensky.[182]

Varonka stressed the consistent efforts of the VBR in advocating for the interests of Belarusians, despite the lack of funds for organizing a broad campaign. Contrasting this to the BOK, a latecomer on the Belarusian political scene, he reminded the delegates to prioritize the tasks of local power organization and to formulate clear positions regarding the peace negotiations, the redistribution of land, and the occupation of Belarusian territories. The power of the people's commissars in Petrograd was to be recognized only if it did not contradict Belarusian self-determination intentions.[183] An editorial in *Vol'naja Bielarus'* concurred with Varonka, stating that the Bolshevik government was rapidly losing its credibility by instigating unnecessary social unrest. It noted that this internal matter of Russian politics became a concern for Belarusians as soon as the Bolsheviks started to use Belarusian territories in their trade for peace. The newspaper protested against the possible division of Belarus and "resolutely warned" that this would not be tolerated.[184]

The West-Russist group of *oblastniki* and their sympathizers at the Congress were more reserved, but the positions of some of them underwent a slight evolution. This can be traced back to the statement made by their leader Kančar on December 15. On behalf of the BOK he recognized the "Petrograd authority of the commissars," but stressed that once local Belarusian power was established, it would be recognized as well.[185] Kančar admitted that the Belarusian Bolsheviks experienced a turning point and started to follow their nation. In a manner typical of the BOK, he still exaggerated the threat of "imperialist Poles," but at the same time, most likely having the Minsk Bolsheviks in mind, he also criticized the "Bolshevik autocracy" which ruled by a "whip."[186] The leader of the *oblastniki*

---

[182]   *Belorusskaia Rada*, no. 12, December 21, 1917, 51.

[183]   *Belorusskaia Rada*, no. 12, December 21, 1917, 51–52.

[184]   *Vol'naja Bielarus'*, no. 35, December 21, 1917, 1.

[185]   *Belorusskaia Rada*, no. 12, December 21, 1917, 51.

[186]   *Belorusskaia Rada*, no. 11, December 17, 1917, reprinted in "Usiebielaruski Zjezd 1917 hoda: svedčannie sučasnika," *Bielaruski histaryčny časopis*, no. 3 (1993): 67–68.

expressed his disappointment in the revolution, as in his opinion it was assuming a chaotic character. Hinting at the problematic legitimacy of the Obliskomzap, Kančar noted that Belarus had its own Bolsheviks as opposed to non-local strangers. He called on the delegates to stop all internal party struggles, as the only question of importance at the Congress, the same as at the peace negotiations, was "to be or not to be" for Belarus.[187] Yet, in Kančar's interpretation, it also had to be without any "collaboration with the bourgeoisie."[188]

Still, the Petrograd Belarusians continued to slow down the work of the Congress. During the general meeting on December 16, when the Congress had already been in session for ten days, a certain Jafremaŭ suggested to return again to the question about its goals and tasks. The *oblastnik* Vazila, speaking on behalf of the Mahilioŭ province, added that the Congress was not authorized to solve the issue of organizing power in Belarus and that other congresses would be required in the future.[189] These statements provoked a large discussion in response. Burbis of the BSH reminded the delegates that they had gathered for the Congress with the clear aim to "build a better future for the Belarusian people. Those who tell us that we do not need power are blurring our vision."[190] In regard to Vazila's comments, Mamon'ka from the 12th Army bitterly noted that doubts about the competences and authority of the Congress expressed by the Presidium deputy chair, rather than an ordinary delegate, were especially disappointing. Greeted with applause by the audience, Aliaksiuk, on behalf of the CBVR, asked for the support of the "revolutionary democratic power."[191]

Delegates from the military section of the Congress were particularly offended by Vazila's suggestion to take time and postpone important decisions. Pointing to the intrigues and internal struggle that had marked the Congress since its very first days, they equated all delays with sabotage and called for the resolute actions of "real revolutionaries." In his disappointment, Jezavitaŭ even referred to the delegates who played down the issue of self-determination as "black sheep." This provoked the Mahilioŭ group to demand Jezavitaŭ's exclusion from the Congress, yet the incident was over after voting revealed that they were outnumbered: 170 delegates supported Jezavitaŭ, while 90 delegates voted for his exclusion.[192]

---

[187]　*Belorusskaia Rada*, no. 11, December 17, 1917, 68.
[188]　*Belorusskaia Rada*, no. 12, December 21, 1917, 52.
[189]　*Belorusskaia Rada*, no. 12, December 21, 1917, 52.
[190]　*Belorusskaia Rada*, no. 12, December 21, 1917, 53.
[191]　*Belorusskaia Rada*, no. 12, December 21, 1917, 53.
[192]　*Belorusskaia Rada*, no. 12, December 21, 1917, 53.

However, these numbers are significant as they show that the *oblastniki* were not a marginal group and enjoyed some support among the delegates.

The issue of the organization of power was picked up soon thereafter by another BOK member, Selivanaŭ, who expressed his distrust of the Minsk-based national organizations and continued stressing the internal divisions of the Congress. This provoked another series of passionate and patriotic responses. For instance, Kachanovič, speaking on behalf of the Mahilioŭ province teachers, also regretted the lack of unity at the Congress, but urged the delegates to act without delay, pointing out that otherwise Germany or Polish legions would decide the fate of Belarus. In Falski's opinion, the situation in Belarus required the Congress to take over responsibility for the country, and he considered it to be fully authorized to do so. Kascevič dismissed as an intrigue the question of whether the Congress was competent enough to decide on a state structure. Delegates from Hrodna province added that they were sent to Minsk not to discuss such insignificant issues as the competencies of the Congress, but to determine the fate of Belarus, establish democratic rule, send a delegation to the peace conference, decide on the formation of a national army, and instigate the immediate transfer of land to the people.[193]

The debates on December 16 were summed up by a socialist faction resolution, which essentially followed the opinion of the majority: delays were considered counterproductive. Obviously, the delegates were also unsure whether they would be able to organize another congress. It was suggested to follow the example of Ukraine, which had not even had such a representative gathering, yet had managed to get international recognition. However, according to the protocols, at this moment the meeting suddenly switched over to a discussion of the refugee issue. The debates on self-determination continued the next day.[194]

Dispersal of the Congress

The delegates were aware of the persistent danger of the Congress's dissolution. Jezavitaŭ specifically noted that it had struggled for its existence since the very first day.[195] Vasil' Zacharka pointed out that the activities of the BOK members along with the Bolsheviks from the Obliskomzap caused discord and confusion among the delegates. In addition to the destabilizing internal disagreements and conflicts,

---

[193] *Belorusskaia Rada*, no. 12, December 21, 1917, 54.
[194] *Belorusskaia Rada*, no. 12, December 21, 1917, 55.
[195] NARB, f. 325, vop. 1, spr. 6, ark. 14, 15.

Belarusian national organizations failed to find in their ranks a person with good managerial and leaderships skills to direct and guide the work of the Congress, as demonstrated by the constant re-elections to the chair of the Congress.[196]

Without knowing that it would be the last day of the Congress, the unsuspecting delegates met again on the morning of December 17 in the hall of the Belarusian National House (formerly the Minsk Nobility Association building), resuming the discussion on the goals and tasks of the Congress. An unnamed delegate from Mahilioŭ province expressed his disagreement with Kachanovič (both of them represented the teachers of that province), declaring that it was not yet time to create a republic. He recognized as competencies of the Congress only the ability to set up a local power of soldiers', workers', and peasants' deputies as an *oblast'*-level authority.[197] The military representatives, including war invalids, as well as the delegates from Vil'nia and Hrodna provinces, continued to make straightforward demands for declaring a democratic republic, albeit still as a part of a future federation with the democratic Russian republic. The Mahilioŭ group and the *oblastniki* loudly protested against the inclusion of this item in the resolution. During a break in the meeting, it was discovered that one of the delegates had fake credentials and everyone else had to undergo the procedure of mandate verification, thus terminating the debates.[198]

The meeting resumed at about 1:00 a.m. on December 18, with a reading of the resolution adopted the previous evening by the general meeting of the Congress. Its first point stated the following:

> Exercising the right to self-determination, declared by the Russian Revolution, and approving democratic republican governance within the boundaries of Belarusian territories in order to save the homeland and to prevent its division and the possibility of separation from the Russian democratic federative republic, the First All-Belarusian Congress decides to form out of its ranks the organ of local power—the All-Belarusian Council of Peasants', Soldiers', and Workers' Deputies, which is temporarily to act as the highest power in the country, entering into relations with the central power, which is responsible to the Soviet of the Workers', Soldiers', and Peasants' Deputies.[199]

The entire resolution consisted of fifteen points. Further provisions stipulated that the new organ of power was designed to implement decisions and resolutions of the Congress with the authorization to prepare the Belarusian Constituent

---

[196] Zacharka, "Haloŭnyja momanty bielaruskaha ruchu," 26.
[197] *Belorusskaia Rada*, no. 12, December 21, 1917, 55–56.
[198] *Belorusskaia Rada*, no. 12, December 21, 1917, 56–57.
[199] *Belorusskaia Rada*, no. 12, December 21, 1917, 57.

Assembly, which was to decide the future of the country. In order to strengthen its authority, the new Council was to start with the formation of Belarusian army units immediately. Representatives of the Belarusian provisional power were to be sent to the peace negotiations to defend the interests of a united and indivisible Belarus.[200]

The resolution makes it clear that the Congress was establishing a new Belarusian organ of power to replace the Bolshevik-controlled Obliskomzap. Despite the statements of some delegates calling for a proclamation of a republic, the document appears to be very moderate in character and does not hint at a declaration of independence. On the contrary, just as the *oblastniki* intended, the final decision was delayed until the national Constituent Assembly that was to determine the future of the Belarusian republic. It demonstrates that Belarusian activists were assuming responsibility for the future of their country, but had to take into account the opinions of more conservative groups within the Congress. The adoption of a consensus resolution reflected a point on which everyone agreed, namely, that the Belarusian people themselves had the right to decide the fate of their country, rather than the Bolshevik military authorities. Further, the proposed decision on the national army units signaled that the Congress was moving on a course towards establishing statehood. This might explain why the report from *Vol'naja Bielarus'* provided an emotional description of the Congress dissolution as an interrupted proclamation of a republic.[201]

The resolution of December 17 was the last official document of the Congress, as at around 2:00 a.m. on December 18 its work was interrupted by two representatives of the Obliskomzap, Krivoshein[202] and Rezausskii, who introduced themselves

---

[200] *Belorusskaia Rada*, no. 12, December 21, 1917, 57.

[201] "Razhon Usiebielaruskaha Zjezdu," *Vol'naja Bielarus'*, no. 36, December 31, 1931, 2.

[202] Nikolai Krivoshein (1885–1936)—not to be confused with his namesake, another Nikolai Krivoshein, who in the 1920s was a member of the illegal anti-Soviet military organization *Zialiony Dub*, which led a guerilla war against the Bolsheviks on Belarusian territories. The Bolshevik Nikolai Krivoshein, notoriously known as one of the chief figures in the dispersion of the All-Belarusian Congress, had served on the Western front since the start of the First World War. In 1917, he became a member of the Military-Revolutionary Committee of the Western Front in Minsk and chaired the Executive Committee of the pro-Bolshevik gathering of the peasant deputies of Minsk and Vil'nia provinces in November. In December 1918, he became the garrison commander in Minsk. In 1936, Krivoshein wrote his memoirs in which he positioned himself in the main role during the establishment of Soviet power in Belarus. He was immediately accused of counterrevolutionary activities and sentenced to death. See Sergei Krapivin, "Provokatory i pogromshchiki dekabria 1917-go," *Narodnaja Volia*, December 30, 2010, http://www.nv-online.info/by/140/printed/25693 (Accessed August 19, 2015). The Bolshevik Nikolai Krivoshein is

as "garrison commander" and "commissar of the Western oblast," respectively. They were accompanied by the commander of the First Revolutionary Regiment of the Minsk Soviet, Remnev, and armed soldiers.[203] Denying the request made by the chair of the Congress, Sierada, to present their credentials, the Bolsheviks declared that the building was surrounded by the military. While Hryb was trying to resolve the issue with these unexpected arrivals, the delegates proceeded to vote on the resolution. The first point was supported unanimously, yet the voting procedure on the remaining parts of the resolution was again interrupted by Krivoshein. Having his identity finally confirmed by two delegates, he demanded a time slot for an urgent statement. Krivoshein's rambling speech made it at once clear to everyone that he was drunk. Eventually, his comrade Rezausskii cut him short, declaring that the Congress was closed. Armed soldiers were ordered to arrest the entire Presidium of the Congress and remove it from the building.[204] According to the memoirs of the Bolshevik Knorin, they acted on orders received from Miasnikov, who was the most resolute among the Minsk Bolshevik leaders in his opposition to the All-Belarusian Congress.[205]

Delegates present at the meeting reacted to these developments with a burst of indignation. Even the pro-Bolshevik members of the Congress considered the actions of Krivoshein and Rezausskii to be illegal, violating the interests of the Belarusian people. In response, the Congress quickly proceeded with the election of a second Presidium, which managed only to adopt a protest resolution, while ensconced behind barricades made of furniture, before being arrested as well. The Congress was powerless against the Bolsheviks, as it did not have any guards to protect itself. National army units had not been formed and loyal soldiers were absent from Minsk. The only instance of active resistance occurred when the drunken Krivoshein tried to force Zinaida Jurjeva, a delegate from the BOK and a member of the newly elected second Presidium, to join him for a ride in a car. Apparently, Jurjeva either beat him up or threatened to shoot him.[206]

---

also not to be confused with the Soviet General Semion Krivoshein (1899–1978) who along with Heinz Guderian participated in the joint Soviet-German military parade in 1941 in Brest.

[203] Makar Kraŭcoŭ, "Razhon. Uspamin," *Bielaruskae žyccio*, March 18, 1920.

[204] *Belorusskaia Rada*, no. 12, December 21, 1917, 58; "Razhon Usiebielaruskaha Zjezdu," *Vol'naja Bielarus'*, no. 36, December 31, 1917, 2.

[205] NARB, f. 35, vop. 1, spr. 71, ark. 20, reprinted in V. D. Selemenev, ed., *1 ianvariia 1919 goda: vremennoe raboche-krest'ianskoe sovetskoe pravitel'stvo Belorussii: dokumenty i materialy* (Minsk: Limarius, 2005), 231.

[206] Skalaban, "Usiebielaruski Zjezd," 69; Makar Kraŭcoŭ, "Razhon: Uspamin," *Bielaruskae žyccio*, March 18, 1920.

The remaining delegates followed their arrested colleagues, accompanying their departure with revolutionary songs and a funeral march. Cavalry with machine-guns were waiting outside to escort each group of delegates to their houses. Some marched along Padhornaja Street to the building of the Commercial School, where the headquarters of the Council of the People's Commissars were located and where the arrested were transported.[207] By 5:00 a.m. on December 18, 1917, the All-Belarusian Congress had been dissolved.[208] The next day, a detachment of soldiers from the regiment of the Minsk Soviet under the command of Remnev raided the offices of the VBR, CBVR, BSH, and Belarusian cultural organizations, detaining the members of the Military Rada.[209]

Delegates of the Congress attempted to continue working underground. They gathered on December 18 to protest the violence, condemning the "false socialists" led by Krivoshein and demanding true national self-determination. They called for the establishment of a "Belarusian Democratic Republic within the boundaries of a Russian federation."[210] The Council of the Congress was acknowledged as an executive organ of the Congress, entrusted with the task of implementing all its decisions. It replaced all national organizations, including the BOK, VBR, and others. The CBVR was preserved as a subordinate organ of the Council, which declared the convocation of a second All-Belarusian Congress to be its chief priority.[211] The Council met on December 20 to elect an Executive Committee of seventeen members, which was later expanded by the inclusion of the representatives of the national minorities and the CBVR. However, they had trouble coordinating their activities and even in maintaining effective communication links between all of its members in the underground.[212]

---

[207] Padhornaja is currently Karl Marx Street in central Minsk. The Commercial School was located in the area of the current main campus of the Belarusian State University. See Zachar Šybeka, *Minsk sto hadoŭ tamu* (Minsk: Bielarus', 2007), 288, 290.

[208] *Belorusskaia Rada*, no. 12, December 21, 1917, 59; Vieras, *Ja pomniu ŭsio*, 61.

[209] *Belorusskaia Rada*, no. 12, December 21, 1917, 60.

[210] *Belorusskaia Rada*, no. 1, January 13, 1918, reprinted in "Usiebielaruski Zjezd 1917 hoda: svedčannie sučasnika," *Bielaruski histaryčny časopis*, no. 4 (1993): 61.

[211] Ibid., 60.

[212] NARB, f. 325, vop. 1, spr. 21, ark. 86; NARB, f. 567, vop. 1, spr. 11, ark. 3.

Statistics and Representation

Both memoirs of the participants and historical research generally agree that the total number of delegates at the First All-Belarusian Congress tallied 1872, out of whom 1167 had voting rights, while the remaining 705 had consultation rights.[213] Recently, it has been suggested that these numbers should be regarded with more skepticism, based on the assumption that all of these people could not have physically fit into the building of the Minsk city theatre.[214] These doubts appear to be ungrounded, as the theatre was not the only place where the Congress convened. Due to the large numbers of delegates, some meetings were moved to the halls of the Minsk Nobility Association, located across the street from the theatre.[215] On December 10, the Congress decided to requisition the building, declaring it to be national property.[216]

The violent dissolution of the Congress by the Bolsheviks prevented the delegates from completing their work, but there are no reasons for historians to deny their presence in Minsk and suggest that their numbers were inflated to benefit a "nationalist mythology."[217] Furthermore, this statement is not corroborated by the available statistical data, collected by the credentials commission of the All-Belarusian Congress, which was in charge of issuing the mandates for the delegates and keeping records on the social and political profiles of the participants. These materials had already been analyzed by Piotra Krečeŭski in early 1918 in a report of the Congress, published in the first issue of *Belorusskaia Rada* in 1918. However, most issues of this newspaper could not reach the readers, as they were destroyed on the orders of the printing facility administration shortly after being printed. Consequently, this analysis was published again later in the spring of 1918 by *Bielaruski Šliach*.[218]

---

[213] Cvikievič, *Kratkii ocherk*, 9; Turuk, *Belorusskoe dvizhenie*, 38; Siamenčyk, *Hramadska-palityčnae žyccio*, 106; Šybeka, *Narys historyi Bielarusi*, 190; M. V. Doŭnar-Zapoľski, *Historyja Bielarusi* (Minsk: Bielaruskaja encyklapedyja imia P. Broŭki, 1994), 479; I. Ihnacenka, "Nacyjanaľny ruch. Usiebielaruski Zjezd i jaho razhon," in *Historyja Bielarusi ŭ šasci tamach*, vol. 5, ed. Michail P. Kasciuk (Minsk: VP Ekaperspektyva, 2005), 92.

[214] See endnote 47, Rudling, *The Rise and Fall of Belarusian Nationalism*, 339.

[215] *Belorusskaia Rada*, no. 8, December 12, 1917, reprinted in "Usiebielaruski Zjezd 1917 hoda: svedčannie sučasnika," *Bielaruski histaryčny časopis*, no. 2 (1993): 51. The Minsk Nobility Association building was located on the corner of Padhornaja and Petrapaŭlaŭskaja streets, currently the corner of Marx and Engels streets. The building was not preserved. See Šybeka, *Minsk sto hadoŭ tamu*, 201.

[216] Document No. 0064 "Pratakol no. 19 ahuľnaha pasiedžannia Usiebielaruskaha Zjezdu ŭ Mensku 10.12.1917," in Šupa, *Archivy Bielaruskaj Narodnaj Respubliki*, 36.

[217] Endnote 47, Rudling, *The Rise and Fall of Belarusian Nationalism*, 339.

[218] Skalaban, "Usiebielaruski Zjezd," 70. See also "Bielaruski Konhres," *Bielaruski Šliach*, no. 25,

Krečeŭski's report explicitly stated that in the period from December 5 to 17, 1917, the credentials commission issued 1167 mandates for delegates with voting rights, and 705 mandates for those with consultative rights. Out of this number, civilians received 812 mandates with voting rights and 344 mandates with consultative rights, while military representatives had 355 and 361 mandates, respectively. Delegates from districts, zemstvos, and cities had 445 mandates with voting rights, while socialist parties and professional and political organizations were represented by 367 delegates qualified to vote. Krečeŭski explained the considerable number of mandates without voting rights by the insufficient information about the Congress in the provincial organizations, as some of them failed to provide their delegates with adequate credentials in order to receive full mandates.[219]

An analysis of the social and political profiles of the congress delegates was based on a representative sample of 357 preserved questionnaires. The remaining documentation was destroyed by the Bolsheviks during the dispersal of the Military Rada. Furthermore, not all of the questionnaires of the credentials commission had been filled in, due to the premature dissolution of the Congress.[220] Available data on the social origin of the delegates reveals that the total number of 357 included 101 peasants, 149 soldiers and sailors, 16 workers, 38 teachers, 29 refugee peasants, and 29 representatives of the intelligentsia. The age of the delegates varied between 19 and 62, but an overwhelming majority was found in the age group between 20 and 40 years old: 86 delegates were aged between 20 and 25 years old, 106 between 25 and 30, and 123 between 30 and 40. Most of them had various degrees of education, which was to be expected, as communities and organizations would strive to send the most qualified people to the Congress. Graduates of the people's schools were represented by 129 persons, another 45 delegates attended various city schools or adult education institutions, while a further 31 and 25 participants of the congress were graduates of teachers' seminaries and universities, respectively.[221]

Politically, the Congress gathered together the representatives of various parties: among the 357 delegates 33 were from the BSH, 6 from the BNPS, 31 identified as Bolsheviks, 73 as Socialist-Revolutionaries, and 57 as Left Socialist-Revolutionaries. Another 57 delegates described themselves as sympathizers of

---

April 22, 1918, 1.

[219] "Bielaruski Konhres," *Bielaruski Šliach*, no. 25, April 22, 1918, 1.

[220] "Bielaruski Konhres," *Bielaruski Šliach*, no. 25, April 22, 1918, 1.

[221] "Bielaruski Konhres," *Bielaruski Šliach*, no. 25, April 22, 1918, 1.

either the SR or the Bolshevik party, while 79 delegates were not affiliated with any party.[222] With regard to this variety, Cvikievič called the Congress a "true parade of the democratic forces of Belarus."[223]It is obvious that politically it was dominated by the Socialist-Revolutionaries, who were popular among both peasants and soldiers of peasant origin. The number of the BSH-affiliated delegates most likely reflected its better party standing within Minsk and the province, where it had stronger positions in comparison to the eastern, more Russified provinces. The comparable numbers of the pro-Bolshevik delegates indicated their influence over the military of the Western front. It is also likely that these numbers could have been interpreted as a warning sign by the radical Minsk Bolsheviks, who realized that 31 delegates were not enough to control the proceedings of the Congress, in contrast to their recent series of orchestrated gatherings of peasants', workers', and soldiers' representatives in November, where they secured their own predominance by manipulating the membership in order to provide a shade of legitimization for the Obliskomzap.

Conclusion

In the second half of 1917, several overlapping initiatives to organize power in Belarus emerged. First, the Belarusian national movement reorganized itself again around the Great Belarusian Rada in Minsk. The new Rada had more potential for success, as it was based on a broad democratic coalition platform, emphasizing the unity of the whole of Belarus and its people, whose interests it intended to represent and protect. Second, the Belarusian Oblast' Committee at the All-Russian Soviet of Peasants' Deputies emerged as the most influential of the Belarusian organizations in Russia, whereas the political weight of the Moscow-based Belarusian People's Hramada notably decreased. Operating from Petrograd and maintaining close links with the new Bolshevik authorities, the BOK enjoyed financial support from the new power and hoped to profit politically in Belarus.

Last but not least, in the aftermath of the October Revolution, the Bolsheviks proceeded with solidifying their positions in strategically important areas of the Western front, which at that time ran through Belarusian territories from north to south. The Military-Revolutionary Committee of the Western Front established the Oblast' Executive Committee of the Soviets of Workers', Soldiers', and Peasants'

---

[222] "Bielaruski Konhres," *Bielaruski Šliach*, no. 25, April 22, 1918, 1.
[223] Cvikievič, *Kratkii ocherk*, 9.

Deputies of the Western Oblast' and Front (Obliskomzap), effectively replacing previous civilian authorities with military powers. The local Belarusian population was denied representation in this new administration, which was clearly oriented towards military goals and interests, in line with the overall trend in this region during the First World War. The Minsk Bolsheviks did not hesitate to demonstrate their outright hostility to Belarusian national aspirations, while their comrades in Petrograd were still referring to the progressive slogans of self-determination, or the rights of nationalities to secession, in order to manipulate their political opponents.

In these circumstances, the convocation of the All-Belarusian Congress in December of 1917 was a combined achievement of all Belarusian organizations, regardless of their political preferences. It was designed to provide a legitimate alternative to the militarized Bolshevik power structures of the Western front. Analysis of preserved congress protocols indicates the socialist backgrounds of the majority of the delegates, who recognized the principle of soviet power, but specifically objected to the interpretation of its principles by the Minsk Bolsheviks. Despite the fact that the VBR was able to enforce its own plan of having the Congress in Minsk, the rivalry between the VBR and the BOK was defining for its proceedings, resulting in disruptive internal discussions, as the *oblastniki* faction constantly questioned the authority of the Congress and attempted to slow down its work. Meanwhile the supporters of Belarusian national self-determination urged the delegates to assume responsibility for the fate of their homeland, pointing out the dangers of more influential foreign political actors interested in implementing their own agendas on Belarusian territories.

Defined by these debates, Congress resolutions were conciliatory in character. The last resolution of the Congress was a rather moderate compromise to reconcile all the factions around the points on which they could agree. It did not go further than making calls for autonomy, thus reflecting the dominant trend of 1917. More importantly, it explicitly denied giving recognition to the hastily organized Bolshevik military authorities over Belarusian territories. A majority of the delegates could not accept that strangers and foreigners were voluntarily setting up governing structures and usurping power. Thus, the attitude of the most representative gathering of Belarusians can be interpreted as a cautious first step in the direction of their own independent statehood. Yet, only the subsequent violent dispersion of the Congress can be regarded as a major turning point, forcing national activists to acknowledge greater responsibilities for the future of their homeland. The circumstances of the Congress's dissolution eventually overshadowed the initial goals of the organizers and exercised greater influence both on the course of historical events and on the image of the Congress, constructed in its aftermath.

Chapter 6

Belarusian Statehood in the Making: The BDR and Soviet Belarus

Under what conditions did the idea of a separate Belarusian nation-state emerge, what meaning did it have for the Belarusian national movement, and how was it implemented? The answer to these questions lies in the crucial period in the history of Belarusian statehood in 1918. Firstly, it is associated with the independence proclamation of the Belarusian Democratic Republic (*Bielaruskaja Narodnaja Respublika*, BDR) on March 25, 1918, in Minsk. Secondly, the rival Soviet project, emerging in 1919, is also traced back to 1918. At that time, the Soviet state reoriented itself towards the appropriation of the Belarusian national movement and, combined with the efforts of the left-wing Belarusian socialists in Russia, contributed to the development of a parallel notion of Belarusian statehood, leading to the proclamation of the Socialist Soviet Republic of Belarus (SSRB) on January 1, 1919, in Smolensk.

This chapter traces the dual origins of Belarusian statehood by providing a comparative perspective of the early state- and nation-building efforts of the Belarusian national activists in 1918, both from the national and the Bolshevik-friendly camps. The latter were represented by the Belarusian organizations in Petrograd and Moscow that grouped around the Belarusian National Commissariat (Bielnackam), under the auspices of the central Bolshevik authorities in early 1918. It gradually started to position itself as an alternative force to the Minsk-based Belarusian national elites, by expanding its own political activities, publishing a newspaper, and engaging in a humanitarian mission with the numerous Belarusian refugees, who were still residing in Russia. Politically, the Belarusian socialists in Russia accepted cooptation into the Bolshevik state and party structures, hoping to achieve a Soviet-based Belarusian state.

Their political adversaries in Minsk were the former delegates of the All-Belarusian Congress, which had been violently dissolved by the Bolshevik authorities of the Western front. Belarusian activists reorganized around the Congress Council, which attempted to capitalize on the lack of coordinated actions between the Minsk Bolsheviks and the central authorities in Petrograd. However, the break in the Brest-Litovsk peace talks and the advance of the German armies to the east in February 1918 changed the balance of forces in the region. The subsequent German occupation of the Belarusian territories ended the first brief period of Soviet power in Belarus, presenting new opportunities for the national movement. Following the inclusion of minorities as well as municipal and zemstvo members, the Congress Council transformed into the Rada (Council) of the BDR in February 1918. Its ranks were soon expanded by the Belarusian national activists from the Great Belarusian Rada in Vil'nia, representing western Belarus within the German-occupied zone of Ober Ost. In contrast to the Belarusian Bolsheviks in Russia and the Obliskomzap, the Rada of the BDR could claim more legitimacy as the democratically elected representative body of the Belarusian people, as much as it was feasible under the conditions of war and revolution. It proclaimed the independence of the first Belarusian state, yet was forced to struggle with the occupation authorities for the recognition of its demands.

Historical evaluations of the BDR often highlight its insufficient state authority and dependence on German toleration. For instance, echoing some of the critical evaluations of the first Belarusian state as an "annex of the occupation regime"[1] and a "virtual republic,"[2] Per Anders Rudling describes it as a "powerful fiction,"[3] which turned to be attractive for the nationalist believers and did not lose its appeal with time. This approach to the BDR focuses on its lack of state attributes, first and foremost—a monopoly on power, indispensable for a modern state according to Max Weber's definition.[4] This chapter will approach the discussion of the BDR from a different angle, moving away from the discussion of state attributes and whether it could be defined as a real state or not, towards an analysis of the overall trends that its proclamation revealed about Belarusian national politics in 1918.

This chapter focuses on two currents of the Belarusian movement, one in Minsk and the other in Russia, and their approaches to the state- and nation-building process during 1918. However, a discussion of Belarusian statehood in the making during 1918 also requires the context of interactions between the German Empire and Soviet Russia. Both referred extensively to the new principle of national self-determination, and both consistently abused it for their own ends, limiting the options available to the Belarusian national activists. Moreover, the

---

[1]   V. A. Krutalevich, *O Belorusskoi Narodnoi Respublike* (Minsk: Pravo i ekonomika, 2005), 205.

[2]   Aleh Lickievič, "Bielaruskaja virtualnaja respublika," *Bielaruskaja Dumka*, no. 3 (2008): 68.

[3]   Rudling, *The Rise and Fall of Belarusian Nationalism*, 121.

[4]   Rudling, *The Rise and Fall of Belarusian Nationalism*, 121–22.

clash of German and Soviet interests over Belarusian territories in the winter of 1918 was complicated by a local military factor: the presence of the First Polish Corps in eastern Belarus. It increased the instability and militarization of the region, preventing Belarusians from establishing control over key cities and expanding Belarusian military units, thus further weakening Belarusian claims on political power on the eve of the German occupation in 1918.

"One Hundred Days" of Soviet Power in Belarus

During November 1917, Soviet power gradually established its authority in most of the large cities and towns of the unoccupied parts of eastern Belarus. The Bolsheviks benefited from considerable support from the 2nd, 3rd, and 10th armies of the Western front, which still numbered about 1.5 million soldiers. In late November 1917, the Minsk Bolsheviks established the Oblast' Executive Committee of the Soviets of Workers', Soldiers', and Peasants' Deputies of the Western Oblast' and Front (Obliskomzap), claiming authority over the Minsk, Mahilioŭ, and Viciebsk provinces, along with parts of Vil'nia province, as well as over the whole area of the Western front. However, the actual power of the Obliskomzap at this time was rather limited. It extended effectively only over the front areas in parts of Minsk and Vil'nia provinces. The position of the Obliskomzap was soon weakened by Lenin's Decree on Peace, which led to demobilization from the Russian army and narrowed the organization's support base among the soldiers. The Soviet of People's Commissars of the Western Oblast' and Front acted as the Obliskomzap's executive organ of power. These two major Soviet institutions on the Belarusian territories remained in place until February 19, 1918, when the Bolsheviks hastily fled from Minsk due to the new German offensive, which started after Trotsky failed to secure a peace settlement during the negotiations with Germany at Brest-Litovsk.[5]

The First All-Belarusian Congress, convening in Minsk on December 5–17 (N.S. 18–31), 1917, and gathering representatives of various political currents within the Belarusian national milieu, extensively discussed possible forms of state building. Debates led to a compromise resolution, uniting different factions of

---

5   Ignatenko and Shtykhov, *Istoriia Belorusskoi SSR*, 239; Z. Žylunovič, "Liuty—Kastryčnik u biela-ruskim nacyjanalnym ruchu," in *Bielarus': Narysy historyi, ekanomiki, kul'turnaha i revoliucyjnaha ruchu*, ed. A. Stašeŭski, Z. Žylunovič, U. Ihnatoŭski (Minsk: Vydannie Centralnaha Kamitetu Bielaruskaje Savieckaje Socyjalistyčnaje Respubliki, 1924), 200.

the Congress in recognizing the need to establish its own organ of local power in Belarus to replace the militarized Obliskomzap, which was controlled entirely by the front Bolsheviks. At the same time, the Congress did not display firm intentions towards separation from Russia, refraining from discussing possible independence and remaining faithful to the principle of Belarusian autonomy. Nevertheless, Minsk Bolshevik authorities actively interfered in the work of the Congress from the day of its opening. At first, they carried out subversive provocations among the congress delegates, aiming to disrupt the proceedings. After the Bolsheviks failed to sabotage the Congress from within, the Obliskomzap used the Congress resolution on the establishment of local power as an excuse for its violent dissolution in the early hours of December 18, 1917.[6]

By January 1918, the Obliskomzap had ensured the precarious position of the Belarusian movement in Minsk, depriving it of any public influence and eliminating it as a threat. Even the cultural and educational activities declined, especially compared to the summer and fall of 1917.[7] According to the memoirs of Wacław Solski, a Polish socialist and a member of the Military-Revolutionary Committee of the Western Front, who was in close contact with the Minsk Bolsheviks during 1917–1918 and cooperated with them in the Minsk Soviet, the main concern for the Obliskomzap in January 1918 was not Belarusian nationalism, but rather the relations with the Minsk City Duma. It was the only intact "pre-October" institution operating in the city by January 1918 and still included representatives of various political parties. For a while, it even managed to hold meetings and debates open for the public. The Obliskomzap temporarily tolerated the existence of the City Duma, hoping for its assistance in food procurement.[8] Only on January 22, 1918, did the Minsk Soviet, chaired by Karl Lander, issue a decree dissolving the City Duma and taking over its responsibilities. Described as an "organizing center of counterrevolutionary elements," the City Duma was accused of waging a political struggle against the parties that supported Soviet power.[9] According to Solski, the deputies refused to obey this order and remained in session throughout the night, awaiting the arrival of the soldiers. Eventually, the intimidated deputies

---

6   Zacharka, "Haloŭnyja momanty bielaruskaha ruchu," 26–27.
7   Turuk, *Belorusskoe dvizhenie*, 40.
8   Solski and Khomich, *1917 god v Zapadnoi oblasti*, 201–3.
9   Document No. 30 "Dekret Minskogo Soveta o rospuske gorodskoi dumy i upravy i peredachi Minskomu Sovetu funktsii upravleniia gorodom," in V. I. Adamushko, ed., *Minskii gorodskoi Sovet deputatov: 1917–2012: Dokumenty i materialy* (Minsk: Belorusskii dom pechati, 2012), 42.

left in the morning and did not convene again.[10] Solidifying their grip on power in Minsk, the Western front Bolsheviks proceeded with the dissolution of the Minsk Municipal Food Committee on January 24, 1918, on the grounds of its "bourgeois" majority, which allegedly encouraged "free criminal speculation."[11]

However, Soviet power was far from stable, as instances of armed clashes with the Belarusian militia units in Viciebsk demonstrated. One of the bigger incidents took place after the Bolsheviks attempted a raid on the cathedral and military warehouses in the city.[12] On February 6, 1918, a reinforced unit of the Red Guards attacked the building where the Viciebsk Belarusian organizations were located. All correspondence and finances of the Belarusian Rada of the Northern Front, the Viciebsk Belarusian Rada, and the BSH were confiscated. The eyewitness report of K. Chadkievič unmasked the "Bolshevik self-determination of peoples" as "the dispersal and crushing of revolutionary-democratic organizations."[13] Fearing a German advance, the Bolsheviks briefly left Viciebsk in early February 1918, only to return after the German armies failed to reach the city.[14] The work of Belarusian organizations in Viciebsk was paralyzed henceforth. The Rada of the Northern Front was dissolved and only the Viciebsk BSH section, headed by Michail Mialeška, attempted to operate illegally from underground. Securing their power claims in Viciebsk, the Bolsheviks relied on the First Polish Revolutionary Regiment, which belonged to the Red Army and was hostile towards the Belarusian national movement.[15]

The formation of Bolshevik-loyal Polish military units was authorized by Miasnikov in late November 1917, as Soviet power aimed to neutralize the independent activities of the First Polish Corps,[16] which posed serious security concerns for the Bolsheviks in Belarus. The history of the First Polish Corps dates back to the summer of 1917, when the Russian military command allowed the creation of Polish military units in Russia. It immediately attracted high numbers of soldiers of Polish origin, who were serving in the Russian army during the First

[10] Solski, *1917 god v Zapadnoi oblasti*, 204. See also Document No. 56 "Iz vospominanii K. I. Landera 1917 god," in Adamushko, *Minskii gorodskoi Sovet deputatov*, 72.
[11] Document No. 31 "Postanovlenie Minskogo Soveta o rospuske Minskogo gorodskogo prodovol'stvennogo komiteta," in Adamushko, *Minskii gorodskoi Sovet deputatov*, 42.
[12] BDAMLIM, f. 3, vop. 1, spr. 137, ark. 115.
[13] BDAMLIM, f. 3, vop. 1, spr. 137, ark. 116 adv.
[14] Latyšonak, *Žaŭnery BNR*, 61.
[15] NARB, f. 325, vop. 1, spr. 8, ark. 35, 35 adv.
[16] Siamenčyk, *Hramadska-palityčnae žyccio*, 89.

World War.[17] Within a few months, the First Polish Corps under the command of General Józef Dowbór-Muśnicki numbered about 30,000 soldiers.[18] Anti-cipating leaving for Poland at the first suitable opportunity, the Polish troops preferred to maintain a neutral position. However, at the time of the October takeover by the Bolsheviks, they declared their readiness to protect the population of Minsk, should it be required.[19] Following the decisions of the Second Congress of Polish Soldiers of the Western Front, which took place from November 13 to 18, 1917 and which supported the expansion of the Polish military units "for the protection of the lives and properties of the population in the areas where Polish troops were stationed,"[20] Polish units started to interfere in local affairs in order to protect the estates of the Polish landowners during the Bolshevik-led pogroms.[21]

The Military-Revolutionary Committee of the Western Front asked Commander-in-Chief Krylenko to disband the Corps under the excuse that its soldiers were assisting the local landowners, instead of granting the land committees free access to the estates. In November 1917, the Polish Corps headquarters were ordered to move away from Minsk. At that time, most of the Polish units were stationed in eastern Belarus, in the area of Rahačoŭ, Žlobin, and Babrujsk. At first, the Bolshevik strategy aimed to divide the Polish forces from within, by promoting the creation of alternative, "proletarian" Polish units. Simultaneously, the Bolsheviks initiated a denigration campaign against the First Polish Corps in the press. The disruption of Polish supply lines followed, culminating in provocations of a direct nature.[22]

On January 20, 1918, the commander of the Western front, Miasnikov, ordered the dissolution of the Polish Corps, offering its soldiers a chance to join the Red Army. Dowbór-Muśnicki was labeled an "enemy of the revolution," while all Polish officers caught with weapons were to be tried immediately and shot should they show any signs of resistance.[23] In January 1918, Soviet power did not yet possess enough resources to defeat the Poles, as the Western front was in the process of an uncontrolled demobilization. Commander-in-Chief Krylenko

---

17   Sukiennicki and Siekierski, *East Central Europe during World War I*, 330.
18   Józef Dowbor-Muśnicki, *Moje wspomnienia* (Poznań: Nakładem Przewodnika Katolickiego, 1936), 104.
19   "U Minsku," *Vol'naja Bielarus'*, no. 29, November 14, 1917, 4.
20   Siamenčyk, *Hramadska-palityčnae žyccio*, 88.
21   Józef Dowbór-Muśnicki, *Krótki szkic do historji I-go Polskiego Korpusu*. Cz. 2 (Warsaw: Placówka, 1919), 68–71, cited in Sukiennicki and Siekierski, *East Central Europe during World War I*, 465.
22   Siamenčyk, *Hramadska-palityčnae žyccio*, 88–90.
23   Siamenčyk, *Hramadska-palityčnae žyccio*, 93–94.

was struggling to keep Stavka intact in order to maintain a sufficient amount of available old army units to fight the Polish Corps, which in January 1918 still numbered around 14,000 soldiers, while the number of Red Army volunteers was only about 1,500.[24]

In contrast to the First Polish Corps, Belarusian attempts to organize military units were more modest, suffering both from the Bolshevik-imposed restrictions and competition with the better organized Poles. The Central Belarusian Military Rada (*Central'naja Bielaruskaja Vajskovaja Rada*, CBVR)[25] was formed only in late October 1917 and had to work under unfavorable circumstances, as already on December 8, 1917, Krylenko issued an order halting the process of nationalization in the army and banning all national activities in the front zone.[26] The CBVR continued to operate without official approval, focusing on promoting the national cause and establishing Belarusian committees in the army. Remarkably, this process was more successful not in Belarus, but among the numerous Belarusians who served at the distant Romanian front,[27] which still did not recognize the authority of Krylenko as the Commander-in-Chief. The leadership of the Romanian front therefore did not object to the nationalizing process, viewing it as a lesser evil to the Bolshevization of the soldiers.[28]

Within Belarus, the deputy chair of the CBVR, Kanstancin Jezavitaŭ, along with some younger officers, tried to accelerate the formation of the Belarusian units. An unexpected complication, however, arose within the CBVR itself, when they had to confront General Kipryjan Kandratovič,[29] who was in charge of organizing the Belarusian military units. As an older member of the military,

---

[24] Sanborn, *Imperial Apocalypse*, 228.

[25] See Chapter 4 for details on the activities of the CBVR.

[26] NARB, f. 325, vop. 1, spr. 21, ark. 42.

[27] Belarusian units at the Romanian front included the 4th Army Corps, transformed into the Belarusian Infantry Division, two Belarusian militia squads, and the Belarusian National Hussar Regiment. After Romania signed peace with Germany, the latter requested the disbanding of the national units. All soldiers were decommissioned and the transfer of the units to Belarus was no longer feasible. See Document No. 0177 "List bielaruskaha kamisara Rumynskaha frontu K. Mancevička Narodnamu Sakrataryjatu BDR," in Šupa, *Archivy Bielaruskaj Narodnaj Respubliki*, 76.

[28] Latyšonak, *Žaŭnery BNR*, 54–55.

[29] General Kipryjan Kandratovič (1859–1932), a native of the Lida region in Belarus, was a graduate of the prestigious Nicholas General Staff Academy. Together with Józef Dowbór-Muśnicki, Kandratovič participated in the Russo-Japanese war (1904–1905), commanded a separate corps in Eastern Prussia during the First World War, was active in the CBVR, and served as a defense minister in the BDR government in 1918. See Leanid Laŭreš, "Heneral Kandratovič: dva imhnenni viečnasci," *Naša Slova*, no. 12, March 19, 2014, 6.

he had a corresponding mentality of subordination to orders. In particular, Kandratovič was not inclined to allow any independent initiatives in army matters without explicit orders from above. In this situation, only the efforts of the local Belarusian front committees led to some partial progress with the First Belarusian Regiment, originally numbering about 350 soldiers. However, in early December 1917, following Krylenko's order prohibiting nationalization processes in the army, this regiment was merged with the 289th Reserve Infantry Regiment.[30]

According to Kanstancin Jezavitaŭ, by the time the CBVR managed to force Kandratovič out from his position of authority, a lot of time had been wasted, allowing the Bolsheviks to strengthen their position in Minsk. The Western front command and Miasnikov in particular displayed outright hostility toward the Belarusian military units. Fearing that Belarus might follow Ukraine, which started a war against the Bolsheviks, the Obliskomzap authorities resolved to prevent similar developments in Belarus. Due to the short-term absence of Krylenko from Stavka in December 1917, Miasnikov temporarily became the acting Commander-in-Chief, using his new authority to concentrate more Bolshevik-loyal troops in Minsk and to suppress the formation of the Belarusian military units.[31]

Other adversaries of the CBVR were the Poles. After the February Revolution, Minsk served as an important political center for Polish nationalists on the unoccupied Belarusian territories. Since 1915, large numbers of Polish refugees had settled in the cities of eastern Belarus, significantly changing their demographic outlook and influencing national politics during this revolutionary period. The re-establishment of the Minsk Catholic diocese in 1917 and the active participation of local Poles in public life benefited the process of Polish national consolidation, creating competition for the Belarusian nation-building efforts. For instance, throughout 1917, the Polish political club engaged in the organization of meetings and lectures, while the Polish Educational Society of the Minsk Region (*Polska Macierz Szkolna Ziemi Mińskiej*) took responsibility for the opening of elementary schools, libraries, and reading rooms. The Polish Council of the Minsk Province (*Rada Polska Ziemi Mińskiej*), established in May 1917, pursued similar tasks. More importantly, all Polish organizations, including the socialists, supported the idea of a Polish state. This common goal allowed them to maintain a high degree of cohesion and national unity, which other national minorities often lacked, as, for instance, Jews, who at that time were widely involved in the activities of the All-Russian parties.[32]

---

[30] Latyšonak, *Žaŭnery BNR*, 51.
[31] K. Jezavitaŭ, "Bielaruskaja Vajskovaja Rada," *Kryvič*, no. 1 (7), 1924: 42–43.
[32] Tarasiuk, *Między nadzieją a niepokojem*, 111; Siamenčyk, *Hramadska-palityčnae žyccio*, 108–9.

In early 1918, the Polish Military Organization (*Polska Organizacja Wojskowa*, POW) in Minsk closely monitored all steps undertaken by the CBVR. The POW was subordinated to the Polish Council, which directed the actions of Dowbór-Muśnicki's Corps and enjoyed the support of Polish landowners from Belarus and Lithuania. Many of the POW members held important positions in the Western front headquarters and maintained personal contacts with Miasnikov. Jezavitaŭ noted their extremely hostile attitude towards the CBVR and suspected that the Poles might have influenced the decision of the Western front command, taken around January 20, 1918, to transfer the 289th Reserve Infantry Regiment out of Minsk to guard railways in the provinces. Consisting of mostly Belarusian soldiers, the regiment was spread out over a large territory between Minsk, Smolensk, Viciebsk and further east, thus significantly reducing the Belarusian military presence in Minsk.[33]

Jezavitaŭ was also concerned about the First Polish Corps' activities in eastern Belarus, in the area of Bychaŭ, Rahačoŭ, and Babrujsk. In particular, he feared a Polish takeover of Babrujsk, where a large fortress and a military warehouse were located. Their estimated capacity was sufficient to sustain the existence of several military corps. Since the poorly guarded warehouse was an easy target, Jezavitaŭ planned to turn Babrujsk into a base for Belarusian military units. In January 1918, he sent out telegrams, urging already existing Belarusian units to send people to Babrujsk.[34] Yet, only one Belarusian squadron directly clashed with the Polish Corps, failing to prevent the Polish occupation of Babrujsk on January 20, 1918. The city fortress and military warehouses became the center of Dowbór-Muśnicki's operations in the region.[35] On February 19, 1918, Polish soldiers advanced west towards Asipovičy, gaining control over the main road leading to Minsk. To the east of Babrujsk, they managed to force the Bolshevik units back beyond the Dnepr River in the vicinity of Rahačoŭ and Žlobin.[36] Thus,

---

[33] Kanstancin Jezavitaŭ, "Bielaruskaja Vajskovaja Central'naja Rada," *Kryvič*, no. 9, 1925: 80–92.

[34] NARB, f. 325, vop. 1, spr. 21, ark. 58.

[35] Latyšonak, *Žaŭnery BNR*, 55.

[36] Due to the large numbers of Polish officers in the Russian army, the First Polish Corps included in its ranks special elite officer legions. Among the officers serving in the Corps was Władysław Anders, who would lead the Polish Armed Forces in the East in 1941. In March 1918, the First Polish Corps took an oath of loyalty to the Regency Council in Warsaw. Polish soldiers left Belarusian territories in late May 1918, following the ultimatum of the German occupation authorities to General Dowbór-Muśnicki to evacuate the Babrujsk fortress and leave behind all weapons, or face the superior forces of the German 10th Army. See Ihar Mel'nikaŭ, "Zabyty korpus zabytaha henerala," *Novy Čas Online*, http://159.253.18.178/poviaz_casou/zabyty_ korpus_zabytaha_hienier/ (Accessed November 10, 2015).

in addition to Soviet Russia and Germany, the First Polish Corps temporarily turned into another external player on the Belarusian territories in early 1918.

Realignment of the Belarusian National Forces in 1918

Following the dispersal of the All-Belarusian Congress by the Bolshevik authorities, the congress participants who could avoid arrest, gathered in the early morning of December 18, 1917, in the buildings of the Libava-Romenskaja railroad. They decided to transform the Congress Council[37] into a provisional local executive power, expanding it by the inclusion of peasants', workers', and soldiers' representatives as well as national minorities. Further, the meeting agreed that the Belarusian Oblast' Committee (BOK), the Great Belarusian Rada (VBR), the Regional Bureau, and other organizations which had participated in the organization of the Congress, were to transfer their responsibilities as well as their properties to the Congress Council. The CBVR was kept intact in the capacity of a subordinate body to the Council, entrusted with the task of implementing all decisions and resolutions of the Congress. The Second All-Belarusian Congress was to be called as soon as possible, following the resolution of December 17, 1917.[38]

The Council immediately formed an Executive Committee, chaired by Jazep Varonka. This institution was to take over executive power in Belarus in case of favorable conditions for such a transition. Until that moment, the whereabouts of the Executive Committee was to be kept secret. From December 18 (N.S. 31), 1917 until February 19, 1918, it existed illegally, emerging from underground only when the Obliskomzap Bolshevik authorities left Minsk due to the German advance.[39] The leaders of the Congress Council were subject to political persecution by the Obliskomzap. For instance, its chair, Jazep Varonka, was arrested twice in the first half of January 1918.[40] Nevertheless, even in its illegal position, the Executive Committee was considered to be the single legitimate organ of power formed by a popular representation of the Belarusian people and taking responsibility for their political future after the dissolution of the All-Belarusian Congress.[41]

---

[37] According to Jazep Varonka, it included thirty-six persons. See Document No. 0065 "Spis siabroŭ Rady 1-ha Usiebielaruskaha Zjezdu," in Šupa, *Archivy Bielaruskaj Narodnaj Respubliki*, 37–38.

[38] See Prilozhenie No. 17 "Postanovlenie Soveta Siezda," in Turuk, *Belorusskoe dvizhenie*, 110.

[39] Turuk, *Belorusskoe dvizhenie*, 110.

[40] Ladyseŭ and Bryhadzin, *Pamiž Uschodam i Zachadam*, 66.

[41] Cvikievič, *Kratkii ocherk*, 11.

The head of the CBVR, Symon Rak-Michajloŭski, stressed the need for constant communication with the Executive Committee, noting that the priorities had to focus on "solidarity in building up the agitation-political department."[42] Rak-Michajloŭski correctly observed that the Belarusian movement had to establish better public visibility. He argued that the best way to do this was to demonstrate the existence of national demands to the civilian and military powers by producing as many protest resolutions from various localities as possible. He noted that previously neither the Bolshevik authorities nor the media had received enough information about Belarusian interests and demands. According to the head of the CBVR, "while all other nationalities literally 'bombed' everyone[43] with their protests and resolutions, raising their voice all over the Russian republic, we remained silent. Now we have to speak up and raise our voice all at once, as the existence of Belarus is under a mortal threat."[44] The dissolution of the Congress, the persecution of the Executive Committee and members of the CBVR, along with the ban on the organization of Belarusian army units were identified as the main themes for the protest resolutions.[45]

This call did not remain unheeded. Deputies of the Minsk City Duma condemned the violence against the First All-Belarusian Congress already on December 18.[46] The Executive Committee of the Congress Council refuted Trotsky's references to the Congress as a gathering instigated by the "agrarians" who allegedly attempted to rob the working people of their rights to the land. A corresponding disclaimer was sent out to all newspaper offices for dissemination.[47] Complaints against the actions of the Western oblast' commissars were signed by Belarusian soldiers and the civilian population in Smolensk.[48] Socialist parties in Minsk, Viciebsk, Odesa, Petrograd, along with the soldiers of the South-Western front, also protested against the dissolution of the All-Belarusian Congress.[49]

---

[42] LMAVB, RS, f. 21, b. 2209, l. 1.

[43] In original: "vsekh, vsekh, vsekh"–the usual form of address in proclamations during the revolutionary period.

[44] LMAVB, RS, f. 21, b. 2209, l. 1.

[45] LMAVB, RS, f. 21, b. 2209, l. 1.

[46] Siamenčyk, *Hramadska-palityčnae žyccio*, 108–9.

[47] Document No. 0075 "Redaktsiiam vsekh gazet," in Šupa, *Archivy Bielaruskaj Narodnaj Respubliki*, 42–43.

[48] LMAVB, RS, f. 21, b. 2209, l. 4 r.

[49] Document No. 5 "Dokladnaia zapiska 'Sovetskaia vlast' v Belorussii,'" in V. D. Selemenev, ed., *1 ianvariia 1919 goda: vremennoe raboche-krest'ianskoe sovetskoe pravitel'stvo Belorussii: dokumenty i materialy* (Minsk: Limarius, 2005), 213.

In the aftermath of the All-Belarusian Congress's dissolution, the Minsk Bolsheviks raided the CBVR offices in the former Governor's House in the early hours of December 20, 1917.[50] According to Jezavitaŭ's eyewitness account, the Bolsheviks apparently did not feel confident as they chose to act under cover of night once again and were accompanied with armored vehicles and a cavalry unit. The Soviet of the People's Commissars confiscated the Governor's House, previously used by the CBVR and the Congress Council.[51] The latter managed to requisition another building, located at Palicejskaja[52] Street and continued working underground.[53]

Celebrating their "triumph," the Bolsheviks organized a mass military event in Minsk on December 20, 1917. They gathered the Minsk garrison and their new loyal troops around the Governor's House, parading regiments with orchestras, armored vehicles, and cavalry under the slogans of strengthening Soviet power and combating "international imperialism" and the "bourgeois Constituent Assembly." Belarusian affairs, its leaders, and supporters were denigrated in all speeches.[54] The Minsk Bolsheviks also used their control over the media to slander the Congress and its participants, labeling them as counterrevolutionaries and provocateurs. The official statement of the Obliskomzap concerning the Congress's dissolution was based on the accusation of the latter's intentions "to create a separate parallel nationalistic power and insubordination to the existing Soviet power."[55]

Since the initiative in the dissolution of the Congress had been taken by the Commander of the Western Front, Aleksandr Miasnikov, and the chair of the Soviet of People's Commissars of the Western Oblast' and Front, Karl Lander, without explicit orders from above, Belarusian national activists still counted on the central authorities in Petrograd to take their side in the conflict with the

---

[50]   It was located on Sabornaja Square, currently Freedom Square.

[51]   During 1917, the building was used by the authorities of the Provisional Government, later serving as a base for the VBR and the CBVR. Located on Governor's Square in the center of Minsk, it represented a symbol of power and authority. Since the Bolsheviks in 1917 had been confined to the Commercial School located in the peripheral area near the railway station, possession of the Governor's House bore an obvious symbolic value for them in asserting their rule in Minsk. See Solski, *1917 god v Zapadnoi oblasti*, 39.

[52]   Currently Janka Kupala Street. On Minsk toponymy in the early twentieth century, see Ivan Sacukievič, "Tapanimija vulic i ploščaŭ Mienska ŭ XIX–pačatku XX st." http://philology.by/ page/minsk-toponyms-19-beginning-20-centuries (Accessed November 14, 2015).

[53]   Kanstancin Jezavitaŭ, "Bielaruskaja Vajskovaja Rada," *Kryvič*, no. 1 (7), 1924: 43–44.

[54]   Siamenčyk, *Hramadska-palityčnae žyccio*, 109; Kanstancin Jezavitaŭ, "Bielaruskaja Vajskovaja Rada," *Kryvič*, no. 1 (7), 1924: 44.

[55]   *Sovetskaia pravda*, no. 15, December 19, 1917.

Bolsheviks of the Western front. Belarusian organizations and socialist parties addressed their protests to the Council of the People's Commissars of the Russian Soviet Federative Socialist Republic (RSFSR), and personally to the Commissar of Nationalities, Joseph Stalin. Nevertheless, none of these steps could shake the position of the Obliskomzap, especially since Stalin chose not to interfere in the actions of the Western front commanders.[56] The Petrograd authorities only tried to save their image, as they had initially sanctioned the convocation of the Congress. Belarusian organizations in Petrograd and Moscow, as well as the Executive Committee of the Congress Council in Minsk, were reassured that the Petrograd Council of the People's Commissars recognized the rights of nations to self-determination. Krylenko even received an order to start negotiations with the CBVR.[57]

The Executive Committee of the CBVR sent Kanstancin Jezavitaŭ and Ivan Sierada to meet Krylenko on December 29, 1917. The Soviet Commander-in-Chief's behavior was hostile, as he constantly referred to the independence intentions of the Ukrainians, revealing his concerns that the Belarusians would follow their southern neighbors on this path. Krylenko announced solidarity with Miasnikov, and refused to recognize national military units. Jezavitaŭ and Sierada refuted the accusations of the "bourgeois" character of the CBVR and the Congress Council, requesting that the Commander-in-Chief support the principle of national self-determination and allow the formation of the Belarusian army. Eventually, Krylenko agreed to a compromise solution of establishing Belarusian units within the future Red Army. Yet, this step did not mean that the central authorities were interested in supporting Belarusian initiatives. An explanation for Krylenko's permission is to be found not in the persuasiveness of the CBVR delegation, but rather in his strained personal relations with Miasnikov. As the commander of the Western front, Miasnikov had trouble subordinating himself to Krylenko's authority and often tried to dictate to him the course of actions, which resulted in feelings of mutual dislike. Apparently, Miasnikov learned about the plans of the CBVR to modify the regulations on Red Army organization in order to transform its Belarusian units into Belarusian National Guards, and requested that Krylenko revoke his permission. Asserting his authority as the Commander-in-Chief, Krylenko refused to obey Miasnikov, and allowed the CBVR to continue

---

[56] Document No. 5 "Dokladnaia zapiska 'Sovetskaia vlast' v Belorussii,'" in Selemenev, *1 ianvariia 1919 goda*, 212–13.

[57] Latyšonak, *Žaŭnery BNR*, 53.

its work until mid-January 1918. Yet, in practice, Miasnikov had more means of interference, preventing any of the vague agreements from being implemented. Forced to appoint a special commission to deal with the creation of the Belarusian units, he deliberately chose members who would paralyze its work.[58]

By late January 1918, alarmed by the activities of the Polish and Ukrainian military forces, the Bolshevik authorities decided to neutralize the Belarusian attempts at creating army units by dissolving the CBVR, arresting its members, and closing down its newspaper, *Belorusskaia Rada*. On January 31, 1918, soldiers sent from Stavka in Mahilioŭ, assisted by the Minsk Bolsheviks, encircled the building of the CBVR and arrested the head of the military section, Jezavitaŭ, and the secretary, Vasil' Zacharka. On the following day, four additional arrests were made.[59] All arrested were escorted to the hotel *L'Europe* in the vicinity of the Governor's House, where the Cheka headquarters were located. Nevertheless, the CBVR did not stop working, as the Minsk Bolsheviks had enough resources to arrest only six persons, while the overall number of CBVR members exceeded one hundred and not all of them were based in Minsk.[60]

Both the Obliskomzap and the central Bolshevik authorities in Petrograd supported the crackdown on the CBVR. The Minsk Bolsheviks formally justified the arrests by referring to intercepted telegrams sent by Jezavitaŭ. His calls to Belarusian soldiers to head to Babrujsk and take over its fortress along with the military warehouses were interpreted as evidence of the CBVR's connections with the "Polish legionnaires." At the level of central power, the attack on the CBVR coincided with the decision of the Bolshevik authorities in Petrograd to take control over the Belarusian question from above. The declaration of Ukrainian independence prompted Soviet power towards more resolute actions against the Belarusian national movement and its appropriation. The establishment of the Belarusian National Commissariat at the People's Commissariat of Nationalities on January 31, 1918, was one of the first steps in this direction.[61] The Minsk Bolsheviks in turn planned to legalize their authority in Belarus by creating a counterweight to the All-Belarusian Congress. In order to link the Obliskomzap with the local Soviets in a closer and more legitimate manner, the Bolsheviks were preparing for the convocation of an oblast' congress of the Belarusian provinces

58   NARB, f. 325, vop. 1, spr. 21, ark. 42–43, 52; Kanstancin Jezavitaŭ, "Bielaruskaja Vajskovaja Central'naja Rada," *Kryvič*, no. 9, 1925: 82–83.
59   Latyšonak, *Žaŭnery BNR*, 55.
60   Kanstancin Jezavitaŭ, "Bielaruskaja Vajskovaja Central'naja Rada," *Kryvič*, no. 9, 1925, 89–90.
61   Michaluk, *Białoruska Republika Ludowa*, 223–24; Latyšonak, *Žaŭnery BNR*, 56.

in mid-February 1918.[62] However, the rapid German advance interfered with the implementation of these plans.

The "Second" German Occupation of the Belarusian Territories

After the Soviet delegation left Brest-Litovsk on February 10, 1918, without signing a peace treaty, the German Empire interpreted its departure as the end of the armistice and thus resumed military actions. Trotsky's strategy of "neither war, nor peace" backfired, and it would have placed the Bolshevik regime on the verge of collapse, had Germany decided to proceed with a more aggressive approach. Yet, the direction of the German Eastern policy in 1918 was neither straightforward nor clear, as it was determined by the fluctuations between the annexationist drive of the German High Command, embodied by Ludendorff, and the more cautious approach of the diplomatic circles, represented by Foreign Minister Richard von Kühlmann. The latter did not want to take any steps that could potentially result in the overthrow of the Bolshevik power, as it would have harmed German interests in the region. Even though German diplomats despised the Bolsheviks, the latter were still considered to be the only party interested in finding an acceptable solution through negotiations. This was especially important for Germany in 1918, as it wanted to spare soldiers and resources in the East, prioritizing military efforts on the Western front. Kühlmann considered the weak and uncertain position of the Bolshevik regime to be beneficial for extracting maximum benefits. His practical approach contrasted with the views of the military, which was eager to continue with the successful German advance. Eventually, Wilhelm II agreed with the strategy suggested by the Foreign Ministry and chancellor Hertling, choosing to keep the Bolshevik government in place as the only party willing to negotiate.[63]

The German 10th Army under the command of Erich von Falkenhayn started its advance on February 18, 1918, moving east through the Belarusian territories.[64] At the same time, the units of the First Polish Corps under the command of Dowbór-Muśnicki left Babrujsk, heading west towards Minsk. Neither of the armies encountered resistance, as by this time demobilization and high desertion rates had significantly depleted the ranks of the Russian Western front, whose commanders along with the Obliskomzap hurriedly abandoned

---

[62] Siamenčyk, *Hramadska-palityčnae žyccio*, 116–17.
[63] Baumgart, *Deutsche Ostpolitik 1918*, 82–84.
[64] Baumgart, *Deutsche Ostpolitik 1918*, 24–26.

Minsk.[65] The Council of People's Commissars of the Western Oblast' and Front held an emergency meeting on February 18, 1918, at which everyone agreed to evacuate to Smolensk. Miasnikov was barely able to leave in time, as the railway workers refused to assist the Bolsheviks in the evacuation process.[66]

The arrested members of the CBVR, among them Jezavitaŭ, Zacharka, and Mamon'ka, left prison and immediately called an emergency meeting of the Executive Committee of the CBVR. It decided to transfer power in Minsk to the Council of the First All-Belarusian Congress. On February 19, 1918, it retook possession of the Governor's House[67] and announced in the press its decision to remain in Minsk, calling upon the Belarusian population to unite around the national democratic organizations. Belarusian military units and civilian militia took over the responsibility of guaranteeing order in the city after it was abandoned by the commissars of the Western Oblast' and Front. All arrested Belarusian activists were released and sessions of the Minsk City Duma were resumed.[68]

By the evening of February 19, Belarusian forces controlled large sections of the city, including the armory on Maskoŭskaja Street, the Governor's House, and the building of the Cheka, located in the center. Jezavitaŭ became the commandant of Minsk. Simultaneously, the Poles also made an attempt to claim power in Minsk. Ignacy Matuszewski from the First Polish Corps was appointed as another commandant of Minsk, while the soldiers under his command were fighting the Bolsheviks and disarming the Belarusian units at the same time.[69] The confrontation continued throughout the day of February 20, until Polish forces controlled the armory on Maskoŭskaja Street and the railway station. The Belarusian units managed to hold the central part of the city around the Governor's House. Both Belarusians and Poles hoped for prompt reinforcements in order to eliminate the stalemate. Until then, they temporarily divided spheres of influence in Minsk, even though the first units of the German army had already started arriving in the city on February 21.[70]

According to a representative of the Ukrainian government, M. Lebedynec, reporting from Minsk, the Belarusians failed to establish control over the whole

[65] Ladyseŭ and Bryhadzin, *Pamiž Uschodam i Zachadam*, 67.
[66] Document No. 0095 "Zahad načalnika Libava-Romenskaj čyhunki za 2.03.1918 u sprave evakuacyi čyhunki z Miensku ŭ Maskvu," in Šupa, *Archivy Bielaruskaj Narodnaj Respubliki*, 50.
[67] *Vol'naja Bielarus'*, no. 6, February 24, 1918, 48.
[68] Document No. 0081 "Infarmacyja dlia druku za 19.02.1918," in Šupa, *Archivy Bielaruskaj Narodnaj Respubliki*, 45–46.
[69] Latyšonak, *Žaŭnery BNR*, 58–59.
[70] Latyšonak, *Žaŭnery BNR*, 60.

city and oust the Polish legionnaires due to the evident and regrettable lack of human and financial resources. The report correctly identified internal squabbles within the Belarusian national milieu and the insufficient consolidation of the national forces during 1917 as the chief reasons for this weakness during the crucial period of the power vacuum.[71] This also harmed the image of the Belarusian movement in the eyes of the German military administration, which did not regard it as a strong political factor in the region.

Despite organizational problems and the disruptive presence of Dowbór-Muśnicki's soldiers in Minsk, Belarusian authorities represented themselves as the only legitimate power in Minsk in the period from February 18 to 25, 1918, as best as they could.[72] On February 21, the First Constituent Charter declared the full rights of the Belarusian people to self-determination. The Executive Committee of the First All-Belarusian Congress Council, expanded by the inclusion of the national minorities' representatives, assumed provisional power in Belarus until the convocation of the democratic Belarusian Constituent Assembly. It formed the first Belarusian government, known as the People's Secretariat. Chaired by Jazep Varonka, it consisted of fourteen members, who were responsible for internal affairs (I. Makrejeŭ[73]), external affairs (Varonka), the military (Jezavitaŭ), finances (G. Belkind), education (A. Smolič), the judiciary (E. Belevič), agriculture (Tamaš Hryb), the economy (I. Sierada), social security (Paluta Badunova), and other administrative areas.[74]

The future fate of Belarusian state-building initiatives was closely connected to the Brest-Litovsk peace treaty. Demoralized by the successful German advance to the east in late February 1918, the Bolsheviks agreed to peace on March 3, 1918. With regard to the Belarusian territories, article three of the peace treaty was particularly important, as it foresaw the establishment of a future border between Russia and Germany, where Russia was to give up the territories to the west of an agreed line running west of Tallinn, through Daugavpils, to Pružany. This line roughly coincided with the borders of the front at the time of the

---

[71]   NARB, f. 325, vop. 1, spr. 19, ark. 145.

[72]   Turuk, *Belorusskoe dvizhenie*, 41.

[73]   Makrejeŭ and Belkind represented the All-Russian Socialist Revolutionaries and left the government in April 1918, as the party did not agree with the proclamation of Belarusian independence. See *Dziannica*, no. 10, April 30, 1918, 4; Document No. 0173 "Chronika dlia hazetaŭ [za 3.04.1918]," in Šupa, *Archivy Bielaruskaj Narodnaj Respubliki*, 73–74.

[74]   NARB, f. 325, vop. 1, spr. 21, ark. 100; see also Document No. 0089 "Abvestka Narodnaho Sekretaryjatu Bielarusi No. 3 za 23.02.1918," in Šupa, *Archivy Bielaruskaj Narodnaj Respubliki*, 48–49.

armistice, signed on December 15, 1917, which excluded the central and eastern Belarusian territories from the German sphere of influence. Russia was to refrain from interference in the internal matters of the areas to the west of the agreed line, which included Hrodna and Vil'nia provinces along with the Baltic region, whose fate was to be determined by Germany.[75] However, by March 1918 German armies had already advanced further east of the agreed border, occupying most of the Belarusian territories, including Polack, Barysaŭ, Rečyca, Mahilioŭ, and Homieĺ.[76] Germany promised to evacuate the areas located to the east of the proposed border only after the conclusion of a general peace and a complete Russian demobilization.[77]

Thus, the Brest peace treaty and the German advance resulted in a new division of the Belarusian territories in 1918: the western areas of the "first" German occupation in Ober Ost, also known as the lands "behind the trenches"; the territories of the "second" occupation in central Belarus around Minsk, which faced an unpredictable and unclear future; and, finally, the Bolshevik-held territories in the east around the major city of Viciebsk.[78] As most of the Belarusian lands were located in areas which were to be ceded to Russia after the conclusion of the general peace, Germany did not engage in fake state-building here as it did in the Baltics. Moreover, the supplemental treaty, signed by the Central Powers and Soviet Russia on August 27, 1918, contained an article on separatist movements, wherein Germany promised that it would "neither cause nor support the formation of independent states in those territories."[79]

The political implications of the Brest-Litovsk peace treaty were reinforced by its character as a "bread treaty" for the Central Powers, desperate for resources to support their war effort, which influenced the decision to take advantage of Ukraine.[80] With German assistance, the Ukrainian Rada was reinstated in its position in March 1918, and the Bolsheviks were ousted from the country. However, the socialist-dominated Rada was soon replaced by the more agreeable

---

[75] "Friedensvertrag von Brest-Litowsk," in *Quellen zu den deutsch-sowjetischen Beziehungen 1917–1945*, ed. Horst Günther Linke (Darmstadt: Wissenschaftliche Buchgesellschaft, 1998), 54.

[76] John W. Wheeler-Bennett, *Brest-Litovsk: The Forgotten Peace, March 1918* (New York: Norton Library, 1971) 271, 274; *Homan*, no. 19, March 5, 1918, 4.

[77] "Friedensvertrag von Brest-Litowsk," 54–55.

[78] Document No. 0112 "Vypiska z pratakolu pasiedžannia Mienskaj Haradzkoj Dumy za 18.03.1918," in Šupa, *Archivy Bielaruskaj Narodnaj Respubliki*, 56.

[79] *Supplementary Treaty to the Treaty of Peace between Russia and the Central Powers*, in Wheeler-Bennett, *Brest-Litovsk*, 429.

[80] Grelka, *Die ukrainische Nationalbewegung*, 80.

pro-German regime of Hetman Skoropadsky.[81] In contrast to Ukraine, Belarus lacked vast economic potential that could have prompted Germany to pay more attention to the local national movement. While the German authorities were to some degree familiar with the Belarusians in Ober Ost, they were not inclined even to differentiate between Belarusians and Great-Russians in the areas of the "second" occupation, indefinitely postponing discussions of this issue.[82] The uneven development of the Belarusian national movement and the low numbers of national activists continued to harm its image. In this respect, the "dual power" of Belarusians and Poles over Minsk on the eve of the German takeover of the city clearly demonstrated insufficient organization and a lack of military potential, turning the Belarusian movement in the eyes of the German officials into a minor local factor, which was insignificant in terms of *Realpolitik*.

Initially, relations between the Belarusian institutions and the German military authorities of the 10th Army, which established full control over Minsk on February 25, 1918, did not look promising. The new power disarmed the existing Belarusian military units and confiscated the Governor's House as well as the possessions of the Belarusian People's Secretariat,[83] including the latter's funds (more than 300,000 rubles), which the People's Secretariat acquired from the state treasury after the Bolshevik withdrawal from Minsk.[84] The German authorities were unwilling to tolerate Belarusian claims, forcing the People's Secretariat and the Executive Committee of the Congress Council to give up the functions of an acting power and to assume the role of a political center, advocating Belarusian interests.[85] In this manner, Belarusian institutions were effectively reduced to a local national representation with consultative tasks.[86]

---

[81]   Piotr Stefan Wandycz, *The Lands of Partitioned Poland, 1795–1918* (Seattle: University of Washington Press, 1974), 363.

[82]   Document No. 0185 "List Jazepa Varonki (Miensk) Ivanu i Antonu Luckievičam (Vil'nia) za 5.04.1918," in Šupa, *Archivy Bielaruskaj Narodnaj Respubliki*, 78.

[83]   Latyšonak, *Žaŭnery BNR*, 61–62.

[84]   Document No. 0788 "List Narodnaha Sakrataryjatu BDR Haloŭnamu Kamandavanniu X Armii za 5.08.1918," in Šupa, *Archivy Bielaruskaj Narodnaj Respubliki*, 228.

[85]   Cvikievič, *Kratkii ocherk*, 13.

[86]   Varonko, *Bielaruski ruch*, 11.

Establishment of the BDR and the Proclamation of Independence

From the Belarusian perspective, the Brest peace treaty signed between Germany and Soviet Russia on March 3, 1918, was an outright violation of the decisions of the First All-Belarusian Congress against territorial divisions. Economically, all Belarusian lands faced an uncertain future, as Soviet Russia and Germany agreed to refrain from war damage payments, transferring this burden onto the local populations. Thus, the dispersal of the All-Belarusian Congress by the Bolsheviks and their subsequent neglect of the Belarusian question during the Brest-Litovsk peace negotiations led the Belarusian national elites to believe that only separation from Bolshevik Russia could secure their national interests and grant access to international politics.[87] They argued that only the proclamation of a Belarusian state could avert the external threats and political ambitions of neighboring nations. Among the latter, Aliaksandr Cvikievič singled out Lithuanian attempts to appropriate the Vil'nia and Hrodna regions, Ukrainian claims towards the areas in the south, in the Palesse region, and, last but not least, Polish aspirations to create a strong nation-state with the inclusion of ethnically Belarusian territories.[88]

On March 9, 1918, the Second Constituent Charter proclaimed Belarus a democratic republic (Bielaruskaja Narodnaja Respublika, henceforth BDR). The declared borders of the new state included the areas of settlement of ethnic Belarusians, as well as territories with their numerical predominance, while all other nationalities were assured of national autonomy rights. The future constitution was to be adopted by the Constituent Sejm of Belarus.[89] The People's Secretariat remained in the capacity of an executive power organ.[90] It immediately sought assistance from and alliance with other democratic forces in Minsk in an attempt to expand its political influence. For instance, discussing the circumstances of the BDR proclamation in the Minsk City Duma, Jazep Varonka noted that the Second Constituent Charter considered the interests of all nations and pointed out the practical achievements of the Congress Council in maintaining order in the city during the Bolshevik evacuation. At this stage, the Minsk City Duma did not object to cooperation and agreed to send its representatives to the People's Secretariat, supporting it financially with 10,000 rubles.[91]

---

[87] Cvikievič, *Kratkii ocherk*, 14–15.
[88] Document No. 0112 "Vypiska z pratakolu pasiedžannia Mienskaj Haradzkoj Dumy za 18.03.1918," in Šupa, *Archivy Bielaruskaj Narodnaj Respubliki*, 56–57.
[89] Document No. 0101 "II-ja Ŭstaŭnaja Hramata Vykanaŭčaha Kamitetu Rady Pieršaha Ŭsiebielaruskaha Zjezdu za 9.03.1918," in Šupa, *Archivy Bielaruskaj Narodnaj Respubliki*, 52.
[90] Ibid.
[91] Document No. 0112 "Vypiska z pratakolu pasiedžannia Mienskaj Haradzkoj Dumy za 18.03.1918," in Šupa, *Archivy Bielaruskaj Narodnaj Respubliki*, 56–57.

The legislative power of the newly proclaimed BDR was temporarily delegated to the Council of the All-Belarusian Congress, or the Rada[92] of the BDR, as it was known henceforth.[93] The first chair of the Rada was Ivan Sierada, while Jazep Varonka served as his deputy.[94] On the eve of the independence proclamation on March 25, 1918, the core of the Rada consisted of the members of the Congress Council (twenty-seven persons), expanded by the inclusion of national minorities[95] as well as municipal and zemstvo representatives.[96] It incorporated various political currents and not all of them supported the idea to separate from Russia and to switch political orientation towards cooperation with the new German authorities.

On March 24, 1918, Ivan Sierada opened the session of the Rada, welcoming the delegates of the Great Belarusian Rada from Vil'nia—the brothers Anton and Ivan Luckievič, Janka Stankievič, and Jazep Turkievič, who finally received permission to travel from Vil'nia to Minsk. Thus, after three years of almost no communication, Belarusian national activists from Ober Ost could reunite with their counterparts from Minsk.[97] By that time, the Great Belarusian Rada in Vil'nia, established in late January 1918, actively promoted the idea of the indivisibility of all ethnic Belarusian lands and the creation of a separate state. After several years of German occupation, accompanied by the experiences of interaction with Lithuanian and Polish national movements in the region, the Belarusian elites in Ober Ost were the first to depart from the idea of maintaining ties to Russia, while the BDR Rada had still not achieved unity on this issue. With the encouragement of the Vil'nia Belarusians, the BSH members of the Rada proposed to discuss the proclamation of independence of the new Belarusian republic. In contrast to the Congress Council faction, which offered full support for this proposition, other factions within the Rada were divided over this issue, spending the whole night

---

[92]   In English: Council.

[93]   Document No. 0101 "II-ja Üstaŭnaja Hramata Vykanaŭčaha Kamitetu Rady Pieršaha Ŭsiebielaruskaha Zjezdu za 9.03.1918," in Šupa, *Archivy Bielaruskaj Narodnaj Respubliki*, 52.

[94]   Turuk, *Belorusskoe dvizhenie*, 42.

[95]   Here some tensions arose due to Polish demands for a larger representation. Out of fifteen places, seven were assigned to Jews, four—to Poles, two—to Russians, and one place each for Ukrainians and Lithuanians. The Polish Council of the Minsk Province petitioned the head of the People's Secretariat, Varonka, demanding ten places instead of four. Factions of the Rada considered the Polish demands to be ungrounded, yet they failed to reach an agreement on this issue as the Poles along with their four minority places already had four representatives in the group of cities and zemstvos. See *Bielaruski Šliach*, no. 31, April 29, 1918, 1.

[96]   Document No. 0131 "Schema pradstaŭnictva ŭ Radzie BDR u dzien' pryniaccia pastanovy ab niezaležnasci 25.03.1918," in Šupa, *Archivy Bielaruskaj Narodnaj Respubliki*, 63.

[97]   Luckievič, *Da historyi bielaruskaha ruchu*, 102.

in heated debates.[98] Disagreements over the independence proclamation already indicated deep internal divisions within the Rada, foreshadowing its future instability.

In particular, the BSH pro-independence faction encountered the opposition of the Socialist Revolutionaries, who enjoyed support within the Minsk City Duma and the zemstvos.[99] Municipal institutions in Belarus were generally dominated by the All-Russian parties[100] which could not accept the idea of Belarusian separation from Russia. Later, in 1918, they declared their intention to unite in the Oblast' Union of Zemstvos and Cities of Belarus as an alternative to the Rada and the People's Secretariat, which, in their opinion, "had forgotten the real needs of the Belarusian people."[101] This group also actively used the local Minsk press to force the Rada to take a step back and proclaim the declarative character of its decision on independence.[102]

However, the vote of the municipal and zemstvo delegates was not unanimous. The same applied to national minorities' delegates. The Bund voted against Belarusian independence, while the United Jewish Socialist Workers' Party and Poalei Zion abstained from voting.[103] These parties were reluctant to support independence, which they interpreted as a step towards the further dispersion of the Jewish nation. They were more likely to accept the concept of "national personal autonomy."[104] However, some of the Jewish socialists spoke in favor of Belarusian independence.[105]

At six in the morning on March 25, 1918, a majority of the Rada finally approved the proposition of the BSH. The Third Constituent Charter proclaimed the independence of the BDR, renouncing all previous state ties, which "enabled a foreign government to sign the Brest agreement in the name of Belarus," arbitrarily dividing its territories with no respect for the will of the people. The BDR government strove to revise the Brest-Litovsk peace treaty and declared that the borders of the new state extended to all ethnographically Belarusian territories, inclusive of Mahilioŭ, Minsk, and Hrodna (with the city of Białystok) provinces,

---

[98] NARB, f. 325, vop. 1, spr. 21, ark. 118.
[99] NARB, f. 567, vop. 1, spr. 11, ark. 6.
[100] These parties triumphed during the electoral campaigns of 1917 in eastern Belarus and Minsk. See *Vol'naja Bielarus'*, no. 13, August 11, 1917, 2.
[101] NARB, f. 325, vop. 1, spr. 19, ark. 68.
[102] "Skrypty šovinisty," *Bielaruski Šliach*, no. 16, April 11, 1918, 1.
[103] NARB, f. 325, vop. 1, spr. 21, ark. 118.
[104] See Chapter 4.
[105] Luckievič, *Da historyi bielaruskaha ruchu*, 104, 248.

along with parts of Vil'nia, Viciebsk, Smolensk, and Chernihiv provinces.[106] These claims were based on the *Ethnographic Map of the Belarusian Tribe*, developed by Jaŭchim Karski in 1903. Since it was the first map treating Belarusian as a separate language, it acquired political meaning in the revolutionary period, when national activists needed a precise definition of the future nation-state's borders. Karski used linguistic criteria of the spread of Belarusian dialects for the development of his map, and Belarusian national activists eagerly used it for political aims in claiming more territories. In 1918, Karski's map served as the foundation for a special cartographic commission of the BDR, which developed a detailed map of the BDR to be presented at the Paris peace conference in 1919.[107]

Even though the territorial claims of the new state reflected the boldest dreams of Belarusian nationalists, in reality, the BDR desperately lacked armed forces to protect its declared borders, let alone reach them and establish an effective authority outside of Minsk. Even news of its independence proclamation apparently reached many places in a form that caused surprise and misunderstandings. For instance, in June 1918, Kanstancin Jezavitaŭ reported to the People's Secretariat about the situation in Viciebsk, noting that the news of Belarusian independence generated fears among the local population, although these were able to be put to rest.[108] Similar reactions were also recorded in Kojdanava, not far from Minsk, most likely due to the lack of efficient communication, as the People's Secretariat had directed that its representative be sent to Kojdanava to inform the locals about the Belarusian movement.[109]

Internationally, the ambitions of the first Belarusian state antagonized its neighbors and were perceived as threats to the interests of Soviet Russia, Germany, Ukraine, and Lithuania in the region. More importantly, the first Belarusian government had no support from the German occupational authorities, who reacted negatively to the independence proclamation. They also could not accept any calls to renounce the Brest treaty. In their eyes, the Rada of the BDR was a purely socialist and therefore untrustworthy institution.[110] Therefore, attempts to receive official diplomatic recognition of the BDR by Germany remained

---

[106]   NARB, f. 325, vop. 1, spr. 21, ark. 124.

[107]   Michaluk, *Białoruska Republika Ludowa*, 244–45, 255–63.

[108]   Document No. 57 "Pratakol No. 49 pasiadžennia Naradnaha Sakrataryjata BNR," in Horny and Buča, ed., *Archivy Bielaruskaj Narodnaj Respubliki*, 139.

[109]   Document No. 16 "Pratakol No. 12 pasiadžennia Naradnaha Sakrataryjata BNR," in Horny and Buča, ed., *Archivy Bielaruskaj Narodnaj Respubliki.*, 47–49.

[110]   Rudling, *The Rise and Fall of Belarusian Nationalism*, 84.

unsuccessful.[111] However, in contrast to the Berlin civilian authorities, the German military powers in Minsk were inclined to show more flexibility towards the Belarusian question. First, as has been pointed out, the military command had its own vision of Eastern policy and second, the occupation authorities were concerned about practical issues surrounding the establishment of the occupation regime. As soon as the Germans stopped perceiving the Belarusian factor as a threat, relations gradually stabilized. In May 1918, the commander of the German 10th Army, General Erich von Falkenhayn, appeared rather sympathetic to the representatives of the BDR government, vaguely promising the "desired political outcome" and reassuring them that the Rada was to act as an intermediary between the occupation authorities and the Belarusian people.[112]

Even though the German occupation authorities did not share political power with the BDR institutions, they were willing to delegate some responsibilities to the Belarusians to facilitate governance of the newly occupied territories. Following the visit of the head of the People's Secretariat Varonka to the German Chief of Staff von Stapff on June 21, 1918, the German army command agreed to introduce positions of special Belarusian advisers in the district commandants' offices. The authority to appoint these advisers belonged to the People's Secretariat. Yet, the sole purpose of this concession was to improve the regulation of relations between the army and the local population.[113] The same applied to the assistance with refugee repatriation and the issue of sending Orthodox priests to the Vil'nia and Hrodna provinces,[114] where the local population had been deprived of spiritual services since 1915, when almost all Orthodox priests were evacuated east.[115] Echoing the approaches implemented in Ober Ost, the German authorities did not object to Belarusian cultural and educational activities.[116]

On the other hand, the refusal of the German military authorities to tolerate the formation of Belarusian army units even by November 1918[117] indicates that the German involvement in Belarusian national politics was consistently

---

[111]   Aliaksandr Cichamiraŭ, "Bielarus' u palitycy viaducych dziaržaŭ Zachadu (1914–1945 hh.)," *Białoruskie Zeszyty Historyczne*, no. 15 (2001): 171.

[112]   NARB, f. 325, vop. 1, spr. 8, ark. 53.

[113]   NARB, f. 325, vop. 1, spr. 19, ark. 304.

[114]   In 1918, German administrative reports pointed out that the Belarusian population in Białystok region was "thankful" to the authorities for the return of priests, who resumed regular Orthodox church services. See BArch, PH 30-III/5, 24.

[115]   See Chapter 1.

[116]   NARB, f. 325, vop. 1, spr. 19, ark. 304 adv.

[117]   Cichamiraŭ, "Bielarus' u palitycy," 172–73.

determined by the pragmatic everyday needs of running an effective occupation regime, rather than in assisting another anti-Russian national force. Germany adhered to the Brest-Litovsk peace treaty and its supplemental agreements, where it was obligated not to support any local separatist movements to the east of the future border with Soviet Russia. Consequently, Belarusian territories located in the areas of the new or "second" German occupation in 1918 were to be ceded to Russia under the terms of the Brest-Litovsk treaty, and were treated as a temporary trophy. This circumstance precluded expansion of Belarusian political power under German occupation.

Small German concessions did not influence the vague political and legal status of the BDR, yet they allowed Belarusian activists to continue promoting the national cause among the population. The BDR government was convinced that evidence of its support by Belarusian society would facilitate the task of achieving international recognition for the young Belarusian state.[118] In particular, the BDR institutions focused on financing Belarusian periodicals, religious and children's books, and Belarusian primers and school textbooks, as well as extending support to the existing Belarusian publishing initiative in Vil'nia. One of the major projects in the educational sphere was the construction of a Belarusian high school in Budslaŭ (Vilejka district).[119] The People's Secretariat also elevated the Belarusian language to the status of an official state language, stipulating that all official acts, documents, and correspondence should appear in Belarusian.[120]

Yet, financial difficulties limited these activities significantly, and even the daily newspaper *Bielaruski Šliach* appeared irregularly.[121] After German authorities confiscated more than 300,000 rubles from the People's Secretariat on February 25, 1918, the latter struggled to find sources of funding, relying primarily on Ukrainian trade and loans.[122] Moreover, the existing restrictions on travel between Ober Ost and the areas of the so-called "second occupation"[123] complicated communication between the BDR institutions in Minsk and the national activists in Vil'nia. The same applied to the national work in the provinces of Ober Ost,

---

[118] Michaluk, *Białoruska Republika Ludowa*, 327.
[119] Document No. 0596 "Spravazdača kasy Narodnaha Sakrataryjatu za peryjad 30.03–1.07.1918," in Šupa, *Archivy Bielaruskaj Narodnaj Respubliki*, 196–97.
[120] Document No. 0173 "Hronika dlia hazetaŭ," in Šupa, *Archivy Bielaruskaj Narodnaj Respubliki*, 74.
[121] Document No. 0712 "Chadajnictva Bielaruskaha Vydavieckaha Tavarystva ŭ Miensku 'Zaranka' pierad NS BNR za 25.07.1918," in Šupa, *Archivy Bielaruskaj Narodnaj Respubliki*, 215.
[122] Document No. 0596 "Spravazdača kasy Narodnaha Sakrataryjatu za peryjad 30.03–1.07.1918," in Šupa, *Archivy Bielaruskaj Narodnaj Respubliki*, 196.
[123] BArch, PH 30-III/5, 8 r.

where, according to German administrative reports compiled in September 1918, the ethnically Belarusian population failed to present itself as a politically organized force.[124]

BDR between Germany and Russia: Political Crisis of 1918

German neglect of the Belarusian question highlighted the need to consolidate the national movement and to turn it into a more formidable political factor. Since the insufficient political power of the BDR was recognized even in the contemporary Belarusian press,[125] the Rada of the BDR was actively looking for allies in the spring of 1918. Efforts to find common ground with the representatives of municipalities and zemstvos revealed fundamental differences, as these institutions were dominated by the All-Russian parties. Therefore, they could not accept the idea of separation from Russia. However, the need to secure Belarusian interests under German occupation dictated a greater degree of independent action. Therefore, the efforts of the Rada were directed towards the consolidation of the existing Belarusian national milieu, as demonstrated by the start of cooperation with the Minsk Belarusian Representation. Both shared more common patriotic goals in contrast to the Russian-sympathizing municipal and zemstvo members.

The Minsk Belarusian Representation was a new organization of a moderate, centrist current. Founded on February 25, 1918, it united People's Socialists, Christian Democrats, and unaffiliated persons, who were excluded from the BSH-dominated national politics in the second half of 1917.[126] The Representation positioned itself as an heir to the Belarusian National Committee (BNK)[127] and was even chaired by its former head, Raman Skirmunt, while the presidium included General Kandratovič, Orthodox archpriest Kulčycki, Paviel Aliaksiuk, Aliaksandr

---

[124] BArch, PH 30-III/5, 24.

[125] See "Čarodnaje zadanne," *Bielaruski Šliach*, no. 16, April 11, 1918, 1.

[126] Vincent Hadleŭski, "Z bielaruskaha palityčnaha žyccia ŭ Miensku ŭ 1917–18 hh.," *Spadčyna*, no. 5 (1997): 28–30.

[127] The BNK was the first short-lived organizational structure of Belarusian national activists in the period between March and July 1917. It united two major Belarusian parties, the BSH and the BNPS (Belarusian People's Party of Socialists). Both were socialist in character, yet the BNPS included more moderates and emphasized national development rather than prioritizing social issues. As the result of the disagreements between these parties in July 1917, the People's Socialists were largely excluded from decision-making and from the organizational activities of the Belarusian movement, while the BNK was replaced with the Central Rada of Belarusian Organizations, where the BSH played the leading role. See Chapter 4 for a detailed analysis.

Ulasaŭ,[128] Roman Catholic priest Vincent Hadleŭski, and the former head of the Minsk section of the Society for the Aid of War Victims, Viktar Čavusaŭ.[129] The Representation was conceptualized as a national interparty organization, promoting the political, cultural, and economic revival of Belarus. Supporting the coalition of socialists from the BSH and Belarusian national democracy, as the moderates defined themselves,[130] the Representation prioritized Belarusian statehood within the declared ethnographic borders, the promotion of Belarusian education, and the normalization of relations with neighboring nations.[131]

Members of the Representation recognized that independence was to be treated as a practical matter in politics. They pointed out that the Rada of the BDR did not have better options than to interact and to work with the new authorities, hoping to convince them to share power in civilian matters. Such a form of cooperation could potentially secure national self-determination rights and enhance the chances of achieving sovereignty in the future.[132] From these rather realistic positions, the Minsk Belarusian Representation supported cooperation with the German occupation authorities, yet at the same time emphasized Belarusian independence as the ultimate goal.[133]

The position of the Representation and the reorientation towards Germany did not enjoy popularity among the Belarusian socialists, who constituted the majority of the Rada. The chair of the People's Secretariat, Jazep Varonka, was direct in admitting that he did not trust Skirmunt, Aliaksiuk, and Hadleŭski.[134] Another BSH activist, Tamaš Hryb, was even more resolute in his evaluations, referring to the Representation as an organization of "landowners and nobles," aiming to undermine the unity of the national front.[135] This statement holds true only if Hryb's interpretation of the "national front" implies the unchallenged leadership status of the BSH within Belarusian national politics, which it enjoyed since July 1917. In this regard, the inclusion of moderates posed a problem for the dominance of the BSH, yet from a long-term perspective it diversified and democratized the Belarusian movement.

---

128   Editor-in-chief of the first Belarusian newspaper *Naša Niva* during 1906–1914.
129   Hadleŭski, "Z bielaruskaha palityčnaha žyccia," 30–31.
130   "Try Centry," *Bielaruski Šliach*, no. 16, April 11, 1918, 1.
131   "Adozva Mienskaha Bielaruskaha Predstaŭnictva," *Vol'naja Bielarus'*, no. 10, March 24, 1918, 79.
132   *Bielaruski Šliach*, no. 5, March 28, 1918, 1; NARB, f. 325, vop. 1, spr. 21, ark. 86.
133   "Adozva Mienskaha Bielaruskaha Predstaŭnictva," *Vol'naja Bielarus'*, no. 10, March 24, 1918, 79.
134   Document No. 0303 "List Jazepa Varonki Antonu Luckievičui za 27.04.1918," in Šupa, *Archivy Bielaruskaj Narodnaj Respubliki*, 132.
135   NARB, f. 567, vop. 1, spr. 11, ark. 4.

The Great Belarusian Rada in Vil'nia welcomed this step, trying to reconcile both groups and shift the emphasis towards the more important task of state-building, instead of focusing on the differences in social programs.[136] Political cooperation among the Belarusian national forces could also stabilize the Rada, providing it with an absolute pro-independence majority.[137] Brothers Ivan and Anton Luckievič argued that it could improve the image of the BDR in the eyes of the German authorities.[138] Another reason for their sympathies appears to have been the closeness of the Minsk moderates to the political views of the Vil'nia Belarusians, echoing the latter's visions of a common Belarusian-Lithuanian state. The program of the Minsk Representation, published in *Vol'naja Bielarus'* in March 1918, called for the settling of Belarusian-Lithuanian ties "on the basis of common state-building together with Kurland in order to restore the old trade routes to the sea."[139] The April statement on the positions of the Representation was more specific, calling for a "union with Lithuania and Kurland, reviving the ancient independent Belarusian-Lithuanian statehood."[140]

However, in contrast to the Ober Ost Belarusians, the idea of a federation of the successor nations of the Grand Duchy of Lithuania did not find any support or understanding in eastern Belarus. People from this region were generally more reluctant to terminate all ties to Russia, often demonstrating a lack of national-oriented thinking. For instance, when Mitrafan Doŭnar-Zapol'ski, an historian and ethnographer by profession, proposed to negotiate with the Germans a possible project of a regional federation of Belarus, Ukraine, and Lithuania, he faced opposition from a certain Trempovič, who protested against a "final" separation from Russia. Instead, he wanted Belarus to participate in the future construction of "Great Russia," implying that it should have declared support for the Whites in fighting the Bolsheviks in the civil war.[141] Even the head of the People's Secretariat, Jazep Varonka, did not exclude federation with the Russian state in its non-Soviet version.[142]

---

[136] Luckievič, *Da historyi bielaruskaha ruchu*, 169.
[137] Document No. 0195 "Čarnavik lista Antona Luckieviča (Vil'nia) siabram Mienskaha Bielaruskaha Pradstaŭnictva (Miensk) za 7.04.1918," in Šupa, *Archivy Bielaruskaj Narodnaj Respubliki*, 87–88.
[138] Ibid.
[139] "Adozva Mienskaha Bielaruskaha Predstaŭnictva," *Vol'naja Bielarus'*, no. 10, March 24, 1918, 79.
[140] "Try centry," *Bielaruski Šliach*, no. 16, April 11, 1918, 1.
[141] Document No. 0488 "Pratakol No. 15 pasiedžannia delehacyi NS BDR u sprave pieramovaŭ za 10.06.1918," in Šupa, *Archivy Bielaruskaj Narodnaj Respubliki*, 173.
[142] Luckievič, *Da historyi bielaruskaha ruchu*, 300–301.

The Rada of the BDR, originating from the All-Belarusian Congress, consisted primarily of national activists from eastern Belarus with a similar thinking. Eventually it influenced the cooperation efforts of the Minsk Representation and the Rada, and for a while it seemed that they might succeed. With the assistance of the Vil'nia Belarusians, the whole Representation was incorporated into the Rada of the BDR on April 12, 1918.[143] The leading members of the BSH, including Jazep Varonka and Arkadz' Smolič, agreed to cooperation, yet the left wing of the party protested.[144] Within the Rada, the Representation formed the faction of the center, second in size after the biggest faction of the bloc, which included the Congress Council members and the BSH. The left wing of the BSH, consisting of Tamaš Hryb, Paluta Badunova, and six others, in protest against the inclusion of the moderates, formed a separate SR faction.[145]

The rift within the BSH, leading to its division, deepened on April 25, 1918, after the Rada sent a telegram to the German Kaiser Wilhelm II. By that time, Germany had already recognized the new Ukrainian state in the course of the Brest-Litovsk peace talks, followed by the recognition of Lithuania on April 23, 1918. Hoping to achieve a similar recognition of the BDR and to increase its visibility in international politics, Raman Skirmunt, the head of the Minsk Representation and new member of the Rada, acted as the main initiator of contacting the Kaiser. As the Rada of the BDR was previously involved in interactions with the German government,[146] the fact of sending a telegram to the Kaiser was not an extraordinary step as such. The debates developed around its contents rather than the need to send it.[147]

The final version, authored by Jazep Varonka, who managed to dismiss Skirmunt's draft,[148] described the Rada as the legitimate representation of the Belarusian people and thanked the Kaiser for the "liberation from foreign rule

---

143   Hadleŭski, "Z bielaruskaha palityčnaha žyccia," 32.
144   NARB, f. 567, vop. 1, spr. 11, ark. 6.
145   NARB, f. 325, vop. 1, spr. 21, ark. 252.
146   The People's Secretariat had sent a telegram to the German chancellor Hertling in March 1918, requesting participation in the decision-making process on the Belarusian territories. See *Vol'naja Bielarus'*, no. 10, March 24, 1918, 79. See also Document No. 0186 "Memaryjal Narodnaha Sekretaryjatu BDR Imperskamu Kancleru Niamieččyny za 5.04.1918," in Šupa, *Archivy Bielaruskaj Narodnaj Respubliki*, 79–84.
147   Hadleŭski, "Z bielaruskaha palityčnaha žyccia," 34–35.
148   See Document No. 0303 "List Jazepa Varonki Antonu Luckievičovi za 27.04.1918," in Šupa, *Archivy Bielaruskaj Narodnaj Respubliki*, 132.

and anarchy."[149] With regard to the independence and indivisibility of Belarus, proclaimed in the Third Constituent Charter, the Rada asked the German Empire for protection and guarantees of territorial integrity. The telegram was signed by the chair of the Rada, Ivan Sierada, the head of the People's Secretariat, Varonka, and Rada members Skirmunt, Aŭsianik, Aliaksiuk, Krečeŭski, and Liosik.[150]

The majority of the Rada voted in favor of the telegram, while only four members were against and another four abstained. Although it remained unanswered, as Germany was not inclined to revise the Brest peace commitments,[151] it had far-reaching consequences for the internal stability of the BDR. The telegram caused discord within the Belarusian movement, destroying the apparently temporary unity of interests. The major party, the BSH, split into three groups: the left wing, inspired by the anti-German positions of Badunova and Hryb, formed the Belarusian Party of the Socialist-Revolutionaries (*Bielaruskaja Partyja Sacyjalistaŭ-Revalucyjaneraŭ*, BPSR). Politically it was close to the Russian Socialist Revolutionaries and Belarusian Bolsheviks, focusing on land redistribution, rather than state-building activities. It still supported the BSH national program, yet did not consider it a priority. This position secured the BPSR considerable support among the peasantry, which were primarily concerned about the land issue.[152]

The Belarusian Social Democratic Party (*Bielaruskaja Sacyjal-Demakratyčnaja Partyja*, BSDP) was formed by the centrists within the BSH, joined by the Vil'nia Social Democratic Workers' Group. Led by Anton Luckievič, Arkadz' Smolič, and Ivan Kraskoŭski, it promoted Belarusian independence, a democratic form of government, and nationalization of the land by means of social reforms.[153] Finally, the smallest of all three BSH successors, the Belarusian Party of the Socialists-Federalists (*Bielaruskaja Partyja Sacyjalistaŭ-Federalistaŭ*, BPSF), formed around Jazep Varonka with the support of Kanstancin Ezavitaŭ, Vasil Zacharka, Ivan Sierada, and Anton Aŭsianik.[154] It focused on balancing major social and national issues, and promoting an independent Belarus in a possible federation with a democratic Russia, but not with its Bolshevik version.[155] Two of the successors to

---

[149] NARB, f. 325, vop. 1, spr. 21, ark. 146.
[150] NARB, f. 325, vop. 1, spr. 21, ark. 146.
[151] Hadleŭski, "Z bielaruskaha palityčnaha žyccia," 36.
[152] Michaluk, *Białoruska Republika Ludowa*, 299–300.
[153] Michaluk, *Białoruska Republika Ludowa*, 300.
[154] Luckievič, *Da historyi bielaruskaha ruchu*, 169.
[155] Luckievič, *Da historyi bielaruskaha ruchu*, 300–301.

the BSH, the more radical leftist BPSR with Hryb and the BPSF with Varonka, appear to have been in clear opposition to the moderate current, while other socialists and the BSDP, including the Luckievič brothers, Liosik, Harun, and Smolič, demonstrated more flexibility to compromise and cooperate.[156]

Divisions within the BSH deepened the political crisis of the BDR government. On April 12, 1918, in the same session when the Minsk Belarusian Representation was coopted into the Rada, Varonka had already discussed the options for restructuring the People's Secretariat. He argued for a more efficient cabinet system to replace the ad hoc Secretariat formed on the eve of the German takeover of Minsk. Taking into account the inclusion of moderates into the governing structures of the BDR,[157] the majority of the Rada proceeded with voting for a coalition cabinet "for the sake of Belarusian statehood."[158] Raman Skirmunt was entrusted with the task of forming the new People's Secretariat after the announcement of the Varonka government's resignation on May 14. The replacement of Varonka's socialist-dominated Secretariat with a moderate government was aimed at facilitating relations with the German occupation authorities. Yet, the formation of the new government was delayed until the summer. Skirmunt's inclination to settle the land question through agricultural reforms and his reluctance to nationalize the land did not win him support in the Rada. Moreover, his failure to address Polish-Belarusian relations caused reservations among the left wing of the Rada, complicating the formation of the cabinet.[159]

A crisis broke out on July 9, 1918, when the Rada of the BDR officially confirmed the mandate of Skirmunt's government. The moderate faction of the Rada was also able to prevail against the socialist faction in the minor question of deciding against the creation of special commissions within the Rada.[160] In defiance, Varonka's Secretariat met on July 13 and confronted the members of the new cabinet, Astroŭski and Aliaksiuk, over the issue of power transfer.[161]

---

[156] Anatol' Sidarevič, "Urady BNR i kabinet Ramana Skirmunta," *ARCHE*, no. 4 (2008): 121.
[157] To reflect the political cooperation with the Minsk Representation, the Rada of the BDR also reelected its presidium. The new coalition presidium was chaired by Jazep Liosik, who replaced Ivan Sierada. Smolič and Ulasaŭ were elected to serve as his deputies. NARB, f. 325, vop. 1, spr. 8, ark. 39, 39 adv.
[158] Document No. 0213 "Karotkaja spravazdača z 5-ha pasiedžannia II sesii Rady BDR za 12.04.1918," in Šupa, *Archivy Bielaruskaj Narodnaj Respubliki*, 92.
[159] Michaluk, *Białoruska Republika Ludowa*, 315–16.
[160] Sidarevič, "Urady BNR," 118–20. The commissions within the Rada were nevertheless created in August 1918. See Document No. 0784 "Chronika dlia hazet. Miensk, 5.08.1918," in Šupa, *Archivy Bielaruskaj Narodnaj Respubliki*, 227.
[161] NARB, f. 325, vop. 1, spr. 7, ark. 77, 78.

The Belarusian historian Anatol' Sidarevič has suggested several explanations for Varonka's actions. One of the concerns was the perception that the moderates were taking the lead, instead of enforcing the agreement on the coalition government. In addition, Varonka might have resented the loss of his position in the government, reinforced by his personal dislike of Skirmunt and Aliaksiuk.[162]

The left-wing BSH successor parties undermined the chances of political consolidation within the governing institutions of the BDR in 1918. The BPSR and the BPSF did not trust Skirmunt's government, accusing it of Polonophile tendencies, although the Minsk Representation did not make any statements regarding Poland. In fact, its orientation was anti-Russian, offering new ways of building Belarusian statehood with regard to the existing political circumstances, which at that time favored a pro-German direction. Yet, the Belarusian left wing was extremely suspicious of the Poles, using the exaggeration of a perceived Polish threat[163] for the construction of a powerful image of the national "other." This reasoning often denied the local Poles the right of being represented in the Belarusian government. An exclusivist way of thinking of the nation and a lack of confidence was characteristic for the BPSR and BPSF, as in their understanding being Belarusian was invariably connected to peasant origins. Eventually, such a stereotypical approach made them suspicious even towards the Belarusian national activists who belonged to the Roman Catholic faith.[164]

The internal crisis of Belarusian national politics was complicated by the international situation. In foreign policy, Skirmunt prioritized international recognition of the Belarusian state, which was dependent on the positions of either Russia or Germany. Since Russia did not welcome the proclamation of BDR independence and still planned on a forced "federation" with the Soviet state,[165] Skirmunt's reasoning in favor of a German orientation offered more room for maneuver for the Belarusian state. However, by mid-1918 Germany was focused on its Western front and did not intend to destabilize the situation in the East by violating its agreements with Russia.[166]

---

[162] Sidarevič, "Urady BNR," 122.
[163] For instance, Varonka was especially adamant about perceived Polish threats in his speech on July 9, 1918, accusing "certain new local elements" of enlisting into the ranks of the Belarusian nation after the failure of Polish forces to gain power in Minsk. See NARB, f. 325, vop. 1, spr. 8, ark. 83.
[164] Michaluk, *Białoruska Republika Ludowa*, 320.
[165] See Document No. 1038 "Pro memoria Nadzvyčajnaj Delegacyi Rady BDR (Kieŭ) Narodnamu Sakrataryjatu BDR (Miensk)," in Šupa, *Archivy Bielaruskaj Narodnaj Respubliki*, 269.
[166] Rudovič, "Bielaruski dzejač z vialikich panoŭ," 34.

The tendency to move out of the Russian orbit was continued by the third People's Secretariat, which promptly replaced Skirmunt's government on July 22. Chaired by Ivan Sierada, it appeared less controversial for the Belarusian socialists, but in essence continued to focus on relations with the German authorities. Looking for a detour route to achieve recognition of the BDR by Germany, Sierada's government attempted to establish closer ties to Ukraine—another newcomer on the political map of Europe. However, in contrast to the BDR, Ukraine enjoyed German support.[167] A delegation led by Aliaksandr Cvikievič had already travelled to Kyiv in April 1918.[168] Along with the recognition of the BDR and finding a regional ally, its main task was to secure financial assistance.[169] However, initial discussions were dominated by the issue of the BDR's southern border with Ukraine and in particular, Ukrainian ambitions towards the contested Palesse region.[170]

Between September and November 1918, up until the last days of Skoropadsky's regime, BDR delegations continued to negotiate the issue of the recognition of independence by Ukraine. Anton Luckievič discussed this question with the Ukrainian foreign minister Doroshenko, offering to create a common front against the Bolsheviks and suggesting the creation of a regional federation. Ukrainian authorities assured the delegation only of their sympathies towards the BDR, but refused to recognize its independence until there was an agreement from the German side. Doroshenko offered financial assistance and promised to act as an intermediary in establishing contacts with Berlin. Yet at the same time, the Ukrainians appropriated the region of western Palesse and used their relations with the BDR to exercise pressure on Soviet Russia, threatening to recognize the Belarusian state should Russia refuse to transfer the eastern Palesse areas to Ukraine.[171] Thus, the international situation was not favorable for the BDR, leaving it powerless and without any reliable allies in the region.

---

[167] *Bielaruski Šliach*, no. 5, March 28, 1918, 1.

[168] The delegation was able to establish diplomatic and economic ties: Belarusian consulates operated in Kyiv and Odesa, and a Belarusian Commerce Chamber opened in Kyiv. See Turuk, *Belorusskoe dvizhenie*, 44.

[169] Tacciana Paŭlava, "Asnoŭnyja napramki zniešnepalityčnaj dzejnasci BNR u 1918–1920 hh.," *Białoruskie Zeszyty Historyczne*, no. 15 (2001): 80.

[170] Belarusian-Ukrainian border negotiations and the arguments of both sides are discussed in detail by Dorota Michaluk. See Michaluk, *Białoruska Republika Ludowa*, 247–57.

[171] Michaluk, *Białoruska Republika Ludowa*, 324–26.

Soviet Version: The Belarusian National Commissariat

The divisions within the BSH, which affected BDR governance, date back to the 3rd Congress of the party, which was held between October 14 and 20, 1917, in Minsk. It resulted in the first serious crisis within the main Belarusian political party, caused by the uncompromising positions of its left wing, which antagonized the majority of the party by advocating socialism over the program of national consolidation.[172] The left wing of the BSH received support from the Petrograd section of the party and the Belarusian Social Democrats in Russia, represented by the Belarusian Social Democratic Workers' Party (*Bielaruskaja Sacyjal-Demakratyčnaja Rabočaja Partyja,* BSDRP).[173] Together they became the foundation of the Belarusian political forces operating in Soviet Russia during 1918.

In early 1918, all Russian-based Belarusian socialists had to decide how to engage in national politics and whether to do so under the auspices of the Soviet government or not. Their options were limited by either hopeless confrontation with Soviet power or a faint chance at Belarusian self-determination, albeit directed and controlled from above. Bolshevik regime consolidation did not leave them much of a choice. The dissolution of the All-Belarusian Congress on December 18, 1917, made it clear that the Bolsheviks were determined to hold onto power by any means. On the other hand, some flexibility that the Bolsheviks demonstrated in handling the national issue attracted many non-Russian socialists. Unlike their adversaries in the Civil War who fought for the "one and indivisible" Russia, the Bolsheviks recognized the potential of national movements as tools to strengthen Soviet power. National minorities were allowed a symbolic representation in the government, along with the prospects of participation in the decision-making process within the People's Commissariat for Nationality Affairs (Narkomnats). In essence, the Narkomnats was an improvised institution, created as a recruitment tool for national elites who were willing to collaborate with the Bolsheviks and ensure mass support for Soviet power in the non-Russian regions.[174]

---

[172] Žylunovič, "Liuty—Kastryčnik," 193.

[173] The party's roots are traced back to the Petrograd conference of the BSH in June 1917. Led by Alaiksandr Čarviakoŭ, the BSDRP took shape in late September 1917, incorporating members of the Narva organization of the BSH. At first, it existed as a separate party with representation in the Bolshevik party committee. In March 1918, the BSDRP merged with the Russian Communist Party and was reduced to the status of a section within the latter. Its members later made careers in the government of the BSSR. See Anatol' Sidarevič, "Da historyi Bielaruskaj Sacyjalistyčnaj Hramady: ahliad krynicaŭ," *ARCHE,* no. 4 (2006): 158; Ladyseŭ and Bryhadzin, *Pamiž Uschodam i Zachadam,* 42; Turuk, *Belorusskoe dvizhenie,* 47–48.

[174] Smith, *The Bolsheviks and the National Question,* 31. On Narkomnats and its place within the early Soviet government structures, see Stephen Blank, *The Sorcerer as Apprentice: Stalin as*

In the Belarusian case, the trend towards the Soviet cooptation of national elites became evident with the decision to establish the Belarusian National Commissariat (*Bielaruski Nacyjanal'ny Kamisaryjat*, Bielnackam) in Petrograd as a subdivision of the Narkomnats on January 31, 1918, following the attack on the CBVR and its members in Minsk. From the Bolshevik perspective, it was to provide an institutional legitimation for their appropriation of Belarusian nationalism.[175] The left wing of the BSH and the Belarusian Social Democrats in Russia formed the core of the Bielnackam, treating it as an opportunity to advance the Belarusian national cause within the Soviet state. Being aware that wartime destruction made it hardly possible for Belarus to survive as an independent state without assistance of the great powers, the majority of Belarusian socialists in Petrograd agreed that state-building remained their priority, even if it was to be built under close Soviet supervision and in connection with Russia. The prospect of holding the Second All-Belarusian Congress further reinforced the decision of Belarusian socialists to cooperate with Soviet power. Yet, in exchange, they had to give up their own independent roles and recognize the rights of the Soviet government to decide all crucial aspects of the Belarusian state-building process.[176]

Cooperation with the Soviet authorities promised some additional incentives and immediate benefits, including financial assistance for publishing activities, access to refugee relief funds, and the formal possibility to join the Soviet governing institutions. Being aware of these opportunities, the general meeting of the Petrograd section of the BSH and BSDRP sent a delegation to the central Soviet government already in early January 1918 to negotiate possible assistance options. Starting from February 1918, Belarusian socialists in Russia continued their activities within the institutional structures of Bielnackam, headed by A. Čarviakoŭ, one of the organizers and leaders of the BSDRP. Zmicier Žylunovič from the left wing of the BSH served as the chief secretary of the new organization. In March 1918, along with other Soviet state institutions, Bielnackam moved to Moscow and started publishing its own newspaper, *Dziannica*, there. Branches of Bielnackam existed in Petrograd, Viciebsk, Smolensk, and Saratov, focusing on the spread of Soviet propaganda among ethnic Belarusians.[177]

Commissar of Nationalities, 1917–1924 (Westport: Greenwood Press, 1994), 7–29.

[175] Michaluk, *Białoruska Republika Ludowa*, 223–24; Latyšonak, *Žaŭnery BNR*, 56.

[176] Ryhor Laz'ko, "Bielnackam i Narkamnac: pieršy prykry vopyt uzaemaadnosin (studzien'–červien' 1918 h.)," *Bielaruski histaryčny časopis*, no. 2 (2012): 6–7.

[177] Siarhiej Siniak, "Bielaruskae pytanne i kanflikt bielaruskich aktyvistaŭ Maskvy i Pietrahrada (1918–1919 hh.)," *Bielaruski histaryčny časopis*, no. 2 (2012): 17. "O deiatel'nosti Belarusskago Natsional'nogo Komissariata," *Dziannica*, no. 11, May 1, 1918, 1.

Some Bielnackam members supported the creation of an independent Belarusian state, while others sympathized with Marxist internationalism, denigrating the BDR.[178] For instance, Jaŭsej Kančar, the former head of the Belarusian Oblast' Committee, did not object to the BDR. Speaking on the occasion of a Belarusian refugees meeting in Petrograd on April 14, 1918, which was attended by about 8,000 people according to *Dziannica*, Kančar commended the efforts of the Executive Committee of the First All-Belarusian Congress towards securing the existence of a Belarusian republic.[179] However, in the course of 1918, the positions of the Belarusian socialists in Russia towards the BDR became more confrontational. Bielnackam started presenting itself as a superior solution to the BDR, aspiring to the status of a new Belarusian political center. Zmicier Žylunovič in particular was keen on attacking the BDR and his former party colleagues from the BSH.[180]

Even though the Bielnackam was careful not to demand full participation in the decision-making process regarding the governance of the Belarusian territories,[181] it gradually emerged in the role of an alternative to the former Obliskomzap Bolsheviks. The latter fled from the advancing Germans to Smolensk, which became the center of the Western oblast' and included territories of Smolensk, Viciebsk, and Mahilioŭ provinces in April 1918. The Obliskomzap transformed into the Executive Committee of the Western Oblast' (Oblastiskomzap), headed by Miasnikov.[182] The new Bolshevik institution retained extremely anti-Belarusian positions, opposing even the officially approved activities of the Bielnackam. For instance, in September 1918, it resisted the latter's proposition to rename the Western oblast' to the "Belarusian oblast'"[183] and to transfer power over

---

[178] This tendency reflected divisions among the Bolshevik leadership, which did not have a clear idea on settling the nationality question after the October Revolution. While Lenin argued for a gradual road towards socialism allowing for nationalities to complete all stages of historical development as suggested by Marx, other Bolsheviks, among them Bukharin and Piatakov, interpreted the principle of national self-determination as being counterproductive and emphasized economic factors as crucial instruments for the construction of socialism. Francine Hirsch terms these two currents as ethnographic and economic paradigms, respectively, arguing that Soviet nationality policy developed as a result of the competition between these two approaches. See Francine Hirsch, *Empire of Nations: Ethnographic Knowledge and the Making of the Soviet Union* (Ithaca: Cornell University Press, 2005), 64–65. Laz'ko, "Bielnackam i Narkamnac," 11.

[179] *Dziannica*, no. 11, May 1, 1918, 3.

[180] Laz'ko, "Bielnackam i Narkamnac," 11–12.

[181] "O deiatel'nosti Belarusskago Natsional'nogo Komissariata," *Dziannica*, no. 11, May 1, 1918, 1.

[182] Ignatenko, *Istoriia Belorusskoi SSR*, 245.

[183] It was renamed the Western Commune instead.

the unoccupied territories of Viciebsk, Mahilioŭ, parts of Smolensk, Orel, and Pskov provinces with ethnic Belarusian populations to the representatives of the Belarusian peasants and workers. The Smolensk Bolsheviks immediately labeled Bielnackam's activities as "chauvinistic" and "counterrevolutionary," interfering in its work on the unoccupied Belarusian territories.[184] For instance, despite the requests of the local population, not a single Belarusian school was opened in the eastern Belarusian districts under Soviet power. Publication of Belarusian books was not possible there either, and the ban extended even to the publication of translated Communist propaganda materials.[185] The Smolensk department of the Bielnackam was promptly closed by the Executive Committee of the Western Oblast' already in June 1918.[186] The branch in Viciebsk was able to continue working under pressure until late 1918, when it was also dissolved on the orders of the Viciebsk Committee of the Communist party.[187]

These experiences of the Bielnackam reflect the consistently hostile reactions of the official leadership of the Western Oblast' towards Belarusian national demands. More generally, these tensions also demonstrate the overall problematic position of the Narkomnats in the system of the Soviet government, caused by the vaguely defined role of this ministry. The Bolshevik authorities treated it primarily as a subordinate organ of the central government, while the representatives of the non-Russian nationalities interpreted their inclusion into the Narkomnats as recognition of their expertise in national politics, treating it as a tool of political advocacy.[188]

The case of the Bielnackam can be interpreted as a confirmation of this trend, illustrating the growing frustrations and disillusionment of the Soviet-coopted national elites as they realized their subordinate positions. For instance, in the spring of 1918 the Bielnackam's Military Department optimistically planned for the creation of Belarusian detachments within the Red Army, pursuing a similar tactic as the CBVR in January 1918. However, this plan was never implemented. Moreover, the Military Department itself was soon disbanded,[189] forcing the Bielnackam to switch its focus towards cultural and humanitarian tasks.

---

[184] See Document No. 5 "Dokladnaia zapiska 'Sovetskaia vlast' v Belorussii,'" in Selemenev, *1 ianvariia 1919 goda*, 218.

[185] Ibid.

[186] Laz'ko, "Bielnackam i Narkamnac," 8.

[187] *Dziannica*, no. 42, December 17, 1918, 3.

[188] Smith, *The Bolsheviks and the National Question*, 32.

[189] Laz'ko, "Bielnackam i Narkamnac," 7–8.

Deprived of the opportunity to expand its activities on the Belarusian territories, Bielnackam turned its attention to the Belarusian refugees in Russia. Due to the slow evolution of modern Belarusian nationalism in the pre-war years, the refugees had been barely exposed to any comprehensive national agitation at home. Displacement and resettlement only worsened the situation, as Belarusians in Russia did not possess their own stable national refugee organizations throughout the First World War. Consequently, they did not show any particular interest in national politics. Motivated only by the primary concern of returning home, Belarusian refugees did not attach any particular value to national identifications and often did not hesitate in declaring their belonging to different nationalities,[190] making use of the services offered by the Polish and Lithuanian National Commissariats, which had been established prior to the Bielnackam.[191] A representative of the Bielnackam, reporting from the Saratov province, noted that Belarusian Catholics residing there apparently were "taken over" by Polish national refugee organizations, while the Orthodox remained an unorganized "inert mass" in terms of political participation, still in need of being educated about "civil and national self-consciousness."[192] Left without connections to their homeland, Belarusian refugees in Russia often lived in an information vacuum. The report from Saratov province also mentioned that even by 1918 Belarusian refugees had still not been informed about the political situation in Belarus and Russia.[193]

Throughout 1918, Bielnackam emissaries visited various districts in the Russian provinces, attempting to overcome these signs of "national indifference." Emphasizing Bielnackam's attention to the specific needs and concerns of Belarusians, they organized committees for the Belarusian refugees, distributed political brochures, and recruited activists to continue their work on the local level.[194] For some of the refugees, these contacts with the Bielnackam might have been the first encounter with the Belarusian national idea, even if it was in Soviet "packaging."

In practical terms, by the fall of 1918, the Refugee Department of the Bielnackam assisted in the repatriation of about 70,000 people[195] (the majority of them,

---

190 NARB, f. 4, vop. 1, spr. 68, ark. 34.
191 Laz'ko, "Bielnackam i Narkamnac," 6.
192 NARB, f. 4, vop. 1, spr. 67, ark. 4.
193 NARB, f. 4, vop. 1, spr. 67, ark. 4.
194 NARB, f. 4, vop. 1, spr. 67, ark. 4 adv.
195 The exact number of Belarusian refugees in Russia during the First World War remains unknown, since the official statistics assigned Belarusians together with Ukrainians into the category of "Great Russians." Researchers suggest that a total of about 1.4 million people were evacuated

about 50,000, were natives of Hrodna province).[196] The Cultural-Educational Department of the Bielnackam negotiated with the central government on the issue of the re-evacuation of pedagogical institutions to Belarus and established contacts with Belarusian teachers, instructing them on how to organize and run cultural groups.[197]

Despite the lack of support from the central government and insufficient funding,[198] the Bielnackam expanded its activities beyond Petrograd and Moscow, making a serious attempt to establish targeted relief for the Belarusian refugees in Russia and to promote Belarusian national identity among these people for the first time. Bielnackam's attention to the practical needs of the refugees, along with promises of material benefits enjoyed by other nationalities, popularized the option of identifying as Belarusian among the refugees. In this manner, it pioneered and advanced the national cause among the Belarusian refugees in Russia, who had been neglected over the course of the entire First World War.

Towards Belarusian Soviet Statehood

Belarusian Bolsheviks from the Bielnackam made an attempt to solidify their status within the central party structures already in May 1918. They aspired towards the establishment of a separate Belarusian section in the Central Committee of the Communist party, since the only official organization of Belarusian Communists at that time had been the district-level local Petrograd section. Yet, the Central Committee refused the request and an official Belarusian Communist organization in Moscow, along with sections in other cities, emerged only in November 1918.[199] Soon thereafter it called for a conference of the Belarusian Communist sections to be held on December 21–23, declaring the creation of a Belarusian Soviet Republic in the capacity of "an outpost of the Russian revolution" to be a priority task.[200] The conference concluded with the election of Zmicier Žylunovič as chair

---

from the Vil'nia, Hrodna, Minsk, Viciebsk, and Mahilioŭ provinces, where the majority of the ethnically Belarusian population resided. See Gatrell, *A Whole Empire Walking*, 212–14; Mironowicz, Tokć, and Radzik, *Zmiana struktury narodowościowej*, 24–26.

[196] NARB, f. 4, vop. 1, spr. 67, ark. 105.

[197] NARB, f. 4, vop. 1, spr. 67, ark. 105.

[198] Document No. 5 "Dokladnaia zapiska 'Sovetskaia vlast' v Belorussii,'" in Selemenev, *1 ianvariia 1919*, 216–17.

[199] Laz'ko, "Bielnackam i Narkamnac," 14.

[200] Document No. 5 "Dokladnaia zapiska 'Sovetskaia vlast' v Belorussii,'" in Selemenev, *1 ianvariia 1919*, 220.

of the Bielnackam and the head of the Belarusian sections within the RKP(b) (Russian Communist Party [Bolsheviks]).[201]

The German defeat in the First World War on November 11, 1918, resulted in the subsequent annulment of the Brest peace treaty on November 13 and the return of Soviet power to Minsk and the central regions of Belarus. This posed a new set of problems and threats for the Belarusian national activists. The future status of the Belarusian territories remained unclear up until late December 1918. In contrast to the BDR government, which was evacuated from Minsk and moved to Hrodna, where German armies remained until the early spring of 1919,[202] the Belarusian Communists in Russia saw a chance to advance their struggle for Belarusian Soviet statehood. They wanted to seize the initiative from the Western oblast' Bolsheviks, who in their own words "protected only the oblast' structures, but not the nation."[203] The central Soviet government remained undecided on the issue until the end of 1918. Eventually, it was the international situation in the region that prompted it to create revolutionary governments on the territories vacated by the German armies, as was the case with Soviet Lithuania, Latvia, and also Belarus.

The Russian Bolsheviks expected that the German defeat in the First World War would revitalize national aspirations in the borderlands, encouraged by the previous German policies of fostering anti-Russian moods among the local national movements. To neutralize it, the Central Committee of the Communist Party decided to employ a similar strategy by creating a *cordon sanitaire* of buffer republics.[204] Lenin himself mentioned to the Smolensk Bolsheviks that the Belarusian republic was to be designed as a buffer state at the border to the West.[205] The Belarusian Soviet state was thus conceptualized from above as a counterbalance to the newly created independent Polish state, as well as to Ukraine, where Bolsheviks were concerned about existing and potentially

---

[201] Siniak, "Bielaruskae pytanne," 22.

[202] Andrej Čarniakevič, *Naradženne bielaruskaj Harodni: Z historyi nacyjanal'naha ruchu 1909–1939 hadoŭ* (Minsk: Vydavec A. M. Januškievič, 2015), 25–27.

[203] Document No. 12a "Protokol No. 12 zasedaniia TsB KPB ot 31/1," in Selemenev, *1 ianvariia 1919*, 92.

[204] Document No. 30 "Protocol No. 10 zasedaniia Central'nogo Biuro Kommunisticheskoi partii (bolshevikov) Belorusii," in V. I. Adamushko et al., eds., *Vitebskaia guberniia, 1917–1924 gg.: Dokumenty i materialy* (Vitebsk: Vitebskaia oblastnaia tipografiia, 2012), 98.

[205] Document No. 12a "Protokol No. 12 zasedaniia TsB KPB ot 31/1," in Selemenev, *1 ianvariia 1919*, 92.

destabilizing "nationalist tendencies."[206] Furthermore, the Soviet government had doubts about the feasibility of the project of Soviet Lithuania, exacerbated by the ambitions of some Polish political forces to restore the 1772 pre-partition Commonwealth borders.[207] As a side effect, support for Belarusian statehood could improve the image of the Soviet state as a protector of non-Russian nationalities. Later, it evolved into one of the strategies to weaken the Polish state from within. Known as "the Piedmont principle," this approach influenced the development of nationality policy in the Belarusian Soviet state during the interwar period.[208]

At the same time, the Bolsheviks realized that the establishment of Soviet Belarus "would strongly encourage national-chauvinistic dreams."[209] Adol'f Ioffe, a member of the Central Committee of the RKP(b), warned that without strong control, "bourgeois elements will use national slogans to confuse proletarian self-consciousness, as is happening in Poland."[210] With these reservations in mind, the People's Commissar of Nationalities, Stalin, kept the Belarusian state-building process under close supervision and control, interfering whenever necessary. On December 25, 1918, he met with Žylunovič and his party colleagues to discuss the proclamation manifesto of the new republic[211] and handed down the list of ministers for the first Belarusian Soviet government.[212] He specifically pointed out the subordinate position of the future Central Bureau of the Belarusian Communist Party to the central Soviet institutions.[213]

On the same day, the Central Committee of the RKP(b) sent a telegram to the Smolensk Communists, ordering the formation of the Belarusian Soviet government.[214] Being aware of the anti-Belarusian positions of the Western oblast' administration, the Belarusian Communists tried to negotiate with Stalin the composition of the future government, yet Stalin sided with Miasnikov, forcing Žylunovič and the Belarusian Communists to obey the Central Committee and

---

[206] Hirsch, *Empire of Nations*, 150.
[207] Šybeka, *Narys historyi Bielarusi*, 212.
[208] Hirsch, *Empire of Nations*, 150; Rudling, *The Rise and Fall of Belarusian Nationalism*, 139–40; Martin, *The Affirmative Action Empire*, 9.
[209] Document No. 30 "Protokol No. 10 zasedaniia Tsentral'nogo Biuro Kommunisticheskoi partii (bolshevikov) Belorusii," in Adamushko, *Vitebskaia guberniia*, 98.
[210] Ibid.
[211] The location of the document with the decision of the TsK to form a Belarusian government remains unknown. See Emanuil Iofe, "Neviadomy Zmicier Žylunovič," *Maladosc'*, no. 780 (November 2012): 89.
[212] Ignatenko, *Istoriia Belorusskoi SSR*, 250.
[213] Šybeka, *Narys historyi Bielarusi*, 212.
[214] Šybeka, *Narys historyi Bielarusi*, 211–12.

agree to be a minority in their own government. The latter was to be composed of seven Belarusian Communists, seven members of the Executive Committee of the Western Oblast', and two members appointed by Moscow.[215]

Meanwhile in Smolensk, the Oblastiskomzap organized the 6th North-Western Regional Conference of the Communist Party and promptly transformed it into the 1st Congress of the Communist Party of Belarus, KP(b)B, declared to be an indivisible part of the RKP(b). The Central Bureau (TsB) of the new party division was headed by Miasnikov.[216] This step effectively sidelined the Belarusian Communist sections within the RKP(b), formed in Moscow in November 1918. When Žylunovič and the delegation of Belarusian Communists arrived in Smolensk, anticipating the meeting of the new government, they found out that Miasnikov had called a meeting of the Central Bureau of the Communist Party of Belarus without waiting for them. Only two Belarusians (Žylunovič and Lahun) were allowed to join the new TsB, outnumbered by thirteen Oblastiskomzap members.[217] Conflict developed immediately, as Žylunovič demanded fair representation of the Belarusian Communists both in the Central Bureau and in the Belarusian government.[218]

According to the protocol of the first meeting of the Central Bureau of the KP(b)B on December 31, 1918, the Oblastiskomzap Communists ignored Žylunovič's requests to include the representatives of the Belarusian Communist section from Moscow into the new TsB, refusing even to recognize them as a legitimate party section.[219] In protest, Žylunovič walked out of the meeting and submitted a complaint to the central authorities.[220] Apparently, as compensation for Miasnikov's manipulations with the new TsB, Žylunovič requested to exclude three Smolensk Communists from the Belarusian government (Miasnikov, Kalmanovich, and Pikel). Yet, Stalin refused and left the Belarusian Communists outnumbered in their own government.[221] Eventually, they had to obey all

---

[215]   Document No. 5 "Dokladnaia zapiska 'Sovetskaia vlast' v Belorussii,'" in Selemenev, *1 ianvariia 1919*, 221.

[216]   Šybeka, *Narys historyi Bielarusi*, 212.

[217]   Document No. 5 "Dokladnaia zapiska 'Sovetskaia vlast' v Belorussii,'" in Selemenev, *1 ianvariia 1919*, 221.

[218]   Iofe, "Neviadomy Zmicier Žylunovič," 89.

[219]   Document No. 1 "Protokol No. 1 zasedaniia Tsentral'nogo Biuro Kommunisticheskoi partii (bolshevikov) Belorussii 31 dekabria 1918 goda," in Selemenev, *1 ianvariia 1919*, 46–48.

[220]   Document No. 5 "Dokladnaia zapiska 'Sovetskaia vlast' v Belorussii,'" in Selemenev, *1 ianvariia 1919*, 221.

[221]   Iofe, "Neviadomy Zmicier Žylunovič," 90.

decisions issued by the Central Committee, as it predictably sided with Miasnikov, who became its primary liaison in Belarus, receiving direct orders from Moscow regarding the organization of the Belarusian government.[222] Following Miasnikov's initiative, the new TsB and the Belarusian Communists held another meeting, which decided to issue a manifesto of the Provisional Worker-Peasant Soviet Government of Belarus on January 1, 1919. The text of the official proclamation of the Soviet Socialist Republic of Belarus (SSRB) was coordinated with Moscow and was signed by only five members of the new government, including Žylunovič, Čarviakoŭ, Miasnikov, Ivanov, and Reingold. It appeared in the press on January 2, 1919, first in Russian, and only later in Belarusian translation.[223]

In order to consolidate power over the newly created SSRB and to eliminate all possible competition from the Belarusian Communists, Miasnikov and his Central Bureau outlawed the Belarusian Communist sections of the RKP(b) on January 15, 1919, explaining this step by their alleged "nationalist agitation" and intentions to "disorganize local Communist and Soviet work."[224] Arrests of several Belarusian Bolsheviks followed. In a grim coincidence, they were ordered by the head of the Minsk garrison Krivoshein, who commanded the violent dissolution of the All-Belarusian Congress on December 18, 1917. Western oblast' Communists did not hesitate to test their power by any means, and were known for their mocking of Belarusian national culture in the press. The opening of national schools and the publication of newspapers in Belarusian was considered to be superfluous.[225]

Official legitimization of the puppet Soviet Belarusian statehood was provided through the All-Belarusian Congress of Soviets of Workers', Peasants', and Soldiers' Deputies, which took place in Minsk from February 2 to 3, 1919. All delegates were loyal party appointees, and none directly elected by the Belarusian population. The congress formed a Central Executive Committee. Belarusian Communists were excluded from this institution, while its presidium, chaired by Miasnikov, de facto received the authority of a government. More importantly,

---

[222]   Document No. 4 "Protokol zasedaniia Tsentral'nogo Biuro Kommunisticheskoi partii Belorussii 3 ianvaria 1919 goda," in Selemenev, *1 ianvariia 1919*, 51.

[223]   Document No. 5 "Dokladnaia zapiska "Sovetskaia vlast' v Belorussii," in Selemenev, *1 ianvariia 1919*, 222; Document No. 1 "Manifest Časovaha Rabotniča-Sialianskaha Saveckaha Urada Bielarusi," in ibid., 13–16.

[224]   Document No. 7 "Protokol No. 7 zasedaniia Tsentral'nogo Biuro Kommunisticheskoi partii (bolshevikov) Belorussii ot 15 ianvaria 1919 goda," in Selemenev, *1 ianvariia 1919*, 65.

[225]   Document No. 5 "Dokladnaia zapiska "Sovetskaia vlast' v Belorussii," in Selemenev, *1 ianvariia 1919*, 226–28.

the congress decided to unite the western parts of Soviet Belarus with the Minsk, Hrodna and parts of Vil'nia provinces into one republic with Soviet Lithuania, while the eastern Belarusian territories along with the Mahilioŭ, Viciebsk, and Smolensk provinces were transferred to Russia.[226]

The motivations of the central Soviet authorities are summarized in the statement of the representative of the Central Committee Ioffe, who feared that even the mere fact of establishing statehood in the region with weak nationalism could ignite and catalyze national mobilization processes, threatening to transform "the proletarian republic into a bourgeois republic" and endanger Soviet class politics. These considerations led him to believe that national forces could be controlled by a "divide and rule" strategy, where the size of the buffer states was to be limited.[227] As a result, the division of the SSRB and the merger of the remaining Belarusian territories with Soviet Lithuania effectively ended the brief period of the first Belarusian Soviet statehood and established another short-lived buffer state, which was to fall victim to the advancing Polish armies already by the spring of 1919.

Throughout 1918, the Bielnackam and Belarusian Bolsheviks tried to establish Belarusian Soviet statehood. However, it did not take them long to realize that the Bolsheviks were not willing to share any of the decision-making power. The Bielnackam was not able to boast any great successes in political advocacy, failing to influence Soviet policymaking in relation to Belarus and to establish any effective representation on the eastern Belarusian territories, losing the political struggle against the Western oblast' Communist functionaries. The status of the Bielnackam within the Soviet state was in certain respects reminiscent of the experiences of the BDR under German occupation, yet in contrast to Germany, Soviet Russia had clear long-term intentions of keeping Belarusian territories in its possession, and therefore paid close attention to political control over the Belarusian socialists. By early 1919, the Smolensk Communists with the support of the Central Committee were able to neutralize all efforts of the Belarusian Bolsheviks and assume actual power over the Belarusian territories, deciding their fate as they pleased.

---

[226] Šybeka, *Narys historyi Bielarusi*, 214–20; Turuk, *Belorusskoe dvizhenie*, 51.

[227] Document No. 10a "Protokol No. 10 zasedaniia TsB ot 22/1," in Selemenev, *1 ianvariia 1919*, 81–82.

Conclusion

The analysis presented in this chapter suggests that the BDR played the role of a political center which defended Belarusian interests, and strove to become a state to the degree that this was possible under the conditions of 1918. In this capacity, the BDR prioritized Belarusian national interests, departing from Russia-oriented state-building concepts. It continued national mobilization work among the population, popularizing the Belarusian language and advancing cultural and educational activities. In contrast to the Bolshevik military front authorities which claimed power over Belarus, the first Belarusian state derived its legitimacy from the First All-Belarusian Congress. The BDR established a state tradition, the first foundation myth, and a point of reference for future national activists, and it should be evaluated first and foremost in terms of its lasting legacies for the Belarusian national movement.

Yet, the BDR also suffered from a number of fundamental flaws, preventing its evolution into a fully functional nation-state. The principal weakness of the BDR was the lack of physical military power. This marginalized the Belarusian national movement both in the eyes of Germany and Soviet Russia, preventing the BDR from establishing itself as a subject of international politics in the region. Furthermore, the provisions of the Brest-Litovsk peace treaty deprived the BDR of the protection of the great powers. Germany strictly adhered to its agreement with Soviet Russia, concentrating on the war effort on the Western front and taking advantage of the resources in the conquered Eastern Europe. In this regard, Ukraine was exploited as a principal pressure factor on Soviet Russia and played the key role in the "bread peace" scheme. It managed to sign a separate peace with the Central Powers and emerged as the primary beneficiary of political concessions. By contrast, Belarus was excluded from the German sphere of influence and was treated as a hostage to secure implementation of the Brest treaty. Consequently, the German occupation authorities effectively obstructed all attempts of the BDR to achieve recognition and acquire more political power throughout 1918. These circumstances left the first Belarusian state unable to defend itself after the German withdrawal from the Belarusian territories by late 1918.

Internally, the BDR was further weakened by the lack of agreement among the freshly-minted Belarusian statesmen, which translated into the transient and unstable nature of several BDR governments during 1918. Echoing the history of the Belarusian National Committee in 1917, the socialists demonstrated an unwillingness to cooperate with the moderates. The oldest Belarusian party, the BSH, split over this issue into three smaller parties, leading to the further fragmentation and marginalization of Belarusian politics. The fate of the moderates, who in 1918 gathered around the Minsk Belarusian Representation, was even more dramatic. Lacking strong organizational structures and facing hostility from the socialist part of the Belarusian national milieu, the moderates failed to consolidate as a political force.

At the same time, the Belarusian left-wing socialists, who were based in Russia, did not lose hope of advancing a Soviet version of Belarusian statehood, taking advantage of the flexible Soviet approach to nationalities policy. Adapting to the unexpected levels of nationalism in the former tsarist Russia, the Bolsheviks attempted to use its potential in order to strengthen Soviet power in the non-Russian borderlands. In the Belarusian case, the aftermath of the First All-Belarusian Congress influenced the Bolshevik decision to coopt national elites and appropriate the national movement. On the other hand, construction of the Belarusian Soviet state cannot be attributed exclusively to the need to control and use nationalism.

The lack of formal state attributes is even more apparent in the case of the first Belarusian Soviet state than in that of the BDR, as the emergence of the SSRB was completely dependent on the will of the central Soviet government in Moscow and on the actions of the Bolsheviks from the former Obliskomzap structures, known for their anti-Belarusian positions. Misled by the illusions of cooptation into the Soviet governing structures, Belarusian Communists were excluded from decision-making processes. The SSRB was conceptualized, managed, and redesigned by the central Bolshevik authorities and their proxies in Smolensk as a buffer state. Its rapid merger with Soviet Lithuania concluded the first short-lived episode of Belarusian statehood on a Soviet basis. In sum, strategic concerns to secure the western borders of the first socialist state through the creation of a chain of loyal puppet states defined Soviet strategy in Belarusian state-building in much the same way as they had in the German *Ostpolitik*.

Concluding Remarks

Among all the successor nations of the Polish-Lithuanian Commonwealth, Belarusians were the last to make the transition from the early modern version of patriotism, inclusive and non-national in character, to their own modern national project. Persistent loyalty to the old Commonwealth hindered the self-perception of Belarusian elites. On the other hand, the population which was to be nationalized was also inclined to choose non-national forms of identification. At this time, people were more concerned with matters of everyday survival, often choosing a vague and therefore convenient local form of identity, instead of consciously identifying as Belarusians. Last but not least, national activists opted for a particular emphasis on peasant culture in the modern Belarusian national project. Suffering from negative connotations, this feature turned out to be detrimental to its image and thus failed to attract the majority of society. Thus, the national elites did not have enough time to consolidate their support among the masses before the outbreak of the First World War, which created a window of opportunity for stateless nations seeking to free themselves from imperial rule.

With the start of the Great War, an unexpected demographic crisis, new territorial divisions, and major power shifts all negatively impacted on the Belarusian national movement. Suddenly scattered across the Russian Empire and the German-occupied lands, national activists lacked a distinctive center, and were forced to operate from various locations, without proper communication and exchange between them. The first and by far the most important among these centers was located in Vil'nia, where Belarusian publishing and cultural activities flourished in the pre-war decade. Weakened by evacuation and resettlement, the Belarusian national milieu in Vil'nia under German occupation was nevertheless the most progressive in terms of developing Belarusian ethnic particularism. Benefiting from the cultural and educational concessions of the German military administration to the non-Russian nationalities, Belarusian national elites promoted a range of schooling and publishing initiatives aiming to nationalize the peasantry and strengthen their own positions, while facing the competing Lithuanian and Polish national projects. Politically, Vil'nia Belarusians pioneered the concept of Belarusian independence, as they were the first to recognize the futility of the plans for a federation with neighboring nations.

Yet, the prospects of retaining Vil'nia for the Belarusians waned with the turn in German *Ostpolitik* in 1917, which started to favor Lithuanian national ambitions. In the wake of the February Revolution, Belarusian national elites in Minsk suddenly came to the foreground, facing the dilemma of establishing a firm presence in a city, where the Belarusian national milieu had remained marginalized due to the extensive Russification policies of the nineteenth century. The start of the First World War in 1914 and the introduction of martial law, along with the arrival of Russian armies and Polish refugees, further minimized the space for negotiating Belarusian national interests between 1914 and early 1917. Only after the February Revolution was the Belarusian national movement in Minsk and eastern Belarus legalized and able to use the liberalization of political life and new freedoms for its nation-building activities. However, the revolution also left less time for the national elites, who were at once confronted with a variety of tasks, such as promoting Belarusian national consciousness among various segments of the population, involving the masses in the political process, and creating their own national narrative, while competing with the All-Russian parties and organizations.

In early 1917, Belarusian national activists were still euphoric about revolutionary freedoms and hopeful for a strong federation of autonomous states in a future democratic Russia, yet a number of factors influenced their actions as the year of revolution progressed. The physical dispersal of Belarusians as a result of massive population displacement and migration caused by the war complicated the initial conditions for national mobilization. Since Belarusian refugees were officially considered to be Great Russians, their national relief organizations were weak and under-financed. The national movement remained fragmented due to the political irreconcilability of the Belarusian socialists, along with their inability to agree on compromise solutions to benefit a Belarusian national project. The socialists, who aspired to leadership positions, prioritized social aspects over the national program and underestimated the implications of maintaining ties to Russia, where the Bolsheviks were consolidating their grip on power and were unlikely to tolerate the independent actions of local national activists, as demonstrated by the forcible dissolution of the All-Belarusian Congress in late 1917. In other words, the dominant positions of the socialists contributed to the internal instability of the Belarusian parties and organizations. This trend came to the foreground in early 1917 and continued throughout 1918, impacting on all major Belarusian state-building initiatives.

The year 1918 represented a turning point for the Belarusian national movement in its transition towards the practical implementation of statehood projects, despite the unfavorable international situation. In fact, the latter accelerated this process, which can be traced back to the resolutions of the First All-Belarusian Congress in late December 1917, refusing to recognize the self-appointed Bolshevik powers of the Western front. However, the Congress did not resolve the issue of possible separation from the ephemeral future Russian democratic state. Only the signing of the Brest-Litovsk peace treaty by Germany and Soviet Russia without Belarusian participation finally convinced Belarusian national elites of the need to take responsibility for their homeland, and to proclaim the BDR on March 9, 1918, followed by the declaration of its independence on March 25, 1918.

In 1918, supporters of the Belarusian state encountered the fierce opposition of those who could not imagine severing all ties to Russia. The latter current represented the third center of Belarusian national mobilization, which was located in Russia, where over a million ethnic Belarusians found temporary refuge from the privations of war and occupation. The Belarusian national milieu in Petrograd and Moscow connected all projects of Belarusian self-determination with Russia, believing in the possibility of joining either a democratic federation of states of the former Russian Empire, or the Soviet state in the status of an autonomous unit or a separate region.

From a realistic point of view and taking into account the political situation in the region by 1918, the chances that Belarusian national activists could achieve complete sovereignty without allying with some of the greater powers remained slim. The circumstances of the BDR proclamation hinted at the option of choosing Germany as an ally, however, neither Germany nor the Belarusian movement at that time were genuinely interested in such an alliance. By 1918, Germany had already found leverage against Russia in the region, while the Belarusian national milieu suffered a further loss of its integrity due to the anti-German prejudices and pro-Russian sentiments which divided moderates and socialists. Eventually, the idea of Belarusian statehood and the goals of Belarusian national activists were appropriated by the Bolsheviks, who used concessions to nationalities to secure their hold on power. They took over the unsuspecting Belarusian Bolsheviks, who believed in the idea of a Belarusian state under Soviet patronage. Yet, by early 1919, it had already become apparent that the Bolsheviks intended to use Belarusian statehood only as a buffer to protect the Soviet state.

In the long run, the establishment of Soviet rule determined the evolution of the Belarusian national project throughout the twentieth century. Belarusian statehood was embedded in socialist paradigms, while the rival conception of the BDR was exiled and forced to remain in the background. However, seen from a different angle, Belarusian nationalists succeeded because a new political unit appeared on the map of Europe. Even though the Soviet state (mis)used it to achieve its own political ends, it nevertheless established a continuous statehood tradition, surviving throughout the twentieth century and serving as a basis for the creation of the independent Belarusian state after the fall of the Soviet Union.

Bibliography

Archival collections:

Bielaruski Dziaržaŭny Archiŭ-Muzej Litaratury i Mastactva (BDAMLIM) [Belarusian State Archive-Museum of Literature and Art]

    F. 3 Kalekcyja dakumentaŭ addziela rukapisaŭ Bielaruskaha muzeja im. I. Luckieviča ŭ h. Vil'nia

Bundesarchiv Freiburg (BArch)

    PH 30-III/2 Oberbefehlshaber Ost

    PH 30-III/3 Militärverwaltung Litauen

    PH 30-III/5 Kaiserliche Militärverwaltungen und Militärmissionen

Lietuvos Centrinis Valstybės Archyvas (LCVA) [Lithuanian Central State Archive]

    F. 582 Baltarusių Liaudies Respublikos ministrų kabinetas

    F. 368 Baltarusių laikraščių redakcijų dokumentų kolekcija

    F. 361 Draugija nukentejusiems nuo karo šelpti

Lietuvos Mokslų Akademijos Vrublevskių Biblioteka, Rankrašču Skyrius (LMAVB, RS) [Wroblewski Library of the Lithuanian Academy of Sciences, Manuscripts Department]

    F. 21 Vilniaus Baltarusių fondas

    F. 23 Vokiečių okupacija Lietuvoje 1914–1918 m.

Lietuvos Valstybės Istorijos Archyvas (LVIA) [Lithuanian State Historical Archive]

    F. 641 Lietuvos karinės valdybos viršininkas

Nacyjanal'ny Archiŭ Respubliki Bielarus' (NARB) [National Archive of the Republic of Belarus]

    F. 325 Rada narodnych ministraŭ BDR, h. Minsk

    F. 4 Bielaruski Nacyjanal'ny Kamisaryjat (Belnackam)

    F. 567 Hryb Tamaš Tamaševič

Nacyjanal'ny Histaryčny Archiŭ Bielarusi (NHAB) [National Historical Archive of Belarus]

    F. 511 Minskae Hubernskae addzialennie Taccianinskaha Kamitetu

    F. 700 Minski Hubernski Kamitet Usierasijskaha Zemskaha Sajuzu

Printed sources:

Adamushko, V. I., ed. *Minskii gorodskoi Sovet deputatov: 1917–2012: Dokumenty i materialy.* Minsk: Belorusskii dom pechati, 2012.

Adamushko, V. I., V. D. Sokolova, V. P. Selemenev, N. E. Kokhanko, V. E. Kalesnik, D. N. Kazachenok, N. A. Zhigalov et al., eds. *Vitebskaia guberniia, 1917–1924 gg.: Dokumenty i materialy.* Vitebsk: Vitebskaia oblastnaia tipografiia, 2012.

Browder, Robert Paul, and Aleksandr Fyodorovich Kerensky. *The Russian Provisional Government, 1917: Documents.* Stanford, CA: Stanford University Press, 1961.

Gimžauskas, Edmundas, ed. *Lietuva vokiečių okupacijoje Pirmojo pasaulinio karo metais, 1915–1918: Lietuvos nepriklausomos valstybės genezė; Dokumentų rinkinys.* Vilnius: Lietuvos istorijos instituto leidykla, 2006.

Horny, Aliaksandr, and Andrej Buča, eds. *Archivy Bielaruskaj Narodnaj Respubliki.* Vol. 2, Book 1, Minsk: Knihazbor, 2021.

Proceedings of the Brest-Litovsk Peace Conference: The Peace Negotiations Between Russia and the Central Powers, 21 November, 1917–3 March, 1918. Washington: U.S. G.P.O., 1918.

Šupa, Siarhiej, ed. *Archivy Bielaruskaj Narodnaj Respubliki.* Vilnius: Bielaruski instytut navuki i mastactva, 1998.

Newspapers and periodicals:

Befehls- und Verordnungsblatt Ober Ost
Belorusskaia Rada
Bielarus'
Bielarus
Bielaruskae Žyccio
Bielaruski Šliach
Biulleten' Belorusskoi Rady XII armii
Dziannica
Dziennik Wileński
Homan
Kryvič
Naša Slova
Polymia
Sialianskaja Praŭda
Vitebskoe Slovo
Vol'naja Bielarus'
Zeitung der 10. Armee
Verordnungsblatt der Deutschen Verwaltung für Litauen

Reference works:

Bič, M. V., ed. *Encyklapedyja Historyi Bielarusi.* Minsk: Bielaruskaja Encyklapedyja imia Pietrusia Broŭki, 1994.

Bič, Michas', Natallia Hardzienka, Radzim Harecki, Uladzimir Konan, Arsen' Lis, Leanid Lojka, Adam Maldzis et al., eds. *Histaryčny šliach bielaruskaj nacyi i dzjaržavy.* Minsk: Medisont, 2006.

Kasciuk, Michail P., ed. *Historyja Bielarusi u šasci tamach.* Vols. 1–6. Minsk: VP Ekaperspektyva, 2005.

Secondary sources:

Aliachnovič, Francišak. *Bielaruski teatr*. Vilnius: Vydannie Bielaruskaha Hramadzianskaha Sabrannia, 1924.

Ambrosovich, Petr. "K 90-letiiu Vsebelorusskogo siezda." *Białoruskie Zeszyty Historyczne* 29 (2008): 229–50.

Anderson, Benedict R. *Imagined Communities: Reflections on the Origin and Spread of Nationalism*. London: Verso, 2006.

Azarov, A. I., ed. *Iz istorii ustanovleniia sovetskoi vlasti v Belorussii i obrazovaniia BSSR: dokumenty i materialy po istorii Belorussii*. Vol. 4. Minsk: Izddatel'stvo Akademii Nauk BSSR, 1954.

Bachinger, Bernhard, and Wolfram Dornik, eds. *Jenseits des Schützengrabes: Der Erste Weltkrieg im Osten: Erfahrung—Wahrnehmung—Kontext*. Innsbruck: Studien Verlag 2013.

Bahdanovič, Maksim. *Vybranyja tvory*. Minsk: Bielaruski knihazbor, 1996.

Bairašauskaitė, Tamara. "Lietuvos bajorės ir žemėvalda: nuosavybės santykiai I XIX amžiaus antroje pusėje." *Lietuvos istorijos studijos*, no. 32 (December 2013): 84–98.

Bakhturina, A. Iu. *Okrainy Rossijskoj imperii: gosudarstvennoe upravlenie i natsionalnaia politika v gody pervoi mirovoi voiny (1914–1917 gg.)*. Moscow: Rosspen, 2004.

Balkelis, Tomas. "A Dirty War: The Armed Polish-Lithuanian Conflict and Its Impact on Nation-Making in Lithuania, 1919–23." *Acta Poloniae Historica* 121 (August 2020): 227–59.

———. *The Making of Modern Lithuania*. New York: Routledge, 2009.

Bardach, Juliusz. *O dawnej i niedawnej Litwie*. Poznań: Wydawnictwo Naukowe Uniwersytetu im. Adama Mickiewicza w Poznaniu, 1988.

Barthel, Christopher. "Contesting the Russian Borderlands: The German Military Administration of Occupied Lithuania, 1915–1918." PhD Dissertation, Brown University, 2011.

Bauer, Henning, Andreas Kappeler, and Brigitte Roth, eds. *Die Nationalitäten des Russischen Reiches in der Volkszählung von 1897*. Vol. B, *Ausgewählte Daten zur sozio-ethnischen Struktur des russischen Reiches: Erste Auswertungen der Kölner NFR-Datenbank*. Stuttgart: Steiner, 1991.

Baumgart, Winfried. *Deutsche Ostpolitik 1918*. Vienna: Oldenbourg, 1966.

Bechtel, Delphine. "The Russian Jewish Intelligentsia and Modern Yiddish Culture." In *Nationalism, Zionism and Ethnic Mobilization of the Jews in 1900 and Beyond*, edited by Michael Berkowitz, 213–26. Leiden: Brill, 2004.

Bekus, Nelly. "Nationalism and Socialism: 'Phase D' in the Belarusian Nation-Building." *Nationalities Papers* 38, no. 6 (November 2010): 829–46.

Beliavina, V. N. *Belarus' v gody Pervoi mirovoi voiny*. Minsk: Belarus', 2013.

Bemporad, Elissa. *Becoming Soviet Jews: The Bolshevik Experiment in Minsk*. Bloomington: Indiana University Press, 2013.

Biadulia, Z. *Žydy na Bielarusi: Bytavyja štrychi*. Miensk: Drukarnia Ja. A. Hrynbliata, 1918.

Bjork, James E. *Neither German nor Pole: Catholicism and National Indifference in a Central European Borderland*. Ann Arbor: University of Michigan Press, 2008.

Blaščak, Tomaš, *Belarusy ŭ Litoŭskaj Respublicy (1918–1940)*. Smolensk: Inbelkult, 2022.

Böhler, Jochen. "Generals and Warlords, Revolutionaries and Nation State Builders." In *Legacies of Violence: Eastern Europe's First World War*, edited by Jochen Böhler, Włodzimierz Borodziej, and Joachim von Puttkamer, 51–68. Munich: Oldenbourg Verlag, 2014.

Bohn, Thomas M., Victor Shadurski, and Albert Weber, eds. *Ein weißer Fleck in Europa: Die Imagination der Belarus als einer Kontaktzone zwischen Ost und West*. Bielefeld: Transcript, 2011.

Brensztein, Michał. *Spisy ludności m. Wilna za okupacji niemieckiej od d. 1 listopada 1915*. Biblioteka Delegacji Rad Polskich Litwy i Białej Rus. Warsaw: Warszawska Drukarnia Wydawnicza, 1919.

Bulgakov, Valer. *Istoriia belorusskogo natsionalizma*. Vilnius: Institut belorusistiki, 2006.

Buraczok, Maciej. *Dudka Biełaruskaja*. Kraków: Wł. L. Anczyc i Ska, 1891. http://knihi.com/Francisak_Bahusevic/Dudka_bielaruskaja.html#chapter1 (Accessed March 28, 2016).

Čarniakievič, Andrej. *Naradženne bielaruskaj Harodni: Z historyi nacyjanal'naha ruchu 1909–1939 hadoŭ*. Minsk: Januškievič, 2015.

———. "Partret na fone interjera: štodzionnaje žyccio bielaruskaha dzejača ŭ Hrodna." In *Białoruś w XX stuleciu: w kręgu kultury i polityki*, edited by Dorota Michaluk, 137–60. Toruń: Wydawnictwo Naukowe Uniwersytetu Mikołaja Kopernika, 2007.

Chadanionak, V. M. *Sacyjalna-ekanamičnae stanovišča nasiel'nictva neakupiravanaj terytoryi Bielarusi ŭ hady Pieršaj susvietnaj vajny (kastryčnik 1915–kastryčnik 1917 hh.)*. Viciebsk: UA VDTU, 2015.

Chadasievič, Hanna. "Magdalena Radzivil—patryjotka nacyjanalnaha i relihijnaha adradžennia." In *Bielarus' i Hermanija: historyja i sučasnasc': Materyjaly mižnarodnaj navukovaj kanferencyi*. Vol. 7, Book 1, edited by A. Kavalienia, 8–82. Minsk: MDLU, 2009.

Cherepitsa, Valerii N. *Gorod-krepost' Grodno v gody Pervoj mirovoj vojny: Meropriiatiia grazhdanskikh i voennykh vlastei po obespecheniiu oboronosposobnosti i zhiznedeiatel'nosti*. Minsk: Bielaruskaja Encyklapedyja imia Pietrusia Broŭki, 2009.

Chernev, Borislav. *Twilight of Empire: The Brest-Litovsk Conference and the Remaking of East-Central Europe, 1917–1918*. Toronto: University of Toronto Press, 2019.

Cherniavskaia, Iulia. *Belorusy: Ot "tuteishikh" k natsii*. Minsk: FUAinform, 2010.

Cichamiraŭ, Aliaksandr. "Bielarus' u palitycy viadučych dziaržaŭ Zachadu (1914–1945 hh.)." *Białoruskie Zeszyty Historyczne*, no. 15 (2001): 168–88.

Cvikievič [Tsvikevich], A. *Kratkii ocherk vozniknoveniia Belarusskoi narodnoi respubliki*. Kyiv: n. p., 1918.

Demm, Eberhard. *Ostpolitik und Propaganda im Ersten Weltkrieg*. Frankfurt am Main: P. Lang, 2002.

Dolbilov, M. D. *Russkii krai, chuzhaia vera: Etnokonfessional'naia politika imperii v Litve i Belorussii pri Aleksandre II*. Moscow: Novoe literaturnoe obozrenie, 2010.

Dolbilov, M. D. and A. I. Miller. *Zapadnye okrainy Rossiiskoi imperii.* Moscow: Novoe literaturnoe obozrenie, 2006.

Doŭnar-Zapol'ski, M. V. *Historyja Bielarusi.* Minsk: Bielaruskaja encyklapedyja imia Pietrusia Broŭki, 1994.

Dowbor-Muśnicki, Józef. *Moje wspomnienia.* Poznań: Nakładem Przewodnika Katolickiego, 1936.

Dubeiko, Irina. *Zabytaia voina.* Minsk: Medisont, 2014.

Eidintas, Alfonsas, Vytautas Žalys, and Edvardas Tuskenis. *Lithuania in European Politics: The Years of the First Republic, 1918–1940.* New York: St. Martin's Press, 1999.

Eisfeld, Alfred, Guido Hausmann, and Dietmar Neutatz, eds. *Besetzt, interniert, deportiert: Der Erste Weltkrieg und die deutsche, jüdische, polnische und ukrainische Zivilbevölkerung im östlichen Europa.* Essen: Klartext, 2013.

Erickson, John. *The Soviet High Command: A Military-Political History, 1918–1941.* London: Frank Cass, 2001.

Fedyshyn, Oleh. *Germany's Drive to the East and the Ukrainian Revolution, 1917–1918.* New Brunswick: Rutgers University Press, 1971.

Frame, Murray, Boris Kolonitskii, Steven G. Marks, and Melissa K. Stockdale, eds. *Russian Culture in War and Revolution, 1914–22.* Bloomington, IN: Slavica Publishers, 2014.

Ganzenmüller, Jörg. *Russische Staatsgewalt und Polnischer Adel: Elitenintegration und Staatsausbau im Westen des Zarenreiches (1772–1850).* Cologne: Böhlau Verlag, 2013.

Gapova, Elena. "The Woman Question and National Projects in Soviet Byelorussia and Western Belarus (1921–1939)." In *Zwischen Kriegen: Nationen, Nationalismen und Geschlechterverhältnisse in Mittel- und Osteuropa, 1918–1939*, edited by Johanna Gehmacher, Elizabeth Harvey, and Sophia Kemlein, 105–28. Osnabrück: Fibre, 2004.

Gatrell, Peter. *Russia's First World War: A Social and Economic History.* Harlow: Pearson/Longman, 2005.

———. *A Whole Empire Walking: Refugees in Russia During World War I.* Bloomington, IN: Indiana University Press, 1999.

Gerwarth, Robert. *Vanquished: Why the First World War Failed to End (1917–1923).* London: Allen Lane, 2016.

Gimžauskas, Edmundas. *Bielaruski faktar pry farmavanni litoŭskaj dziaržavy ŭ 1915–1923 hh.* Białystok: Bielaruskae histaryčnae tavarystva, 2012.

Głogowska, Helena. *Białoruś 1914–1929: kultura pod presją polityki.* Białystok: Białoruskie Towarzystwo Historyczne, 1996.

Gomółka, Krystyna. *Między Polską a Rosją: Białoruś w koncepcjach polskich ugrupowań politycznych 1918–1922.* Warsaw: Gryf, 1994.

Graf, Daniel. "Military Rule behind the Russian Front, 1914–1917: The Political Ramifications." *Jahrbücher für Geschichte Osteuropas* 22, no. 3 (1974): 390–411.

Gräfe, Karl-Heinz. *Vom Donnerkreuz zum Hakenkreuz: Die baltischen Staaten zwischen Diktatur und Okkupation.* Berlin: Ed. Organon, 2010.

Grelka, Frank. *Die ukrainische Nationalbewegung unter deutscher Besatzungsherrschaft 1918 und 1941/42*. Wiesbaden: Harrassowitz Verlag, 2005.

Griffante, Andrea. *Children, Poverty and Nationalism in Lithuania, 1900–1940*. Cham: Palgrave Macmillan, 2019. https://doi.org/10.1007/978-3-030-30870-4

Gumz, Jonathan E. "Losing Control: The Norm of Occupation in Eastern Europe during the First World War." In *Legacies of Violence: Eastern Europe's First World War*, edited by Jochen Böhler, Włodzimierz Borodziej, and Joachim von Puttkamer, 69–87. Munich: Oldenbourg Verlag, 2014.

Guthier, Steven L. *The Belorussians: National Identification and Assimilation, 1897–1970*. Ann Arbor, MI: Center for Russian and East European Studies, University of Michigan, 1977.

Hadleŭski, Vincent. "Z bielaruskaha palityčnaha žyccia ŭ Miensku ŭ 1917–18 hh." *Spadčyna* 5 (1997): 18–39.

Hagen, Mark von. "The Entangled Eastern Front in the First World War." In *The Empire and Nationalism at War*, edited by Eric Lohr, Vera Tolz, Alexander Semyonov, and Mark von Hagen, 9–48. Bloomington, IN: Slavica Publishers, 2014.

———. *War in a European Borderland: Occupations and Occupation Plans in Galicia and Ukraine, 1914–1918*. Seattle: Herbert J. Ellison Center for Russian, East European, and Central Asian Studies, University of Washington, 2007.

Hirsch, Francine. *Empire of Nations: Ethnographic Knowledge and the Making of the Soviet Union*. Ithaca, NY: Cornell University Press, 2005.

Holovchenko, V. I., and V. F. Soldatenko. *Ukrains'ke pytannia v roky Pershoi svitovoi viiny*. Kyiv: Parlaments'ke vydavnytstvo, 2009.

Holquist, Peter. *Making War, Forging Revolution: Russia's Continuum of Crisis, 1914–1921*. Cambridge, MA: Harvard University Press, 2002.

Horak, Stephan M. *The First Treaty of World War I: Ukraine's Treaty with the Central Powers of February 9, 1918*. Boulder, CO: East European Monographs, 1988.

Hroch, Miroslav. *Social Preconditions of National Revival in Europe: A Comparative Analysis of the Social Composition of Patriotic Groups among the Smaller European Nations*. New York: Columbia University Press, 2000.

Hryckievič, Anatol'. *Vybranaje*. Minsk: Knihazbor, 2012.

Ignatenko, I. M., and G. V. Shtykhov. *Istoriia Belorusskoi SSR*. Minsk: Nauka i tekhnika, 1977.

Ihnatoŭski, U. "Vialiki Kastryčnik na Bielarusi." In *Bielarus': Narysy historyi, ekanomiki, kul'turnaha i revoliucyjnaha ruchu*, edited by A. Staševski, Z. Žylunovič, and U. Ihnatoŭski, 195–214. Minsk: Vydannie Centralnaha Komitetu Bielaruskaje Savieckaje Socyjalistyčnaje Respubliki, 1924.

Iofe, Emanuil. "Neviadomy Zmicier Žylunovič." *Maladosc'* no. 780 (November 2012): 87–94.

Jäger, Walter. *Weissruthenien: Land, Bewohner, Geschichte, Volkswirtschaft, Kultur, Dichtung*. Berlin: K. Curtius, 1919.

Jekabsons, Eriks. "Belorusy v Latvii v 1918–1940 godakh." In *Bielaruskaja dyjaspara jak pasrednica ŭ dyjalohu cyvilizacyj: Materyjaly III Mižnarodnaha kanhresa bielarusistaŭ*, 47–71. Minsk: Bielaruski knihazbor, 2001.

Jezavitaŭ, Kanstancin. "Pieršy Ŭsebielaruski Kanhres." *Bielaruskaja Minuŭščyna*, no. 1 (1993): 25–29.

Kachanovič, Michail. "Mahilioŭcy i niezaležnasc' Bielarusi (Maje ŭspaminy)." *Spadčyna* 6 (1997): 3–5.

Kalesnik, N. E. *Belorusskoe obshchestvo v Petrograde po okazaniiu pomoshchi postradavshim ot voiny, 1916–1918: mezharkhivnyi spravochnik*. Minsk: NARB, 2008.

Kalinoŭski, Kastus', and Henadz' Kisialoŭ. *Za našuju vol'nasc': tvory, dakumenty*. Minsk: Bielaruski knihazbor, 1999.

Kancher, Evsevii. "Iz istorii Grazhdanskoi voiny v Belorussii v 1917–1920 gg. Fragmenty 5-oi glavy." *Bielaruskaja Dumka*, no. 1 (2010): 92–97.

Kappeler, Andreas. *Der schwierige Weg zur Nation: Beiträge zur neueren Geschichte der Ukraine*. Vienna: Böhlau, 2003.

———. *The Russian Empire: A Multiethnic History*. Harlow: Longman, 2001.

Kasmach, Lizaveta. "Between Local and National: The Case of Eastern Belarus in 1917," *Journal of Belarusian Studies* 8, no. 2 (2017): 5–31.

Kazharski, Aliaksej. "Belarus' New Political Nation? 2020 Anti-Authoritarian Protests as Identity Building." *New Perspectives* 29, no. 1 (2021): 69–79.

Khavkin, Boris. "Russland gegen Deutschland: Die Ostfront des Ersten Weltkrieges in den Jahren 1914 bis 1915." In *Die vergessene Front—der Osten 1914/15: Ereignis, Wirkung, Nachwirkung*, edited by Gerhard Paul Gross, 65–85. Paderborn: Schöningh, 2006.

Kit, Barys. *Ciarnovy šliach: Uspaminy*. Frankfurt am Main: n. p., 2001.

Klamrot, Kurt, and Ales' Smaliančuk, "Horadnia 1916 na staronkach Dzionnika rotmistra Kurta Klamrota," *Horad Sviatoha Huberta*, no. 6 (2012): 41–85.

Kohut, Zenon E., Bohdan Y. Nebesio, and Myroslav Yurkevich. *Historical Dictionary of Ukraine*. Lanham, MD: Scarecrow Press, 2005.

Kratkii otchet o deiiatel'nosti Minskago Gubernskago Komiteta V. Z. S. za 1916 god. Minsk: Tipografiia B. L. Kaplana, 1917.

Kravtsevich, Aleksandr, Aleksandr Smolenchuk, and Sergei Tokt'. *Belorusy: natsiia Pogranich'ia*. Vilnius: EGU, 2011.

Krutalevich, V. A. *O Belorusskoi Narodnoi Respublike*. Minsk: Pravo i ekonomika, 2005.

Kukushkin, Vadim. *From Peasants to Labourers: Ukrainian and Belarusan Immigration from the Russian Empire to Canada*. Montreal: McGill-Queen's University Press, 2007.

Kulakevich, Tatsiana. "National Awakening in Belarus: Elite Ideology to 'Nation' Practice," *SAIS Review of International Affairs* 40, no. 2 (2020): 97–110.

Kvit, Serhii. *Dmytro Dontsov: ideolohichnyi portret*. Lviv: Halyts'ka vydavnycha spilka, 2013.

Ladyseŭ, U. F., and P. I. Bryhadzin. *Pamiž Uschodam i Zachadam: Stanaŭlenne dziaržaŭnasci i terytaryjalnaj celasnasci Bielarusi (1917–1939)*. Minsk: BDU, 2003.

Lapanovič, S. F. *Dzejnasc' dziaržaŭnych i hramadskich arhanizacyj pa akazanni dapamohi bežancam u Bielarusi ŭ hady Pieršaj susvietnaj vajny (1914–kastryčnik 1917 h.)*. Minsk: Akademija MUS, 2010.

Lastoŭski, Vaclaŭ. *Karotkaja historyja Biełarusi z 40 rysunkami.* Vilnius: Drukarnia Marcina Kuchty, 1910.

———. *Rodnyja ziarniaty: Knižka dlia škoľnaga čytannia.* Vilnius: Homan, 1916.

Latyšonak, Aleh. *Žaŭnery BNR.* Białystok: Bielaruskae Histaryčnaje Tavarystva, 2009. Originally published as Łatyszonek, Oleg. *Białoruskie formacje wojskowe, 1917–1923.* Białystok: Białoruskie Towarzystwo Historyczne, 1995.

Laz'ko, Ryhor. "Belnackam i Narkamnac: pieršy prykry vopyt uzaemaadnosin (studzien'– červien' 1918 h.)." *Bielaruski histaryčny časopis,* no. 2 (2012): 6–15.

Lehnstaedt, Stephan. "Fluctuating between 'Utilisation' and Exploitation: Occupied East Central Europe during the First World War." In *Legacies of Violence: Eastern Europe's First World War,* edited by Jochen Böhler, Włodzimierz Borodziej, and Joachim von Puttkamer, 89–112. Munich: Oldenbourg Verlag, 2014.

Lemke, M. K. *250 dnei v tsarskoi stavke 1914–1915.* Minsk: Kharvest, 2003.

Liachoŭski, Uladzimir. *Ad homanaŭcaŭ da hajsakoŭ: čynnasc' bielaruskich maladzevych arhanizacyj u 2-j palovie XIX st.–I-j palovie XX st. (da 1939 h.).* Białystok: Bielaruskae histaryčnaje tavarystva, 2012.

———. *Škoľnaja adukacyja ŭ Bielarusi padčas niameckaj akupacyi (1915–1918 h.).* Vilnius: Instytut bielarusistyki: 2010.

Lickievič, Aleh. "Bielaruskaja virtualnaja respublika." *Bielaruskaja Dumka,* no. 3 (2008): 68–73.

Lieven, Dominic. *The End of Tsarist Russia: The March to World War I and Revolution.* New York: Viking, 2015.

Linde, Gerd. *Die deutsche Politik in Litauen im Ersten Weltkrieg.* Wiesbaden: O. Harrassowitz, 1965.

Lindner, Rainer. *Historiker und Herrschaft: Nationsbildung und Geschichtspolitik in Weissrussland im 19. und 20. Jahrhundert.* Munich: R. Oldenbourg, 1999.

Linke, Horst Günther, ed. *Quellen zu den deutsch-sowjetischen Beziehungen 1917–1945.* Darmstadt: Wissenschaftliche Buchgesellschaft, 1998.

Litwa za rządów ks. Isenburga. Kraków: Nakł. Krakowskiego Oddziału Zjednoczenia Narodowego, 1919.

Liulevicius, Vejas G. *War Land on the Eastern Front: Culture, National Identity and German Occupation in World War I.* Cambridge: Cambridge University Press, 2000.

Lohr, Eric. *Nationalizing the Russian Empire: The Campaign against Enemy Aliens during World War I.* Cambridge, MA: Harvard University Press, 2003.

———. "War Nationalism." In *The Empire and Nationalism at War,* edited by Eric Lohr, Vera Tolz, Alexander Semyonov, and Mark von Hagen, 91–107. Bloomington, IN: Slavica Publishers, 2014.

Lopata, Raimundas. "The Lithuanian Card in Russian Policy, 1914–1917." *Jahrbücher für Geschichte Osteuropas,* no. 3 (1994): 340–54.

Luba Vitaľ, ed. *Bežanstva 1915 hoda.* Białystok: Prahramnaja rada tydniovika "Niva," 2000.

Lubachko, Ivan S. *Belorussia under Soviet Rule, 1917–1957.* Lexington, KY: University Press of Kentucky, 1972.

Luckievič, Anton. *Da historyi bielaruskaha ruchu: vybranyja tvory*, edited by Anatol' Sidarevič. Minsk: Bielaruski knihazbor, 2003.

———. *Vybranyja tvory: Prablemy kultury, litaratury i mastactva*. Minsk: Knihazbor, 2006.

Ludendorff, Erich. *Meine Kriegserinnerungen, 1914–1918, mit zahlreichen Skizzen und Plänen*. Berlin: E.S. Mittler und Sohn, 1919.

Magosci, Paul Robert. *A History of Ukraine*. Toronto: University of Toronto Press, 2010.

Mark, Rudolf A. "Die nationale Bewegung der Weißrussen im 19. und zu Beginn des 20. Jahrhunderts." *Jahrbücher für Geschichte Osteuropas* 42, no. 4 (1994): 493–509.

Marková, Alena. *Sovětská bělorusizace jako cesta k národu: iluze nebo realita?* Prague: NLN, Nakladatelství Lidové noviny, 2012.

Marples, David. "Belarusian Studies in the West." *Belarusian Review* 27, no. 1 (Spring 2015): 2–3.

Martin, Terry. *The Affirmative Action Empire: Nations and Nationalism in the Soviet Union, 1923–1939*. Ithaca, NY: Cornell University Press, 2001.

Mel'nikaŭ, Ihar. "Zabyty korpus zabytaha henerala." *Novy Čas Online*, http://159.253.18.178/poviaz_casou/zabyty_korpus_zabytaha_hienier/ (Accessed November 10, 2015).

Menning, Bruce W. "War Planning and Initial Operations in the Russian Context." In *War Planning 1914*, edited by Richard F. Hamilton and Holger H. Herwig, 80–142. Cambridge: Cambridge University Press, 2010.

Miadziolka, Paŭlina. *Sciežkami žyccia*. Minsk: Mastackaja litaratura, 1974.

Michaluk, Dorota, and Per Anders Rudling. "From the Grand Duchy of Lithuania to the Belarusian Democratic Republic: The Idea of Belarusian Statehood during the German Occupation of Belarusian Lands, 1915–1919." *Journal of Belarusian Studies* 7, no. 2 (2014): 3–36.

Michaluk, Dorota. *Białoruska Republika Ludowa, 1918–1920: u podstaw białoruskiej państwowości*. Toruń: Wydawnictwo Naukowe Uniwersytetu Mikołaja Kopernika, 2010.

Mikalaevič, Aliaksandr. "Bežancy Pieršaj susvietnaj vajny." *Spadčyna*, no. 3 (1994): 17–21.

Mikietyński, Piotr. *Niemiecka droga ku Mitteleuropie: Polityka II Rzeszy wobec Królestwa Polskiego (1914–1916)*. Kraków: Towarzystwo Wydawnicze "Historia Iagellonica," 2009.

Miknys, Rimantas, and Darius Staliūnas. "The 'Old' and 'New' Lithuanians: Collective Identity Types in Lithuania at the Turn of the Nineteenth and Twentieth Centuries." In *Forgotten Pages in Baltic History: Diversity and Inclusion*, edited by Martyn Housden and David J. Smitt, 35–48. Amsterdam, New York: Rodopi, 2011.

Miknys, Rimantas. "Michał Römer, krajowcy a idea zjednoczenia Europy w pierwszej połowie XX wieku." In *O nowy kształt Europy: XX-wieczne koncepcje federalistyczne w Europie Środkowo-Wschodniej i ich implikacje dla dyskusji o przyszłości Europy*, edited by Jerzy Kłoczowski and Sławomir Łukasiewicz, 94–109. Lublin: Instytut Europy Środkowo-Wschodniej, 2003.

Miller, Alexei. "The Role of the First World War in the Competition between Ukrainian and All-Russian Nationalism." In *The Empire and Nationalism at War*, edited by Eric Lohr,

Vera Tolz, Alexander Semyonov, and Mark von Hagen, 73–89. Bloomington, IN: Slavica Publishers, 2014.

——. *The Romanov Empire and Nationalism: Essays in the Methodology of Historical Research.* Budapest–New York: CEU Press, 2008.

——. "The Romanov Empire and the Russian Nation." In *Nationalizing Empires*, edited by Alexei I. Miller and Stefan Berger, 309–68. Budapest–New York: CEU Press, 2015.

Miller, Alexei, and Oksana Ostapchuk. "The Latin and Cyrillic Alphabets in Ukrainian National Discourse and in the Language Policy of Empires." In *A Laboratory of Transnational History: Ukraine and Recent Ukrainian Historiography*, edited by Heorhii Kasianov and Philipp Ther, 171–210. Budapest–New York: CEU Press, 2009.

Mironowicz, Eugeniusz. *Białorusini i Ukraińcy w polityce obozu piłsudczykowskiego.* Białystok: Wydawnictwo Uniwersyteckie Trans Humana, 2007.

Mironowicz, Eugeniusz, Siarhiej Tokć, and Ryszard Radzik. *Zmiana struktury narodowościowej na pograniczu polsko-białoruskim w XX wieku.* Białystok: Wydawnictwo Uniwersytetu w Białymstoku, 2005.

Münkler, Herfried. "Spiel mit dem Feuer: Die 'Politik der revolutionären Infektion' im Ersten Weltkrieg." *Osteuropa* 64, nos. 2–4 (February–April 2014): 109–26.

Nadsan, Aliaksandar. *Kniahinia Radzivil i sprava adradžennia Unii ŭ Bielarusi.* Minsk: Biblijateka časopisa Bielaruski Histaryčny Ahliad, 2006.

Nagornaia, Oksana S. *Drugoi voennyi opyt: Rossiiskie voennoplennye Pervoi mirovoi voiny v Germanii (1914–1922).* Moscow: Novyi Khronograf, 2010.

Naumann, Friedrich. *Mitteleuropa.* Berlin: G. Reimer, 1916.

Nikol'skii, E. A. *Zapiski o proshlom.* Moscow: Russkii put', 2007.

Otchet o deiatelnosti Litovskogo Obshchestva po okazaniiu pomoshchi postradavshim ot voiny za vremia s 22 noiabria 1914 po 1 iiulia 1915 g. Petrograd: Nauchnoe delo, 1916.

Paškievič, Ales'. "Symon Rak-Michajloŭski: staronki žyccia i dzejnasci." *Kuferak Vilenščyny* 12, no. 1 (2007): 4–30.

Paškievič, Ales', and Andrej Čarniakievič. "Stary niamecki ahent ci bac'ka radzimickaha narodu?" *ARCHE*, no. 4 (2005): 147–65.

Paŭlava, Tacciana. "Asnoŭnyja napramki zniešnepalityčnaj dzejnasci BNR u 1918–1920 hh." *Białoruskie Zeszyty Historyczne*, no. 15 (2001): 76–85.

Plokhy, Serhii, *Lost Kingdom: The Quest for Empire and the Making of the Russian Nation from 1470 to the Present.* New York: Basic Books, 2017.

Płygawko, Danuta. *Sienkiewicz w Szwajcarii: Z dziejów akcji ratunkowej dla Polski w czasie pierwszej wojny światowej.* Poznań: Wydawnictwo Naukowe Uniwersytetu im. Adama Mickiewicza w Poznaniu, 1986.

Ponarski, Zenowiusz. "Konfederacja Wielkiego Księstwa Litewskiego 1915–1916." *Białoruskie Zeszyty Historyczne*, no. 10 (1998): 56–67.

Porter, Brian. *When Nationalism Began to Hate: Imagining Modern Politics in Nineteenth-Century Poland.* New York: Oxford University Press, 2000.

Presseabteilung Ober Ost. *Das Land Ober Ost: Deutsche Arbeit in den Verwaltungsgebieten Kurland, Litauen und Bialystok-Grodno.* [Kowno]: Verlag der Presseabteilung Ober Ost, 1917.

Radkey, Oliver H. *Russia Goes to the Polls: The Election to the All-Russian Constituent Assembly, 1917.* Ithaca, NY: Cornell University Press, 1990.

Radzik, Ryšard. *Vytoki sučasnaj bielaruskasci: Bielarusy na fone nacyiatvorčych pracesaŭ u Centralna-Uschodniaj Europe 19 st.* Minsk: Medysont, 2012. Originally published as Radzik, Ryszard. *Między zbiorowością etniczną a wspólnotą narodową: Białorusini na tle przemian narodowych w Europie Środkowo-Wschodniej XIX stulecia.* Lublin: Wydawnictwo Uniwersytetu Marii Curie-Skłodowskiej, 2000.

Renan, Ernest. "What Is a Nation?" In *Becoming National: A Reader*, edited by Geoff Eley and Ronald Grigor Suny, 42–56. New York: Oxford University Press, 1996.

Richter, Klaus. *Fragmentation in East Central Europe: Poland and the Baltics 1915–1929.* Oxford: Oxford University Press, 2020.

Romanowski, Andrzej. "The Year 1905 and the Revival of Polish Culture between the Neman and the Dnepr." *Canadian Slavonic Papers/Revue Canadienne Des Slavistes* 41, no. 1 (1999): 45–67.

Roshwald, Aviel. *Ethnic Nationalism and the Fall of Empires: Central Europe, Russia and the Middle East, 1914–1923.* London: Routledge, 2000.

Rudling, Per Anders. *The Rise and Fall of Belarusian Nationalism, 1906–1931.* Pittsburgh, PA: University of Pittsburgh Press, 2014.

Rudovič, Stanislaŭ. "Bielarus' u čas Pieršaj susvietnaj vajny: Aspiekty etnapalityčnaj historyi." In *Białoruś w XX stuleciu: w kręgu kultury i polityki*, edited by Dorota Michaluk, 100–112. Toruń: Wydawnictwo Naukowe Uniwersytetu Mikołaja Kopernika, 2007.

———. "...Bielaruski dzejač z vialikich panoŭ: Epizody palityčnaj bijahrafii Ramana Skirmunta." In *Histaryčny almanach*, 14–37. Hrodna: Bielaruskae histaryčnaje tavarystva, 1999.

———. *Čas vybaru: Prablema samavyznačennia Belarusi ŭ 1917 hodzie.* Minsk: Technalohija, 2001.

———. "Zachodnierusizm va ŭmovach revalucyi 1917 hoda: Pamiž imperskasciu i bielaruskaj idejaj." *Białoruskie Zeszyty Historyczne*, no. 16 (2001): 55–68.

Rudovich, Stanislav. "Rozhdenie Soveta." In *Minskii gorodskoi Sovet deputatov: 1917–2012: Dokumenty i materialy*, edited by V. I. Adamushko, 6–9. Minsk: Belorusskii dom pechati, 2012.

Rust, Christian. "Self-Determination at the Beginning of 1918 and the German Reaction." *Lithuanian Historical Studies* 13 (January 2008): 41–66.

Safronovas, Vasilijus. "Zum Wandel des räumlichen Begriffs 'Litauen' im deutschsprachigen Diskurs während und nach dem Ersten Weltkrieg." *Forschungen zur Baltischen Geschichte* 10 (June 2015): 109–35.

Sanborn, Joshua. *Imperial Apocalypse: The Great War and the Destruction of the Russian Empire.* Oxford: Oxford University Press, 2014.

———. "War of Decolonization." In *The Empire and Nationalism at War*, edited by Eric Lohr, Vera Tolz, Alexander Semyonov, and Mark von Hagen, 49–71. Bloomington, IN: Slavica Publishers, 2014.

Savchenko, Andrew. *Belarus: A Perpetual Borderland*. Leiden: Brill, 2009.

Savicki, Jan. "Michał Römer wobec problemów narodowościowych ziem Litewsko-białoruskich na początku XX wieku." In *Krajowość—tradycje zgody narodow w dobie nacjonalizmu: Materiały z międzynarodowej konferencji naukowej w Insytucie Historii UAM w Poznaniu (11–12 maja 1998)*, edited by Jan Jurkiewicz, 71–85. Poznań: Instytut Historii UAM, 1999.

Selemenev, V. D., ed. *I ianvariia 1919 goda: vremennoe raboche-krest'ianskoe sovetskoe pravitel'stvo Belorussii: dokumenty i materialy*. Minsk: Limarius, 2005.

Senn, Alfred Erich. *The Emergence of Modern Lithuania*. New York: Columbia University Press, 1959.

Serhiichuk, Volodymyr. "Mykhailo Hrushevs'kyi i ukrainstvo Petrohradu." *Ukrains'kyi Istoryk* 34, no. 1/4 (April 1997): 187–91.

Shchavlinskii, Nikolai. "Deiatel'nost' belorusskikh natsionalnykh organizatsii v Kieve i Odesse v 1917–1918 godakh." *Ukrains'kii istorichnii zbirnik*, no. 12 (2009): 176–82.

———. "Deiiatel'nost' Belorusskogo obshchestva v Petrograde po okazaniiu pomoshchi poter-pevshim ot voiny v 1916–1918 godakh." *Bielaruskaja Dumka*, no. 6 (2013): 62–65.

Shubin, Aleksandr. "The Treaty of Brest-Litovsk: Russia and Ukraine," *Lithuanian Historical Studies* 13 (January 2008): 75–100.

Siamenčyk, M. Ja. *Hramadska-palityčnae žyccio na Bielarusi ŭ peryjad Liutaŭskaj i Kastryčnickaj revaliucyi: sakavik 1917- sakavik 1918 hh*. Minsk: Bielaruski dziaržaŭny pedahahičny univer-sitet imia Maksima Tanka, 2001.

Sidarevič, Anatoľ. "Anton Luckievič: Ad krajovas'ci da niezaležnictva (1916–1918)." *ARCHE*, nos. 1–2 (2006): 80–91.

———. "Da historyi Bielaruskaj Sacyjalistyčnaj Hramady: Ahliad krynicaŭ." *ARCHE*, no. 4 (2006): 153–74.

———, ed. *Pra Ivana Luckieviča: Uspaminy, sviedčanni*. Minsk: Knihazbor, 2007.

———. "Urady BNR i kabinet Ramana Skirmunta." *ARCHE*, no. 4 (2008): 108–26.

Siegel, Jennifer. *For Peace and Money: French and British Money in the Service of Tsars and Commissars*. New York: Oxford University Press, 2014.

Siemakowicz, Marian. "Polityka władz rosyjskich, niemieckich i polskich wobec szkolnictwa białoruskiego w latach 1903–1922." *Białoruskie Zeszyty Historyczne*, no. 7 (1997): 23–48.

Sienkevich, Victor. "Łastoŭski the Historian and His Historical Views." *Journal of Belarusian Studies* 5, nos. 3–4 (1984): 3–13.

Silitski, Vitaľ, and Jan Zaprudnik. *Historical Dictionary of Belarus*. Lanham, MD: Scarecrow Press, 2007.

Siniak, Siarhiej. "Bielaruskae pytanne i kanflikt bielaruskich aktyvistaŭ Maskvy i Pietrahrada (1918–1919 hh.)." *Bielaruski histaryčny časopis*, no. 2 (2012): 16–24.

Sirutavičius Vladas, Darius Staliūnas, and Jurgita Šiaučiūnaitė-Verbickienė. *The History of Jews in Lithuania: From the Middle Ages to the 1990s*. Paderborn: Ferdinand Schöningh, 2020.

Skalaban, Vitaľ. "Jaŭsiej Kančar—palityk, historyk, memuaryst." *Bielaruskaja Dumka*, no. 1 (2010): 88–97.

Skalaban, Vitaľ. "Usiebielaruski Zjezd 1917 hoda: Perspektyvy vyvučennia." *Białoruskie Zeszyty Historyczne*, no. 15 (2001): 63–75.

Smaliančuk, Aliaksandr. "Kastus' Kalinoŭski and the Belarusian National Idea: Research Problems." *Journal of Belarusian Studies* 7, no. 3 (2015): 70–78.

———. "Krajovaść vis-à-vis Belarusian and Lithuanian National Movements in the Early 20th Century." In *Belarus and Its Neighbors: Historical Perceptions and Political Constructs: International Conference Papers*, edited by Ales' Lahvinec and Taciana Čulickaja, 69–80. Warsaw: Uczelnia Łazarskiego, 2013.

———. "Licvinstva, zachodnerusizm i bielaruskaja ideja XIX–pačatak XX st." In *Białoruś w XX stuleciu: W kręgu kultury i polityki*, edited by Dorota Michaluk, 55–68. Toruń: Wydawnictwo Naukowe Uniwersytetu Mikołaja Kopernika, 2007.

———. *Pamiž krajovasciu i nacyjanalnaj idejaj: Polski ruch na bielaruskich i litoŭskich zemliach 1864–liuty 1917*. St. Petersburg: Neŭski prasciah, 2004.

———. *Raman Skirmunt (1868–1939): Žycciapis hramadzianina Kraju*. Minsk: Vydaviec Zmicier Kolas, 2018.

———. *Vol'nyja muliary ŭ bielaruskaj historyi: Kaniec XVIII–pačatak XX st*. Vilnius: Gudas, 2005.

Smith, Jeremy. *The Bolsheviks and the National Question, 1917–23*. New York: St. Martin's Press, 1999.

Smol'ianinov, M. M. *Belarus' v pervoi mirovoi voine 1914–1918*. Minsk: Bielaruskaja navuka, 2014.

Snapkoŭskaja, Sviatlana. *Adukacyjnaja palityka i škola na Bielarusi ŭ kancy XIX–pačatku XX stst*. Minsk: Ministerstva Adukacyi Respubliki Bielarus', Nacyjanal'ny Instytut Adukacyi, 1998.

Snyder, Timothy. *The Reconstruction of Nations: Poland, Ukraine, Lithuania, Belarus, 1569–1999*. New Haven: Yale University Press, 2003.

Solak, Zbigniew. *Między Polską a Litwą: Życie i działalność Michała Römera, 1880–1920*. Kraków: Wydawnictwo Arcana, 2004.

Solski, Wacław, and S. N. Khomich. *1917 god v Zapadnoi oblasti i na Zapadnom fronte*. Minsk: Tesei, 2004.

Staliūnas, Darius. *Enemies for a Day: Antisemitism and Anti-Jewish Violence in Lithuania under the Tsars*. Budapest–New York: CEU Press, 2014.

———. "Making a National Capital out of a Multiethnic City: Lithuanians and Vilnius in Late Imperial Russia." *Ab Imperio*, no. 1 (2014): 157–75.

———. *Making Russians: Meaning and Practice of Russification in Lithuania and Belarus after 1863*. Amsterdam: Rodopi, 2007.

Stankievič, Adam. *Z Boham da Bielarusi: Zbor tvoraŭ*. Vilnius: Instytut bielarusistyki, 2008.

Stone, David R. *The Russian Army in the Great War: The Eastern Front, 1914–1917*. Lawrence, KS: University Press of Kansas, 2015.

Stone, Norman. *The Eastern Front, 1914–1917*. New York: Scribner, 1975.

Strazhas, A. *Deutsche Ostpolitik im Ersten Weltkrieg: Der Fall Ober Ost 1915–1917*. Wiesbaden: Harrassowitz, 1993.

Struck, Hermann, and Herbert Eulenberg. *Skizzen aus Litauen, Weissrussland und Kurland*. Berlin: George Stilke, 1916.

Sukiennicki, Wiktor, and Maciej Siekierski. *East Central Europe during World War I: From Foreign Domination to National Independence.* Vol. 1. New York: Columbia University Press, 1984.

Surmač, Hanna. "Bielaruski zahraničny archiŭ." *Bielaruskaja Miniuŭščyna,* no. 1 (1993): 18–23.

Survilla, Paula M. "Retrospective Positions and Introspective Critiques: A Belarusist in the Academic Trenches." *Belarusian Review* 27, no. 1 (Spring 2015): 11–16.

Šupa, Siarhiej. "Bielaruskaja Narodnaja Republika i jaje archivy." In *Archivy Bielaruskaj Narodnaj Respubliki,* edited by Siarhiej Šupa, v–xviii. Vilnius: Bielaruski instytut navuki i mastactva, 1998.

Šybeka, Zachar. *Minsk sto hadoŭ tamu.* Minsk: Bielarus', 2007.

———. "Z historyi bielaruskich maraŭ pra Vil'niu: Peryjad niameckaj akupacyi, 1915–1918 hh." In *Harady Bielarusi ŭ kanteksce palityki, ekanomiki, kult'ury: Zbornik navukovych artykulaŭ,* edited by I. P. Kren' and I. V. Sorkina, 170–80. Hrodna: HrDU, 2007.

Szpoper, Dariusz. *Gente Lithuana, Natione Lithuana: Myśl polityczna i działalność Konstancji Skirmuntt (1851–1934).* Gdańsk: Arche, 2009.

Tarasiuk, Dariusz. *Między nadzieją a niepokojem: Działalność społeczno-kulturalna i polityczna Polaków na wschodniej Białorusi w latach 1905–1918.* Lublin: Wyd. Uniwersytetu Marii Curie-Skłodowskiej, 2007.

Tauber, Joachim. "German Eastern Policy, 1917–1918." *Lithuanian Historical Studies* 13, no. 1 (January 2008): 67–74.

———. "The View from the Top: German Soldiers and Lithuania in the Two World Wars." In *Forgotten Pages in Baltic History: Diversity and Inclusion,* edited by Martyn Housden and David J. Smitt, 211–37. Amsterdam, New York: Rodopi, 2011.

Tereshkovich, P. V. *Etnicheskaia istoriia Belarusi XIX–nachala XX v. v kontekste Tsentralno-Vostochnoi Evropy.* Minsk: BGU, 2004.

Tokt', Sergei. "Latinitsa ili kirillitsa: problema vybora alfavita v belorusskom natsional'nom dvizhenii vo vtoroi polovine XIX-nachale XX veka." *Ab Imperio,* no. 2 (2005): 297–319.

Tumanova, Anastasia S. "The Public and the Organization of Aid to Refugees during World War I." *Russian Studies in History* 51, no. 3 (Winter 2012): 81–107.

Turonak, Jury. *Madernaja historyja Bielarusi.* Vilnius: Instytut bielarusistyki, 2008.

Turonek, Jerzy. *Białoruś pod okupacją niemiecką.* Warsaw: Książka i Wiedza, 1993.

Turuk, F. *Belorusskoe dvizhenie: Ocherk istorii natsionalnogo i revoliutsionnogo dvizheniia belorussov.* Moscow: Gosudarstvennoe izdatelstvo, 1921.

Utgof, Valentina. "In Search of National Support: Belarusian Refugees in World War One and the People's Republic of Belarus." In *Homelands: War, Population and Statehood in Eastern Europe and Russia, 1918–1924,* edited by Nick Baron and Peter Gatrell, 33–73. London: Anthem Press, 2004.

Vakar, Nicholas P. *Belorussia: The Making of a Nation—A Case Study.* Cambridge, MA: Harvard University Press, 1956.

Varonko, Ja. *Bielaruski ruch ad 1917 da 1920 hodu: Karotki ahliad*. Koŭna: n. p., 1920.

Vesialkoŭski, Jury. *Bielarus' u Pieršaj Susvietnaj vajne: Histaryčny narys*. Białystok-London: n. p., 1996.

Vieras, Zos'ka. *Ja pomniu ŭsio: Uspaminy, listy*. Hrodna–Wrocław: Haradzienskaja biblijateka, 2013.

Vitan-Dubiejkaŭskaja, Julijana. *Maje ŭspaminy*. Vilnius: Niezaležnaje vydaviectva Technalohija, 1994.

Volkava, Volha. "Ziemie białoruskie pod niemiecką okupacją w okresie I wojny światowej." In *Pierwsza Niemiecka Okupacja: Królestwo Polskie I Kresy Wschodnie Pod Okupacją Mocarstw Centralnych 1914–1918*, edited by Grzegorz Kucharczyk, 669–824. Warsaw: Instytut Historii PAN, 2019.

Völker-Verteilung in West-Russland. [Kowno]: Verlag der Kownoer Zeitung, 1916.

Wade, Rex A. *The Russian Revolution, 1917*. Cambridge: Cambridge University Press, 2005.

Wandycz, Piotr Stefan. *The Lands of Partitioned Poland, 1795–1918*. Seattle: University of Washington Press, 1974.

Wasilewski, Leon. *Litwa i Białoruś: przeszłość, teraźniejszość, tendencje rozwojowe*. Kraków: Ksiażka, 1912.

Weeks, Theodore. *Nation and State in Late Imperial Russia: Nationalism and Russification on the Western Frontier, 1863–1914*. DeKalb, IL: Northern Illinois University Press, 1996.

———. "Religion and Russification: Russian Language in the Catholic Churches of the 'Northwest Provinces' after 1863." *Kritika: Explorations in Russian and Eurasian History 2*, no. 1 (2001): 87–110.

———. "'Us' or 'Them'? Belarusians and Official Russia, 1863–1914." *Nationalities Papers 31*, no. 2 (June 2003): 211–24.

———. *Vilnius between Nations, 1795–2000*. DeKalb, IL: NIU Press, 2015.

Werdt, Christophe V. "Trans- und multikulturelle Entwicklungspfade am Rande Ostmitteleuropas: Belarus und die Ukraine vor dem Anbruch der Moderne." In *Ein weißer Fleck in Europa: Die Imagination der Belarus als einer Kontaktzone zwischen Ost und West*, edited by Thomas M. Bohn, Victor Shadurski, and Albert Weber, 89–98. Bielefeld: Transcript, 2011.

Westerhoff, Christian. *Zwangsarbeit im Ersten Weltkrieg: Deutsche Arbeitskräftepolitik im besetzten Polen und Litauen 1914–1918*. Paderborn: Schöningh Paderborn, 2012.

Wheeler-Bennett, John W. *Brest-Litovsk: The Forgotten Peace, March 1918*. New York: Norton Library, 1971.

Wimmer, Andreas. *Waves of War: Nationalism, State Formation and Ethnic Exclusion in the Modern World*. New York: Cambridge University Press, 2013.

Wróbel, Piotr. *Kształtowanie się białoruskiej świadomości narodowej a Polska*. Warsaw: Wydawnictwa Uniwersytetu Warszawskiego, 1990.

Yekelchyk, Serhy. *Ukraine: Birth of a Modern Nation*. Oxford: Oxford University Press, 2007.

Zacharka, Vasil'. "Haloŭnyja momanty bielaruskaha ruchu." *Zapisy*, no. 24 (1999): 5–87.

Zadencka, Maria. "Krajowość a strategie elit wobec emancypacji narodowej ludu w końcu XIX i początku XX wieku: Litwa i Białorus, prowincje Bałtyckie, Finlandia." In *Krajowość— tradycje zgody narodow w dobie nacjonalizmu: Materiały z międzynarodowej konferencji naukowej w Insytucie Historii UAM w Poznaniu (11–12 maja 1998)*, edited by Jan Jurkiewicz, 49–61. Poznań: Instytut Historii UAM, 1999.

Zaprudnik, Janka. *Belarus: At a Crossroads in History*. Boulder, CO: Westview Press, 1993.

———. "Da zahadki dziaržaŭnaha archivu BNR u Mikoly Abramčyka." *Zapisy*, no. 32 (2009): 450–76.

Zemke, Hans. *Der Oberbefehlshaber Ost und das Schulwesen im Verwaltungsbereich Litauen während des Weltkrieges*. Berlin: Junker und Dünnhaupt, 1936.

Zetterberg, Seppo. *Die Liga der Fremdvölker Russlands, 1916–1918: Ein Beitrag zu Deutschlands antirussischem Propagandakrieg unter den Fremdvölkern Russlands im ersten Weltkrieg*. Helsinki: Finnische Historische Gesellschaft, 1978.

Zienkiewicz, Tadeusz. *Polskie życie literackie w Mińsku w XIX i na początku XX wieku, do roku 1921*. Olsztyn: Wyższa Szkoła Pedagogiczna, 1997.

Ž., Z. "Z'jezd bielaruskich nacyjanalnych arhanizacyj 25 sakavika 1917 h." *Polymia*, no. 6 (1925): 202–6.

Žylunovič, Z. "Liuty—Kastryčnik u bielaruskim nacyjanalnym ruchu." In *Bielarus': Narysy historyi, ekanomiki, kul'turnaha i revoliucyjnaha ruchu*, edited by A. Stašeŭski, Z. Žylunovič, and U. Ihnatoŭski, 182–94. Minsk: Vydannie Centralnaha Komitetu Bielaruskaje Savieckaje Socyjalistyčnaje Respubliki, 1924.

Index